Nietzsche's *The Anti-Christ*

Edinburgh Critical Guides to Nietzsche
Series editors: Keith Ansell-Pearson and Daniel Conway

Guides you through the writings of Friedrich Nietzsche (1844–1900), one of modernity's most independent, original and seminal minds

The Edinburgh Critical Guides to Nietzsche series brings Nietzsche's writings to life for students, teachers and scholars alike, with each text benefitting from its own dedicated book. Every guide features new research and reflects the most recent developments in Nietzsche scholarship. The authors unlock each work's intricate structure, explore its specific mode of presentation and explain its seminal importance. Whether you are working in contemporary philosophy, political theory, religious studies, psychology, psychoanalysis or literary theory, these guides will help you to fully appreciate Nietzsche's enduring significance for contemporary thought.

Books in the series
Nietzsche's *The Birth of Tragedy from the Spirit of Music*, Tracy B. Strong and Babette Babich
Nietzsche's *Philosophy in the Tragic Age of the Greeks*, Sean Kirkland
Nietzsche's *Unfashionable Observations*, Jeffrey Church
Nietzsche's *Human, All Too Human*, Ruth Abbey
Nietzsche's *Dawn*, Katrina Mitcheson
Nietzsche's *Gay Science*, Robert Miner
Nietzsche's *Thus Spoke Zarathustra*, Charles Bambach
Nietzsche's *Beyond Good and Evil*, Daniel Conway
Nietzsche's *On the Genealogy of Morality*, Robert Guay
Nietzsche's *The Case of Wagner and Nietzsche Contra Wagner*, Ryan Harvey and Aaron Ridley
Nietzsche's *Twilight of the Idols*, Vanessa Lemm
Nietzsche's *The Anti-Christ*, Paul Bishop
Nietzsche's *Ecce Homo*, Matthew Meyer
Nietzsche's *Late Notebooks*, Alan Schrift

Visit our website at edinburghuniversitypress.com/series-edinburgh-critical-guides-to-nietzsche to find out more

Nietzsche's *The Anti-Christ*

A Critical Introduction and Guide

Paul Bishop

EDINBURGH
University Press

Edinburgh University Press is one of the leading university presses in
the UK. We publish academic books and journals in our selected subject
areas across the humanities and social sciences, combining cutting-edge
scholarship with high editorial and production values to produce academic
works of lasting importance. For more information visit our website:
edinburghuniversitypress.com

© Paul Bishop, 2022

Edinburgh University Press Ltd
The Tun – Holyrood Road, 12(2f) Jackson's Entry, Edinburgh EH8 8PJ

Typeset in 11/13 Bembo by
IDSUK (DataConnection) Ltd

A CIP record for this book is available from the British Library

ISBN 978 1 4744 3073 9 (hardback)
ISBN 978 1 4744 3075 3 (webready PDF)
ISBN 978 1 4744 3074 6 (paperback)
ISBN 978 1 4744 3076 0 (epub)

The right of Paul Bishop to be identified as the author of this work has been
asserted in accordance with the Copyright, Designs and Patents Act 1988,
and the Copyright and Related Rights Regulations 2003 (SI No. 2498).

Contents

Acknowledgements	vii
Chronology	viii
Abbreviations	xi
Introduction	1
1. Nietzsche's Biography and Religious Background	16
2. Christ and Anti-Christ in *The Anti-Christ*	38
Composition of *The Anti-Christ*	39
Significance of the figure of anti-Christ	40
Who are the Hyperboreans?	47
Methods (AC §13 and §59)	52
Nietzsche's portrait of Christ (AC §29 and §32)	63
Beweise der Kraft or 'proofs of strength' (AC §32 and §50)	74
3. Nietzsche on Buddhism, the History of Israel and the Loss of the Symbol	80
Nietzsche on Buddhism (AC §§20–3)	82
Nietzsche on the history of Israel (AC §25)	97
Nietzsche on the loss of the symbolic dimension (AC §§31–2)	108
4. Nietzsche on Christianity and the Mysteries	112
Son of Man (AC §34)	113
Kingdom of God (AC §34)	116
Son of God (AC §34 and §37)	118
Nietzsche, Christianity and the Mysteries (AC §37)	121
Nothing to do with Dionysos?	137

5. Nietzsche on Hinduism, the Roman Empire and
   Nobility   147
      Nietzsche on the Lawbook of Manu (AC §§56–7)   148
      Nietzsche on the Roman Empire (AC §58)   167
      Theme of nobility (AC §24, §37, §45 and §§60–2)   182
6. Nietzsche and St Paul   201
      The logic of sacrifice (AC §§39–40)   203
      Paul in *Daybreak* (D §68)   209
      The role of Paul of Tarsus (AC §§41–3)   217
7. Nietzsche on Philology   236
      Nietzsche's critique of philology   236
      Nietzsche's philological strategies   250
8. Conclusion   259

Glossary of Key Terms   269
Guide to Further Reading on *The Anti-Christ*   275
Bibliography   277
Index   306

Acknowledgements

I should like to thank Keith Ansell-Pearson and Daniel Conway for the invitation to contribute to this series of Edinburgh Critical Guides to Nietzsche, and for Dan's comments in particular on the first draft of this manuscript. (I have tried to incorporate as many of his excellent suggestions as I could within the space available, so if there are any particularly clear insights or incisive passages in the book, they are due to him.) I should also like to thank the members of the Graduiertenkolleg 'Europäische Traumkulturen (European Dream-Cultures)' at the Universität des Saarlandes in Saarbrücken for our discussions about Nietzsche during the summer of 2019. I am grateful to Kirsty Wood of EUP for her patience when delivery of the typescript and then submission of the revisions were delayed in turn by university commitments and by the coronavirus pandemic. And, as always, my profound thanks to Helen for being there.

Chronology

1844	Friedrich Wilhelm Nietzsche is born on 15 October in Röcken, Saxony.
1849	Nietzsche's father Ludwig, a Protestant minister, dies of 'softening of the brain'.
1850	Nietzsche's younger brother, Joseph, dies, and the family moves to Naumburg.
1858–64	He attends the elite boarding school Schulpforta on a full scholarship that he received as the orphan of a minister.
1864	Enrols at the University of Bonn to study theology, although he no longer plans to become a minister. He joins a fraternity, but resigns soon after.
1865	Follows the philologist Professor Albrecht Ritschl to the University of Leipzig. He buys a copy of Schopenhauer's *World as Will and Representation* in his landlord's shop.
1865	Refuses to take Communion during his Easter visit home to Naumburg.
1866	Publishes an essay on Theognis in a philological journal edited by Ritschl.
1867	Enlists in an artillery regiment after managing to pass a physical exam.
1868	Injures himself while riding. Reads Kuno Fischer's book on Kant. Meets Richard Wagner in a café in Leipzig, through the mediation of Mrs Ritschl. After his 24th birthday becomes emancipated from his guardian.

1869	Appointed Extraordinary Professor of Classical Philology in Basel on Ritschl's recommendation. Renounces Prussian citizenship. Begins frequent visits to Wagner in nearby Tribschen.
1870	Volunteers as a medical orderly in the Franco-Prussian War, but after two months becomes ill with dysentery and diphtheria.
1872	Publishes his first, controversial book, *The Birth of Tragedy out of the Spirit of Music*. Accompanies Wagner to Bayreuth for the laying of the foundation stone for the new opera house.
1873	Meets Paul Rée in Basel.
1873–75	Publishes *Unfashionable Observations*. Relationship with Wagner begins to sour.
1876	Begins working with Peter Gast, who takes dictation for an essay on Wagner. Visits the Bayreuth Festival and sees Wagner for the last time in Sorrento.
1878	Publishes the first part of *Human, All Too Human*.
1879	Publishes the two additions to *Human, All Too Human*. Resigns from Basel with a small pension. Begins a long period of wandering, mostly through Italy and Switzerland, staying in off-season boarding houses.
1881	Publishes *Daybreak*.
1882	His friendship with Paul Rée ends. Publishes the first edition of *The Gay Science*. In April travels to Rome, meets Lou Salomé, and proposes marriage to her. She declines and the relationship ends badly.
1883–84	Publishes *Thus Spoke Zarathustra*.
1884	Breaks with his sister Elisabeth over her fiancé's anti-Semitism.
1886	Publishes *Beyond Good and Evil*. Plans new editions of previous works, for which he writes five new prefaces, among other material.
1887	Writes *On the Genealogy of Morality* in July and August. It is published in November in an edition of 600 copies. He pays for the printing himself.
1888	Publishes *The Case of Wagner*. Writes *The Anti-Christ*, *Ecce Homo*, *Nietzsche Contra Wagner* and *Twilight of the Idols*.

1889	Suffers a breakdown and collapses in Turin, after writing megalomaniacal postcards to many friends and celebrities. He is retrieved by his friend Franz Overbeck, who takes him to Basel. Nietzsche's mother then takes him to an asylum in Jena.
1890	Nietzsche is moved to his mother's apartment in Jena, and then to Naumburg. His sister Elisabeth returns to Germany from Paraguay. She later takes control of her brother's literary estate.
1894	Elisabeth founds the Nietzsche Archive, which houses Nietzsche and his papers.
1896	Elisabeth moves Nietzsche and the Archive to Weimar.
1900	Dies in Weimar on 25 August.

Abbreviations

Biblical and other texts

DRV Douay-Rheims Version
KJV King James Version
NJB New Jerusalem Bible, Wansbrough 1985
OT   Old Testament
NT   New Testament

Nietzsche: editions

BAW *Frühe Schriften*, Nietzsche 1994 [1933–40]
KGW *Werke: Kritische Gesamtausgabe*, Nietzsche 1975–
KSA *Sämtliche Werke: Kritische Studienausgabe*, Nietzsche 1967–77; 1988
KSB *Sämtliche Briefe: Kritische Studienausgabe*, Nietzsche 1975–84
NK   *Nietzsche-Kommentar*, Neymeyr 2020 [= 1/2]; Schmidt and Kaufmann 2015 [= 3/1]; Sommer 2016 [= 5/1]; Sommer 2012 [= 6/1]; Sommer 2013 [= 6/2].
W   *Werke in drei Bänden*, Nietzsche 1966

Nietzsche: individual works

AC   *The Anti-Christ*, Nietzsche 1920
AOM *Assorted Opinions and Maxims*, in Nietzsche 1908; 1986

BGE   *Beyond Good and Evil*, Nietzsche 1968a
BT   *The Birth of Tragedy*, Nietzsche 1968a
CW   *The Case of Wagner*, Nietzsche 1899
D   *Daybreak*, Nietzsche 1924a
EH   *Ecce Homo*, Nietzsche 1911; 1992
GM   *On the Genealogy of Morals*, Nietzsche 1968a
GS   *The Gay Science*, Nietzsche 1924b
HAH   *Human, All Too Human*, Nietzsche 1908; 1986
NCW   *Nietzsche contra Wagner*, Nietzsche 1899
TI   *Twilight of the Idols*, Nietzsche 1899; 1968b
TSZ   *Thus Spoke Zarathustra*, Nietzsche 1969
UM   *Untimely Meditations*, Nietzsche 1983
WP   *The Will to Power*, Nietzsche 1968c [indexed to passages in KSA]
WS   *The Wanderer and his Shadow*, in Nietzsche 1908; 1986

Introduction

In the middle of the nineteenth century, the English poet and cultural critic Matthew Arnold (1822–88) wrote his famous poem 'Dover Beach' (1867). Full of melancholy and nostalgia, the poem opens with an evocation of the moonlit English coast:

> The sea is calm tonight.
> The tide is full, the moon lies fair
> Upon the straits; on the French coast the light
> Gleams and is gone; the cliffs of England stand,
> Glimmering and vast, out in the tranquil bay.
> Come to the window, sweet is the night-air!
> [. . .]
> The Sea of Faith
> Was once, too, at the full, and round earth's shore
> Lay like the folds of a bright girdle furled.
> But now I only hear
> Its melancholy, long, withdrawing roar,
> Retreating, to the breath
> Of the night-wind, down the vast edges drear
> And naked shingles of the world. (Hayward [ed.] 1964: 645–6)[1]

As the poem unfolds, it becomes clear that it is a lament for the disappearance of a metaphysical or supernatural world, in which the 'sea of faith' is, like the ebbing tide, in slow but remorseless retreat. Arnold's poem is completely in line with the lament for

---

[1] For further discussion, see Wilson 1999: 255–78.

the disappearance of the pagan world so memorably expressed in Friedrich Schiller's poem 'The Gods of Greece' (Schiller 1844: 16–21).

Tellingly, Nietzsche uses an image strikingly similar to Arnold's in his third *Untimely Meditation*, 'Schopenhauer as Educator' (1874):

> The waters of religion are ebbing away and leaving behind swamps or stagnant pools; the nations are again drawing away from one another in the most hostile fashion and long to tear one another to pieces. The sciences, pursued without any restraint and in a spirit of the blindest laissez faire, are shattering and dissolving all firmly held belief [. . .] Everything, contemporary art and science included, serves the coming barbarism. (UM §4)

In 1984 this motif of the 'sea of faith' was used for a series of TV programmes broadcast on BBC television, written and presented by the Cambridge theologian Don Cupitt (Cupitt 1984). (Inspired by this series, an academic network entitled the Sea of Faith Network was established, which continues to hold conferences today.) The programme included – how could it not? – a discussion of Nietzsche, whose prediction and analysis of the decline of religion fitted in perfectly with the theme of the series, even if Nietzsche might not have been so sanguine about Cupitt's project to reconceive Christianity as something to be practised without dogma, as a spiritual path, as an ethic, and as a way of giving meaning to life.

In 1992, the American political scientist and political economist Francis Fukuyama borrowed a Nietzschean motif for the title of his influential book, *The End of History and the Last Man* (1992). Fukuyama argued that the global spread of liberal democracy and Western-style free market capitalism spelled the end of humankind's sociocultural evolution and, in this sense, the end of history. It doesn't get much better than this, Fukuyama was widely perceived as arguing, even though he was already rowing back from some of the confidence of his position by the time he wrote *Trust: Social Virtues and Creation of Prosperity* (1995).

Yet as I write this preface in 2018 (and revise it in 2019/2020), how the picture has changed. The Al-Quaeda terrorist attack on the Twin Towers on 11 September 2001 and the subsequent declaration by the US of the War on Terror; the US-led war in Iraq (2003–10); the global financial crisis (2007–08), considered by some economists to have been the worst financial crisis since the Great Depression of the 1930s; the fallout from the Arab Spring (2010); the outbreak of the Syrian Civil War (2011); the rise of ISIS (2014) and the ongoing refugee crisis; not to mention the coronavirus pandemic – much that appeared to be certain about the modern world-order has been thrown into radical uncertainty. And the decline of religion, which appeared to be one of those certainties, has been rapidly reversed. While the number of churchgoers in the UK might still be on the decline, this is by no means the case in the US, and the global picture is robust: in 2010 there were 2.2 billion Christians around the world, up from 600 million in 1910, and it is predicted that, if current trends continue, by 2050 there will be 2.9 billion Christians – over 30% of the world's population.

Close on Christianity's heels is Islam. Between 1990 and 2010, the number of Muslims increased from 1.1 billion to 1.6 billion people, increasing at an annual average rate of 2.2%. In 2009, it was estimated that Muslims constituted approximately 23% of the world's population, and they are projected to represent over a quarter (26.4%) by 2030. Other calculations suggest that by 2070 the projected Muslim population will equal the Christian population, and that it will outnumber it by the end of the millennium. Thanks to their young age and relatively high fertility rate, the population growth of Muslims worldwide is roughly twice the world's overall population growth. In Germany, such writers as Thilo Sarrasin warn that Islam is eroding the fundamental basis of Western civilisation (Sarrasin 2010; 2018).

So there could not be a better time – or a worse, depending on your point of view – to read Nietzsche's electrifying attack on organised religion in general and on Christianity in particular, provocatively entitled *The Anti-Christ*. Written in 1888, but (because of its controversial tone and content) not published until 1895, it is sobering to reflect on Nietzsche's rhetorical assault on Christianity in the light of the recent rise of religion.

Why did I write this book? In part because I was invited to write it, and this kind of opportunity does not arise very often;

in part because, as Dan Conway has noted, *The Anti-Christ* has received relatively little critical attention and 'remains something of an outlier, an enigma perhaps, even to Nietzsche's most sympathetic readers' (Conway [ed.] 2019: 4); and in part because *The Anti-Christ* has always struck me as one of the most difficult and provocative of Nietzsche's works. Yet despite (or perhaps precisely because of) this fact, it is also one of his most timely (or *zeitgemäß*).[2] So it is a pity that it is so difficult to find a discursive space in which to talk about and discuss it. For at least in the UK, Nietzsche is disappearing from academic discourse at an alarming speed. Departments of philosophy tend to have a focus on analytic philosophy, apart from a few 'blissful islands' where continental philosophy is taught. In departments of German, he is not taught either – because he is 'too difficult' or 'not relevant', to recall some of the phrases used by colleagues or senior managers. Given the entirely understandable sensitivities about not giving offence to people's religious beliefs or cultural norms, Nietzsche's rhetoric can make him highly problematic, not to say downright offensive. His remarks about smelling Jews, for instance, are unacceptable in a twenty-first-century context, although they do not necessarily make him an anti-Semite (as we shall see); the jury is, understandably enough, still out on that question. All in all, both admirers and detractors alike would agree that Nietzsche is not a proponent of affirmative action, that he eschews political correctness, and that he is decidedly not woke. Black Lives Matter? Some of his critics would have us believe that Nietzsche thinks most individual lives don't really matter at all.

As a result, in the current intellectual climate I would find it challenging as a Germanist to teach Nietzsche in any real depth, and certainly not *The Anti-Christ*. (Both the attack on belief and perhaps belief itself are equally problematic, albeit in different ways.) The risk of causing offence is, it seems to me, simply too great; any class would have to be littered with 'trigger warnings', and it is not as if the work does not deliberately set out to offend. Maybe Nietzsche's friends, the theologian Franz Overbeck and

---

[2] For further discussion of the notion of *timeliness*, see Shapiro 2016: 102–10.

the writer Heinrich Köselitz (aka Peter Gast), were right to delay its publication? And yet – surely it is odd that, over a hundred years on, Nietzsche's work is still so controversial. Could it be that Nietzsche's power to shock and to disturb us reveals that he is addressing questions that we don't want to think or talk about, but perhaps should? Maybe Nietzsche himself got it right when, at the beginning of *The Anti-Christ*, he wrote that 'some are born posthumously' (AC Preface), or when, in *Ecce Homo* (another much maligned, much misunderstood work) he asserted, 'I am not a man, I am dynamite' (EH Destiny §1).

So this book has been written *in lieu* of the classes I have not been able to teach, yet out of the conviction that Nietzsche remains in some sense our 'destiny', and that engagement with his work repays the effort involved. In this book I have deliberately avoided taking a personal stance on the question of whether Nietzsche is right or wrong, whether his critique of Christianity is valid or not. The so-called *Gretchenfrage* – named after the episode in Goethe's *Faust*, Part 1, where Margarete asks Faust whether he believes in God or not – is not one that any critic should be obliged to answer, although I have felt the need to explain the context of Nietzsche's arguments in a way that might be unexpected for some. This is because of the situation in which we find ourselves as far as cultural knowledge is concerned, and I know this is a widespread predicament.

In their introduction to the second edition of the *Oxford Dictionary of Christian Art and Architecture*, its editors, Peter and Linda Murray, note that over thirty years' experience of teaching the history of art and architecture has taught them that 'simple lack of knowledge of the Bible, and of Christian doctrine, as well as something of church history and ritual, frequently prevents people from understanding – and even more, appreciating – much of the greatest art which has ever been created' (Murray and Murray 2013: viii). This is a problem which, they rightly say, is 'getting worse', and a similar situation can be recognised in the field of English literature, where 'the words and cadences of the Authorized Version of the Bible, echoed by writers from Shakespeare to Hardy, no longer have the effect intended by the author and, because they are not recognized, their meaning and relevance is lost' (Murray and Murray 2013: viii).

The Murrays recall overhearing someone in the National Gallery in London standing in front of Piero della Francesca's *Baptism of Christ*, and asking his companion, 'What's the pigeon for?' And they relate how an English couple, looking at Leonardo da Vinci's *The Last Supper* in Milan, said to each other, 'I don't know what they are doing, but they seem to be having some sort of a meal.' This second example strikes a chord with me: when we used to teach German poetry to our second-year students, I remember doing a class on Friedrich Hölderlin's poem, *Brot und Wein* ('Bread and Wine'). It is by anyone's standards a difficult poem, so I thought I would try and approach its central theme through the motif in the title. 'What do you associate with bread and wine?', I asked. Someone answered, 'A picnic.'

In Jungian terms, what we are experiencing is a collapse of the symbolic system or 'the death of the symbol'. In a seminar talk given in 1939 to the Guild of Pastoral Psychology in London, C. G. Jung discussed what happens to a symbol when it ceases to be a living one:

> What I have spoken of is, alas, to a great extent the past. We cannot turn the wheel backwards; we cannot go back to the symbolism that is gone. No sooner do you know that this thing is symbolic than you say, 'Oh, well, it presumably means something else.' Doubt has killed it, has devoured it. So you cannot go back. I cannot go back to the Catholic Church, I cannot experience the miracle of the Mass, I know too much about it. I know it is the truth, but it is the truth in a form in which I cannot accept it any more. I cannot say 'This is the Sacrifice of Christ' and see him any more. I cannot. It is no more true to me; it does not express my psychological condition. My psychological condition wants something else. I must have a situation in which that thing becomes true once more. I need a new form. (§632, in Jung 2014: 276)[3]

---

[3] For further discussion, see Giegerich 2004.

This analysis explains why it is important to take Linda and Peter Murray's complaint seriously and not glibly dismiss it as mere snobbery, for a simple lack of knowledge of the Bible, and of Christian doctrine in general, can prevent people from understanding and appreciating Nietzsche too. So in this critical introduction and guide I have taken the time to try and contextualise Nietzsche's ideas historically, as well as to explain the biblical and theological background that Nietzsche so often simply presupposes. He would have assumed that his readers would have automatically 'got' his biblical or theological references, but this is by no means the case today.

As well as exploring Nietzsche's critique in order to understand it better, I have also tried to explore the surprising gaps in what Nietzsche does *not* critique about Christianity. The question of what a writer does *not* say is an important one for Nietzsche – as, after all, he himself notes (TI Expeditions §51) – and it may come as a surprise to some readers to realise that, despite the title of his book, Nietzsche never says anything negative at all about the actual figure of Christ. This absence of criticism of the biblical Jesus extends to apparently not doubting his historical existence, and in this respect Nietzsche might be seen as a rather unusual critic of Christianity. He might even have felt out of place in the Rationalist Union . . .

At the core of this book is the thesis that Nietzsche advances an argument against Christianity on essentially *philological* grounds. This makes his argument sometimes hard to grasp, and it also accounts for its remarkable subtlety in some respects (and its startling absence of subtlety in others). We might expand and explain Nietzsche's argument as running something like this.

First, Judeo-Christianity is based on religious texts that arose in an historical context, but we no longer have full access to the meaning of those texts. For instance, the notion of the 'Messiah', a Hebrew term meaning 'the anointed one', or its Greek equivalent, *Christos* or Χριστός, 'the Christ', carries with it a whole range of associations no longer available to us.

Second, Christianity itself arises from a series of comparative readings, whereby the New Testament takes on its full significance only in relation to the Old. For instance, the liberation from Egypt, the wandering in the desert and the building of the tabernacle in Exodus, or the instructions for offering sacrifice in Numbers, are 'reverse engineered' in the Letter to the Hebrews into 'shadows' or 'types' of the redemptive sacrifice of Christ. This parallel reading is reinforced by the use of scripture in liturgical contexts, for example daily readings from Old and New Testaments at the Mass; the readings from Exodus and Numbers, then the Letter to the Hebrews, in the Office of Readings; and the liturgy on Holy Saturday, which presents an entire sequence of readings from Old and New Testaments so as to reinforce the idea of continuity and a shift from the literal to the 'spiritual'.

This leads to a kind of *just as* approach to the scriptures, exemplified by the way in which Paul (in the First Letter to the Corinthians) derives a warning and a series of lessons from Israel's history (1 Cor. 10:1–13). In Exodus one reads of how the people of Israel are conducted through the desert (Exod. 13:21; cf. Num. 9:21) and of how they pass through the Sea of Reeds (or Red Sea) (Exod. 14:22). One reads of how God gave them manna,[4] and of how the Lord gave the people water out of a rock (Exod. 16:15; 17:5–6). For Paul, the clouds and the passing through the Red Sea become images of baptism, while the manna and the water from the rock become images of the Eucharist:

> For I would not have you ignorant, brethren, that our fathers were all under the cloud, and all passed through the sea: And all in Moses were baptized, in the cloud, and in the sea: And they all eat the same spiritual food: And all drank the same spiritual drink: (and they drank of the spiritual rock that followed them, and the rock was Christ). (1 Cor. 10:1–4)

In the gloss on this passage offered by the English Catholic Bible scholar George Leo Haydock (1774–1849), we read that

---

[4] The philological significance of *manna* recalls how Yahweh, the name of God himself who says I AM THAT I AM, derives from the Hebrew roots HYH/HWH, to 'cause to exist'.

under the conduct of Moses [the Israelites] received baptism in figure, by passing under the cloud and through the sea: and they partook of the body and blood of Christ in figure, by eating of the *manna* (called here a *spiritual food*, because it was a figure of the true bread which comes down from heaven) and drinking the water miraculously brought out of the rock, called here a *spiritual rock*; because it was also a figure of Christ. (Haydock 2006: 1511)

Indeed, in the final line of the passage quoted from 1 Corinthians, an old rabbinic tradition according to which the rock (Num. 20:8) followed Israel in the desert is reinterpreted as a symbol of the pre-existent Christ, already active in the history of Israel (NJB, NT, 1901).

Third, this interpretative principle organises the Christian approach to scripture, as reflected even today in Bertrand Vergely's reading of the accounts of miracles in the New Testament (Vergely 2010: 225–73).[5] By this stage, this kind of *lectio divina* (as it is called in the Benedictine tradition) has completely departed from the philological practices espoused, not just by Nietzsche, but by contemporary text criticism, leading to his repeated expressions of outrage at the way the Church reads the Bible. In the end, Nietzsche can no longer believe, because he thinks he has gained insight into a fraudulent *production of meaning* in the texts, in a way that is comparable with his insight into the *production of morality* in *On the Genealogy of Morals* (1887).

Consequently, the approach taken to *The Anti-Christ* in this critical introduction and guide is, in keeping with the task at hand, essentially thematic. So at the outset a brief overview of Nietzsche's actual progression through the numbered sections of his book might be helpful. Some of the titles used to describe the sections draw on the draft outline of the work found in Nietzsche's unpublished writings or *Nachlass* (see KSA 13, 19[4], 543), which shows just how much of a work-in-progress the text was right up to its final version; others are drawn from the text itself:

---

[5] For an overview of the theological reception of Nietzsche, see Köster 1981/1982; 1998.

Preface
- Nietzsche sets out the requirements for those who want to read this book, and predicts their advent in the future: 'This book belongs to the most rare. Perhaps not one of them is yet alive [. . .] Some are born posthumously' (AC Preface)[6]

§§1–7: 'We Hyperboreans': Opening critique of Christianity[7]
- §1: The Hyperboreans
- §2: Nietzschean catechism

§§8–14: 'For us – against us': Nietzsche's theological and philosophical opponents
- §7: critique of pity
- §§10–11: critique of Kant
- 'The Protestant pastor is the grandfather of German philosophy [. . .] One need only utter the words "Tübingen School" to get an understanding of *what* German philosophy is at bottom – an *underhand* theology' (AC §10)

§§15–19: 'Concept of a religion of *décadence*'
- §15: Christianity founds a 'purely *fictitious world*'
- §§16–19: critique of the Christian idea of God[8]
- §17: God 'from the standpoint of Spinoza', as 'Ideal' and as 'pure spirit' (Hegel), as '*absolutum*' (Fichte), 'as thing-in-itself' (Kant, Schopenhauer): 'The decline of a God: He became a "thing-in-itself"'

§§20–3: 'Buddhism and Christianity'
- 'Both are to be reckoned among the nihilistic religions – they are both religions of decadence – but they are different from each other in a most striking way' (§20)

---

[6] See the draft of this preface in Nietzsche's *Nachlass*, where he writes: 'This book addresses only very few, – human beings who have *become free*, for whom nothing more is forbidden: we have, step by step, won back the right to everything forbidden' (KSA 13, 15[76], 454).

[7] See the draft of these sections in the *Nachlass*, where Nietzsche provocatively suggests that moralists be hanged, and throws a famous line from Goethe's *Faust*, Part Two ('The Mothers! Mothers! It sounds so mysterious', l. 6217), in the face of centuries (indeed, millennia) of philosophers, describing them as a bunch of 'old women' (KSA 13, 23[3], 601–4); cf. 'Sayings of a Hyperborean' (KSA 13, 15[118], 477).

[8] See the draft of these sections in the *Nachlass* entitled 'On the History of the God-Concept' (KSA 13, 17[4], 523–6).

- §23: Nietzsche on the three 'theological virtues' (faith, hope, love)

§§24–7: 'The roots of Christianity':[9] on the origin of Christianity
- 'Here I barely touch on the problem of the *origin* of Christianity' (§24)
- §§25–6: outline of the history of Israel – five stages of denaturalising values:
  - 1 Israel's Yahweh as 'an expression of its consciousness of power, its joy in itself, its hopes for itself' (AC §25)
  - 2 the concept of God is falsified: 'Yahweh is the god of Israel, and *consequently* the god of justice' → 'Yahweh, the god of "justice" – he is in accord with Israel *no more*, he no longer visualizes the national egoism' (AC §25)
  - 3 the concept of morality is falsified: Yahweh becomes 'merely a weapon in the hands of clerical agitators, who interpret all happiness as a reward and all unhappiness as a punishment for obedience or disobedience to him, for "sin"' (AC §25)
  - 4 the history of Israel is falsified: 'the *great* age of Israel became an age of decline' → 'the Exile, with its long series of misfortunes, was transformed into a *punishment* for that great age – during which priests had not yet come into existence' (AC §26)
  - 5 The 'will of God' is revealed in sacred scripture: 'From this time forward things were so arranged that the priest became *indispensable everywhere*; at all the great natural events of life, at birth, at marriage, in sickness, at death, not to say at the *"sacrifice"* (that is, at meal-times), the holy parasite put in his appearance, and proceeded to *denaturize* it – in his own phrase, to "sanctify" it' (AC §26)

---

[9] See the draft title of this section (cf. KSA 14, 440); cf. the earlier fragments, 'On the History of Christianity' (KSA 13, 11[364–6], 160–3).

§§28–35: A psychological sketch of Jesus Christ and his teachings
- §29: Jesus as hero, as genius and as 'idiot'
- §30: critique of Epicurus
- §32: Jesus as fanatic and as 'free spirit'
- 'The life of the saviour was simply a carrying-out of this way of life – and so was his death [. . .] he *knew* that it was only by a *way* of life that one could feel one's self "divine", "blessed", "evangelical", a "child of God". *Not* by "repentance", *not* by "prayer and forgiveness" is the way to God: *only the Gospel way* leads to God – it is *itself* "God"!' (AC §33)

§§36–8: Excursus on history of Christianity as falsification of Jesus's teachings
- §38: critique of Bismarck and Wilhelm II: 'What was formerly merely sickly now becomes indecent – it is indecent to be a Christian today [. . .] Even someone who makes the most modest pretensions to integrity *must* know that a theologian, a priest, a pope of today not only errs when he speaks, but actually *lies* [. . .] The priest knows, as everyone knows, that there is longer any "God", or any "sinner", or any "saviour" – that "free will" and the "moral order of the world" are *lies*'

§§39–46: The 'true' history of Christianity
- §42: critique of St Paul
- §43: critique of doctrine of immortality
- §§44–5: critique of the Gospels: 'Let us not be led astray: they say "judge not", and yet they condemn to hell whoever stands in their way. In letting God sit in judgment they judge themselves [. . .] The fact is that the conscious conceit of the chosen here disguises itself as modesty: it is in this way that they, the "community", the "good and just", range themselves, once and for *always*, on one side, the side of "the truth" – and the rest of humankind, "the world", on the other' (AC §44)
- §45: link between argument of *The Anti-Christ* and Nietzsche's critique of 'slave morality' in *On the Genealogy of Morals*

- defence of Pontius Pilate as 'the only *one* figure worthy of honour' in the NT (AC §46)

§§47–9: Recapitulation of central argument and emphasis on philology

- §47: Christianity is rejected, not because God does not exist (in history or nature) but for essentially philological reasons: 'As a matter of fact no one can be a *philologian* or a physician without being also *Antichrist[ian]*'
- §48: satirical reading of the Book of Genesis

§§50–5: A psychological sketch of believers, especially martyrs and fanatics

- §52: 'Another characteristic of the theologian is his *unfitness for philology* [. . .] the art of reading with profit – the capacity for absorbing facts *without* interpreting them falsely, and *without* losing caution, patience and subtlety in the effort to understand them. Philology as *ephexis* [i.e., 'suspension of judgment' or 'scepticism'] in interpretation'
- §53: 'In the very tone in which a martyr flings what he fancies to be true in the face of the world there appears so low a grade of intellectual honesty and such *insensibility* to the problem of "truth", that it is never necessary to refute a martyr. Truth is not something that one person has and another person does not: at best, only peasants, or peasant apostles like Luther, can think of truth in any such way'[10]

§§56–7: Contrast between Christianity and the Lawbook of Manu[11]

- §57: three physiological types → (a) spiritual people (the few); (b) custodians of law or guardians; (c) the mediocre

§§58–61: Political implications of Christianity

---

[10] See the draft passage in the *Nachlass* about 'martyrs' under the title 'Will to truth' (KSA 13, 15[52], 442–4).

[11] See the draft section entitled 'On a Critique of the Lawbook of Manu'; here as elsewhere, Nietzsche inserts his discussion of this work into his ongoing engagement with Plato: 'Here the most cold-blooded sober-mindedness [*Besonnenheit*] was at work, the same kind of sober-mindedness that a Plato had when he was devising his *Republic* [. . .] Plato is entirely in the spirit of Manu: he was initiated in Egypt' (KSA 13, 15[45], 440 and 14[191], 378).

- §58: lament for the fall of Roman Empire as *aere perennius* [i.e., 'more enduring than bronze']; defence of Epicurus
- §59: key importance of ancient Romans → methods
- §§59–60: Islamic culture
- §61: the Renaissance and critique of Luther and the Reformation: '*Cesare Borgia as pope* [. . .] that would have been the sort of triumph that *I* alone am longing for today'; 'Luther saw only the *depravity* of the papacy at the very moment when the opposite was becoming apparent: the old corruption, the *peccatum originale* [i.e., 'original sin'], Christianity itself, *no longer* occupied the papal chair! Instead there was life! Instead there was the triumph of life! Instead there was the great yea to all lofty, beautiful, daring things! . . . And Luther *restored the Church*: he attacked it'

§62: Final condemnation of Christianity and its '"humanitarian" blessings'
- rejection of 'the worm of sin' and 'an art of self-violation'
- 'The "equality of souls before God" – this fraud, this *pretext* for the rancour of all the base-minded – this explosive concept, ending in revolution, the modern idea, and the notion of overthrowing the whole social order – this is *Christian* dynamite'

'Law Against Christianity'
1. Every type of anti-nature is a vice
2. Any participation in religious services is an assassination attempt on public morality
3. Sacred locations for Christianity should be eradicated
4. Christian teaching on chastity is a public instigation to anti-nature
5. The Christian priest is a Chandala, i.e., he should be ostracised, starved, driven into every sort of desert
6. The 'holy' history is an accursed history, and such terms as 'God', 'saviour', 'redeemer', 'saint' should be used as terms of abuse
7. The rest follows from this (i.e., the Christian religion should be exterminated?)

This Critical Guide tries to bring out a plea for the reinvigoration of philology as the main theme of *The Anti-Christ*. Indeed, in many of Nietzsche's writings after *Thus Spoke Zarathustra* (1883–85), as well as such earlier ones as *Daybreak* (1881), Nietzsche's frequent accusation levelled at his opponents is one of poor or lazy philology, that is, of failing to read carefully the 'texts' (in all senses of the word) that are in front of them. (Nietzsche believes that, a lot of the time, we *don't want to see* the awful truth.) In this respect, *The Anti-Christ* is not only typical of, but also represents the culmination of Nietzsche's argumentational approach.

Consequently, this book begins by examining Nietzsche's biography against the religious background of his own life. The next four chapters examine key aspects of Nietzsche's argument in *The Anti-Christ*, beginning with the mysterious figures of anti-Christ and the Hyperboreans (AC §§1–2), the importance for Nietzsche of methods (AC §13 and §59), and his portrait of Christ (AC §29 and §32). I then contrast Nietzsche's attitude to Christianity with his attitude to Buddhism (AC §§20–3), what he says about the history of Israel (AC §25), and the huge emphasis placed by Nietzsche in *The Anti-Christ* (AC §§31–2) on the loss of symbolic dimension in our understanding of religion. In particular, Nietzsche is interested in such categories as the 'Son of Man', the 'Son of God' and the 'Kingdom of God', as well as the link between Christianity and the ancient Greek mysteries. Next I examine Nietzsche's praise of the so-called 'Lawbook' of Manu (AC §§56–7), his remarks on the Roman Empire (AC §58), and the recurrent theme in *The Anti-Christ* of nobility. I then consider Nietzsche's attitude to St Paul (D §68 and AC §§31–43), and investigate its problems. In the final chapter, I offer an examination of the importance for Nietzsche of philology – and its importance for the construction of the New Testament as well; and in the conclusion I argue for the timeliness of *The Anti-Christ*, despite or precisely because it is one of Nietzsche's most controversial works. Overall, the approach of this critical introduction and guide aims to make *The Anti-Christ*, this most controversial of all Nietzsche's works, accessible to readers of all faiths – and none.

1
Nietzsche's Biography and Religious Background

There [are] morning-thinkers, there are afternoon-thinkers, there are night-owls. Not to be forgotten is the most noble species: *those of midday*, – those in whom the great Pan is steadfastly asleep. There all light falls vertically. (KSA 13, 16[28], 489)

As Friedrich Nietzsche was well aware, he was the descendant of a whole line of Christian ministers,[1] and in an early autobiographical sketch he wrote: 'As a plant I was born close to the churchyard, and as a human being in a vicarage.'[2] At 10 o'clock in the morning on Tuesday, 15 October 1844, a child had been born to Franziska Nietzsche, *née* Oehler, and Karl Ludwig Nietzsche, the pastor of the village of Röcken, near Lützen in the eastern part of Germany. On 24 October, the boy was christened Friedrich Wilhelm; his father, on the anniversary of whose own baptism the service had taken place, gave his son the following *Taufspruch* or baptismal motto: 'What manner of child shall this be? And the hand of the Lord was with him' (Luke 1:66). In 1849, when Nietzsche was just five years old, his father died; less than a year later, Nietzsche's younger brother, Ludwig Joseph, died shortly before his second birthday. His

---

[1] See Nietzsche's letter to Heinrich Köselitz of 21 July 1881 (KSB 6, 109).
[2] 'Aus meinem Leben' [1863] (W 3, 107).

father's death, followed by his brother's, left Nietzsche in a household dominated by women: his younger sister (Elisabeth Alexandra); his mother, his grandmother, two unmarried aunts and the family maid. (Looking back, Nietzsche wondered whether it was 'a bad thing that henceforth my entire development did not have a man's eye looking after it'.)[3]

It is tempting to speculate that there might be an important psychoanalytic point here. After all, the analytical psychologist C. G. Jung (1875–1961) made much of the fact that Nietzsche's father had been a clergyman, telling the members of his seminar on Nietzsche's *Zarathustra* that 'you must remember that he was the son of a parson and he had some inheritance presumably', adding – 'I know what *that* means' (Jung 1989: vol. 1, 31). Discussing a line in *Thus Spoke Zarathustra*, 'What the father hath hid cometh out in the son; and oft have I found the son the father's revealed secret' (TSZ I Of the Tarantulas), Jung hailed this remark as 'a very remarkable psychological insight, such as one often finds in *Zarathustra*' (1989: vol. 2, 1095). Being the son of a clergyman meant that Nietzsche had himself been 'the father's unrevealed secret' (1989: vol. 2, 1095). Significantly, Jung went on to say that it was a 'great truth' that 'he can reveal the secret of his mother as well' (1989: vol. 2, 1097), and it is hard not to recall Nietzsche's riddling remark in *Ecce Homo*, 'as my father I have already died, as my mother I still live and grow' (EH Wise §1).

In 1850, the Nietzsche household moved to Naumburg, where Nietzsche attended the local primary school, before attending the grammar school (*Gymnasium*) attached to the cathedral. As a six-year-old, Nietzsche's ability to cite biblical passages and sing hymns earned him the reputation of being *der kleine Pastor* ('the little pastor'). Nevertheless, one of his recent biographers has pointed out that, in his autobiographical writings, Nietzsche virtually never mentions his participation in church services or prayers, and other childhood documents suggest 'decidedly irreligious tendencies' (Blue 2016: 58). For instance, there is a childhood drawing of

---

[3] 'Mein Leben' [1864] (W 3, 117). For further discussion of the impact of women on Nietzsche's life, see Leis 2000.

what looks like the funeral of a turkey (Benders et al. 2000: 21), and three poems from the Naumburg period appear to include passages that are sexual or scatological (KGW I.1: 6–8). Was there, Daniel Blue wonders, a suppressed side of Nietzsche that was beginning to surface (Blue 2016: 58)?

At least in the eyes of his family, Nietzsche was destined to be a church minister, and when he was 14 he was sent to Schulpforta, the famous school that Klopstock and Fichte, among others, had attended. According to Blue, arriving at Schulpforta awakened Nietzsche to the joys of learning and marked the moment when he began to take scholarship seriously (Blue 2016: 93). The pattern of a typical school day involved prayer alternating with study and instruction throughout the day (BAW 1, 119–20), and at Schulpforta Nietzsche developed his love of classics, demonstrating remarkable proficiency in Greek and Latin. And he began to develop his love for classical German literature and the German Romantics.

Two early essays from 1862 show Nietzsche already struggling to free himself from his Christian upbringing (Blue 2016: 139–40). In 'Fate and History', Nietzsche says that 'if we could look upon Christian doctrine and church history with a free, unbiased view, then we would have to express several opinions in opposition to their general ideas', but that 'from our first days confined under the yoke of custom and prejudice, inhibited by the impressions of our childhood in the natural development of our spirit, and determined in the formation of our temperament', it had to be 'considered a transgression if we adopt a freer standpoint in order to make an impartial and timely judgment about religion and Christianity'; 'such an attempt', he adds, 'is not the work of a few weeks, but of a lifetime' (BAW 2, 54).

In 'Freedom of the Will and Fate', Nietzsche strikes a decidedly negative note about Christianity, contrasting 'the people believing in fate [who] are distinguished by force and strength of will' with 'women and men who let things happen according to perversely interpreted Christian tenets – since "God makes all things right" – and allow themselves to be guided by circumstances in a degrading fashion', concluding that, 'in general, "submission to God's will" and "humility" are often nothing but a cloak for cowardly timidity to face destiny with decisiveness' (BAW 2, 60). In an accompanying draft letter, Nietzsche claimed that 'the principal teachings of Christianity express merely the basic truths of the human heart; they are symbols, just as the highest must always be merely a symbol of something still higher', that 'the illusion of the supernatural has placed the human spirit in a false relationship to the earthly world', and that 'humanity [. . .] recognizes in itself "the beginning, the middle, the end of religion"' (BAW 2, 63). In this passage, Blue detects not just shades of Ludwig Feuerbach (1804–72), but an actual quotation from him (Blue 2016: 140).[4]

On his family's side the plan was still for Nietzsche to become a minister, so after Schulpforta he went to university in Bonn to study theology. But his school-leaving dissertation, 'Theognis as a Poet', served as a reminder of what was now his real passion: classical philology. And there is evidence that religious doubts were creeping into Nietzsche's late teenage mind. Already a sketch, dated 18 September 1863, indicates the sense of doubt – and a concomitant sense of liberation – in the 19-year-old Nietzsche:

> And so the human being grows out of everything that used to embrace him; he does not need to break his shackles, for unexpectedly, when a god bids it, they fall away; and where is the ring that in the end still encircles him? Is it the world? Is it God? (W 3, 110)

According to his sister, Elisabeth, differences of opinion in matters of religion led, not surprisingly, to increasing tensions between him and Franziska, his mother. In a remarkably frank letter to his sister, written on 11 June 1865, Nietzsche asked: 'Do we, in our enquiries, seek rest, peace, happiness? No, only truth, however abhorrent and ugly it may be' (KSB 2, 61). And he diagnosed for her the moment of caesura he was facing, in the following dramatic phrase: 'Here the ways of men part: if you want to strive for peace of mind and happiness, then believe; but if you want to be a disciple of truth, then enquire' (KSB 2, 61).

---

[4] For further discussion of these early essays, see Stack 1993.

With this change from theology to philology, the course was set for Nietzsche's promotion to academic stardom. When his favourite lecturer, the great classical scholar Friedrich Ritschl (1806–76), moved from Bonn to Leipzig, Nietzsche decided to switch universities as well; and an autobiographical sketch entitled 'Retrospective View of my Two Years in Leipzig' records Nietzsche's sense of enchantment on arriving in Leipzig, accompanied by his friend Hermann Mushacke (1845–1906) (BAW 3, 293–6). Ritschl's exclamation, 'Look! Nietzsche is here, too!', when he spotted his student among the audience at his inaugural lecture captures the sense of excitement in the intellectual world in Leipzig, shared by Nietzsche until he gradually began to question precisely the value and use of philology (Heise 2000).

During his two years in Leipzig, however, Nietzsche was entirely committed to the ideals of philology: together with fellow students Heinrich Wilhelm Wisser (1843–1935), Wilhelm Heinrich Roscher (1845–1923) and Richard Arnold (1845–1910), he founded a philological society, the *Philologischer Verein*, worked on Theognis and Diogenes Laertius, and met regularly with friends in Café Kintschy to discuss philology and philosophy. Of course, it was while he was at Leipzig that Nietzsche met Richard Wagner (1813–83) in person in the house of the orientalist Hermann Brockhaus (1806–77). In a letter of 8 October 1868, Nietzsche confided to his closest friend, Erwin Rohde (1845–98): 'What appeals to me in Wagner is what appeals to me in Schopenhauer, the ethical atmosphere, the Faustian odor, cross, death, and crypt' (KSB 2, 322).

On the strength of the philological excellence of his publications in the academic journal, the *Rheinisches Museum für Philologie*, Ritschl – one of the co-editors of that journal – urged his colleagues in Basel to appoint Nietzsche to their Chair for Greek language and literature. And so, despite his enthusiasm for his military service in the horseback artillery that began in October 1867, from which he was released a year later because of ill-health, and despite his subsequent plan to abandon philology and study chemistry,[5]

---

[5] See Nietzsche's letter to Rohde of 16 January 1869 (KSB 2, 359–60).

Nietzsche became a classics professor. To be precise, in April 1869 he was appointed Extraordinary Professor of Classical Philology at the University of Basel, at the age of 24. The remarkable speed and extent of Nietzsche's promotion should not be underestimated; nor should his eventual and bitter disillusionment with the profession in which he had been so swiftly advanced, leading him to write the bitingly satirical sentence, 'In the end I would much rather have been a professor at Basel than God.'[6]

After his inaugural lecture on 28 May 1869, later published as 'Homer and Classical Philology', and after a series of addresses – including (in 1870) 'The Greek Music Drama', 'Socrates and Tragedy' and 'The Dionysian World-View' and (in 1871) 'Socrates and Greek Tragedy' – Nietzsche settled down to his professorial duties: to his teaching, his research and socialising with his university colleagues, including the philologists Jacob Mähly (1828–1902) and Hermann Usener (1834–1905). Yet after only a few months, one can detect a note of caution in Nietzsche's correspondence about his future career, and expressions of an increasing dissatisfaction with his life as a professor together with a developing sense of rather different priorities, reflected in his failed application for a chair in philosophy, not philology, in Basel (KSB 3, 175–6 and 193). Just ten years after his appointment, Nietzsche decided to give up his professorship at Basel, and he applied to be released from the post on the grounds of ill-health on 2 May 1879 (KSB 5, 411–12). He had developed, as he told Franz Overbeck (1837–1905) on 3 April 1879, 'a phobia about Basel, a veritable anxiety and inhibition about the bad water, the bad air, the entire depressed essence of this unholy breeding-ground of my sufferings!' (KSB 5, 402).

Although Nietzsche now embarked on an itinerant lifestyle, moving around continental Europe between Italy, France and Switzerland, depending on the season of the year, philology remained a matter of concern to him. For example, in *Human,*

---

[6] See Nietzsche's letter of 6 January 1889, addressed to his former colleague, Jacob Burckhardt (KSB 8, 577).

All Too Human (1878–80), he wrote in an aphorism entitled 'the art of reading':

> The restoration and keeping pure of texts, besides their explanation, carried on in common for hundreds of years, has finally enabled the right methods to be found; the whole of the Middle Ages was absolutely incapable of a strictly philological explanation, that is, of the simple desire to comprehend what an author says—it was an achievement, finding these methods, let it not be undervalued! (HAH I §270)

And in his Preface to *Daybreak* (1881), he observed:

> For philology is that venerable art which exacts from its followers one thing above all – to step to one side, to leave themselves spare moments, to grow silent, to become slow – the leisurely art of the goldsmith applied to language: an art which must carry out slow, fine work, and attains nothing if not *lento*. For this very reason philology is now more desirable than ever before; for this very reason it is the highest attraction and incitement in an age of 'work': that is to say, of hurry, of unseemly and immoderate haste, which is intent upon 'getting things done' at once, even books whether old or new. Philology itself perhaps will not 'get things done' so hurriedly: it teaches how to read *well* [. . .] (D Preface §5)

Elsewhere in this work, Nietzsche explicitly takes issue with 'the philology of Christianity':

> How little Christianity cultivates the sense of honesty can be inferred from the character of the writings of its scholars. They set out their conjectures as audaciously as if they were dogmas and seldom find any difficulty in the interpretation of Scripture. Their continual cry is: 'I am right, for it is written' – and then follows an explanation so shameless and capricious that a philologist, when he hears it, is caught between anger and laughter, asking himself again

and again: Is it possible? Is it honest? Is it even decent? It is only those who never – or always – attend church that underestimate the dishonesty with which this subject is still dealt in Protestant pulpits [. . .] (D §84)

He was equally trenchant about the shortcomings of 'so-called classical education', condemning 'the squandering of our youth when our educators failed to employ those eager, hot and thirsty years to lead us towards knowledge of things but used them for a so-called "classical education"!' (D §195). And as far as classics was concerned, Nietzsche lamented that as a student he had learned nothing about how the ancient Greeks had actually thought, spoken and lived:

Nothing grows clearer to me year by year than that the nature of the Greeks and of antiquity, however simple and universally familiar it may seem to lie before us, is very hard to understand, indeed is hardly accessible at all, and that the facility with which the ancients are usually spoken of is either a piece of frivolity or an inherited arrogance born of thoughtlessness. We are deceived by a similarity of words and concepts: but behind them there always lies concealed a sensation which has to be foreign, incomprehensible or painful to modern sensibility. (D §195)

As we shall see, in *The Anti-Christ* a good number of Nietzsche's arguments about, with and against Christianity turn on philological points. In fact, it is a central argument of this present introductory study that there is a significant element of continuity between Nietzsche's early interest in philology and his critique of Christianity.

At the same time, after he had left Basel, the question of religion advanced to the forefront of Nietzsche's concerns.[7] The entire chapter of *Human, All Too Human* volume 1 (1878) entitled 'The Religious Life' (§§108–44) focuses on religion, and

---

[7] For further discussion of Nietzsche's critique of religion, see Strong 2019.

the following sections are particularly important: §111, 'Origin of Religious Worship'; §126, 'Art and Strength of False Interpretation'; and §§132–5, 'Of the Christian Need of Salvation'. Behind the dramatic presentation in *The Gay Science* (1882, §125) of the 'death of God' lies a complex, nuanced argument about the impossibility – as Nietzsche saw it – of belief. For in volume 1 of *Human, All Too Human*, we already find Nietzsche reflecting at length on what he called 'the religious life'. In a section devoted to the 'origin of religious worship', he examined 'a fundamental conviction' which human beings (or so he argued) 'no longer share' and, as a consequence of which, 'the door to the religious life' is closed 'once for all so far as we are concerned': namely, about *nature and our traffic with nature* (HAH I §111). Or as he put it later, 'the religious instinct is indeed in the process of growing powerfully – but the theistic satisfaction it refuses with deep suspicion' (BGE §53).

In 'the times in which religious life flourished most vigorously', Nietzsche argues in *Human, All Too Human*, 'nothing is yet known of nature's laws' and there is a lack of 'all idea of natural causation'. If it rained, or if the sun shone, this did not happen because of 'natural laws', but rather because someone (or something) wanted it to: a god, perhaps, or a daimon. Hence 'all nature is, in the opinion of religious people, a sum total of the doings of conscious and willing beings, an immense mass of complex volitions'. On this account, the human being is 'the rule' and nature is 'the ruleless' – this is 'the fundamental conviction that dominates crude, religion-producing, early civilizations'. In his philosophy of symbolic forms, Ernst Cassirer (1874–1945) would describe this outlook as 'mythical consciousness'.[8] In the example that Nietzsche provides, 'if a man rows, it is not the oar that moves the boat, but rowing is a magical ceremony whereby a demon is constrained to move the boat!'

By contrast, today we feel 'exactly the opposite': it is we who are 'polyphonic' in our subjectivity, it is we who are (in the striking image used by Zarathustra) 'tormented and bent' by 'invisible

---

[8] See especially 'Particular Categories of Mythical Thinking' (Cassirer 1955: 60–70).

hands', as 'the wind, which we cannot see, torments and bends [the tree] where it wishes' (TSZ I Of the Tree on the Mountainside), whereas it is nature that is uniform, predictable and law-bound. Formerly, the reverse was the case: whereas primitive human beings were governed by 'rule' or 'tradition', nature seemed instead to be 'the domain of freedom, of volition, of higher power, indeed as an ultra-human degree of destiny, as god' (HAH I §111). Hence the rise of *magic*[9] as an attempt to regulate the powers of nature just as the human being is regulated by law: 'The cogitation of the superstitious and magic-deluded man is upon the theme of imposing a law upon nature: and to put it briefly, religious worship is the result of such cogitation' (HAH I §111).

In this section Nietzsche considers, as Cassirer does in the second volume of *The Philosophy of Symbolic Forms*, religion in its most original (and, in this sense, 'primitive') forms. In a subsequent section, however, he turns his attention specifically to Christianity, in a passage that sets up a contrast between antiquity and modernity, between an age of belief and (implicitly) an age of disbelief: 'When on a Sunday morning we hear the old bells ringing, we ask ourselves: Is it possible? All this for a Jew crucified two thousand years ago who said he was God's son?', whereas – as Nietzsche is swift to add – 'the proof of such an assertion is lacking' (HAH I §113). As a consequence of this lack of proof, he continues, 'the Christian religion constitutes in our time a protruding bit of antiquity from very remote ages', and 'that its assertions are still generally believed [. . .] constitutes the oldest relic of this inheritance' (HAH I §113). In the rest of this section, Nietzsche goes on to present a cartoon-sketch version of Christianity, but one that culminates in the proposition that the essence of Christianity is, in fact, no longer understood today:

> A god who begets children by a mortal woman; a sage who demands that no more work be done, that no more justice

---

[9] Cf. Cassirer (1955: 24–5), for the distinction between the 'magical-mythical' and the truly 'religious' worldview.

be administered but that the signs of the approaching end of the world be heeded; a system of justice that accepts an innocent as a vicarious sacrifice in the place of the guilty; a person who bids his disciples drink his blood; prayers for miracles; sins against a god expiated upon a god; fear of a hereafter to which death is the portal [. . .] (HAH I §113)

Above all, 'the figure of the cross as a symbol in an age that no longer knows the purpose and the ignominy of the cross' – when we hear the bells on Sunday morning, 'how ghostly all these things flit before us out of the grave of their primitive antiquity! Is one to believe that such things can still be believed?' (HAH I §113).

In *Daybreak* Nietzsche, in a section entitled 'The Tortures of the Soul', accuses Christianity of having 'turned this world of ours into a fearful habitation by raising the crucifix in all parts and thereby proclaiming the earth to be a place "where the just man is tortured to death"!' (D §77). In particular, Nietzsche criticises the Methodist preacher George Whitefield (or Whitfield) (1714–70), a kind of eighteenth-century Billy Graham, for

> preach[ing] 'like a dying man to the dying', now bitterly weeping, now violently stamping his feet, speaking passionately, in abrupt and incisive tones, without fearing to turn the whole force of his attack upon any one individual present, excluding him from the assembly with excessive harshness – then indeed did it seem as if the earth were being transformed into a 'field of evil' [cf. Ἄτης ἀν λειμῶνα; Empedocles, DK fragment B 121] (D §77)

– or, as R. J. Hollingdale translates it, 'a vale of misery'.

Yet in volume 2 of *Human, All Too Human*, Nietzsche went on to argue that precisely the antiquity of Christianity constitutes its most positive aspect: indeed, Nietzsche even goes so far as to express his *gratitude* to Christianity. This passage should alert us to the complexity and ambiguity of his account of Christian belief:

> Christianity is the religion of antiquity grown old, its presupposition is degenerated ancient cultures; on these it

could and can act as a balm [. . .] If one thinks of the Rome of Juvenal, that poison-toad with the eyes of Venus, one learns what it means to confront the 'world' with a Cross, one comes to respect the quiet Christian community and is grateful that it overran the Graeco-Roman world [. . .] This Christianity as the evening-bell of *good* antiquity, a bell broken and weary yet still sweet-sounding, is a balm to the ears even for him who now wanders through these centuries only as a historian: what must it have been for the men of these centuries themselves! (HAH II AOM §224)

True, Nietzsche goes to argue that, 'for youthful, vigorous barbarians Christianity is *poison*', an objection couched in primarily nationalist terms: 'To implant the teaching of sinfulness and damnation into the heroic, childish and animal soul of the ancient German, for example, is nothing other than to poison it' (HAH II AOM §224). Even here, however, Nietzsche is able to extract something positive from this Christian effect of 'enfeeblement':

One must [. . .] ask what, without this enfeeblement, there would have been left to us of Greek culture! of the entire cultural past of the human race! – for the barbarian races *untouched* by Christianity were capable of doing away with ancient cultures altogether: as, for example, was demonstrated with fearful clarity by the pagan conquerors of Romanized Britain. Christianity was obliged against its will to assist in making the 'world' of antiquity immortal. (HAH II AOM §224)

This idea is recapitulated in Nietzsche's unpublished writings from spring 1884. Here he castigates the Romans for decadence and for giving Christianity the opportunity to rise in Roman society. During the rule of the emperors Nero and Caracalla, 'the paradox arose: the lowest human being is *worth more* than those up there!' In turn, this allowed a particular image of God to establish itself, one that was '*distanced* as far as was possible from the image of what was most powerful – the God on the cross!' (KSA 11, 225[344], 102). As a result, Nietzsche argued that 'the Romans are guilty of the *greatest misfortune of Europe*, the people of *immoderation* – they brought extremes to power and *extreme paradoxes*, like the "God on the cross"', as a consequence of which he concluded: 'One first has to learn to make the distinction: *for* the Greeks, *against* the Romans – *that* is what I call *classical education*' (KSA 11, 25[344], 103). One might here recall Martin Heidegger's assertion that Nietzsche was, leaving Friedrich Hölderlin aside, 'the first [. . .] to release the "classical" from the misinterpretations of classicism and humanism' (Heidegger 1991a: vol. 1, 127).

Overall Nietzsche advances three main objections against – or articulates three problems with – belief in Christianity. The first is *psychological*. In *Human, All Too Human*, a sequence of aphorisms aims to uncover the mechanism behind 'the Christian need of salvation' (HAH I §§132–5). Here Nietzsche undertakes to propound 'some explanation of that process in the soul of a Christian which is termed need of salvation', and to provide 'an explanation, too, free from mythology: hence one purely psychological' (HAH I §132). In these sections Nietzsche offers one of his earliest accounts of the origin of the conscience (an account that he was to revise in *Beyond Good and Evil* [1886] and again in *On the Genealogy of Morals* [1887]). Once we understand how 'the idea of a god', which 'perturbs and discourages as long as it is accepted', actually 'originated' – something which, in Nietzsche's view, 'can no longer, in the present state of comparative ethnological science, be a matter of doubt' – then 'with the insight into the origin of this belief all faith collapses' (HAH I §133). In brief, Nietzsche argues that 'a certain false psychology, a certain kind of imaginativeness in the interpretation of motives and experiences is the essential preliminary to being a Christian and to experiencing the need of salvation', and he concludes that, 'upon gaining an insight into this wandering of the reason and the imagination, one ceases to be a Christian' (HAH I §135). This *psychological* account is extended later into a *genealogical* account of morality (see *On the Genealogy of Morals*).

Second, Nietzsche makes it clear elsewhere that another objection to Christianity is a *philological* one (see Chapter 7 below). As we have seen, in *Daybreak* Nietzsche devoted a section to 'The philology of Christianity' and set out his objections at length (D §84).¹⁰ As an example of Christian textual duplicity, Nietzsche refers to the argument surrounding Psalm 96[95], verse 10, which includes the phrase 'the Lord hath reigned' (DRV), but was translated by St Justin Martyr as 'the Lord haith reigned *from the wood*', an allusion to the Cross (Haydock 2006: 737; Neale and Littledale 1874: vol. 3, 234–5).¹¹ Indeed, Christian writing and the Christian liturgy abounds in examples of the 'typological' or 'christological' interpretation of Scripture, sometimes at quite extravagant lengths; see, for example, the New Testament's almost obsessional interest in Psalm 110[109], with its reference to Melchizedek;¹² or St Paul's application of a verse from Psalm 68[67] to the ascension of Christ and the descent of the Holy Spirit;¹³ or the responsory at Matins for the Feast of the Immaculate Conception in the old Roman Breviary. Implicitly, Nietzsche's philological critique goes even further: can we even begin to imagine the significance for Jews, living in Palestine on the cusp of the first millennium, of such terms as 'Messiah', 'Christ' or 'Son of God'?

Although Nietzsche is conventionally read as straightforwardly and unproblematically atheist, the philological aspect of his critique of Christianity should give us pause for thought. For if, as he asserts in *Twilight of the Idols*, 'we are not getting rid of God because we still believe in grammar' (TI 'Reason' §5), then it is surely also the case that the necessarily linguistic construction of (our sense of) reality implies the inevitable persistence of the divine? As in their highly diverse ways both Heidegger¹⁴

---

[10] See also KSA 9, 4[235] and 6[240], 159 and 261.
[11] See the discussion in Haydock 2006: 737; Neale and Littledale 1874: vol. 3, 234–5.
[12] See Matt. 22:41–6; Acts 2:34–6; 1 Cor. 15:25–6; Heb. 1:13; 10:12–13.
[13] See Eph. 4:7–13, referring to Ps. 68[67]:18, whose original context is the military and religious story of Israel; specifically, King David, the Ark of the Covenant and the return of the troops of Israel from battle.
[14] Compare with Heidegger's observation that 'to relegate the animated, vigorous word to the immobility of a univocal, mechanically programmed sequence of signs would mean the death of language and the petrification and devastation of Dasein', because 'in the very foundations of our being language as resonant signification roots us to our earth and ties us to our world' (Heidegger 1991a: vol. 1, 144, 145).

and Jung[15] argue, the vehicle by means of which transcendence persists, whether one calls it God or Being, is language.

Finally, Nietzsche takes issue with the meaning of the central icon of Christianity – the crucified saviour. His argument here is bound up with his account of St Paul, which he first sets out in *Daybreak* (§68) and to which he later returns in *The Anti-Christ* (§§39–42) (see Chapter 6 below). For Nietzsche, the words attributed in the Gospel of St Matthew to Christ on the cross – 'My God, my God, why has thou forsaken me?' (Matt. 27:46; cf. Ps. 22[21]:1) – are to be understood 'in their deepest sense, as they ought to be understood', as 'evidence of a complete disillusionment and enlightenment over the delusion of his life' (D §114). One may criticise Nietzsche for many things, but one cannot criticise him for not taking Christianity seriously.[16] In *Beyond Good and Evil* he writes:

> Modern men, obtuse to all Christian nomenclature, no longer feel the gruesome superlative that struck a classical taste in the paradoxical formula 'God on the cross'. Never yet and nowhere has there been an equal boldness in inversion, anything as horrible, questioning, and questionable as this formula: it promised a revaluation of all the values of antiquity. (BGE §46)

In the first essay in *On the Genealogy of Morals* Nietzsche returned to this theme:

---

[15] Compare with Jung's argument about the persistence of the Christian outlook in the post-Enlightenment world (see his comments in a Basel Seminar of 1934, cited in Jung 1971: 341–2).

[16] In *Retour à l'émerveillement*, Vergely explains that Nietzsche 'wanted to invent a new piety, founded on the passion for life' (2010: 297), and he cites Nietzsche's definition of a philosopher as 'a human being who constantly experiences, sees, hears, suspects, hopes, and dreams extraordinary things; who is struck by his own thoughts as from outside, as from above and below, as by *his* type of experiences and lightning bolts; who is perhaps himself a storm pregnant with new lightnings [. . .] a being that often runs away from itself, often is afraid of itself – but too inquisitive not to "come to" again – always back to himself' (BGE §292).

And could spiritual subtlety imagine [. . .] anything to equal the enticing, intoxicating, overwhelming, and undermining power of that symbol of the 'holy cross', that ghastly paradox of a 'God on the cross', that mystery of an unimaginable ultimate cruelty and self-crucifixion of God *for the salvation of man?* (GM I §8)

For Nietzsche, the episode of the crucifixion and the symbol of the Cross are of central importance, but for different reasons from those usually advanced by the proponents of Christian belief. In *The Anti-Christ*, for instance, Nietzsche explains what he means when, as part of his anti-Pauline rhetoric, he says that 'in reality there was only one Christian, and he died on the Cross' (AC §39). What emerges here is an image of Christ as a kind of almost Stoic figure:

This 'bearer of glad tidings' died as he lived and *taught* – [. . .] to show mankind how to live. It was a *way of life* he bequeathed to man: his demeanour before the judges, before the officers, before his accusers – his demeanour on the *Cross*. He does not resist; he does not defend his rights; he makes no effort to ward off the most extreme penalty – more, *he invites it* . . . (AC §35)

The behaviour and attitude of Christ are, then, comparable to the story told by Celsus (and recorded by Origen) about Epictetus.[17] On this account, one day his master, Epaphroditus, was twisting Epictetus' leg. Smiling and unmoved, Epictetus warned him to

---

[17] See Origen, *Contra Celsum*, book 7, ch. 53. For Celsus, the Gospel account of Christ's suffering counts *against* belief; in response, Origen argues that 'the silence of Jesus under the scourgings, and amidst all His sufferings, spoke more for His firmness and submission than all that was said by the Greeks when beset by calamity' (*Contra Celsum*, book 7, ch. 55); and he contends that although Epictetus' 'firmness' is 'justly admired', 'his saying when his leg was broken by his master is not to be compared with the marvellous acts and words of Jesus which Celsus refuses to believe; and these words were accompanied by such a divine power, that even to this day they convert not only some of the more ignorant and simple, but many also of the most enlightened of men' (*Contra Celsum*, book 7, ch. 54) (see Roberts, Donaldson and Coxe [eds] 1885: 633).

be careful: 'You will break my leg.' But Epaphroditus carried on, until Epictetus' leg broke. To which Epictetus responded, 'Did I not tell you that you would break it?' (Roberts, Donaldson and Coxe [eds] 1885: 633).

Accordingly, for Nietzsche the exchange related by St Luke between Christ and the Good Thief on the cross (Luke 23:39–42) contains nothing less than 'the whole Gospel'. When the Good Thief says to Christ, 'Indeed this was a just man',[18] and Christ responds, 'Amen, I say to thee, this day thou shalt be with me in paradise' (Luke 23:43), Nietzsche sees an embodiment of a highly specific ethic: '*not* to defend oneself, *not* to show anger, *not* to lay blame', even 'to submit to the evil man – to *love* him' (AC §35). From this moment onwards, however, 'the history of Christianity' is 'the history of a progressively cruder misunderstanding of an *original* symbolism' (AC §37). Indeed, Nietzsche's reading of Christianity in *The Anti-Christ* is an eminently symbolic one. 'If I understand anything at all about this great symbolist, it is this: that he regarded only subjective realities as realities, as "truths" – that he saw everything else, everything natural, temporal, spatial and historical, merely as signs, as materials for parables', and this can be applied to His teachings about 'God' and the 'Kingdom of Heaven':

> The 'kingdom of heaven' is a state of the heart – not something to come 'beyond the world' or 'after death' [. . .] The 'kingdom of God' is not something that men wait for: it had no yesterday and no day after tomorrow, it is not going to come at a 'millennium' – it is an experience of the heart, it is everywhere and it is nowhere . . . (AC §34) (see Chapter 4 below)[19]

---

[18] In fact, the words are spoken by the centurion after Christ expires on the Cross (Luke 23:47). As the commentary to the KSA points out, this lack of biblical knowledge on Nietzsche's part may well have led Fritz Koegel, one of the editors working for the Nietzsche Archive in Weimar, to suppress this passage in the version of *The Anti-Christ* published in the *Großoktav-Ausgabe* of Nietzsche's works (cf. KSA 14, 435 and 442).

[19] Compare with Nietzsche's notebooks for November 1887 to March 1888, where he argues that 'the legend of salvation' wrongly replaces 'the symbolic Now-Time and All-Time, Here and Everywhere', and 'the miracle' replaces the 'psychological symbol' (KSA 13, 11[354–5], 154–5).

In his notebooks for the period from autumn 1885 to autumn 1886, Nietzsche noted that the opposition between Christianity and science was a false one: 'Irony of those who regard Christianity as *overcome* by modern sciences. The Christian judgments of value are thereby absolutely *not* overcome. "Christ on the Cross" is the most sublime symbol – still' (KSA 12, 12, 2[96], 108).

What died on the Cross, then, was 'a new and thoroughly original effort to found a Buddhistic peace movement, and so establish *happiness on earth*' (AC §42) (see Chapter 3 below). Instead, what came to prominence in the rise of Christianity was an attitude and an outlook that Nietzsche sees exemplified in the saying of St Paul, 'But the foolish things of the world hath God chosen, that he may confound the wise: and the weak things of the world hath God chosen, that he may confound the strong' (1 Cor. 1:27), and in the interpretation that Paul gives to the Cross:

> *God on the Cross* – is man always to miss the frightful inner significance of this symbol? – Everything that suffers, everything that hangs on the Cross, is *divine* . . . We all hang on the Cross, consequently *we* are divine . . . We alone are divine . . . Christianity was thus a victory: a nobler attitude of mind was destroyed by it. – Christianity remains to this day the greatest misfortune of humankind. – (AC §51)[20]

And in another passage from the Gospel of St John, where Christ tells the Samaritan woman that 'salvation is of the Jews' (John 4:22),[21] Nietzsche sees further evidence of how, 'with the aid of the small sectarian Christian that stood apart from Judaism, a "world conflagration" might be kindled' and how, 'with the symbol of "God on the Cross", all secret seditions, all the fruits of anarchistic intrigues in the Empire, might be amalmagmated into one immense power' (AC §58). In short, in opposition to the outlook summarised in Horace's dictum, *pulchrum est paucorum*

---

[20] Cf. KSA 11, 25[292], 86. The experience of joining Christ on the Cross is a centrepiece of Jung's visionary-mystical experiences in *The Red Book* (see Jung 2009).
[21] Cf. AC §24; and KSA 9, 3[20], 52 and KSA 12, 10[182], 565.

hominum (i.e., 'beauty is for the few') (AC §57),[22] and politically embodied 'as a lasting monument' (*aere perennius*)[23] in the Roman Empire ('the most magnificent form of organization under difficult conditions which has ever been achieved'), Christianity by contrast, 'as the formula for exceeding *and* summing up the subterranean cults of all varieties, that of Osiris, that of the Great Mother, that of Mithras, for instance', was, for Nietzsche, the 'discernment' or insight in which the 'genius' of St Paul consisted (AC §58) (see Chapter 4 below).[24] Hence Nietzsche's famous opposition at the conclusion of *Ecce Homo* of Dionysos against the Crucified.[25] And in one of the notes in his *Nachlass*, Nietzsche explains precisely what this formula means: that '"the God on the Cross" is a curse on life, a hint to deliver oneself from it', whereas 'Dionysos cut to pieces is a *promise* to life: it will eternally be reborn and come home out of destruction' (KSA 13, 14[89], 267; Nietzsche 2003: 250).

For the journalist (and Anglican priest) Giles Fraser, the intensity of piety and religious practice for which Nietzsche was noted before his turn away from organised religion, like his ability as a six-year-old to cite biblical passages and sing hymns which earned him the nickname of 'the little pastor', reflects the Pietistic upbringing he received from his family and teachers. That upbringing resulted in his 'obsession' with 'the question of human salvation', and his subsequent passionate exploration of 'different ways in which the

---

[22] Horace, *Satires*, I, 9, 44. Cf. HAH II AOM §118.
[23] Horace, *Odes*, III, 30, 1.
[24] Nietzsche's allusions to Horace in these passages are part and parcel of his rhetorical strategy to oppose the classical to the Christian; cf. KSA 12, 10[181], 565: 'How one stands on the New Testament is a test of whether one has any *classical taste* in one's body (cf. Tacitus): anyone who isn't revolted by it, who doesn't honestly and profoundly feel something of a *foeda superstitio*, something from which the hand is snatched away to avoid dirtying it, does not know what is classical' (Nietzsche 2003: 204–5). Strategically Nietzsche aligns his position with Goethe's: 'One must feel the "cross" as Goethe did' (Nietzsche 2003: 205).
[25] Cf. KSA, 13, 16[16], 487: 'We believe in Olympus – and *not* in the "Crucified"'; KSA, 13, 14[89], 265–6: 'Dionysos versus the "Crucified One": there you have the opposition. It's *not* a distinction regarding their martyrdom – just that this martyrdom has a different meaning. Life itself, its eternal fruitfulness and recurrence, conditions torment, destruction, the will to annihilation...' (Nietzsche 2003: 249); and KSA, 13, 14[91], 267: '*Buddha against the "Crucified"*'.

same basic instinct for redemption can be expressed in a world without God' (Fraser 2002: 2).[26] Hence, in Nietzsche's philosophical writings, one finds not so much a critique of belief as a critique of a particular set of beliefs, and his analysis of religion is more subtle than his (still numerous) detractors usually give him credit for.[27] In a fragment from the period November 1887 to March 1888, Nietzsche writes: 'Not for a single hour of my life have I been a Christian: I regard everything I have seen as Christianity, as a *contemptible ambiguity of words*, a real *cowardice* towards all the powers that otherwise rule'; yet he made it clear that his ire was directed not at Christ himself, but at those who speak in his name: 'Christians of general military conscription, of parliamentary suffrage, of newspaper culture and, in the middle of all that, talking about "sin", "redemption", "the beyond", death on the cross – how can one endure such a mess!' (KSA 13, 11[251], 96–7; 2003: 234).

Of all Nietzsche's writings about Christianity, however, the one under discussion in the present book stands out as the most obvious, if only because of its title – *The Anti-Christ*. As a work, it has a complex and difficult genealogy; indeed, as it was published posthumously, we cannot even be sure that it is actually presented in the form in which Nietzsche wanted us to read it (see Chapter 2 below). Yet read it we must, for it speaks so very clearly *to* our time and arguably *of* our time, even if (or especially as) its message is an unwelcome one.

Moreover, it is a work about whose epochal significance Nietzsche himself appears to have been convinced. In *Twilight of the Idols*, a book dated to Turin, 30 September 1888, 'on the day when the first book of the *Revaluation of All Values* was completed', he wrote that, having given humankind 'the most profound book it possesses', i.e., *Thus Spoke Zarathustra* (1883–85), he was now going to give it its 'most independent' (TI Foreword; Expeditions §51). In a letter of 4 October 1888 to Malwida von Meysenbug (1816–1903), he said that 'the first book of my *Revaluation of All Values* is finished', describing it as 'the

---

[26] For further discussion of Nietzsche's Pietist upbringing, see Pernet 1995.
[27] For further discussion, see Fraser 2002; Huskinson 2009.

great philosophical event of all times, with which the history of humankind will be broken into two halves' (KSB 8, 447). In his letter to Paul Deussen (1845–1919) of 26 November 1888, Nietzsche made remarkable claims for himself – 'My life is now reaching its culmination: another couple of years, and the earth will tremble from a great lightning bolt. I swear to you that I have the power to change the *calendar*. There is nothing in existence today that will not be toppled, I am more dynamite than human being' – and for *The Anti-Christ*: 'My *Revaluation of All Values*, with the main title "*The Antichrist*", is finished. In the next two years I shall have to take steps to get the work translated into 7 languages; the *first* edition in each language circa one million copies' (KSB 8: 491–2). And in a letter to the Danish scholar and critic Georg Brandes (1842–1917) (a letter that has only survived in draft form), Nietzsche repeated his lines about splitting the history of the world into two, marking the beginning of a new calendar and being dynamite; he described the work as 'a *deathblow* against *Christianity*' and as 'a *judgment on the world*', albeit one over which there lies 'a grandiose calm and sense of elevation'; and he gave a preview of his 'Law Against Christianity' that would be appended to the work (KSB 8: 500–2).

What are we to make of such remarks? Perhaps instinctively we are inclined to reject them as megalomaniac; on the other hand, they anticipate (in a somewhat extreme form) the rhetoric of our own CVs and 'performance and development reviews', where self-praise is very much the order of the day. Yet how *seriously* should we take them? One way to interpret them is as a gesture that encourages us not to adopt a position of neutrality towards Nietzsche's project in *The Anti-Christ*, or in other words as an expression of concern that his readers might not be sufficiently ashamed of their lingering commitments to Christianity (cf. AC §38). If the production or escalation of shame were a goal of Nietzsche's text, then a feeling of shame might be the proper affective condition with which to consider 'the *authentic* history of Christianity' that begins in section 39 of *The Anti-Christ*: in other words, Nietzsche aspires to an affective-somatic transformation (or, in Tracy Strong's words, *transfiguration*) of his best readers (see Strong 2001).

As Daniel Conway has argued, Nietzche's efforts to nudge his readers towards feelings of shame and expressions of righteous disgust (not least for philological reasons, one might add) are part and parcel of that very transformative effect (Conway 2019 [ed.]: 182, 194, 198–200). Such readers will need to see the world differently – and to feel differently about their place within it. For only then, or so Nietzsche seems to imply, will they begin to work their way out of their remaining investments in Christian morality. Or, as Zarathustra puts it, 'And only where there are graves are there resurrections' (TSZ II 11).

Having examined in this chapter Nietzsche's biography and his religious background, in the next we shall consider the composition of the *The Anti-Christ*, part of the flurry of activity that took place in 1888; recall the significance within the biblical tradition of the figure of anti-Christ; and meet the mythical figures of the Hyperboreans. Then we discuss the crucial issue for Nietzsche of *methods*; outline his portrait in *The Anti-Christ* of its central figure, Jesus; and conclude by examining the technical term, *Beweise der Kraft* or 'proofs of strength', and its broader significance within the economy of the work as a whole.

2
Christ and Anti-Christ in *The Anti-Christ*

The composition of *The Anti-Christ* is closely bound up with that of two other works from 1888, *Twilight of the Idols* and *Ecce Homo*.[1] While he was working on *Twilight of the Idols*, Nietzsche had been drafting plans for a major philosophical work that he intended to call *The Will to Power*, subtitled *Attempt at a Revaluation of All Values*.[2] From these drafts, it looks as if Nietzsche had been intending to write a major, systematic exposition of his philosophy; perhaps a little strange, given his remark that 'a will to a system is a lack of integrity' (TI Maxims §26).

Subsequently, Nietzsche abandoned the title *The Will to Power* (although this did not prevent his sister, Elisabeth Förster-Nietzsche (1846–1935), from editing and publishing a selection of the material left unpublished at his death, known as his *Nachlass*, under precisely this title; nor did it prevent Martin Heidegger from treating this work as if were a legitimate text by Nietzsche). Instead, Nietzsche replaced this title with the former subtitle, *The Revaluation of All Values*, and there is evidence that *The Anti-Christ* was intended as the first of (in total) four parts of this work.[3] A letter written to

---

[1] See Montinari 1972; 1982; translated in Montinari 2003. Before Montinari, these arguments were also brought forward in Horneffer 1907; Kaufmann 1950; and by Karl Schlechta, the editor of the first authentic edition of *The Anti-Christ*, in Schlechta 1966.
[2] See, for instance, KSA 13, 16[86], 515–16 and 18[17], 537–8.
[3] See KSA 13, 9[8], 545.

Heinrich Köselitz (aka Peter Gast) (1864–1918) on 13 February 1888 indicates that Nietzsche had already been planning a work under the title of *Attempt at a Revaluation*, but had been dissatisfied with its progress and had abandoned it (KSB 8, 252).[4] Whatever Nietzsche's plans for the work may have been, it is as a standalone work that we know it – or don't know it – today.

Composition of *The Anti-Christ*

In one draft of the layout of *The Will to Power*, the work opens with a section entitled 'We Hyperboreans: Laying the Foundation Stone of the Problem' (KSA 134, 18[17], 537). Section 1 of *The Anti-Christ* is based on the motif of this mythological Greek race, and this prompts the question as to whether one should think of *The Will to Power* as a work that Nietzsche never wrote, or whether *The Anti-Christ* in some way fulfils the summative function that Nietzsche hoped his *Will-to-Power* project would have.

When he returned to this project in September 1888, Nietzsche envisaged that the four parts would be entitled 1) 'The Anti-Christ: Attempt at a Critique of Christianity'; 2) 'The Free Spirit: Critique of Philosophy as a Nihilistic Movement'; 3) 'The Immoralist: Critique of the Most Fatal Kind of Ignorance'; and 4) 'Dionysos: Philosophy of the Eternal Recurrence' (KSA 13, 19[8], 545). And as the autumn wore on, Nietzsche began firing off letters to his friends, announcing the completion of the *Revaluation* and identifying the work with the text of *The Anti-Christ*. As he told Paul Deussen on 26 November 1888, for instance: 'My *Revaluation of Values* under the main title 'the Anti-Christ' is finished' (KSB 8, 492).[5] Although Nietzsche had sent off the manuscript of *Twilight of the Idols* to his publisher C. G. Naumann in Leipzig, and it duly appeared in January 1889, the manuscript of *The Anti-Christ* was ready for printing by the end of 1888 but was

---

[4] For Nietzsche's text, see KSA 12, 9[1]–10[206], 339–582 and KSA 13, 11[1]–11[417], 9–194.
[5] See also Nietzsche's letters to Georg Brandes of 20 November 1888 (KSB 8, 482) and to Carl Fuchs of 11 December 1888 (KSB 8, 521–2).

never sent to Naumann. Following Nietzsche's mental collapse in the streets of Turin on 3 January 1889 – a collapse which, as likely as not, had physiological rather than (or as well as) psychological causes – *The Anti-Christ* joined *Ecce Homo*, the *Dithyrambs of Dionysos* and *Nietzsche contra Wagner* as one of his *Nachlass* texts.[6]

Given its controversial title and polemical content, Nietzsche's early editors, Franz Overbeck and Heinrich Köselitz, chose to delay its publication; so it did not appear until 1895 when it was published by Fritz Koegel (1860–1904) in volume 8 of the *Großoktavausgabe* of Nietzsche's collected works, and even then with the subtitle 'Attempt at a Critique of Christianity', rather than the one that Nietzsche chose to replace it with when he scored it through and added, in somewhat spiky handwriting, 'A Curse on Christianity'. The first reliable edition appeared in 1956 in volume 2 of Karl Schlechta's three-volume *Werke*; in 1961, Erich Podach published his version of the manuscript, including a text called 'Law against Christianity' which Nietzsche had glued between two blank pages in the manuscript; and the authoritative text (insofar as it is possible to reach scholarly agreement) appeared in *Abteilung* VI, vol. 3, of the *Kritische Gesamtausgabe* edited by Giorgio Colli and Mazzino Montinari, publication of which began in 1967. While there is much for scholars to debate about the composition and final form of *The Anti-Christ*, these are in some respects the least of our worries. To what, for instance, does its title refer?

Significance of the figure of anti-Christ

Der Antichrist could mean 'the anti-Christian' or 'the anti-Christ', the original German being ambiguous. In his 'Attempt at a Self-Criticism' prefaced to the second edition (1886) of *The Birth of Tragedy*, Nietzsche asked, 'who could claim to know the rightful name of the Antichrist?' (§5); in a letter to Malwida von Meysenbug of 3–4 April 1883, Nietzsche had jokingly written: 'Do you want a new name for me? In the language of the

---

[6] For discussion of the links between the speed with which Nietzsche composed *The Anti-Christ* and the philosophical school known as Accelerationism, see Shapiro 2019.

Church: I am - - - - the *Antichrist*' (while adding, 'let's not forget how to laugh!') (KSB 6, 357); in a letter to Franz Overbeck of 26 August 1883, Nietzsche had expressed pleasure at how one of the first readers of *Zarathustra* had seen the work as involving 'the long-awaited "Antichrist"' (KSB 6, 438); and in *Ecce Homo* Nietzsche declared, in a passage full of playful *persiflage*,

> We all know, some of us even from experience, what a 'long-ears' is. Well then, I venture to assert that I have the smallest ears that have ever been seen. This fact is not without interest to women – it seems to me they feel that I understand them better! . . . I am essentially the anti-ass, and on this account alone a monster in the world's history – in Greek, and not only in Greek, I am the *Antichrist*. (EH Books §2)

In which case, if Nietzsche is identifying himself with the anti-Christ – just as, in the title of his autobiographical work, *Ecce Homo*, he is identifying himself with Christ – then we need to consider briefly this theological figure, known in Greek as Ἀντίχριστος (i.e., *antichristos*) and in Hebrew as the 'false messiah'.

After all, the figure of anti-Christ has – aside from its use by Nietzsche – a long history (and a wide range) of cultural implications (Brandes and Schmieder 2010); in fact, in the decade after Nietzsche had been working on *The Anti-Christ*, Wilhelm Bousset (1865–1920), a major figure in the history of religions school (or *religionsgeschichtliche Schule*), published – as part of his work on the history of the Early Church that led in 1913 to *Kyrios Christos: Geschichte des Christusglaubens von den Anfängen des Christentums bis Irenäus* – a study of the figure of the anti-Christ in relation to the apocalyptic traditions of Judaism and Christianity entitled *Der Antichrist in der Ueberlieferung des Judentums, des Neuen Testaments und der alten Kirche* (1895). In this work, Bousset sought to establish a link between the figure of anti-Christ and myths about the primordial dragon while demonstrating an extensive knowledge of Patristic and medieval literature.[7]

---

[7] For a response to Bousset's interpretation of the figure of anti-Christ, see Peerbolte 1996: 6–7, 36.

The expression 'anti-Christ' is found five times in the New Testament, in the first and second letters attributed to St John (1 John 2:18, 22; 4:2–3; 2 John 1:7). In the Second Letter to the Thessalonians, attributed to St Paul, the Thessalonians are warned about the advent of 'a day of revolt' and the revealing of 'the man of sin [. . .], the man of perdition' – a figure 'who opposeth, and is lifted up above all that is called God or worshipped, so that he sitteth in the temple of God, showing himself as if he were God' (2 Thess. 2:1–4). From the way in which this revolt or apostasy (*apostasia*) is mentioned in this letter, it would seem that its contemporary readers already knew something about it (NJB, NT, 1957), but for later readers the matter is not quite so clear. For St Jerome and others, this apostasy or 'falling away' had a political sense and applied to the falling away of other kingdoms that had previously been subject to the Roman Empire. In this sense, the passage offered a reassurance that the day of judgement would not come until other kingdoms had 'fallen away' in a general revolt and destroyed the Roman Empire.

For others, including St John Chrysostom, Theodoret of Cyrus and St Augustine, this falling away or apostasy referred to anti-Christ himself, as one who apostasised from the Christian faith; some applied it to Nero, even though the letter was written under Claudius and before Nero's reign. And for yet others such as St Cyril of Jerusalem (*Catechetical Lectures*, §15), the passage looked much further ahead, referring to a great falling off of numbers from the Catholic Church and its faith. Augustine was not wrong, then, when he wrote in *The City of God* (book 20, ch. 19, §7), 'I own myself altogether ignorant what the apostle means by these words', even if he goes on to relate the exposition to the Roman Empire (Haydock 2006: 1563).

More modern commentaries, such as that of the New Jerusalem Bible, note how this apostasy is due to an individual who is described in three different ways: as the wicked one ('the man of sin' or 'man of lawlessness'), as a being destined to be lost ('the son of perdition'), and – in terms reminiscent of the Great Rebel in the Book of Daniel (11:36) – as the Enemy or the one 'who opposeth'. This figure is identified by later Christian traditions as the figure called (in the letters of John) the anti-Christ. This figure, inasmuch as he will be revealed at the end of time, stands in contrast to Satan, whose tool he is, and who is already at work in secret: 'For the mystery of iniquity already worketh' (2 Thess. 2:7). This wicked one is the instrument through which Satan works, and while wickedness (or 'lawlessness) is already going in, it does so in an underground way, secretly preparing for the great revolt, at which point this lawlessness will work unmasked (NJB, NT, 1957):

> And then that wicked one shall be revealed [. . .] him, Whose coming is according to the working of Satan, in all power, and signs, and lying wonders, And in all seduction of iniquity to them that perish: because they receive not the love of the truth that they might be saved. Therefore God shall send them the operation of error, to believe a lie. (2 Thess. 2:8–10)

These warnings are consistent with those spoken by Christ in his great eschatalogical discourse about the end and the Second Coming, where the disciples are told of the great tribulation of Jerusalem that is to come: 'Then if any man shall say to you: Lo here is Christ, or there, do not believe him. For there shall arise false Christs and false prophets, and shall shew great signs and wonders, insomuch as to deceive (if possible) even the elect. Behold I have told it to you, beforehand' (Matt. 24:24–6; cf. Mark 13:21–3). The figure who is here called *pseudokhristos* or 'false Messiah' puts in a final (and apocalyptic) biblical appearance in the Book of Revelation in the form of the 'first beast' (*thērion*) or the beast from the sea (Rev. 13:1–10), or then again the 'second beast' or the beast from the earth, called the 'false prophet' (Rev. 13:11–17).

Drawing on chapter 7 of the Book of Daniel, written during the persecution of Antioches Epiphanes, these prophecies in the Book of Revelation develop an incredibly dense network of images in relation to the Dragon (i.e., Satan), the first beast from the sea and the second beast from the earth. Most interpretations – indeed, the one provided by Revelation itself (Rev. 17:10, 12–14) – see the beast from the sea as the Roman Empire, its seven heads being the seven hills of Rome as well as seven emperors, of whom five (Nero, Domitian, Severus, Decius, Valerian) have gone, one (Diocletian) is currently alive, and another is the anti-Christ. The rich symbolism of the text invites varying interpretations, and it inspired Nietzsche, too; the chapter of *Thus Spoke Zarathustra* entitled 'The Seven Seals' alludes to the scroll with seven seals broken open by the Lamb (Rev. 5:1–5; 6:1–17), while in *The Anti-Christ* Nietzsche defends precisely the institution that is being attacked in the Book of Revelation and depicted as an idolatrous beast and as the great whore of Babylon, i.e., Rome and the Roman Empire.

Clearly, there is a relation between the anti-Christ and the figure of the devil or Satan, a figure who acquires considerably more significance in Christianity than it possessed in Judaism;[8] this relation need not detain us here. But it is perhaps worth noting that the figure of anti-Christ can also be related to the Gnostic concept of the archon (derived from the Greek ἄρχοντες, i.e., 'principalities' or 'rulers'), the name given to various servants of the Demiurge or 'creator god' in some Gnostic traditions. The revival of interest in this figure reflects the persistence of certain ideas found in Neoplatonism; for instance, in his *Theology of Plato* (book 6, ch. 1), Proclus observes:

> For all the series of the ruling Gods (θεοὶ ἄρχοντες), are collected into the intellectual fabrication as into a summit, and subsist about it. And as all the fountains are the progeny of the intelligible father, and are filled from him with intelligible union, thus likewise, all the orders of the principles or rulers, are suspended according to nature from the demiurgus, and participate from thence of an intellectual life. (Taylor 1995: 394)

And in *On the Mysteries of the Egyptians, Chaldeans, and Assyrians* (ch. 2, §§3–9), attributed to Iamblichus of Apamea, the archons are placed below gods, daimons, angels and archangels, but above

---

[8] For discussion of the figure of anti-Christ, see McGinn 2000; and of the figure of Satan, see Kelly 2006.

heroes and departed 'souls', in the hierarchy of invisible beings (Taylor 1999: 51–9).

Over and above these biblical and pagan antecedents, there is a specifically Nietzschean context to his focus on the figure of the anti-Christ. Towards the end of his second essay in *On the Genealogy of Morals*, Nietzsche tells us who the anti-Christ is: someone who is not just the 'victor over God and nothingness' but who represents 'the great health', that is to say, 'the *redemption* of this reality' (GM II §24; cf. Young 2006: 177). Nietzsche describes this figure who 'some day, in a stronger age than this decaying, self-doubting present [. . .] must yet come to us', as follows:

> The *redeeming man*, of great love and contempt, the creative spirit whose compelling strength will not let him rest in any aloofness or any beyond, whose isolation is misunderstood by the people as if it were flight *from* reality – while it is only his absorption, immersion, penetration *into* reality, so that, when he one day emerges again into the light, he may bring home the *redemption* of this reality; its redemption from the curse that the hitherto reigning ideal has laid upon it. The man of the future, who will redeem us not only from the hitherto reigning ideal but also from that which was bound to grow out of it, the great nausea, the will to nothingness, nihilism; this bellstroke of noon and of the great decision that liberates the will again and restores its goal to the earth and his hope to man; this Antichrist and antinihilist; this victor over God and nothingness – *he must come one day*. – (GM II §12)

Thus Nietzsche expresses his conviction that this figure of the anti-Christ – a figure, one might say, of 'hellenic Harmony' (Berry 2007) – *must come*, with the same certainty that, in his *Nachgesang* to *Beyond Good and Evil*, 'From High Mountains' (1886), he recalls how 'Friend *Zarathustra* came, the guest of guests! / The world now laughs, rent are the draps of fright, / The wedding is at hand of dark and light –' (BGE Aftersong); and, in his poem 'Sils Maria' (1887), he remembers how 'Then, suddenly, friend, one turned into two – / And Zarathustra walked into my view' (GS Songs of Prince Vogelfrei). And so anti-Christ and Zarathustra are complementary figures within the dense network of self-referential remarks that forms the Nietzschean corpus.

In his seminar on *Zarathustra*, Jung related the origin of the legend of the anti-Christ as someone who, as described in the Apocalypse of St John (Rev. 12:14, drawing on Dan. 12:7), rules the earth 'for two times and a half time' to the Zoroastrian teaching that every thousand years or so, a Saoshyant (i.e., 'someone who brings benefit' or a saviour) appears. The anti-Christ, born in practically the same circumstances as Christ as his dark brother, would work very much the same miracles as Christ but in order to seduce humankind (Jung 1998: 12). In Zoroastrian terms, the anti-Christ would be 'a sort of negative Saoshyant, appearing when the positive reign of Christ was coming to an end' (1998: 12).

Even more audaciously, Jung suggests that 'this idea of the Saoshyant [. . .] also entered the mind of Nietzsche': 'His Zarathustra is a Saoshyant who comes after the thousand years are once more fulfilled – of course not quite, but *à peu près*', Jung explains, adding (in a rare flash of Swiss humour): 'It was only 1883, unfortunately, but the heavenly powers are sometimes irregular – perhaps the clock doesn't work regularly in heaven, one doesn't know exactly – so the Saoshyant came a bit earlier, a reincarnation in the form of Zarathustra' (1998: 13). Bolstered by the notion of the archetypal figure of the Wise Old Man, Jung expressed with some certainty that 'from what Nietzsche says about Zarathustra [. . .] he experienced him as an identity within himself that had existed many thousands of years before him, that always had been' (1998: 12).

This idea might well appear ridiculous, but Jung is surely right when he says that 'one knows [. . .] from the writings of Nietzsche – even if one only knows the titles of his works – that he had the idea of an Antichrist very much in mind' and 'makes [. . .] a great story about his anti-Christianity, and takes himself as being an Antichrist incarnate' (1998: 13). He adds that Nietzsche does so 'by no means as a merely destructive devilish brother of Christ [. . .] but as a new Saoshyant', someone who will 'destroy the former values sure enough, but for something better and more ideal, for a morality much higher than the Christian morality'; correspondingly, Nietzsche feels himself 'as a positive Saoshyant, in spite of the fact that he accepts the title of "immoralist" and "Antichrist"' (1998: 13).

Can Jung's approach help make sense of what Nietzsche thinks he is up to in *The Anti-Christ*? After all, in the light of other, possibly better-known attempts to reappraise the legacy of Christianity as a whole and of St Paul in particular, why does Nietzsche think that *his* approach and *his* insights should be taken seriously? And why does Nietzsche think that the 'curse' he pronounces in the subtitle of the work, the 'condemnation' he hands down in its final section (AC §62), will be meaningful for his target audience? Unless he thinks that, in some sense, the message he has is not simply a personal one but comes from, as it were, beyond him?

At the same time, in choosing as his title the figure of the anti-Christ, Nietzsche was echoing the decision of the French theologian Ernest Renan (1823–92) to give the fourth volume of his monumental *Histoire des Origines du Christianisme* (1863–81) the title *L'Antéchrist* (1873), and indeed the decision of the Russian novelist and Symbolist Dmitry Merezhkovsky (1866–1941) to entitle his trilogy of novels *Christ and Antichrist* (1895–1904) – the first of these novels, *The Death of the Gods*, was dedicated to the figure of Julian the Apostate, the second, *Resurrection of the Gods*, was dedicated to the figure of Leonardo da Vinci, and third and final one, *Peter and Alexis*, was dedicated to the figure of Peter the Great as an 'embodied Antichrist'. Yet the first section of *The Anti-Christ* opens with an explicitly classical reference: 'Let us look each other in the face. We are Hyperboreans' (AC §1).

Who are the Hyperboreans?

In Greek mythology, the Hyperboreans were a race of giants who lived 'beyond the North Wind', as their name indicates: *hyper* = 'beyond', *Boreas* = the god of the North Wind. In the Greek worldview, beyond the North Wind meant beyond the most northern point of Greece, i.e., Thrace. In his *Histories* (book 4, §13), Herodotus relates how Aristeas, a Greek poet of the seventh century BCE, described a visit to the land of the Issedones and beyond:

> Aristeas son of Kaystrobios of Proconnesus [. . .] composed verses in which he claims to have been inspired by Phoibos Apollo and to have visited the land of the Issedones. Above

the Issedones, he says, live the Arimaspians, one-eyed men; above them dwell the gold-guarding griffins; and above the griffins, the Hyperboreans, whose land extends all the way to the sea. (Straesser [ed.] 2008: 287)

Further on (in book 4, §§32–3), Herodotus is keen to emphasise how little is known about the Hyperboreans, citing as sources Hesiod, Homer and a tale told on the island of Delos about the gifts sent to them by the Hyperboreans:

About the Hyperboreans, neither the Scythians nor any other inhabitants of this region have anything to say, except perhaps for the Issedones; but I suppose they say nothing about them either, since if they did, the Scythians would repeat it [. . .] The Hyperboreans are mentioned by Hesiod and also by Homer in the *Epigonoi* – if Homer actually did compose those verses. But the Delians have by far the most to say about them. They tell how the Hyperboreans send sacred offerings bound in stalks of wheat to Scythia, and these offerings are received in succession by each neighbouring country until they are brought as far west as the Adriatic Sea. From there they are sent southward [. . .] and finally arrive at Delos. (Straesser [ed.] 2008: 294)

Herodotus describes the journey made by these gifts in some detail, and gives an account of the Delian rites conducted in honour of the Hyperboreans (§34), before relating the Delian myth of Arge and Opis, the early Hyperborean maidens (§35), and concluding with a reference to Abaris, said to have been 'a Hyperborean who went around the whole world carrying an arrow and eating nothing' (§36).

Why does Nietzsche choose to introduce section 1 of *The Anti-Christ* with reference to these mythical giants? There are a variety of reasons. First, to align himself with the classical world, the disappearance of whose values he will lament in this work. Second, to invoke a powerful image of living (and, more important, thinking) 'off the beaten track'. Third, to invoke one of the gods who figured in his earliest major work, *The Birth of Tragedy*, i.e., the god Apollo. Apollo was believed to be venerated by the Hyperboreans, because he spent the winter dwelling with them (Harris 1925). Fourth, because in other contexts Hyperborea functioned as a classical version of Paradise, as Pindar described it (in his tenth Pythian Ode):

> [. . .] Such are their ways that the Muse
> is not banished, but, on every side,
> the dances of maidens and the sounds of the lyre
> and the notes of the flute are ever circling;
> and, with their hair crowned with golden bay-leaves,
> they hold glad revelry; and
> neither sickness nor baneful eld mingleth
> among that chosen people; but, aloof from toil and conflict,
> they dwell afar from the wrath of Nemesis. (Pindar 1927: 293)

Thus Hyperborea joins Thule, the Blissful Islands and other *terræ incognitæ* as places where – according to Pliny, Pindar and Herodotus, as well as Virgil and Cicero – people enjoyed longevity and lives of complete happiness and bliss. And Nietzsche's final reason is because, according to Pindar again, Hyperborea does not actually exist; or, more precisely, it has no physical location, for – in words cited by Nietzsche – 'neither by ships nor by land canst thou find the wondrous road to the trysting-place of the Hyperboreans' (Pindar 1927: 291). In the words of Laurence Lampert, the Hyperboreans have become 'a beautiful symbol of the inaccessible' (1993: 275).

Nietzsche – and, by extension, 'we' – are 'Hyperboreans', inasmuch as he is (and we are – or soon will be?) immune to the kind of modern ideas, a residue of previously Christian ones, that infest late modern European culture.[9] So could it be that Hyperborean alludes to a kind of regime or discipline that will allow modern

---

[9] For further discussion of the pronoun 'we' in Nietzsche's locution 'we Hyperboreans', see the remarks by Dan Conway: 'As he does in many of his post-Zarathustran books, he favors a *first-person plural presumptive* mode of address; although he engages his best readers as if they were (near) equals, partners in an exclusive "we", they have not yet earned the privilege to be addressed as such [. . .] Throughout the text of *The Antichrist*, in fact, he speaks to his best readers not as the selves they currently are, but as the selves they may yet become. In particular, he addresses himself to a "we" that is meant to come into existence and take shape as a consequence of being addressed (and treated) as such' (Conway [ed.] 2019: 187).

human beings to exempt themselves from the standard practices of those other human beings who are contemporary Christians? If so, is the corresponding achievement one that is both cognitive and volitional – once one has seen Christianity for what it is, does one become sufficiently alarmed or even enraged to be able to resist it in body and mind (and, perhaps, soul)?

To put it another way, Hyperborea is a state of mind: to be Hyperborean means to have 'discovered happiness', to 'know the way', to have 'found the exit from a labyrinth of whole millennia', as Nietzsche puts it (AC §1). To this extent, the Hyperboreans are opposed to their antipodes in Nietzsche's worldview, the men and women of modernity. '"I don't know where I am; I am everything that doesn't know where it is," – sighs the modern individual'; this is how Nietzsche presents our world. (We have met this world earlier in Nietzsche's writings, in the form of the *letzter Mensch* whom Zarathustra describes in his Prologue – much to the enthusiasm of his audience in the market-place, which much prefers 'the last human being' to the *Übermensch* Zarathustra proposes.) Even the modern 'free spirit' (elsewhere, an entirely positive concept for Nietzsche) is said to be, in a draft preface to *Human, All Too Human*, 'born unlike its predecessors out of struggle, but rather from the *peace of dissolution*' (KSA 8, 25[2], 484).

What, for Nietzsche, is the problem with modernity? Put simply, it is that modernity makes us 'ill': because modernity is 'lazy peace, cowardly compromise, the whole virtuous dirtiness of the modern yea or nay' (AC §1). In contrast to the Borea or the North Wind of the Hyperboreans, the modern individual is exposed to the southern wind of the *sirocco*, the wind of 'tolerance and *largeur* of the heart that "forgives" everything because it "understands" everything' (AC §1). Instead Nietzsche proposes 'liv[ing] amid the ice rather than among modern virtues and other such southwinds', much as he writes in *Ecce Homo* that in *Human, All Too Human* 'one error after another is calmly laid on ice', so that 'the ideal is not refuted – it *freezes*' (EH HAH §1). This meteorological metaphor inspires in Nietzsche a rhetoric that invokes the idea of far and distant travel, a journey to the very edge of the world, a trip to Hyperborea itself:

Our fate – it was the fullness, the tension, the *storing up* of powers. We thirsted for the lightnings and great deeds; we kept as far away as possible from the happiness of the 'weakling', from 'resignation' . . . There was thunder in our air; nature, as we embodied it, became overcast – *for we had not yet found the way*. The formula of our happiness: A Yea, a Nay, a straight line, a *goal* . . . (AC §1).[10]

This goal is 'the exit from the labyrinth', a phrase that evokes the famous myth of the Minotaur. But it also recalls a motif found in *Ecce Homo*, where Nietzsche asserts that *'good men never tell the truth'*: *'The good taught you false shores and false securities: you were born and kept in the lies of the good. Everything has been distorted and twisted down to its very bottom through the good'* (EH Destiny §4). The labyrinth contains something monstrous, because the truth is (in Nietzsche's view) that we are all caught up in something monstrous, and we all have – one way or another – to find a way out. And when Nietzsche does emerge from the labyrinth and then sets sail in *The Anti-Christ* for Hyperborea, he does so with a catechism.

A 'catechism', derived from the Greek *katēkhein* or 'to instruct orally', is a treatise for instruction in religious principles, usually in a question-and-answer form. The Catholic Church has one, formulated by the Council of Trent and published in 1566 (and republished in a systematically revised form, following the Second Vatican Council, as the *Catechism of the Catholic Church* in 1997). Other churches have catechisms too: there are Lutheran catechisms (such as Luther's Large Catechism of 1529), Reformed catechisms (such as Calvin's Genevan Catechism of 1541, the Heidelberg Catechism of 1563, and the Larger and Shorter Westminster Catechisms) and a plethora of other catechisms. But it will come as no surprise to learn that no one has

---

[10] In *Twilight of the Idols*, Nietzsche uses the same concluding expression as here to bring 'Maxims and Arrows' to a close, i.e., with a maxim that captures the sheer directionality of the arrow (TI Maxims §44).

written a catechism quite like the one Nietzsche presents to his readers in *The Anti-Christ*, section 2. It is, in fact, no exaggeration to call it an *anti-catechism*:

> What is good? – Whatever augments the feeling of power, the will to power, power itself, in man.
> What is evil? – Whatever springs from weakness.
> What is happiness? – The feeling that power increases—that resistance is overcome.
> Not contentment, but more power; not peace at any price, but war; not virtue, but efficiency (virtue in the Renaissance sense, *virtù*, virtue free of moral acid).
> The weak and the botched shall perish: first principle of our charity. And one should help them to it.
> What is more harmful than any vice? – Practical sympathy for the botched and the weak – Christianity . . . (AC §2)

Over the course of this book, we shall have occasion to come back to various aspects of the tenets in this anti-catechism. Yet it is clear that in this opening question-and-answer format, the essence of Nietzsche's critique of Christianity is succinctly stated. So the next question is: how is Nietzsche going to pursue this critique?

Methods (AC §13 and §59)

In section 13, Nietzsche declares that 'the most valuable insights are *methods*'. To understand *The Anti-Christ*, we have to understand its methodology, so we must review this statement with some care. Its immediate context is Nietzsche's assertion at the beginning of this section that invokes one of his most characteristic notions, the idea of 'free spirit'.[11] Here Nietzsche identifies himself entirely with 'free spirit', declaring that '*we ourselves*, we free spirits, are already a "transvaluation of all values", a

---

[11] For further discussion, see Bamford 2015; Meyer 2019.

visualized declaration of *war* and victory against all the old concepts of "true" and "not true"' (AC §13). Nietzsche is going to win his argumentational battle, he believes, because of his secret weapon – *methods*.

In so writing, Nietzsche was not articulating anything new. Some fifteen years earlier in a letter of 13 July 1885 to Franz Overbeck, Nietzsche had written:

> If you could see me sitting amid my books! And what sort of books! In fact, it is only in the last ten years that I have acquired *knowledge*; from philology I basically only learned *methods* (for the terrible antiquated bits and pieces were something I had to get rid of, or as it were 'muck out'). (KSB 7, 67)

In the intervening years, however, Nietzsche had come to appreciate the importance of methods, not least the *genealogical* method, according to which the meaning of an object may be revealed by tracing its origin, which is uncovered by genealogy. For Nietzsche to have arrived at this insight – that methods are the real insights – is no mean feat, given that, in his words, 'all the methods, all the principles of the scientific spirit of today, were the targets for thousands of years of the most profound contempt' (AC §13).

Nietzsche returns to the theme of methods towards the end of *The Anti-Christ* when he explicitly links methodology with the ancient world – a world that, in historical terms, was wiped out with the advent of Christianity. Section 59 begins with a giant sigh: 'The whole labour of the ancient world gone for *naught*: I have no word to describe the feelings that such an enormity arouses in me' (AC §59). What causes Nietzsche such distress is not simply a sense of nostalgia or a love of antiquity: rather, it is because the 'labour' of the ancient world was 'merely preparatory', and had been laying 'the foundations for a work to go on for thousands of years' – in other words, because of the implications for the future. This preparatory work constitutes, in Nietzsche's view, 'the whole *meaning* of antiquity' – and a meaning that has since disappeared. Hence the deep sense of melancholy with which Nietzsche regards not just the Greeks, but also the Romans.[12] Nietzsche summarises the achievements as he sees them of the ancient world as follows:

> All the prerequisites to a learned culture, all the *methods* of science, were already there; man had already perfected the great and incomparable art of reading profitably – the first necessity to the tradition of culture, the unity of the sciences; the natural sciences, in alliance with mathematics and mechanics, were on the right road, – *the sense of fact*, the last and more valuable of all the senses, had its schools, and its traditions were already centuries old! (AC §59)

At first sight it would seem that, in this respect, Nietzsche's thought has been on something of a journey, given his critique in *The Birth of Tragedy* of Socratism and Alexandrianism. Socratism sees the triumph of Socrates, the 'theoretical man'; Alexandrianism sees the triumph of this Socratic culture.

Nietzsche is thinking here of the distinction conventionally made between the Alexandrian period (c. 300 to 30 BCE) of Greek culture and the preceding Attic period (fifth and fourth centuries BCE). That earlier period is associated with the great tragic poets (Aeschylus, Sophocles), with Plato, Aristotle and Thucydides, as well as with such sculptors as Phidias and Praxiteles. By contrast, nothing symbolises the achievement of Alexandria, the great intellectual capital of the Hellenic world, more than its great library – science and scholarship replaced tragedy, philosophy and art as the focus of cultural activity. And this Alexandrian world is, it turns out, our world too, for 'our whole modern world is entangled in the net of Alexandrian culture': 'It proposes as its ideal the theoretical man equipped with the greatest forces of knowledge, and labouring in the service of science, whose archetype and progenitor is Socrates' (BT §18).

Yet it is important to note that, while Nietzsche here opposes the Alexandrian to the Attic as an instance of decadence or degeneration, his real target is not the users of the ancient Library

---

[12] For further discussion, see Bishop (ed.) 2004; Bett 2011.

of Alexandria in pursuit of intellectual inquiry, but 'the Alexandrian man' of today – someone who is 'at bottom a librarian and corrector of proofs, and wretchedly goes blind from the dust of books and from printers' errors' (BT §18). In other words, Nietzsche is not simply equating nineteenth-century Germany with Alexandrian civilisation; rather he is here using Alexandrian civilisation as a code for the worst aspects of nineteenth-century German intellectual or cultural life, whereas in *The Anti-Christ* he opposes Alexandrian culture to the 'theologian instinct' (AC §9), to the theologians' 'unfitness for philology' (AC §52), understood here as 'the art of reading well' (see Chapter 7 below).

Here, too, Nietzsche places 'the great, incomparable art of reading well' ahead of natural science, mathematics and mechanics; and, last but (so it seems) not least, 'the factual sense' or *Thatsachen-Sinn* (NK 6/2, 292). This 'sense of fact' is an aptitude that Nietzsche associates elsewhere with Arthur Schopenhauer (1788–1860). In *Human, All Too Human*, vol. 2, 'Assorted Opinions and Maxims', he cites as an example of Schopenhauer's *Thatsachen-Sinn* his view in *The Two Fundamental Problems of Ethics* that 'insight into the strict necessity of human actions is the boundary-line which separates philosophical minds from the rest' (Schopenhauer 2010: 190; HAH II AOM §33). For Nietzsche, this insight entirely undermines Schopenhauer's claim elsewhere that 'the ultimate and true explanation of the inner essence of the totality of things must closely cohere with the explanation of the ethical significance of human behaviour' (Schopenhauer 2010: 126); whereas in fact, Nietzsche argues, the earlier proposition proves that precisely the reverse is the case. Here is a classic example of the way in which, for Nietzsche, *metaphysics* has directly *moral* implications. And in *The Gay Science*, Nietzsche wonders whether it was Schopenhauer's 'hard matter-of-fact sense, his inclination to clearness and rationality, which often makes him appear so English, and so unlike Germans?' (GS §99). It is in this more general sense that, in *Twilight of the Idols*, Nietzsche praises Thucydides as 'the great summation, the last revelation of that strong, stern, hard matter-of-factness, which was instinctive in the older Hellenes' (TI Ancients §2).

In *The Anti-Christ*, Nietzsche develops this contrast between the past and the present, a methodological *querelle des anciens et des modernes*, which is also a contrast (and a contest) of *values*. Again, what Nietzsche writes here is a reprise of what he had written in *Twilight of the Idols*, where he had proposed that there was 'no better corrective' than Thucydides to 'the pitiable tendency to beautify the Greeks in the direction of the ideal, a tendency which the youth "trained in humanities" carries away with him into life as the reward of his public-school drilling' (TI Ancients §2), and where he laments that 'the psychological tact of the Germans seems to me to be called in question by a whole series of cases' (TI Expeditions §16):

> Is all this properly understood? Every *essential* to the beginning of the work was ready; – and the *most* essential, it cannot be said too often, are methods, and also the most difficult to develop, and the longest opposed by habit and laziness. What we have today reconquered, with unspeakable self-discipline, for ourselves – for certain bad instincts, certain Christian instincts, still lurk in our bodies – that is to say, the keen eye for reality, the cautious hand, patience and seriousness in the smallest things, the whole *integrity* of knowledge – all these things were already there, and had been there for two thousand years! *More*, there was also a refined and excellent tact and taste! *Not* as mere brain-drilling! *Not* as 'German' culture, with its loutish manners! But as body, as bearing, as instinct – in short, as reality . . . *All gone for naught!* Overnight it became merely a memory! – (AC §59)

What has been lost, Nietzsche claims, was something that had been *real*. For him, as for Friedrich Schiller in his poem 'The Gods of Greece' (*Die Götter Griechenlands*) (1788), ancient Greece was not some never-never land. Nor was ancient Rome, which had been concretely and historically present, and present as a *political* fact, as he argued that the case of the Roman Empire demonstrated:

> The Greeks! The Romans! Instinctive nobility, taste, methodical inquiry, genius for organization and administration, faith

in and the *will* to secure the future of man, a great yes to everything entering into the *imperium Romanum* and palpable to all the senses, a grand style that was beyond mere art, but had become reality, truth, *life* . . . (AC §59)

The notion of the 'grand style' is one that had preoccupied Nietzsche for many years. In *Human, All Too Human*, vol. 2, 'The Wanderer and His Shadow', he had (somewhat whimsically, if mysteriously) noted that 'the grand style comes into being when the beautiful wins a victory over the monstrous' (HAH II WS §96), while in *The Gay Science*, in an aphorism under the title 'One thing is needful' (one of Nietzsche's favourite biblical quotations), he observed: 'To "give style" to one's character – that is a grand and a rare art!' (GS §290). And in his *Nachlass* for spring 1884, Nietzsche defines the grand style as consisting in 'contempt for trivial and brief beauty; it is a sense for what is rare and what lasts long' (KSA 11, 25[321], 95).

The phrase 'the grand style' caught the attention of Martin Heidegger (1889–1976), who understood well the importance for Nietzsche of this notion.[13] In his lectures on *The Will to Power as Art*, Heidegger foregrounded two other passages in the *Nachlass* selection subsequently published as *The Will to Power*, associating the 'grand style' with Nietzsche's definition of the 'classical style' as 'a representation of this calm, simplification, abbreviation, concentration – *the highest feeling of power*', as being 'to react slowly; a great consciousness; no feeling of struggle' (WP §799 = KSA 13, 14[46], 240). In another aphorism cited in this context by Heidegger, Nietzsche talks about 'an overpowering of the fullness of life [. . .]; *measure* becomes master; at bottom there is that *calm* of the strong soul that moves slowly and feels repugnance toward what is too lively' and where 'the general rule, the law, is *honored* and *emphasized*: the exception, conversely, is set aside, the nuance obliterated' – in this case 'the firm, powerful, solid, the life that reposes broad and majestic

---

[13] For Heidegger's lecture on 'The Grand Style' given at the University of Freiburg during the winter semester of 1936–37, see Heidegger 1991a: vol. 1, 124–38.

and conceals its strength' pleases (WP §819 = KSA 12, 7[7], 289–90). For Heidegger, as for Nietzsche, there is nothing trivial or unreal about aesthetics: rather, as Heidegger notes, 'the grand style' involves 'the unity of the reciprocal relation of rapture and beauty, of creation, reception, and form'; in the grand style, he concludes, 'the essence of art *becomes actual*' (*in ihm wird das Wesen der Kunst wirklich*) (Heidegger 1991a: vol. 1, 137).

Nietzsche would have agreed with the sentiment of loss, irreparable loss, that suffuses Schiller's poem 'The Gods of Greece', but his tone in *The Anti-Christ* becomes much darker and more savage when he identifies the cause of this loss: 'All overwhelmed in a night, but not by a convulsion of nature! Not trampled to death by Teutons and others of heavy hoof!' (AC §59). It took the English historian Edward Gibbon (1737–94) several volumes to explain the demise of Rome in *The Rise and Fall of the Roman Empire* (6 vols, 1776–88), but his conclusion (in chapter 38, 'General Observations on the Fall of the Roman Empire in the West') was a simple one:

> The story of its ruin is simple and obvious; and, instead of inquiring why the Roman empire was destroyed, we should rather be surprised that it had subsisted so long. The victorious legions, who, in distant wars, acquired the vices of strangers and mercenaries, first oppressed the freedom of the republic, and afterwards violated the majesty of the purple. The emperors, anxious for their personal safety and the public peace, were reduced to the base expedient of corrupting the discipline which rendered them alike formidable to their sovereign and to the enemy; the vigour of the military government was relaxed, and finally dissolved, by the partial institutions of Constantine; and the Roman world was overwhelmed by a deluge of Barbarians. (Gibbon 1840: 442)

One of the reasons for the Barbarian attacks on Rome is usually held to be a mass migration that had been brought about by an invasion of Europe by the Huns in the late fourth century, which had the effect of driving many of the Germanic tribes to the borders of the Roman Empire. The attempt to defend the border weakened the Empire, and when an invading Barbarian army reached the outskirts of Rome, it found the city had been left undefended. Thus in 410 CE, the Visigoths, under the leadership of Alaric I, breached the walls of Rome, entered the capital of the Roman Empire, and sacked it. (Incidentally, this account is not universally accepted by scholars. For instance, the Belgian historian Henri Pirenne (1862–1935) disputed that the Germanic Barbarians had brought the Western Roman Empire to an end, pointing to a continuity of cultural and political power even after those invasions, and arguing that the demise of classical civilisation should be dated much later, in the eighth century – and attributed to Arab expansion.)

Instead of political, strategic, military or economic reasons, however, Nietzsche identifies one cause for Rome's demise – a change of outlook that he characterises as a shift in focus away from this world and on to the next, and which he associates with Christianity (NK 6/2, 292–3). Not that he can even bring himself to name the Christians; instead he has recourse to an invective against nocturnal vampirism:

> But brought to shame by crafty, sneaking, invisible, anaemic vampires! Not conquered, – only sucked dry! . . . Hidden vengefulness, petty envy, became *master!* Everything wretched, intrinsically ailing, and invaded by bad feelings, the whole *ghetto-world* of the soul, was at once on *top!* – (AC §59)

Nietzsche uses this invective rhetoric elsewhere, railing against how 'the concept of guilt and punishment, including the doctrines of "grace", of "salvation", of "forgiveness" – *lies* through and through, and absolutely without psychological reality – were devised to destroy man's *sense of causality*: they are an attack upon the concept of cause and effect!' (AC §49). And he continues:

> And *not* an attack with the fist, with the knife, with honesty in hate and love! On the contrary, one inspired by the most cowardly, the most crafty, the most ignoble of instincts! An

attack of *priests!* An attack of *parasites!* The vampirism of pale, subterranean leeches! (AC §49)

Although this kind of vituperative discourse strikes us as characteristically Nietzschean, it goes back to one of the earliest polemical texts written against Christianity. *Against the Galileans* was written by the Roman Emperor known as Julian the Apostate, and in the fragments that have survived (largely thanks to the equally polemical response by Cyril of Alexandria, *Contra Julianum*) we read:

> And though you would be following a law that is harsh and stern and contains much that is savage and barbarous, instead of our mild and humane laws, and would in other respects be inferior to us, yet you would be more holy and purer than now in your forms of worship. But now it has come to pass that like leeches you have sucked the worst blood from that source and left the purer. (Julian 1923: 375–7)

It is possible that Nietzsche knew this source, but it is more likely that he drew on Renan's study of Marcus Aurelius (1882), whose chapter on the social and political revolution brought about by Christianity opens with this arresting passage (NK 6/2, 232):

> Thus, in proportion as the Empire declines, Christianity rises. During the third century Christianity sucks ancient society like a vampire, drains all its strength, and brings to pass that general enervation, against which the patriotic Emperors are to struggle in vain. Christianity has no need to attack actively; it has but to shut itself up in its churches. It takes its revenge in not serving the state, for it keeps almost to itself alone certain principles without which the state cannot prosper. (Renan 1904: 291)

Of this alleged vampiric tendency, Nietzsche names in *The Anti-Christ* just one example, albeit a famous one – the Church Father St Augustine of Hippo (354–430 CE) (AC §59). In a letter written on 31 March 1885 to his friend, Franz Overbeck, a theologian (and an expert on patristics), Nietzsche explained his dislike of Augustine (NK 6/2, 293):

> I have now been reading, as relaxation, the Confessions of St. Augustine, with much regret that you weren't here. O, what an old rhetorician! How deceptive and eye-rolling! How I laughed! (for instance, about the 'theft' in his youth, basically a student prank) [cf. *Confessions*, book 2, §§3–10]. What psychological deceit! (for instance, when he is talking about the death of his best friend [cf. *Confessions*, book 4, §§4–6], with whom he was *one heart and soul*: that 'he decided to continue to live, so that in this way his friend might *not completely* die' [cf. *Confessions*, book 4, §6]. That kind of thing is *sickeningly* dishonest.) Its philosophical value is zero. *Vulgarized Platonism*, or in other words, a way of thinking that was invented for the highest aristocracy of the soul is adjusted to suit slave natures. Incidentally, in this book one can see the guts of Christianity: I look at it with the curiosity of a radical doctor and physiologist. (KSB 7, 34)

What did Overbeck make of this letter? It is hard to say, because no response has survived (Sommer 1998), but the letter demonstrates well Nietzsche's view of the Christian appropriation of philosophy, as Laurence Lampert has noted (1993: 364).

Lampert links section 59 of *The Anti-Christ* to section 359 in *The Gay Science* which offers a portrait of 'the ill-constituted person' or 'a human being who has turned out badly' (*ein missrathener Mensch*) and who succumbs to 'a habitual state of vengeance and inclination for vengeance' (GS §359); and to the chapter in *Thus Spoke Zarathustra* entitled 'Of the Tarantulas', which pursues this image of the venomous spider with its poisonous substance of revenge (TSZ I 7). In *The Gay Science* Nietzsche remarks that 'out of such born enemies of the spirit there arises now and then the rare specimen of humanity who is honoured by the people under the name of saint or sage', and he specifically mentions Augustine (GS §359). To these practitioners of revenge Nietzsche elsewhere adds Tertullian, Thomas Aquinas (GM I §15) and Luther – as well as Rousseau and Pascal (KSA 12, 9[124], 408).

In fact, in section 59 of *The Anti-Christ* Nietzsche extended his view of Augustine into a judgement about the entire patristic tradition:

> One needs but read any of the Christian agitators, for example, St Augustine, in order to realize, in order to smell, what filthy fellows came to the top. It would be an error, however, to assume that there was any lack of understanding in the leaders of the Christian movement: – ah, but they were clever, clever to the point of holiness, these Fathers of the Church! What they lacked was something quite different. Nature neglected – perhaps forgot – to give them even the most modest endowment of respectable, of upright, of *cleanly* instincts . . . Between ourselves, they are not even men . . . (AC §59)

This passage exemplifies Nietzsche's strategy of frankly *ad hominem* attack, and his preference for metaphors of cleanliness (or, in other cases, olfactory metaphors). What one finds here in his depiction of Augustine is, predictably enough, the reverse of the *positive* example Nietzsche gives us in *Ecce Homo*:

> Now, by what signs are Nature's lucky strokes recognized among men? They are recognized by the fact that any such lucky stroke gladdens our senses; that he is carved from one integral block, which is hard, sweet, and fragrant as well. He enjoys that only which is good for him; his pleasure, his desire, ceases when the limits of that which are good for him are overstepped. He divines remedies for injuries; he knows how to turn serious accidents to his own advantage; that which does not kill him makes him stronger. (EH Wise §2)

And it is a hallmark of the way in which *Ecce Homo* treads the line between half-serious, half-joking remarks that Nietzsche rounds off the rest of the description of the person who has 'turned out well' by observing that he has just described himself. Similarly, *The Anti-Christ* plays fast and loose with the categories of the subjective and the objective by elevating Nietzsche's own personal responses into intellectual-historical evaluations. In this sense, then, *The Anti-Christ* highlights and problematises the claim made in section 13 that 'the most valuable insights are *methods*' by turning Nietzsche's reliance on intuitive insights itself into a method.

Nietzsche's portrait of Christ (AC §29 and §32)

In section 125 of *The Gay Science* we find the famous parable of the madman who announces the death of God.[14] We might describe this 'death' as the first of the reasons that Nietzsche gives for atheism: the simple fact that, in terms of belief and practice, human beings in the West have 'killed' God – that is, as a matter of *fact* they have ceased to believe. A second kind of argument in favour of atheism is proposed in *Human, All Too Human*, volume 1, and we could describe this as a *psychological* argument: Nietzsche argues that 'a definite false psychology, a certain kind of fantasy in the interpretation of motives and experiences is the necessary presupposition for becoming a Christian and for feeling the need of redemption', and he concludes that 'with the insight into this aberration of reason and imagination one ceases to be a Christian' (HAH §135). This psychological account is extended later by Nietzsche into a *genealogical* account of morality (see *On the Genealogy of Morals*): we become aware of the reasons why morality had come into being, and on this basis, we then reject it. For Nietzsche, the killer question is: *have we really become more moral?* (TI Expeditions §37) – and this question can even bring about the death of the deity.

Thus Nietzsche's case against God is clear: for him, it is not simply a question of whether God exists, it is rather that we no longer believe in him. So it is interesting to see how in *The Anti-Christ* Nietzsche approaches the figure of Jesus. For Nietzsche does in fact paint quite a distinct, if idiosyncratic, portrait of Christ. This portrait begins in section 24, where Nietzsche raises

---

[14] For further discussion of the trope of the 'death of God', see Wilson 1999; Young 2003; Osborn 2017.

the question of 'the *origin* of Christianity', a phrase that recalls the vast work by Renan, *Histoire des origines du Christianisme* (8 vols, 1863–83). In respect of its origin, Nietzsche emphasises that 'Christianity is to be understood only by examining the soil from which it sprung – it is not a reaction against Jewish instincts; it is their inevitable product; it is simply one more step in the awe-inspiring logic of the Jews' (AC §24).

On one level, Nietzsche is obviously right: in the New Testament Christ is born as a Jew; he is brought up, lives and dies in the Holy Land; his first followers were all Jews; and, as a text, the New Testament is full of references and allusions to Jewish scripture. On another level, Nietzsche cites the famous passage from the Gospel according to John, where Christ is presented as spending time among Samaritans (a separate ethno-religious group claiming descent from the tribes of Ephraim and of Manasseh, but presented in 2 Kings 17:24–41 as of Assyrian, i.e. non-Yahwistic, origin, and hence people from whom Jews should distance themselves).[15] Speaking with a Samaritan woman at a well, Jesus declares, 'salvation is of the Jews' (John 4:22), and because of this historical background, Christ's conversation with the Samaritan woman would have been, like his parable of the 'good Samaritan' (Luke 10), a cause for consternation, even shock, to his fellow Jews.

As the commentary in the New Jerusalem Bible points out, meetings at wells were a feature of the patriarchal narratives, and wells and springs played an important part in the life and religion of the patriarchal and Exodus periods (NJB, NT, 1751). So this episode is rich in symbolism, since spring water symbolised life as a divine gift, especially in the future messianic age, as well as the life inspired by divine wisdom and by the Law. The gospel narrative develops this symbolism by equating spring water with the

---

[15] The Samaritans were descendants of the mixed Israelite and Assyrian population that arose after the fall of Samaria, the city built by King Omri as the capital of the northern kingdom of Israel, after it had been besieged and captured by the Assyrians in 722–721 BCE; by extension, the name Samaria came to be applied to the region in general. While the Samaritans worshipped according to the Pentateuch or 'five books' of Moses, they offered their sacrifices, not at Jerusalem, but on Mount Gerizim; indeed, they opposed the rebuilding of Jerusalem's city walls undertaken by Nehemiah, and at the time of Jesus they had become figures of hate to the Jews.

gift of the Spirit; in short, it is an extremely significant episode, at the heart of which stands Christ's remark, 'salvation is of the Jews' (John 4:22). In part, this remark reinforces the distinction between the Samaritans and the Jews, only immediately to undermine it by announcing that the distinction will soon be superseded: 'But the hour cometh, and now is, when the true adorers shall adore the Father in spirit and in truth' (John 4:23). In part, it captures the essence of an argument found in Paul's Letter to the Romans, where he discusses the privileges of Israel in relation to the history of salvation (Rom. 9:4–5). Yet for Nietzsche, this remark, which he later cites a second time (AC §58), is to be read in the reductive sense that Christianity is a product of what he calls the 'logic' of Judaism.

Nietzsche introduces a second principle when he writes that

> the psychological type of the Galilean is still to be recognized, but it was only in its most degenerate form (which is at once maimed and overladen with foreign features) that it could serve in the manner in which it has been used: as a type of the *Saviour* of humankind. (AC §24)

Behind the figure of the Saviour, Nietzsche believes that the original picture of the 'Galilean' (one of the expressions used by Renan to refer to the historical Jesus) can be recovered, or that at least some of its outlines can. Across several sections of *The Anti-Christ*, Nietzsche thus offers a portrait of Christ as he, Nietzsche, conceives him.

In fact, in section 29 Nietzsche goes so far as to say he is greatly concerned with or cares about 'the psychological type of the redeemer', suggesting that this type 'might be depicted in the Gospels, in however a mutilated form and however much overladen with extraneous characters – that is, in *spite* of the Gospels' (AC §29). Nietzsche proposes an analogy with the figure of St Francis of Assisi, which 'shows itself in his legends in spite of his legends' (AC §29), a comparison he borrows from Renan's *Vie de Jésus* (= *Histoire des origines du Christianisme*, vol. 1) (NK 6/2, 151). Yet Nietzsche is remarkably ungracious, and even downright rude, about his source, describing Renan as 'this buffoon *in psychologicis*', and dismissing his 'attempts [. . .] to read the Gospels even as the *history* of a "soul"' as 'a hateful sort of psychological thoughtlessness' (AC §29).[16] For Nietzsche, Renan and critics like him have missed the point: 'It is *not* a question of mere truthful evidence as to what he did, what he said and how he actually died; the question is, whether his type is still conceivable, whether it has been handed down to us' (AC §29). In other words: are modern human beings in a position to understand who or what Jesus was?

Nietzsche is swift to reject two key ways in which Renan understood Christ – with reference to the concepts of the genius (in French, *génie*) and the hero (in French, *héros*). These concepts are, in Nietzsche's view, 'the most *inappropriate* concepts imaginable', because 'if anything is unevangelical, it is the concept of a hero' (AC §29). By hero, Nietzsche means the Greek concept of ἥρως (*hērōs*), a hero or warrior figure, such as Hercules, who enjoys a divine or semi-divine status (Nagy 2013). To this extent, it might seem at first sight a highly appropriate concept, so what are Nietzsche's objections? First, in the figure of Jesus Nietzsche sees the exact reverse of the hero – indeed, a kind of anti-hero: 'What the gospels make instinctive is precisely the reverse of all heroic struggle, of all taste for conflict: the very incapacity for resistance is here converted into something moral [. . .] to wit, the blessedness of peace, of gentleness, of the *inability* to be an enemy' (AC §29). To support this reading, Nietzsche turns to one of the great passages of the New Testament, the Sermon on the Mount, and the verse where Christ enjoins the listening crowds 'not to resist evil' (Matt. 5:39): '"Resist not evil!" – the most profound sentence in the gospels, perhaps the true key to them', Nietzsche says (AC §29).

Nietzsche couples this emphasis on a Christian version of *amor fati* (or the love of one's fate) with the vision captured in the New Testament notion of 'glad tidings' (cf. Luke 1:19; 8:1; Acts 13:32; Rom. 10:15), a notion implicit in the very idea of the gospel itself (cf. Matt. 11:5; Luke 4:18; 7:22; 9:6; 20:1). Those 'glad tidings',

---

[16] For an extended critique of Renan, see TI Expeditions §2.

far from being contemptuously dismissed by Nietzsche, are paraphrased by him as follows: 'The true life, the life eternal has been found – it is not merely promised, it is here, it is in *you*; it is the life that lies in love free from all retreats and exclusions, from all keeping of distances' (AC §29). Grasping, rightly, the implication of these 'glad tidings' that 'every one is the child of God' and that 'as the child of God each man is the equal of every other man', Nietzsche emphasises that Jesus 'claims nothing for himself alone', and concludes that, as a consequence, it is incorrect to describe Jesus as a 'hero', given this term's connotations of exclusive divine or semi-divine status.

By the same token, Nietzsche dismisses the other term used by Renan in relation to Jesus, *génie*. In this context, Nietzsche does not mean 'genius' in the sense of the divine element in a human being or a location, such as the *genius* of the emperor in the ancient Roman Imperial cult or the divine spirit of a place, but rather in the sense of a distinguished individual, related to the idea of the *grand homme* (Currie 1974; Onfray 2011a: 13–48). In fact, Nietzsche expounds this sense in the section of *Twilight of the Idols* entitled 'My notion of genius':

> Great men, like great periods, are explosive materials in which an immense force is accumulated; it is always prerequisite for such men, historically and physiologically, that for a long period there has been a collecting, a heaping up, an economising, and a hoarding, with respect to them, that for a long time no explosion has taken place. (TI Expeditions §44)

Interestingly, Nietzsche notes that in the popular imagination there is an intersection between the hero and the genius, but this is, he insists, a mistake:

> The genius – in work, in deed – is necessarily a squanderer; his greatness is *that he expends himself*. The instinct of self-preservation is, as it were, out of gear in the genius; the over-powerful pressure of the outflow of his energies forbids all such care and foresight. People

call this 'sacrifice', they praise the heroism of genius, his indifference to his own welfare, his devotion to an idea, to a great cause, or to his country: it is all misunderstanding, however . . . (TI Expeditions §44)

On the face of it, there might be good reason to apply the term 'genius' in this sense to the figure of Jesus, but Nietzsche rejects this option, on the basis that to do so would reduce the sense of something 'other'. 'Our whole conception of the "spiritual", the whole conception of our civilization', says Nietzsche, 'could have had no meaning in the world that Jesus lived in' (AC §29). So what conception would be appropriate for the world in which Jesus lived?

Nietzsche suggests a startlingly provocative term – 'idiot', albeit used in the physiological sense. Yet Nietzsche does not mean ἰδιώτης, *idiōtēs* (a private citizen or individual) in the ancient Greek sense, or in the sense that Renan writes that 'it would be a great error to imagine that Jesus was what we would call *un ignorant*' (Renan 1863: 31, cited in NK 6/2, 155). Rather it is in the sense that, in Dostoevsky's famous novel that bears this title, Prince Myshkin is an *idiot* (NK 6/2, 156). After all, Nietzsche understands 'idiot' in a specific psychopathological sense:

> We all know there is a morbid sensibility of the tactile nerves which causes those suffering from it to recoil from every touch, and from every effort to grasp a solid object. Brought to its logical conclusion, such a physiological *habitus* becomes an instinctive hatred of all reality, a flight into the 'intangible', into the 'incomprehensible'; a distaste for all formulae, for all conceptions of time and space, for everything established – customs, institutions, the Church —; a feeling of being at home in a world in which no sort of reality survives, a merely 'inner' world, a 'true' world, an 'eternal' world . . . (AC §29)

All of which Nietzsche rounds off with a reference to the famous passage in the Gospel of Luke, 'for, lo, the kingdom of God is within you' (Luke 17:21).

In the following section Nietzsche goes on to expand this condition of 'idiocy' into 'the two *physiological realities* upon and out of which the doctrine of salvation has sprung', that is, an 'instinctive hatred of reality' which is 'the consequence of an extreme susceptibility to pain and irritation – so great that merely to be "touched" becomes unendurable, for every sensation is too profound', and an 'instinctive exclusion of all hostility, all bounds and distances in feeling' which is 'the consequence of an extreme susceptibility to pain and irritation' (AC §30). On this account, then, *noli me tangere* (i.e., 'do not touch me'), the famous words spoken by the post-resurrection Christ in the Gospel of John when Mary Magdalene recognises him (John 20:17), would represent 'a sublime super-development of hedonism upon a thoroughly unsalubrious soil' – hence the proximity for Nietzsche of Christianity to Epicureanism or 'the theory of salvation of paganism' (AC §30). Jesus Christ and Epicurus: two decadents (for further discussion, see Chapters 4 and 6 below).

Nevertheless, there remains something provocative, even bitter, about the term 'idiot', which led Elisabeth Förster-Nietzsche to excise it from the editions of *The Anti-Christ* she published (NK 6/2, 155). It is true that when Petrarch (1304–74) in his *De sui ipsius et multorum ignorantia* (*On His Own Ignorance and That of Many Others*) (1368) denounces those contemporary Venetian intellectuals and Averroists whose 'greatest glory is to make some confused and baffling statements which neither they nor anyone else can understand' and who, 'puffed up with their outlandish fabrications [. . .] are particularly pleased with themselves for having learned the art of lecturing and declaiming about everything, when in fact they know nothing', he does so by suggesting his opponents would accuse Christ of being an idiot (or ignoramus). 'Not daring to make overt professions,' Petrarch wrote, 'they deny our faith in covert protestations, at times using serious and sophistical blasphemies, and at times using distasteful jests or rank and impious jokes'; and 'isn't this the same [. . .] as seeking what is true while rejecting the truth? Or the same as leaving behind the sun, entering into the profound and obscure abysses of the earth, and hoping to find light in the darkness there?'; in short, 'how must a Christian man of letters appear to men who say that our lord and master Christ was an ignoramus?' (cited in NK 6/2, 155; see Petrarca 2008: 152–4).

Yet perhaps the best sense of what Nietzsche might have meant by describing Christ as an idiot can be found in a passage from Meta von Salis-Marschlins's memoir of her friendship with Nietzsche:

> On our second [walk] we suddenly met all my closest friends from the *Alpenrose*, lots of young, cheerful girls all dressed up in bright clothes. The contrast between their carefree charm and the very weighty matter that the philosopher had just been discussing could not have been greater. Dostoevsky's Idiot and the figure of Jesus in the four gospels! (Salis-Marschlins 1987: 64, cited in NK 6/2, 156)

While these young Alpine girls are said to contrast with the 'weightier' matters under discussion, their 'carefree charm' expresses exactly what Nietzsche saw as significant about Dostoevsky's idiot and the gospel Jesus.

Another term used to describe Jesus but rejected by Nietzsche is 'fanatic', on the basis of a contrast he establishes between 'the type of the saviour' and Renan's use of the term *impérieux*, which 'alone is enough to *annul* the type' (AC §32). In the fifth volume of his *History of the Origins of Christianity*, entitled *The Gospels*, Renan describes Christ as 'this young Jew, at once gentle and terrible, distinguished and imperious, naïve and profound, full of the disinterested zeal of a sublime morality and the ardour of an exalted personality' (Renan 1877: 88, cited in NK 6/2, 167). For the 'glad tidings', as Nietzsche understands them, consist precisely in the absence of this and all other contrasts and contradictions: 'the kingdom of heaven belongs to *children*; the faith that is voiced here is no more an embattled faith – it is at hand, it has been from the beginning, it is a sort of recrudescent childishness of the spirit' (AC §32).

In so writing, Nietzsche echoes the words of Christ in the Gospel of Matthew, 'Suffer the little children, and forbid them not to come to me: for the kingdom of heaven is for such' (Matt. 19:14). The sense in which St John Chrysostom reads this passage (*Homilies*, no. 63) is paraphrased by Haydock as follows:

If we would enter into the kingdom of heaven, we must imitate the virtues of little children. Their souls are free from passion; void of every thought of revenge, they approach those that have grieved them as to their best friends [. . .] They seek not beyond what is necessary, they admire not the beauty of the body, they are not grieved at the loss of wordly wealth, therefore does the Saviour of the world say, that theirs is the kingdom of heaven. (Haydock 2006: 1288)

Now, the children in the Gospel of Matthew and the children in John Chrysostom's homily are very different from the child imagined in Nietzsche's *The Will to Power*. 'One would make a fit little boy stare if one asked him: "Would you like to become virtuous?" – but he will open his eyes wide if asked: "Would you like to become stronger than your friends?"' (WP §918 = KSA 13, 15[98], 464). Yet one recalls that the child is the last of the three stages of the metamorphosis of the spirit in *Thus Spoke Zarathustra*, and that in *The Will to Power* Nietzsche invokes the Heraclitean image of a child at play when he writes: '"Play", the useless – as the ideal of him who is overfull of strength, as "childlike." The "childlikeness" of God, παῖς παίζων [*pais paizon*, i.e., a child at play]' (WP §797 = KSA 12, 2[130], 129).[17] Nietzsche spells out the implications of what such a childlike faith would look like:

A faith of this sort is not furious, it does not denounce, it does not defend itself: it does not come with 'the sword' [cf. Matt. 10:34] – it does not realize how it will one day set man against man [cf. Matt. 10:35]. It does not manifest itself either by miracles, or by rewards and promises, or by 'scriptures': it is itself, first and last, its own miracle, its own reward, its own promise, its own 'kingdom of God'. (AC §32)

---

[17] Cf. Heraclitus, DK 22 B 52: 'Eternity is a child at play, playing draughts: the kingdom is a child's' (Barnes 1987: 102). For further discussion of the appropriateness or otherwise of the child motif, see Spariosu 1989: 97, n. 53.

In this passage, Nietzsche alludes to Christ's own words in the Gospel of Matthew which recognise that he, Jesus, will be a cause of dissension. 'Do not think that I am come to send peace upon earth', Christ warns the Twelve, 'I came not to send peace, but the sword' (Matt. 10:34), the sword here being (as Haydock observes) the gospel itself. (In the Letter to the Hebrews, the 'word of God', i.e. the *logos* or Son of God, is described as being 'living and effectual, and more penetrating than any two-edged sword' [Heb. 4:12].) And the continuation of this passage is again echoed by Nietzsche, 'For I am come to set man at variance against man, against his father, and the daughter against her mother, and the daughter-in-law against her mother-in-law' (Matt. 10:35), itself an allusion to the prophet Micah (cf. Mic. 7:6).

Nietzsche bristles at the phrase 'according to the scriptures', a key idea in the New Testament and found in the gospels and Pauline epistles alike. In Mark, Jesus answers a question from one of the scribes as to the greatest commandment of them all by citing scripture (Deut. 6:4–5), a response to which the scribe replies by picking up these allusions to Deuteronomy and making further scriptural allusions, to which in turn Jesus reacts by saying, 'Thou are not far from the kingdom of heaven' (Mark 12:28–34). And when foretelling the denial of Peter, Jesus refers to Zechariah (Zech. 13:7), and makes explicit that he is doing so: 'You will all be scandalized in me this night: for it is written: I will strike the shepherd, and the sheep shall be dispersed' (Mark 14:27). In the Gospel of John, Christ himself cries out, 'He that believeth in me, *as Scripture saith*, out of his belly shall flow rivers of living water' (John 7:38) (although which passages of scripture is unclear); and later in one of the great farewell discourses, Jesus prays to the Father and says, 'Those whom thou gavest me, I have kept: and none of them hath perished, but the son of perdition, *that the Scripture may be fulfilled*' (John 17:12) (although, again, the allusion is unclear). Then again, in his discussion of the resurrection of the dead in the First Letter to the Corinthians, Paul reminds the believers in Corinth that 'Christ died for our sins, *according to the Scriptures*', and that 'he was buried, and that he rose again the third day, *according to the Scriptures*' (1 Cor. 15:3–4). Neither scriptural concordance, nor miracles, rewards, nor promises are characteristics of this kind of faith as Nietzsche conceives it.

How does or how would one communicate such a faith? (The problem of communication is, after all, one that is extensively foregrounded in *Thus Spoke Zarathustra*, with all its parodies of biblical themes and images.) This question is one that Nietzsche addresses head-on:

> This faith does not formulate itself – it simply *lives*, and so guards itself against formulae. To be sure, the accident of environment, of educational background gives prominence to concepts of a certain sort: in primitive Christianity one finds *only* concepts of a Judaeo-Semitic character (– that of eating and drinking at the Last Supper belongs in this category – an idea which, like everything else Jewish, has been badly mauled by the Church). But let us be careful not to see in all this anything more than sign language [*eine Zeichenrede*], semiotics [*eine Semiotik*], an opportunity to speak in parables [*Gleichnissen*]. (AC §32)

Nietzsche's approach here is, curiously enough, akin to the one taken in the twentieth century by the Protestant theologian Rudolf Bultmann (1884–1976), who undertook to 'demythologise' Christianity and reduce it to its theological kernel, its *kerygma*, as he called it.

In a remark whose significance is easily overlooked, Nietzsche says that 'precisely the fact that no word is taken literally is, for this anti-realist, the precondition that he can speak at all' (*Gerade, dass kein Wort wörtlich genommen ist, ist diesem Anti-Realisten die Vorbedingung, um überhaupt reden zu können*) (AC §32). Had Jesus been an Indian, Nietzsche suggests, he would have used concepts from one of the six *āstika* schools of Hindu philosophy, known as Samkhya or Sankhya (*sāṃkhya*); had he been Chinese, he would have used concepts from Taoism, the religious or philosophical tradition said to have been founded by Lao-Tzu, the reputed author of the *Tao Te Ching*. 'In neither case would it have made any difference to him', Nietzsche adds (AC §32).

Yet does this also mean that this faith as Nietzsche presents it could be translated into Nietzschean terms? There is good reason to think that it might, because Nietzsche goes on to talk about

Jesus as a 'free spirit' (AC §32), a category very obviously associated with Nietzschean thought, and as a 'symbolist' (AC §34). 'Using the phrase somewhat loosely', Nietzsche admits, one could call Jesus a 'free spirit', on the basis that 'he cares nothing for what is established: the word *killeth*, anything that is established *killeth*' (AC §32).[18] Instead, repelled by 'every sort of word, formula, law, belief and dogma', Christ 'speaks only of inner things', using the terms 'life', 'truth' or 'light' to speak about 'the innermost' (AC §32). Such a faith is non-discursive, for it lies entirely beyond discourse; as Nietzsche puts it, 'dialectic [*die Dialektik*] is missing, there is no conception that a belief, a "truth", could be grounded in reasons', for '*his* "proofs" are inner "lights", inner feelings of pleasure and self-affirmations, pure "proofs of strength"' (AC §32). By 'proofs of strength' (*Beweise der Kraft*), Nietzsche is referring to a phrase found in the Pauline epistles and with which he had already engaged on previous occasions.[19]

Beweise der Kraft or 'proofs of strength' (AC §32 and §50)

In the First Letter to the Corinthians, Paul begins by addressing himself to the divisions and scandals in the Corinthian church at the time. He seeks to unite the factions in the church and to resolve the dissension among the faithful by reminding them of his own preaching, distinguishing in so doing between the true wisdom and the false. Paul writes:

> And I was with you in weakness, and in fear, and in much trembling: and my speech, and my preaching was not in the persuasive words of human wisdom, but in the shewing of the spirit and power: that your faith might not stand on the wisdom of men, but on the power of God. (1 Cor. 2:3–5)

---

[18] Note the echo here of 2 Cor. 3:6, 'for the letter killeth, but the spirit giveth life' (DRV).
[19] See the commentaries in NK 6/1, 214–15; NK 6/2, 170–1 and 233; and Sommer 2000: 478–8.

In his commentary, Haydock glosses the phrase *the shewing of the spirit and power* with reference to 'the gifts of the Holy Ghost bestowed on those that believed, and the miracles which God wrought by his apostles' as being 'the means God made use of to convert the world, which were of much greater force than human eloquence' (Haydock 2006: 1501–2). The New Jerusalem Bible translates the phrase as 'to demonstrate the convincing power of the Spirit', and in its commentary it sees in these words an allusion to those miracles and outpourings of the Spirit that had accompanied Paul's preaching (NJB, NT, 1893). In Luther's translation, the phrase is translated *in Beweisung des Geistes und der Kraft*, and since the work of Friedrich Schleiermacher (1768–1834), this passage had become very popular in theological and homiletical contexts.[20] For instance, in his essay 'On the Proof of the Spirit and Power' (1777), Gotthold Ephraim Lessing (1729–81) interprets Jesus' warning about false prophets at the end of the Sermon on the Mount, 'By their fruits shall ye know them' (Matt. 7:16; cf. 7:20), by taking as its starting point Origen's argument in his treatise *Against Celsus*, namely: 'because of the prodigious miracles which may be proved to have happened by this argument among many others, that traces of them still remain among those who live according to the will of the Logos' (*Contra Celsum*, i.2; Lessing 1956: 51). In the course of his argument that '*accidental truths of history can never become the proof of necessary truths of reason*', Lessing ponders the effect of pious legends and concludes, 'What does it matter to me whether the legend is true or false? The fruits are excellent' (Lessing 1956: 53, 55).

In the section of the first volume of *Human, All Too Human* devoted to the theme of 'The Religious Life', Nietzsche had commented caustically on this doctrine, dubbing it 'the testimony of pleasure', on the basis that 'the agreeable opinion is accepted as true' (HAH I §120); by implication (and by demonstration in much of the rest of his writing), Nietzsche plainly believes the reverse to be true. He returns to this theme and gives it a much longer treatment in section 347 of *The Gay Science*, entitled

---

[20] See Walter Kaufmann's commentary in Nietzsche 1974: 288, n. 22.

'Believers and their Need of Belief'. The starting point of this reflection is the observation that 'how much faith one requires in order to flourish, how much "fixed opinion" one requires which one does not wish to have shaken, because one clings to it' is 'a measure of the degree of one's strength (or, speaking more plainly, of one's weakness)' (GS §347).

In this aspect of Christianity, now as in the past, Nietzsche finds evidence of a psychological truth: 'For such is man: a theological dogma might be refuted to him a thousand times, – provided, however, that he had need of it, he would again and again accept it as "true", – according to the famous "proof of strength" of which the Bible speaks' (GS §347). Nietzsche goes on to consider the 'longing for certainty' that expresses itself not simply in the persistence of metaphysics, but in the modern form of scientific positivism.

Nietzsche argues that faith of this kind is a reaction and a response to a *lack of will*; in this respect, he argues, Buddhism and Christianity have much in common (see the passages in *The Anti-Christ* comparing Buddhism and Christianity, discussed in Chapter 3 below). Fanaticism, Nietzsche claims, is 'the sole "volitional strength" to which the weak and irresolute can be excited', so that 'when a human being arrives at the fundamental conviction that he *must* be commanded, he becomes "a believer"' (GS §347). By contrast, Nietzsche envisages a will that is so free, so strong, that it can entertain not just doubt, but complete uncertainty, turning this capacity for uncertainty into an index for what he calls 'free spirit':

> Conversely, one could imagine a delight and a power of self-determining, and a freedom of will, whereby a spirit could bid farewell to every belief, to every wish for certainty, accustomed as it would be to support itself on slender cords and possibilities, and to dance even on the verge of abysses. Such a spirit would be *free spirit* par excellence. (GS §347)

The theme of the free spirit returns in *Twilight of the Idols* in the famous encomium of Goethe (TI Expeditions §49), as does the theme of *der Beweis der Kraft*, which Nietzsche playfully reformulates as 'the excess of strength only is the proof of strength'

(TI Foreword). He refers again to the phrase in the context of the psychological explanation he offers for the 'error of imaginary causes' (TI Errors §5). And in *Ecce Homo*, Nietzsche appropriates the phrase for himself when he writes of 'the overcoming of pity' that 'to remain master here, here to keep the *elevation* of one's task clean of the many lower and more shortsighted drives which are active in so-called selfless actions, that is the test, the final test perhaps, which a Zarathustra has to pass – the actual *proof* of his strength' (EH Wise §4).

In a *Nachlass* note from the period summer 1872 to early 1873, part of a series of reflections entitled 'The Philosopher: Reflections on the Struggle of Art and Knowledge', Nietzsche analyses the struggle that takes place internal to the philosopher in terms of a contrast – between, on the one hand, the '*optimistic metaphysics*' of logic, which gradually 'poisons and falsifies everything'; and, on the other, a 'sense of truth' that 'derives from *love*', itself a 'proof of strength' (KSA 7, 19[103], 453; Nietzsche 1995: 36–7). (This expression of '*beatifying truth* out of *love*' is based upon knowledge attained by the individual, 'which he does not need to communicate, but whose ebullient beatitude' compels him to do so. Is Nietzsche talking about religion, or is he talking about himself here . . .?) And in a further *Nachlass* note from spring 1888 entitled 'How Virtue comes to Power', Nietzsche cites Jesus' warning about false prophets at the end of the Sermon on the Mount, 'By their fruits shall ye know them' (Matt. 7:16; cf. 7:20), which he glosses as follows: '"By their fruits shall ye know them" – namely, our "truths": this is the priestly way of reasoning still today' (KSA 13, 15[71], 452). In so responding, Nietzsche rejects both the biblical passage and its Enlightenment equivalent (along with its postmodern version, 'if it feels this good, it must be true').

Following his allusion in section 32 of *The Anti-Christ* to 'proof of strength', Nietzsche refers to it again (and much more extensively) in section 50, where he provides 'a psychology of "belief", of the "believer", for the special benefit of "believers"', and engages at length with the proposition, 'Faith makes blessed: *therefore* it is true' (AC §50; cf. NK 6/2, 233–5). Nietzsche comes to the conclusion that, in fact, the reverse is the case, and in words that recall his preface to *The Anti-Christ* where he calls for readers who have 'an inclination, born of strength, for questions that no one has the courage for; the courage for the *forbidden*; predestination for the labyrinth' (AC Preface), he defines the 'hardest service' as 'the service of truth':

> The experience of all disciplined and profound minds teaches *the contrary*. Man has had to fight for every atom of the truth, and has had to pay for it almost everything that the heart, that human love, that human trust cling to. Greatness of soul is needed for this business: the service of truth is the hardest of all services. – (AC §50)

Thus, for Nietzsche, the meaning of integrity or honesty in all intellectual or spiritual matters involves the following: 'That you are strict with your heart, that you look down on "beautiful feelings", that you make every Yes and No a matter of conscience!' (AC §50). Inverting the formulation found in this section, Nietzsche concludes: 'Faith makes blessed: *therefore*, it lies' (AC §50).

We are so used to reading Nietzsche (or not reading him) that it is easy to overlook the significant fact that he is insisting here on the criterion of truth. Nietzsche is far from advocating any postmodern relativism or embracing an attitude of 'anything goes' – quite the contrary. In the first of his *Essays, Civil and Moral*, entitled 'Of Truth', Francis Bacon (1561–1626) – whose image of the idols inspired the thematic image of Nietzsche's *Twilight of the Idols* – famously wrote '"What is truth?" said jesting Pilate, and would not stay for an answer', referring to the exchange between Christ and Pontius Pilate as recorded by John. Pilate asks Christ, 'Art thou a king then?', to which Christ reples, 'Thou sayest that I am a king. For this was I born, and for this I came into the world, that I should give testimony to the truth: everyone that is of the truth, heareth my voice.' To which Pilate responds, 'What is truth?' (John 18:37–8). For the British analytic philosopher J. L. Austin (1911–60), Bacon's response to this episode captures the prescience of Pilate's remark: '"What is truth?" said jesting Pilate, and would not stay for an answer. Pilate was in advance of his time. For "truth" itself is an abstract noun, a camel, that is, of a logical construction, which cannot get past the eye even of a grammarian' (Austin 2013: 27). Yet one of Nietzsche's translators, R. J. Hollingdale, discovers in Bacon's response a springboard for a meditation on the profundity of Pilate's original question:

> 'What is truth?' said jesting Pilate; and would not stay for an answer. If he had stayed, what answer would he have received? There cannot be any doubt: Jesus would have said: I am the truth. This too is Zarathustra's answer to the question 'what is truth?' For what, at this level, *is* truth, 'the truth'? Isn't it the discovery that no truth is discoverable except the truth which you yourself are? that there is no truth (sense, meaning) in the world except the truth (sense, meaning) *you yourself give it?* (Hollingdale 1969: 25)

Far from dismissing the question, as Pilate does (and so many postmodernists do), Nietzsche is *profoundly*, even *desperately*, concerned with the question of (the) truth.

Yet there is one aspect of the truth that Nietzsche chooses never to address: namely, the question – did Jesus ever exist? Instead, Nietzsche's commitment is to philology as a discipline enabled to prosecute a campaign against Christ for linguistic and scholarly reasons, while in *Ecce Homo* Nietzsche succeeded in recreating himself on a textual level that displays important parallels with the way in which Christ can be said to have come into existence through the Bible. (This is a topic to which we shall return in Chapter 7 below.)

In the next chapter, we consider the contrast that Nietzsche draws in *The Anti-Christ* between Christianity and Buddhism; examine the account that Nietzsche gives of the history of Israel, a lightning-fast sketch of ancient Israel and Judah from their prehistory and the conquest of the land of Canaan (or the Promised Land), via the United Monarchy and the split into the Northern Kingdom and the Kingdom of Judah; and conclude by discussing how Nietzsche's analysis of the loss of the symbolic dimension of life informs his argument about Christianity.

3
Nietzsche on Buddhism, the History of Israel and the Loss of the Symbol

In section 20 of *The Anti-Christ*, Nietzsche introduces the topic of Buddhism for essentially strategic reasons, namely that he does not wish to do an injustice to a religion that is related to Christianity, but that has more believers. One of the problems that confronts us in discussing Nietzsche in relation to Buddhism is that the term 'Buddhism' embraces such a variety and diversity of beliefs, practices and traditions; more than eighteen Buddhist sub-schools of thought exist. Two major branches of Buddhism are generally recognised, known as Theravāda (or, in Pali, 'the School of the Elders') and Mahāyāna (or, in Sanskrit, 'the Great Vehicle'), both of which originated in ancient India at some point between the sixth and fourth centuries BCE, and subsequently spread through large parts of Asia. A third branch, Vajrayāna (or Mantrayāna, esoteric Buddhism or tantric Buddhism), is a tradition that developed in medieval India.

Nietzsche's approach to Buddhism in *The Anti-Christ* is an avowedly *comparative* one, and he acknowledges his debt to scholars who have undertaken work in this area.[1] Two of the main sources

---

[1] For a critique of Nietzsche's comparative approach to Buddhism, Judaism and Brāhmaṇism as 'superficially researched, hermeneutically reckless, and methodologically uncritical', see Panaïoti 2019.

consulted by Nietzsche were those by the German scholar of Indology Hermann Oldenberg (1854–1920), *Buddha: Sein Leben, seine Lehre, seine Gemeinde* (Berlin, 1881), and the German-born but Britain-based and English-speaking philologist and orientalist Max Müller (1823–1900), *Essays*, vol. 1 (translated into German, Leipzig, 1869). Nietzsche's sources were thus exclusively European, if not German, in outlook (NK 6/2, 111). In fact, Nietzsche once wrote that he could become the Buddha of Europe,[2] and his relation to Buddhism has recently come under increasingly close scrutiny.[3] Is, for instance, the town of the Motley Cow, where Zarathustra delivers his first sermon, a literal translation of the name of a town, Kalmasadalmya (or in Pali, Kammasuddamam), that the Buddha visited on his wandering (Mistry 1981: 17)? And is it possible that Nietzsche's knowledge of Buddhism fed elsewhere in *Thus Spoke Zarathustra* into his choice of the motif of the 'blissful islands'? After all, in Mahāyāna Buddhism the tradition centres around a celestial buddha of infinite light and life, known as Amitābha or Amitāyus, who is said to dwell in Sukhāvatī, or the land of utmost bliss (Inagaki [trans.] 2003: 13, 131). In the smaller sutra, the Amitāyus buddha describes the land of utmost bliss, also known as the pure land or the Western paradise, to Elder Śāriputra: 'If you travel westward from here, passing a hundred thousand *koṭis* of buddha lands, you will come to the land called Utmost Bliss, where there is a buddha called Amitāyus'; 'the beings in that land suffer no pain but only pleasures of various kinds'; 'the Buddha's light shines boundlessly and without hindrance over all the world of the ten directions', and 'it is for this reason that he is called Amitābha' (Inagaki [trans.] 2003: 92, 346b–347a). For Jung, the idea of periodicity — expressed in

---

[2] In a note from 1883, Nietzsche writes: 'Of all the European who are living and have lived, I have the *most universal* of souls: Plato Voltaire – this depends on conditions which are not fully in my power but rather in the "nature of things" – I could be the Buddha of Europe: though admittedly an antipode to the Indian Buddha' (KSA, 10, 4[2], 109; translated in Mistry 1981: 1).

[3] For further discussion, see Mistry 1981; Elman 1983; Parkes (ed.) 1991; Morrison 1999; Bazzano 2006; Conche 2007; van der Braak 2010; 2015; Panaïoti 2013; and, most recently, Bonardel 2020 (as well as the references in NK 6/2, 110).

the series of the bodhisattvas as the incarnated idea of the saviour of the world[4] – is reflected in Nietzsche's own experience of the archetypal figure of the wise old man, i.e., of Zarathustra as 'an identity within himself that had existed many thousands of years before him, that always had been' (Jung 1998: 13).

Nietzsche on Buddhism (AC §§20–3)

Nietzsche describes Buddhism and Christianity alike as 'nihilistic' and 'decadent' religions, but the point of the comparison is to show to the disadvantage of Christianity that these aspects are not inevitably ruinous. (Oddly, the centrality of the importance of pity is missing from Nietzsche's account of Buddhism [cf. NK 6/2, 110].) Nietzsche describes Buddhism as being 'a hundred times as realistic as Christianity': 'It is part of its living heritage that it is able to face problems objectively and coolly; it is the product of long centuries of philosophical speculation. The concept "God" was already disposed of before it appeared. Buddhism is the only genuinely *positivistic* religion to be encountered in history' (AC §20). This *positivistic* outlook of Buddhism is reflected in its epistemology, i.e., its theory of knowledge, which Nietzsche characterises as strict phenomenalism. Instead of talking about a 'struggle with *sin*', it talks about a 'struggle with suffering' – and thereby, Nietzsche says, it gives reality its due. Hence, in moral terms, Buddhism is said to occupy the same position as Nietzsche himself does – it is '*beyond* good and evil' (see below) (AC §20).

Nietzsche praises Buddhism for its adherence to two *physiological* facts: first, 'an excessive sensitiveness to sensation, which manifests itself as a refined susceptibility to pain'; and second, 'an extraordinary spiritualization, a too-protracted concern with concepts and logical procedures, under the influence of which the instinct of personality has yielded to a notion of the "impersonal"' (AC §20). In a parenthesis, Nietzsche indicates that he

---

[4] That is, the Buddha Amitābha, the bodhisattva of the past world, the Buddha of clarity and truth; the Śākyamuni Buddha, the bodhisattva of the real, actual world, or Gautama Buddha; and the Maitreya Buddha, the bodhisattva of the coming world, the Buddha of perfect love.

shares these characteristics, and perhaps therefore he shares their outcome, namely that these physiological states tend to produce depression. This depression is something that the Buddha tried to combat by hygienic measures, and Nietzsche lists these as follows:

> A life in the open, a life of travel; moderation in eating and a careful selection of foods; caution in the use of intoxicants; the same caution in arousing any of the passions that foster a bilious habit and heat the blood; finally, no *worry*, either on one's own account or on account of others. (AC §20)

These recommendations chime with those made by Nietzsche in *Ecce Homo* in relation to diet (EH Clever §1), in relation to climate (EH Clever §2) and in relation to recreation (EH Clever §3). In a sense, one could describe Nietzsche's lifestyle as a kind of secular Buddhism. Above all, Buddha is said to have rejected prayer as well as asceticism, and the Buddha's rejection of asceticism is something that Schopenhauer had already noted (Schopenhauer 1966: vol. 2, 607). And the Buddha rejected compulsion or discipline in every form, even within a monastic community, since this would exacerbate precisely the excessive sensitiveness Nietzsche has already mentioned.

As a result, Buddhism does not seek out converts, it is not a proselytising religion; its teachings are antagonistic towards nothing except 'revenge, aversion, *ressentiment*' (AC §20). Nietzsche cites a line from one of the most widely read and best-known Buddhist scriptures, a collection of sayings of the Buddha known as the Dhammapada, 'enmity is not vanquished by enmity' (chapter 1, verse 5). So Buddhism does not reject 'revenge, aversion, *ressentiment*' as *immoral* but instead as *unhealthy*, and it seeks to address these affects with a view to bringing them back into line with its primary, dietetic objective:

> The mental fatigue that [the Buddhist] observes, already plainly displayed in too much 'objectivity' (that is, the individual's diminished sense of self-interest, in loss of equilibrium, loss of 'egoism'), he combats by strong efforts to lead even the spiritual interests back to the ego. In the Buddha's teachings, egoism is a duty [. . .] (AC §20)

One might compare this assessment of Buddhism with Zarathustra's proclamation in 'Of the Three Evil Things' of virtue in terms of 'self-enjoyment' or 'selfishness' — that is, 'the wholesome, healthy selfishness, that springeth from the powerful soul: − / − From the powerful soul, to which the high body appertaineth, the handsome, triumphing, refreshing body, around which everything becometh a mirror: / − The pliant, persuasive body, the dancer, whose symbol and epitome is the self-enjoying soul' (TSZ III 10 §2).

In the story of Martha and Mary, Jesus says that 'one thing is necessary' (Luke 10:42), a phrase taken up on several occasions in his sermons by Meister Eckhart.[5] Nietzsche, too, picks up this phrase, which intrigues him elsewhere (cf. AC §43), and he relates it − relying on the work of Hermann Oldenberg − to the central Buddhist question, 'how can *you* be delivered from suffering?' Nietzsche defines this as 'regulat[ing] and determin[ing] the entire spiritual diet' (AC §20; see Oldenberg 1881), to use an expression coined by the German art historian, archaeologist and classical philologist Adolf Schöll (1805–82) to talk about how Goethe developed 'a careful economy of his inclinations and duties' (Schöll 1882: 65). Nietzsche concludes this section with a sly dig at Socrates, a figure whom he had earlier diagnosed in *Twilight of the Idols* as a 'problem' (TI Socrates §§1–12). Even Socrates, Nietzsche suggests, who 'declared war on pure "scientificity"', nevertheless 'elevated personal egoism, even in the realm of problems, to morality' (AC §20). Yet in *The Anti-Christ* the 'problem of Socrates' appears, as Andreas Urs Sommer notes, to be less virulent than previously (NK 6/2, 115).

Section 21 is structured around the antithesis, as Nietzsche sees it, between Buddhism and Christianity. Aligning himself with widespread eighteenth-century views of Buddhism, including those of the classic French Enlightenment thinker Montesquieu (1689–1755) (NK 6/2, 115), Nietzsche lists the preconditions of this religion: namely, 'a very mild climate, customs of great gentleness

---

[5] In its commentary on this passage, the NJB notes the textual variants, 'but only one thing is needed', 'but only a few things are needed', only to reject them: in this remark, it insists, Jesus 'rises from the material plane ("few things are needed", i.e., for the meal) to the "one thing necessary", which is to listen to the word of God' (NJB, NT, 1707).

and liberality, and *no* militarism', as well as the participation of 'the higher and better-educated classes' (AC §21). Its aims? Nietzsche describes them as 'cheerfulness, quiet, and the absence of desire', adding that these are not simply desiderata but actual achievements: 'Buddhism is not a religion in which perfection is merely an object of aspiration: perfection is actually normal' (AC §21). In the language of Buddhism, such perfection is called Nirvāṇa.

In so saying, Nietzsche is reversing his position as found in such earlier works as *The Gay Science* and *On the Genealogy of Morals*. Here Nietzsche had glossed Nirvana or 'the Oriental Nothingness' as 'mute, benumbed, deaf self-surrender, self-forgetfulness, and self-effacement', i.e., as an expression of the fact that 'confidence in life is gone: life itself has become a *problem*' (GS Preface §3); as '*nothingness*', equating 'the desire for a *unio mystica* with God' with 'the desire of the Buddhist for nothingness, Nirvana – no more!' (GM I §468). And in the third essay of *On the Genealogy of Morals*, Nietzsche returns to this point, comparing the state of *redemption* in Buddhism, Hinduism and Christianity.

For 'the three great religions, which are in other respects so steeped in moralization', Nietzsche claims,

> the supreme state, *redemption* itself, total hypnotization and repose at last achieved, is always accounted the mystery as such for whose expression even the supreme symbols are inadequate, as entry and return into the ground of things, as liberation from all illusion, as 'knowledge', as 'truth', as 'being', as release from all purpose, all desire, all action, as a state *beyond even good and evil.* (GM III §17; my emphasis)

Drawing on the work of the German Indologist Paul Deussen (Deussen 1883; 1887), Nietzsche focuses here on Hinduism, a religion he discusses in *The Anti-Christ* with reference to the Lawbook of Manu (see Chapter 5). Significantly, Nietzsche finds common ground between this conception of God as nothingness and the ethical philosophy of Epicurus: 'Although it is arrayed in Oriental exaggeration, what is expressed is merely the same appraisal as that of the clear, cool, Hellenically cool, but suffering Epicurus: the hypnotic sense of nothingness, the repose of deepest sleep, in short *absence of suffering*' (GM III §570).

What for Nietzsche in *The Gay Science* and *On the Genealogy of Morals* I is something negative, and in *On the Genealogy of Morals* III is something ambivalent, is in *The Anti-Christ* valued entirely positively; not least in comparison with Christianity, to his continuing critique of which Nietzsche devotes the rest of section 21. Rather than expressing the goals of the higher and educated classes, in Christianity 'the instincts of the subjugated and the oppressed' are said always to 'come to the fore' (AC §21). On Nietzsche's account, these instincts express themselves in five ways: first, in 'the discussion of sin, self-criticism, and inquisitions of conscience' as a means of passing the time; second, prayer as a means of pumping up the emotion produced by a 'great power' (i.e., God); third, grace as a gift without which the highest good is unattainable; fourth, a lack of 'open dealings', reflected in a preference for 'concealment and the darkened room [*der Versteck*]'; and fifth, returning to a point made in section 20, an absence of hygiene.

Nietzsche exemplifies this final point with reference to Córdoba, a city in Andalusia in southern Spain that was conquered by Muslim armies in the eighth century and became the capital of the Caliphate of Córdoba, otherwise known as al-Andalus (i.e., Muslim Spain or Islamic Iberia). Under Muslim rule, al-Andalus became a beacon of learning, making important advances in astronomy, pharmacology, surgery and trigonometry, and Córdoba became a leading cultural and economic centre in Europe and indeed the Islamic world. Caliph Al-Hakam II opened medical schools, universities and libraries, but what Nietzsche concentrates on are its public baths. (Nietzsche might have mentioned the architectural damage inflicted on the Great Mosque of Córdoba when it was converted to a Roman Catholic cathedral, a process that involved the insertion of a Renaissance-style cathedral nave in the sixteenth century, but for him, the baths are more important.) During the *Reconquista*, Córdoba returned to Christian rule in 1236, and after the expulsion of the Muslims, Nietzsche notes, its 270 public baths were closed.[6]

---

[6] Nietzsche's source of information for this statistic is most likely Müller 1885–87: vol. 2, 508, which gives a figure of 300 public baths (cited in NK 6/2, 118).

This move serves Nietzsche as an example of how 'the body is despised and hygiene is denounced as sensual; the Church even ranges itself against cleanliness' (AC §21).[7]

Further to these five characteristics, Nietzsche lists three more – a cruelty towards the self and others; a hatred of those who do not believe; and a will to persecute (AC §21), a series of charges that he had earlier made in his analysis of the ascetic and the saint in *Human, All Too Human*, vol. 1, §141, in the conclusion to which he had cited the German Romantic poet Novalis (1772–1801): 'It is rather astonishing that the association of lust, religion and cruelty during all these years has not caused humankind to pay more attention to the intimate character of their relationship and to their common aims' (Novalis 1978: 765; NK 6/2, 118). Nietzsche summarises his case against Christianity in pathological terms, derived from *Inquiries into Human Faculty and its Development* (1883) by the Victorian English scientist and polymath Francis Galton (1822–1911) (NK 6/2, 118), and reflecting Nietzsche's more general use in *The Anti-Christ* of a discourse of medicine:

> Sombre and disquieting ideas are in the foreground; the most esteemed states of mind, bearing the most respectable names are epileptoid; the diet is so regulated as to engender morbid symptoms and over-stimulate the nerves. Christian, again, is all deadly enmity to the rulers of the earth, to the 'aristocratic' – along with a sort of secret rivalry with them (– one resigns one's 'body' to them – one wants *only* one's 'soul' . . .). And Christian is hatred of all the senses, of joy in the senses, of joy in general . . . (AC §21)

In section 22, Nietzsche continues his comparison of Buddhism and Christianity. As Andreas Urs Sommer points out, when Nietzsche begins his series of historical sketches of the development of Christianity, he tends to efface the process of Hellenisation undergone by Christianity in favour of an emphasis

---

[7] Examples of how, historically, the Church ranged itself against cleanliness had been enumerated by Feuerbach in his unfinished treatise 'On Eudaimonism'; see Bishop 2009.

on its immediate Jewish roots. It is as if, Sommer suggests, there were an immediate jump from the world of the Palestinian ghetto to the missionary campaigns to convert the Goths, the Vandals, the Langobards and the Franks (NK 6/2, 119). At the beginning of this section, Nietzsche declares:

> When Christianity departed from its native soil, that of the lowest orders, the *underworld* of the ancient world, and began seeking power among barbarian peoples, it no longer had to deal with *exhausted* men, but with men still inwardly savage and capable of self torture – in brief, strong men, but bungled men. Here, unlike in the case of the Buddhists, the cause of discontent with self, suffering through self, is not merely a general sensitiveness and susceptibility to pain, but, on the contrary, an inordinate thirst for inflicting pain on others, a tendency to obtain subjective satisfaction in hostile deeds and ideas. (AC §22)

What is missing from this account, of course, is the rich intellectual life of late Hellenistic, late Roman culture, in which a subtle Greek dogmatic thought – from Origen to Athanasius of Alexandria – gradually developed, so that to accuse Christianity of 'the disdain of the intellect and of culture' (AC §22) is fundamentally to misrepresent it in the most egregious way (NK 6/2, 119). Yet this leap from Palestine to the 'barbarians' serves an important dual function: on the one hand, it allows Nietzsche to present Buddhism as an appropriate form of religion for aristocratic decadence and decline; on the other, he can absolve the Roman Empire of responsibility for the rise and spread of Christianity. (In fact, in section 60 Nietzsche presents the Roman Empire as a *victim* of Christianity [NK 6/2, 119].) Nietzsche's critique runs as follows:

> Christianity had to embrace *barbaric* concepts and valuations in order to obtain mastery over barbarians: of such sort, for example, are the sacrifices of the first-born, the drinking of blood as a sacrament, the disdain of the intellect and of culture; torture in all its forms, whether bodily or not; the whole pomp of the cult. Buddhism is a religion

for peoples in a further state of development, for races that have become kind, gentle and over-spiritualized (– Europe is not yet ripe for it –): it is a summons that takes them back to peace and cheerfulness, to a careful rationing of the spirit, to a certain hardening of the body. (AC §22)

Most of the accusations levelled against Christianity here – the drinking of blood in Communion (a point emphasised in Julius Wellhausen's *Skizzen und Vorarbeiten*, vol. 3: *Reste arabischen Heidenthums* (Berlin, 1887) – cf. KSA 13, 11[292], 113; KSA 13, 11[293], 113–14), great pomp, torture of all kinds – could be described as general *topoi* of Enlightenment anti-clericalism, as could the overarching accusation of 'disdain of the intellect and culture'. The practice of the sacrifice of the first-born was widespread in ancient Middle Eastern religions, as Nietzsche plainly knew; in *Beyond Good and Evil*, he notes that 'there is a great ladder of religious cruelty, with many rungs' (BGE §55), and he identifies three of these, all of which have to do with sacrifice.[8]

The first of these rungs involves the sacrifice of the first-born:

Once one sacrificed human beings to one's god, perhaps precisely those whom one loved most: the sacrifices of the first-born in all prehistoric religions belong here, as well as the sacrifice of the Emperor Tiberius in the Mithras grotto of the isle of Capri, that most gruesome of all anachronisms. (BGE, §257)[9]

Yet the point about the sacrifice of the first-born draws in particular on the work of the Austrian cultural historian Julius Lippert (1839–1909). In a letter to Franz Overbeck of 10 April 1886, Nietzsche recommended Lippert's *Christenthum, Volksglaube und Volksbrauch: Geschichtliche Entwicklung ihres Vorstellungsinhaltes* (1882), describing

---

[8] For further discussion, see NK 5/1, 353–7.
[9] The episode to which Nietzsche is alluding is in Suetonius's *Lives of the Caesars*. See *The Twelve Lives of the Caesars*, book 3, 'Tiberius', §§40–4; Suetonius 1913–14: 351–5. On Nietzsche's interest in Mithras, see Köhler 2002: 103–9.

it as a work 'which no one in Germany wants to know about, yet which contains much of *my* way of thinking about religion and a good number of suggestive facts' (KSB 7, 171).[10] Indeed, in *Die Religionen der europäischen Culturvölker, der Litauer, Slaven, Germanen, Griechen und Römer* (1881), Lippert argued as follows:

> It cannot be denied that Christianity, by involving a '*sacrifice*' that can be made everywhere, on the one hand fell back on the most gruesome feelings of prehistoric times, and on the other provided the primordial sacrifice with its mildest 'solution' in terms of its demands on people, and provided infinitely much for the human demand that had grown so great and reconciled many people. The Christian 'sacrifice' – this expression is still valid – is in itself a real, a terribly great and bloody sacrifice, the greatest of all huge sacrifices that, according to the sentiments of people used to this way of thinking, had to have the power to bring about every kind of atonement – the ancient sacrifice *of the first-born*, and in this case of something that cannot be surpassed, of the first-born of the progenitor of the entire world. (Lippert 1881: 483, cited in NK 6/2, 120–1)

Drawing on one of his favourite (and most provocative) images, the beast of prey (cf. TI 'Improvers' §2), which echoes Thomas Hobbes's description of human beings in the natural state (cf. NK 6/1, 362), Nietzsche sums up the difference between Christianity and Buddhism as follows:

> Christianity aims at mastering *beasts of prey*; its modus operandi is to make them *ill* – to make feeble is the Christian recipe for taming, for 'civilizing'. Buddhism is a religion for the closing, over-wearied stages of civilization. Christianity appears before civilization has so much as begun – under certain circumstances it lays the very foundations thereof. (AC §22)

---

[10] For further discussion, see Orsucci 1996: 217–20, 294–7.

This concluding remark hints at a positive evaluation of Christianity, even in the midst of this wholescale critique; and this single remark would become the starting point of a vast psychological project of explaining the historical role of Christianity in the development of human culture for Jung in his *Transformations and Symbols of the Libido* (1911–12).

In section 23, Nietzsche restates his argument in favour of Buddhism rather than Christianity: it is 'a hundred times more austere, more honest, more objective' (AC §23). Its honesty is revealed in its attitude towards that greatest of all moral and philosophical problems, suffering: 'It no longer has to *justify* its pains, its susceptibility to suffering, by interpreting these things in terms of sin – it simply says, as it simply thinks, "I suffer"' (AC §23). By contrast, the barbarian view – which is, for Nietzsche, the Christian view – has to have recourse to the notion of the devil in order to explain suffering (AC §23). The rest of this section represents Nietzsche's reckoning with the three theological virtues (or, as he calls them, the three Christian 'ingenuities') – faith, hope and charity (or love).[11]

First of all, faith:

> In the first place, [Christianity] knows that it is of very little consequence whether a thing is true or not, so long as it is *believed* to be true. Truth and *faith*: here we have two wholly distinct worlds of ideas, almost two diametrically *opposite* worlds – the road to the one and the road to the other lie miles apart. (AC §23)

In his *Metamorphoses* (book 9, l. 711), Ovid had introduced the notion of the 'pious fraud' or *pia fraus*, and Nietzsche had referred to this idea several times elsewhere (NK 6/1, 371–2). In *Human, All Too Human*, vol. 2, 'Assorted Opinions and Maxims', section 299, and in *Daybreak*, section 27, Nietzsche had used the idea in the context, first, of politics and, second, of interpersonal relations. In *Twilight of the Idols*, Nietzsche claimed that 'a small and modest

---

[11] *Catechism of the Catholic Church* (1997), §1813; cf. 1 Cor. 13:13.

matter after all, the so-called *pia fraus*' had given him access to the problem of the following proposition: namely, that 'in order to *create* morality, it is necessary to have the absolute will to the contrary' (TI 'Improvers' §5). Thus the *pia fraus* was, he added, 'the heritage of all philosophers and priests who have "improved" humankind', and 'neither Manu, nor Plato, nor Confucius, nor the Jewish and Christian teachers, have ever doubted of their *right* to use falsehood' (TI 'Improvers' §5).[12] Similarly, in *The Anti-Christ* Nietzsche repeats this charge: 'To understand this fact thoroughly – this is almost enough, in the Orient, to *make* one a sage. The Brahmins knew it, Plato knew it, every student of the esoteric knows it' (AC §23).

In Plato's *Republic*, Socrates presents the 'noble lie' (γενναῖον ψεῦδος, *gennaion pseudos*, literally 'a lie or wrong opinion about origin') in the form of the myth or parable of the metals, a fictional account of the origin of the three social classes that constitute the state as Plato conceives it (*Republic*, book 3, 414e–15c). What matters, as Socrates is keen to emphasise, is not whether the tale is true, but that it is believed: for believing this myth 'would have a good effect, making them more inclined to care for the state and one another' (book 3, 415c–d). This, then, is the noble lie, understood as 'a contrivance for one of those falsehoods that come into being in case of need, of which we were just now talking, some noble one' (414b–c). The problem with the noble lie, on Nietzsche's account, is that it leads to untruth:

> When, for example, someone gets any *pleasure* out of the notion that he has been saved from sin, it is not necessary for him to be actually sinful, but merely to *feel* sinful. But when *faith* is thus exalted above everything else, it necessarily follows that reason, knowledge and patient inquiry have to be discredited: the road to truth becomes a forbidden road. (AC §23)

---

[12] Among these 'improvers' of humankind Nietzsche would also have included Immanuel Kant (1724–1804), whose 'priestly' philosophy (and Nietzsche's critique of it) are discussed in Loeb 2019.

So much for faith and (in Nietzsche's view) its opposite, truth. What about the second theological virtue, hope? As a culture, we in the West tend to set a lot of store by hope, but this is not universally the case, as Nietzsche shows. He does so in the form of an allusion to the story of Pandora's box, as told in Hesiod's *Works and Days* (ll. 90–105):

> For ere this the tribes of men lived on earth remote and free from ills and hard toil and heavy sicknesses which bring the Fates upon men; for in misery men grow old quickly. But the woman took off the great lid of the jar with her hands and scattered all these and her thought caused sorrow and mischief to men. Only Hope remained there in an unbreakable home within under the rim of the great jar, and did not fly out at the door; for ere that, the lid of the jar stopped her, by the will of Aegis-holding Zeus who gathers the clouds. But the rest, countless plagues, wander amongst men; for earth is full of evils, and the sea is full. Of themselves diseases come upon men continually by day and by night, bringing mischief to mortals silently; for wise Zeus took away speech from them. So is there no way to escape the will of Zeus. (Hesiod 1982: 9)

Usually, this story is read in such a way that hope is *not* regarded as an evil, and in his commentary on Hesiod's *Theogony*, Georg Friedrich Schömann (1793–1879) leaves the question open (Schömann 1868: 213; cited in NK 6/2, 124). Unusually – one might even say, controversially – Nietzsche interprets hope as the evil of evils:

> Hope, in its stronger forms, is a great deal more powerful *stimulans* to life than any sort of realized joy can be. Man must be sustained in suffering by a hope so high that no conflict can *satisfy* it: a hope reaching out beyond this world. (Precisely because of this power that hope has of making the suffering hold out, the Greeks regarded it as the evil of evils, as the most *malign* of evils; it remained behind at the source of all evil.) (AC §23)

Instead, what Nietzsche urges us to have through the mouth of his Zarathustra is not just hope, but the 'highest hope' – a major motif of his *Thus Spoke Zarathustra*.[13]

Finally, Nietzsche turns his attention to the third of the theological virtues, charity or love:

> In order that *love* may be possible, God must become a person; in order that the lower instincts may take a hand in the matter God must be young. To satisfy the ardour of the woman a beautiful saint must appear on the scene, and to satisfy that of the men there must be a virgin. These things are necessary if Christianity is to assume lordship over a soil on which some Aphrodite or Adonis cult has already established a notion as to what a cult ought to be. To insist upon *chastity* greatly strengthens the vehemence and subjectivity of the religious instinct – it makes the cult warmer, more enthusiastic, more soulful. (AC §23)

The cult of Adonis is a cult of the dying-and-reborn god, akin to the Egyptian Osiris, the Semitic Tammuz, or (some would say) the figure of Christ. Born to Smyrna, who was turned into a myrrh tree after conceiving Adonis through an incestuous relationship with her father, Adonis is so beautiful that Aphrodite falls in love with him. She entrusts him to Persephone, the queen of the underworld, who is likewise struck by his beauty and refuses to return him to Aphrodite. Zeus intervenes to decide that Adonis will spend a third of the year with Persephone in the underworld, a third with Aphrodite, and a third as he chooses. Adonis is killed by a wild boar while out hunting, and dies in Aphrodite's arms. She sprinkles his blood with nectar, and so the anemone came into being, a flower whose petals fly away in the wind.

In the account of the cult offered by Walter Burkert (1931–2015),

> Women sit by the gate weeping for Tammuz, or they offer incense to Baal on roof-tops and plant pleasant plants. These

---

[13] See TSZ Prologue §5; TSZ I 8; TSZ I 22 §3; TSZ II 7; TSZ II 11; TSZ III 10 §2; TSZ IV 11.

are the very features of the Adonis legend: which is celebrated on flat roof-tops on which sherds sown with quickly germinating green salading are placed, Adonis gardens [. . .] the climax is loud lamentation for the dead god. (Burkert 1985: 177)

In other words, the association between Adonis and the feminine is central to this cult: 'In Greece, the special function of the Adonis legend is as an opportunity for the unbridled expression of emotion in the strictly circumscribed life of women, in contrast to the rigid order of polis and family with the official women's festivals in honour of Demeter' (Burkert 1985: 177).

The cult of Adonis had interested Nietzsche since his lectures in Basel on *Der Gottesdienst der Griechen* (given in winter 1876–77 and winter 1877–78; KGW, vol. II.5, 355–520). In *Marc-Aurèle et la fin du monde antique* (1882) Renan mentioned Adonis in the context of the religious syncretism from which Christianity emerged (NK 6/2, 125). A more likely source for Nietzsche, however, is *L'irréligion de l'avenir* (1887) by Jean-Marie Guyau (1854–88), who writes about Christianity in the following terms:

Christianity is the most anthropomorphic belief in existence, for it is the one of all others which, after having conceived the most elevated idea of God, abases it, without degrading it, to the most human of human conditions [. . .] What is there astonishing in the fact that Christ has been and is still the great seducer of souls? [. . .] It is possible that from the birth of Christianity down to the present day there has not been one single woman of an exalted piety whose heart has not first beat for her God, for Jesus, for the most lovable and loving type that the human mind has ever conceived. (Guyau 1897: 134–5, cited in NK 6/2, 124–5)

Precisely this psychological dynamic is something that Nietzsche understood well, as becomes clear from the concluding lines of this section:

Love is the state in which man sees things most decidedly as they are *not*. The force of illusion reaches its highest here, and so does the capacity for sweetening, for *transfiguring*. When a man is in love he endures more than at any other time; he submits to anything. The problem was to devise a religion which would allow one to love: by this means the worst that life has to offer is overcome – it is scarcely even noticed. (AC §23)

Looking back at his analysis of the three theological virtues, what do they tell us about Nietzsche's view of Buddhism? To be sure, one might doubt the extent to which he was qualified to discuss Buddhism: his knowledge was largely derived from nineteenth-century sources, such as the work of Paul Deussen. He also refers to Buddhism in a totalising, globalising way, as if there were just one form of the religion called 'Buddhism', rather than a variety of traditions, beliefs and practices. Moreover, Nietzsche's attitude towards Buddhism shifts: in *The Gay Science* and in the first essay in *On the Genealogy of Morals*, he values Buddhism negatively, as an expression of nihilism. In *The Anti-Christ*, however, he values Buddhism more positively, as a foil to his arch-enemy, Christianity. By describing Buddhism as a 'positivistic' religion (AC §20; cf. §23), Nietzsche is adopting a topos of contemporary studies on Buddhism (NK 6/2, 111): Max Müller, for instance, wrote that sufficient had been written in the West about Buddhism 'to frighten priests by seeing themselves anticipated in auricular confession, beads, and tonsure by the Lamas of Tibet, and to disconcert philosophers by finding themselves outbid in positivism and nihilism by the inmates of Chinese monasteries' (Müller 1881: 168); Friedrich von Hellwald (1842–92) remarked that 'over the course of time Buddhistic doctrine developed an idealism as well as a materialism, a positivism as well as nihilism' (von Hellwald 1877: 189); and Gustav Teichmüller (1832–88) observed that Buddhism 'behaves towards appearances (Sankhara) in a positivistic way' (Teichmüller 1882: 357). All in all, Nietzsche's discussion of Buddhism tells us less about Buddhism that it does about the way Nietzsche is prepared at all costs to portray Christianity in the most negative light possible. Whether such an approach is compatible with the principle of 'right speech' as part of the Noble Eightfold Path, and hence with the spirit of Buddhism itself, is something we must leave open at this point.

In short, even if Nietzsche remains convinced that Buddhism is a nihilistic religion, in *The Anti-Christ* he registers a distinct preference for it over Christianity as being, so to speak, more honestly nihilistic. That is, Buddhism offers and brooks no 'moral' interpretation of suffering, whereas Christianity is not merely nihilistic, but insists on compounding this suffering by labelling its sufferers as 'sinners'. In terms of the taxonomy of nihilism offered in the *Nachlass* (WP §22 = KSA 12, 9[35], 350), both Buddhism and Christianity are 'passive' as opposed to 'active' nihilism; Christianity, however, is further along the scale of decline and retreat of the spirit.

Indeed, as Françoise Bonardel has recently argued, Buddhism – far from preaching a 'euthanasia of the will' (to borrow a phrase from Schopenhauer's *The World as Will and Representation*, vol. 2, ch. 49, 'The Road to Salvation') and colluding with the dark cloud of nihilism that was beginning (as Nietzsche argued) to cover Europe – actually coincides with the self-overcoming of nihilism envisaged by Nietzsche (and, in his wake, Martin Heidegger and Ernst Jünger [1895–1998]). On this account, the paradoxical *Überwindung* of nihilism can be fruitfully illuminated by the Buddhist vision of *śūnyatā* (i.e., emptiness, vacuity or voidness); and thus, far from being an obstacle because of its supposed nihilism, Buddhism could make an important contribution to working out a Nietzschean vision of a post-Christian world (Bonardel 2020).

Nietzsche on the history of Israel (AC §25)

In section 25 of *The Anti-Christ*, Nietzsche presents a brief overview of the history of Israel; a history, he writes, which is 'invaluable', because it is 'typical' – typical of a process he calls the 'denaturalisation' (*Entnatürlichung*) of 'natural values', i.e., the values of nature (*Naturwerthe*). In other words, the reader is advised to expect an overview that is both historical and polemical. Nietzsche undertakes to highlight five facts or aspects that illustrate this denaturalisation of natural values.[14]

---

[14] For further discussion of Nietzsche's account of the history of Israel and his use of Wellhausen in particular, see Stern 2019; and for a discussion of Wellhausen's standing today, see Nicholson 2002.

In presenting this overview, Nietzsche's account draws on the work of the German biblical scholar and orientalist Julius Wellhausen (1844–1918), particularly his *Prolegomena to the History of Ancient Israel* (Berlin, 1882; 3rd edn, 1886; 5th German edn, 1899) and the first volume of his *Skizzen und Vorarbeiten* (1884–99) (NK 6/2, 130). Wellhausen's academic path mirrored Nietzsche's, inasmuch as he was a theologian who became a philologist. In 1872, the year in which Nietzsche published *The Birth of Tragedy*, Wellhausen was apppointed Professor of Theology at Greifswald; ten years later, however, in 1882 (three years after Nietzsche had resigned from his professorship at Basel) Wellhausen resigned from the theology faculty and moved to Halle where he became a Professor of Oriental Languages, then to Marburg in 1885, and finally to Göttingen in 1892.

In his *Prolegomena to the History of Israel*, Wellhausen undertook to understand the first five books of the Bible, the Pentateuch, in their historico-social context. Along with Karl Heinrich Graf (1815–69), Wellhausen was one of the pioneers of the so-called 'documentary hypothesis', according to which the Pentateuch was not written by a single author, traditionally identified as Moses. Rather, it is a compound of four narrative sources, referred to as the Yahwistic source (J), the Elohistic source (E), the Deuteronomic source (D) and the Priestly Code (P). While this account is still widely accepted, it is rejected by some and subject to extensive modification by others (NJB, OT, 7–11). In Nietzsche's day, however, it was cutting-edge theory – and, as a philologist, Nietzsche aligned himself with its implicitly historical (and historicising) approach to sacred scripture.

Nietzsche's account commences relatively late in the history of Israel, to the extent that this history can be reconstructed from existing biblical and archaeological sources. Around 2000 BCE, a figure called Abram (Abraham) leaves Ur, an important Sumerian city in ancient Mesopotamia (in what is now southern Iraq), and sets off for Canaan (Palestine). Thus begins the time of the patriarchs, associated until around 1680 BCE with the figures of Isaac, Jacob and Joseph. When Jacob's family settles in Egypt, the centuries spent by Israel in Egypt begin and, after the death of Joseph, the years of slavery. In around 1280 BCE the exodus is said to have taken place, initiating decades of wandering in the desert. This period is associated with the figures of Moses, then Joshua, the former associated with masterminding the exodus and the latter with the fall of Jericho with which the conquest of Canaan begins.

Towards the end of the 1300s BCE, the judges appear – charismatic rulers or military leaders who ruthlessly implemented the will of Yahweh; the institution of this form of rule is narrated in Exod. 18:13–27. This period, lasting until around 1050 BCE, is associated with such figures as Gideon, Samson and Samuel. With King Saul, consecrated by Samuel (1 Sam. 9:26–10:8) after the people ask for a king (1 Sam. 8:1–9) and Yahweh concedes to their demands for a monarchy to be instituted (1 Sam. 8:10–22), the era of Israel's kings begins. During the unhappy reign of Saul (1050–1010 BCE), which seems to confirm Yahweh's misgivings about this form of government, David sings his psalms, is anointed (1 Sam. 16:1–13), takes flight to escape Saul's jealousy (1 Sam. 19:8–21:1) and becomes an outlaw (1 Sam. 22–6); after living among the Philistines (1 Sam. 27–31), he is in turn anointed king (1010–970 BCE) (2 Sam. 2:1–4; 5:1–5). David is followed on the throne, not without much intrigue over the succession, by Solomon (970–928 BCE) (1 Kings 1:28–40), who commences the building of the Temple in Jerusalem (1 Kings 5:15–9:25).

It is at this point, when Israel enters its golden age, that Nietzsche's account begins. Here is his description of the first aspect of the 'denaturalisation' of 'natural values' he wishes to foreground:

> Originally, and above all in the time of the monarchy, Israel maintained the right attitude of things, which is to say, its natural attitude. Its Yahweh was an expression of its consciousness of power, its joy in itself, its hopes for itself: to him the Jews looked for victory and salvation and through him they expected nature to give them whatever was necessary to their existence – above all, rain. (AC §25)

Nietzsche's statements coincide with current thinking at the time about the religious milieu out of which the figure of Yahweh as the god of Israel emerged in the thirteenth century BCE. In Canaanite culture, the chief god, El, coexisted along with a pantheon of other deities, including Baal, the god of rain. In the course of time Yahweh came to be identified as El, at the same time assimilating the military and rain-providing aspects of Baal, while the figure of Baal himself became anathematised.

The outcome of this process can be seen in the ninth century BCE, in the famous story of the great drought which opens the Elijah cycle in the First Book of Kings. Elijah prophesies to Ahab, king of Israel, that there will be a drought (1 Kings 17:1), implicitly as a punishment for deserting Yahweh and following Baal (1 Kings 16:32–3; 17:16–19). To resolve the situation, Elijah challenges the prophets of Baal to call on their god to set fire to a sacrifice prepared on an altar on the top of Mount Carmel, but their cries to Baal apparently go unheard. 'Cry with a louder voice', Elijah mocks them, in terms that Nietzsche takes up and uses in his passage about the death of God in *The Gay Science* (§125): 'Perhaps he is talking, or in an inn, or on a journey; or perhaps he is asleep, and must be awaked' (1 Kings 18:27). Then it is Elijah's turn; even though the sacrifice is doused in water, Yahweh's fire falls on it and consumes it entirely, whereupon Elijah urges the people to seize the prophets of Baal and slaughter them. With this vindication of the power of Yahweh, the drought immediately comes to an end.

Over time and with the emergence of kingship and a concomitantly stronger sense of a national state, Yahweh becomes the national god of Israel, supreme over the other gods while absorbing their positive traits. After the ninth century BCE, the worship of Yahweh focused on annual festivals, celebrating key moments in agricultural life, i.e., the birthing of lambs, the cereal harvest and the fruit harvest – moments that coincided with events in Israel's national myth, i.e., the exodus from Egypt, the giving of the law at Sinai and the wanderings in the wilderness: the three festivals of Passover, Shavuot and Sukkot. The final step comes in the crisis of the exile, when even the existence of other deities comes to be denied.

According to Nietzsche, this attitude towards *nature* also involves an attitude of *justice*:

Yahweh is the god of Israel, and *consequently* the god of justice: this is the logic of every race that has power in its hands and a good conscience in the use of it. In the religious ceremonial of the Jews both aspects of this self-approval stand revealed. The nation is grateful for the benign procession of the seasons, and for the good fortune attending its herds and its crops. (AC §25)

On Nietzsche's account, 'this state of things remained' (as the second fact illustrating the 'denaturalisation' of 'natural values') 'the ideal for a long while, even if it had been robbed of validity by tragic blows: anarchy within and the Assyrian without' (AC §25). Here Nietzsche is thinking of the division of the kingdom into the northern kingdom of Israel and the southern kingdom of Judah in around 930 BCE (1 Kings 12–14). The reigns of Jeroboam I (928–910 BCE), Omri (885–874 BCE) and Ahab (874–853 BCE) in the north correspond to the reigns in the south of Rehoboam (928–913 BCE), Asa (911–870 BCE) and Jehosophat (873–848 BCE) as kings of Judah; in the north, the great prophetic figures of Elijah and Elisha emerge, overshadowing the end of the First Book of Kings (chs 17–19 and 21) and the beginning of the Second Book (2 Kings 2:2–13:21).

As Nietzsche suggests, this period is marked by the rise of Assyria: following the reign in the north of Jeroboam II (793–753 BCE) and during the reign of Hoshea (732–723 BCE), the fall of Samara to the Assyrians in 722/721 marks the end of the northern kingdom of Israel, and the Israelites are taken to Assyria. In the south, the end of the reign of Uzziah (791–740 BCE) coincides with the calling of Isaiah, the great prophet who rises to prominence during the reign of Hezekiah (729–687 BCE). The Assyrians are a problem for the kingdom of Judah as well, besieging Jerusalem around 700 BCE. In his account of this aspect of Israel's history, Nietzsche specifically mentions the figure of the Messianic servant found in the writings of Isaiah, albeit in a typically jaundiced way: 'But the people still retained, as a projection of their highest yearnings, that vision of a king who was at once gallant warrior and an upright judge – a vision best visualised in the typical prophet (i.e., critic and satirist of the moment), Isaiah' (AC §25).

One of the four great prophets – in fact, in the words of Ecclesiasticus, *the* 'great prophet' (Ecclus. 48:25) – Isaiah was born around 765 BCE, receiving his prophetic vocation while in the Temple in Jerusalem in the year of King Uzziah's death, 740 BCE (Isa. 6). His activity as a prophet lasted over forty years, but the text as we have it consists of the work of several writers, referred to as Proto-Isaiah (chs 1–40), Deutero-Isaiah or Second Isaiah (chs 40–55) and Trito-Isaiah or Third Isaiah or a composite collection of writers (chs 56–66). The reasons for this division are essentially philological: on linguistic grounds, it is argued, chapters 40–55 cannot be the work of someone writing in the eighth century, and in fact the historical setting is two centuries later, when Jerusalem has been captured, the people have been taken into captivity in Babylon, and when Cyrus is emerging on to the political stage where he will prove to be the instrument of their salvation (see below). Earlier biblical commentators found no problem in this, since Isaiah is, after all, meant to be a prophet; but more recent commentators are less sure. It would not be impossible, the commentary in the NJB concedes, 'for God in his omnipotence to transport a prophet into the distant future, cut him off from the present and change his thoughts and images' – perhaps in the way that Habbakuk is transported by his hair to Daniel? – but this possibility is rejected, on the grounds that this would presuppose 'a split in [Isaiah's] personality and a disregard for the contemporaries to whom he had been sent' that would be 'contrary to the very nature of prophecy which touches the future only in function of the present' (NJB, OT, 1169). Or could it be that Isaiah was, as Nietzsche puts it, a 'critic and satirist of the moment' (AC §25)?

Following military successes in Tyre, which they besieged between 724 and 720 BCE, and in Damascus, which they conquered in 732 BCE, and the growth of their power in the region, the ascent of the Assyrians goes into reverse at this point, due to the rise of Babylon as a power. In 612 BCE, Nineveh, the Assyrian capital, falls to the Babylonians; later, they defeat Egypt at Carchemish. Despite the religious reform introduced by King Josiah following the 'discovery' of the book of the Law, and despite the warnings of two major prophets, Jeremiah and

Ezekiel, disaster strikes. In 597 BCE Nebuchadnezzar II conquers Jerusalem, taking King Jehoiachan and the people into exile, and in 587 BCE Jerusalem and the Temple are destroyed by Nebuchadnezzar and the Babylonians, and the Judeans are taken to Babylon; Judah is now in exile. Yet the prophecies of Daniel, who had already been taken hostage and removed to Babylon in 605 BCE, point to the reversal in turn of the Babylonians' fortunes: with the rise of Cyrus of Persia, the events 'foretold' in the warning dream and the madness of Nebuchadnezzar (Dan. 3:31–4:34) and in the sinister events at Belshazzar's feast 'become true': in 583 BCE Babylon falls to the Medes and the Persians, and Cyrus allows the Jews to return home.

All these cataclysmic events form the backdrop to the third, fourth and fifth aspects of the 'denaturalisation' of 'natural values' in Nietzsche's account. These historical disasters for the Jewish people meant that 'every hope remained unfulfilled', for 'the old god no longer *could* do what he used to' (AC §25). At this historical stage, Yahweh no longer intervenes as he had done, smiting the Egyptians with plagues, defeating the Amalekites and ensuring victory at Jericho. Consequently this became, in part, the task of the prophets, both major and minor: to explain why Yahweh has seemingly rejected his people.

What should have happened now, Nietzsche writes, is that Yahweh 'should have been abandoned' (AC §25), but instead something else took place: 'The conception of him was *changed* – the conception of him was *denaturized*; this was the price that had to paid for keeping him' (AC §25). This 'denaturalisation' takes the form of a *universalisation* of Yahweh: instead of being a god of nature who had become a national god, he now becomes the one, sole God of all humankind. Thus monotheism in its true sense is born. Initially it had been accepted that other nations had their own gods, while Israel had Yahweh. But the understanding of Yahweh as the most powerful of gods and his insistence on being exclusively honoured began a transition from a specific to a more abstract conception. No longer exclusive to Israel, to its land and its shrines, Yahweh becomes a god for other nations too; hence his repeated injunctions to abandon foreign cults and destroy their idols.

At the end of this development lies full-blown monotheism and the god of the philosophers. We can see this transition in the Book of Isaiah, whose second chapter has a vision of everlasting peace – 'And in the last days the mountain of the house of the Lord shall be prepared on the top of the mountain, and it shall be exalted above the hills, and all nations shall flow unto it' (Isa. 2:2) – while in chapter 44 there is an explicit affirmation that there is only one God: 'Thus saith the Lord, the king of Israel, and his Redeemer, the Lord of hosts: I am the first, and I am the last, and besides me there is no God' (Isa. 44:6; cf. 45:21–2). Such a God may be called transcendent or, in the language of the prophets, 'holy' (NJB, OT, 1163)[15] – and it is a conception that Nietzsche utterly rejects.

In section 25, Nietzsche describes this next aspect of the history of Israel thus: 'Yahweh, the god of "justice" – he is in accord with Israel *no more*, he no longer visualizes national egoism; he is now a god only conditionally' (AC §25). For Nietzsche, the monotheistic conception of God is the weakest possible one that can be imagined. The most abstract statement of this abstract monotheism can be found in Spinoza who, in his *Ethics*, defines God as 'a being absolutely infinite – that is, a substance consisting in infinite attributes',[16] and talks about *amor intellectualis dei* or the intellectual love of God.[17] In *The Gay Science*, Nietzsche is openly contemptuous about what he calls this 'philosophizing vampirism', this reduction of the concept of God to 'nothing but bones and their rattling [. . .] categories, formulae, *words*': 'what is *amor*, what *deus*, when they have lost every drop of blood?', he asks (GS §372).

At this point, an historical account would relate how, in the period from 540 BCE onwards, the return begins: Zerubbabel and the main party of exiles return, the Temple in Jerusalem is rebuilt, followed by the return of Ezra and then the return of Nehemiah, who

---

[15] The category of 'the holy' plays a key role in the most famous work of the theologian and scholar of religion Rudolf Otto (1869–1937), *The Idea of the Holy*, first published in German in 1917 as *Das Heilige: Über das Irrationale in der Idee des Göttlichen und sein Verhältnis zum Rationalen*.

[16] *Ethics*, part 1, definition 1 (Spinoza 1955: 46).

[17] *Ethics*, part 5, proposition 32, corollary; proposition 33 (Spinoza 1955: 263–4).

rebuilds the city walls of Jerusalem, so that after many years in exile a remnant of God's people returns and restores the Promised Land. By contrast, Nietzsche's account chooses a very different emphasis:

> The public notion of this god now becomes merely a weapon in the hands of clerical agitators, who interpret all happiness as a reward and all unhappiness as a punishment for obedience or disobedience to him, for 'sin': that most fraudulent of all imaginable interpretations, whereby a 'moral order of the world' is set up, and the fundamental concepts, 'cause' and 'effect', are stood on their heads. (AC §25)

The notion of *Entnatürlichung* recalls Nietzsche's description of morality as 'anti-nature' (*Widernatur*) as the title of a section in *Twilight of the Idols*, a term which he explains as follows: 'Antinatural morality, on the other hand (i.e., almost every morality which has hitherto been taught, reverenced, and preached), directs itself straight against the instincts of life' (TI Morality §4). And in another section of that work entitled 'The Four Great Errors', he attacks the idea of a *sittliche Weltordnung* or 'moral world-order', arguing that 'Christianity is the hangman's metaphysics' (TI Errors §7).

The four errors of this section are 'mistaking cause for consequence', 'false causality', 'imaginary causes', and – the subject of this section – the error of 'free will', and all of them, but especially the fourth, are associated with Nietzsche's critique of 'priests and legislators in morals' (TI Errors §1). On Nietzsche's account, 'the dogma of will has principally been invented for the purpose of punishment, i.e., with the intention of *finding guilty*' (TI Errors §7). He explains the logic of this position, which for him is summarised in the phrase concerning a 'moral world-order', as follows:

> The whole of old psychology, will-psychology, would have been impossible but for the fact that its originators (the priests at the head of the old commonwealths) wanted to create for themselves a right to impose punishment or a right for God to do so [. . .] There is not in our eyes any more fundamental antagonism than that of theologians, who, with the notion of a 'moral order of the world', go

on tainting the innocence of becoming with 'punishment' and 'guilt'. (TI Errors §7)

Likewise, in *The Anti-Christ* Nietzsche insists that a belief in an '*anti-natural*' (*widernatürliche*) causality informs the 'un-nature' (*Unnatur*) that arises as a consequence:

> Once natural causation has been swept out of the world by doctrines of reward and punishment some sort of *un*natural causation becomes necessary: and all other varieties of denial of nature follow it. A god who *demands* – in place of a god who helps, who gives counsel, who is at bottom merely a name for every happy inspiration of courage and self-reliance . . . (AC §25)

In so arguing, Nietzsche is in effect restating his argument in *Twilight of the Idols* that next to 'this depravity of reason', i.e., mistaking the consequence for the cause – an error that is said to belong to 'the most ancient and the most modern habitudes of the human race', and bears the names 'religion' and 'morality' (TI Errors §1) – and next to the error of a false causality, there is the error of 'imaginary causes', under the concept of which 'the whole domain of morality and religion' falls (TI Errors §6). Or to put it another way, morality and religion 'belong entirely to the *psychology of error*: in every individual case cause and consequence are confounded; or truth is confounded with the result of what is believed to be true; or a condition of consciousness is confounded with the causation of this condition' (TI Errors §6).

The psychological dimension of this argument – so important for Nietzsche's argumentation in *The Anti-Christ* – is one that, in *Twilight of the Idols*, Nietzsche takes very seriously. In section 4 of 'The Four Great Errors', he illustrates the error of imaginary causes with reference to how dreams operate. Say the sleeper hears a gunshot in the distance: a whole elaborate dream-narrative is woven around this sensation, in the light of which the gunshot appears as a *cause*. What Nietzsche calls a 'cause-creating drive' is at work in this example (TI Errors §4).

This is not the only time that Nietzsche has recourse to dreams to illustrate what he means by the work of 'the totality of *drives*' that constitutes the being of the individual. In one of the most important sections of *Daybreak*, entitled 'Experience and Invention', Nietzsche discusses how the 'inventions' of our dream life give 'free play and scope' to our instincts and drives (D §119). Our dreams are 'interpretations of our nervous irritations during sleep, *very free* and arbitrary interpretations of the movements of our blood and intestines, and the pressure of our arm and the bed coverings, or the sound of a church bell, weathercocks, night-revellers, and so on' (D §119). In this aphorism in *Daybreak*, Nietzsche argues that 'waking life does not have this *freedom* of interpretation possessed by dream life' (D §119), but in *Twilight of the Idols* Nietzsche is more ready to explore the similarity in mechanisms between sleeping and waking life (TI Errors §4). Why should the exercise of these drives in general and the cause-creating drive in particular be such a problem? Because, for Nietzsche, this drive can become caught up with another drive, one that is inimical to life. In Freud's later thinking, just such a drive is called the 'death-drive' and associated with the mythological figure of Thanatos.

On Nietzsche's account, it is an anti-vital drive that lies at the root of morality and turns into 'the actual poisoner and calumniator of life' (TI Errors §6). Correspondingly, in *The Anti-Christ* Nietzsche brings section 25 (in which he interprets the history of Israel as the history of a denaturalisation of natural values) to a conclusion by naming as his real target morality:

> *Morality* is no longer a reflection of the conditions which make for the sound life and development of the people; instead it has become abstract and in opposition to life – a fundamental perversion of the imagination, an 'evil eye' on all things. *What* is Jewish, *what* is Christian morality? Chance robbed of its innocence; unhappiness polluted with the idea of 'sin'; well-being represented as a danger, as a 'temptation'; a physiological disorder produced by the canker worm of conscience . . . (AC §25)

By offering this historical account, Nietzsche has, in fact, been laying the groundwork for his psychological, or even physiological, account of religion in general and Christianity in particular.

In this respect, too, *The Anti-Christ* re-rehearses arguments put forward in *Twilight of the Idols* about morality as anti-nature, particularly its accusation that 'the praxis of the Church is *inimical to life*' (TI Morality §1) and its portrayal of what it calls the 'castration' or 'extirpation' of the instincts or desires (TI Morality §2). Correspondingly, in *Twilight of the Idols* Nietzsche famously describes Christianity as 'the hangman's metaphysics' (TI Errors §7), and he explicates the verdict in one of the greatest passages of that work, in which he asks, 'What alone can *our* teaching be?', and concludes: 'We deny God, we deny responsibility by denying God; it is only *thereby* that we save the world' (TI Errors §8). Over and against the religious and transcendental redemption of the world proposed by Christianity, Nietzsche places its immanent (or aesthetic) redemption – but it is a redemption nevertheless.

Nietzsche on the loss of the symbolic dimension (AC §§31–2)

In *Human, All Too Human*, Nietzsche remarks on the importance of 'little unpretentious truths' that have been discovered by 'rigorous method', arguing that 'the characteristic of an advanced civilization' is 'to set a higher value upon little, simple truths, ascertained by scientific method, than upon the pleasing and magnificent errors originating in metaphysical and æsthetic epochs and peoples' (HAH I §3). On this account, it is a mark of 'higher culture' to have moved away from the symbolic: 'Formerly the mind was not brought into play through the medium of exact thought' and 'its serious business lay in the working out of forms and symbols' (HAH I §3). But this, he asserts, has changed, and 'any seriousness in symbolism is at present the indication of a deficient education' (HAH I §3). So what, then, has replaced the symbolic? The answer, it seems, is science:

> The reverers of forms, indeed, with their standards of beauty and taste, may have good reason to laugh when the

appreciation of little truths and the scientific spirit begin to prevail, but that will be only because their eyes are not yet opened to the charm of the utmost simplicity of form or because men though reared in the rightly appreciative spirit, will still not be fully permeated by it, so that they continue unwittingly imitating ancient forms (and that ill enough, as anybody does who no longer feels any interest in a thing). (HAH I §3)

And at this stage in his philosophical trajectory, Nietzsche appears to welcome the dismantling of the symbol:

As our very acts become more intellectual, our tendencies more rational, and our judgment, for example, as to what seems reasonable, is very different from what it was a hundred years ago: so the forms of our lives grow ever more *intellectual* and, to the old fashioned eye, perhaps, *uglier*, but only because it cannot see that the realm of inner, rational beauty [*das Reich der inneren, geistigen Schönheit*] always spreads and deepens, and to what extent we may all now accord the eye of insight [*der geistreiche Blick*] greater value than the fairest structure or the sublimest edifice. (HAH I §3)

This scientific move on Nietzsche's part entails, for instance, a rejection of astrology and related disciplines: 'It is presumable that the objects of the religious, moral, aesthetic and logical notions pertain simply to the superficialities of things, although man flatters himself with the thought that here at least he is getting to the heart of the cosmos', Nietzsche argues, adding: 'He deceives himself because these things have power to make him so happy and so wretched, and so he evinces, in this respect, the same conceit that characterizes astrology' (HAH I §4). At the same time, and for the same reasons, it entails a rejection of conventional morality: for 'astrology presupposes that the heavenly bodies are regulated in their movements in harmony with the destiny of mortals: the moral man presupposes that that which concerns himself most nearly must also be the heart and soul of things' (HAH I §4). Yet a decade later in *The Anti-Christ*, it is precisely the symbolic dimension of Christianity that constitutes, in Nietzsche's eyes, its greatest value.

In section 31, Nietzsche discusses 'that strange and sickly world into which the Gospels lead us' and the difficulties the first disciples must have faced understanding it, which led to them becoming (as he puts it) 'coarsened':

> The first disciples, in particular, must have been forced to translate an existence visible only in symbols and incomprehensibilities into their own crudity, in order to understand it at all – in their sight the type could take on reality only after it had been recast in a familiar mould . . . The prophet, the Messiah, the future judge, the teacher of morals, the worker of wonders, John the Baptist – all these merely presented chances to misunderstand it . . . (AC §31)[18]

Now, in section 32, Nietzsche warns against seeing theological doctrines, such as the notion of the 'kingdom of God' or the eating and drinking at the Last Supper, in anything other than symbolic terms. In fact, he explicitly warns that one 'should be careful not see in all this anything more than sign language [*eine Zeichenrede*], semiotics [*eine Semiotik*], an opportunity to speak in parables [*Gleichnissen*]' (AC §32). Applying, albeit 'somewhat loosely', the term 'free spirit' to Christ, Nietzsche argues that Christ 'cares nothing for what is established: the word *killeth*, anything that is established *killeth*' (AC §32).[19] Instead, repelled by 'every sort of word, formula, law, belief and dogma', Christ 'speaks only of inner things', using the terms 'life', 'truth' or 'light' to speak about 'the innermost' (AC §32). As for everything else, however, 'the whole of reality, all nature, even language, has significance only as a sign [*Zeichen*], as allegory [*Gleichnis*]', and for this reason Nietzsche describes this standpoint as 'a symbolism [*Symbolik*] *par excellence*', which stands 'outside all religion, all notions of worship, all history, all natural science, all worldly experience, all knowledge,

---

[18] For further discussion of the notion of the symbol in this context, see Musurillo 1957.
[19] Note the echo here of 2 Cor. 3:6, 'for the letter killeth, but the spirit giveth life'.

all politics, all psychology, all books, all art' (AC §32). Indeed, by describing this 'knowledge' (*Wissen*) as '*pure ignorance*' (*reine Thorheit*), Nietzsche brings the figure of Christ into proximity with the medieval figure of Parzival (or at least Wagner's Parsifal), who was characterised by just such a 'pure ignorance' (although, in his original manuscript, Nietzsche had written 'entirely stupid lack of knowledge').[20]

After an excursus in section 33 on how the concepts of guilt, punishment and reward are entirely lacking in the psychology of the Gospels, in section 34 Nietzsche returns to his analysis of Christ as a 'great symbolist' (*grosser Symbolist*), the greatness of whose symbolism lies in the fact that 'he regarded only *subjective* realities as realities, as "truths" – that he *saw* everything else, everything natural, temporal, spatial and historical, merely as signs [*Zeichen*], merely as materials for parables [*Gleichnissen*]' (AC §34). The sort of theological concepts that Nietzsche suggests should be regarded in a 'symbolic' way include the 'Son of Man' and the 'kingdom of Heaven', each of which he interprets in a way that can safely be described as unorthodox, as we shall explore in the following chapter. In it we examine such problematic terms in biblical theology as the 'Son of Man', the 'kingdom of God' and the 'son of God', before embarking on a short tour of the ancient Mysteries and Nietzsche's initial interest in the figure of Dionysos. These topics matter, because Nietzsche's own treatment of them is highly allusive, assuming a knowledge on the part of the reader that may not be so common these days, yet is essential for understanding the full significance of his argument in *The Anti-Christ*.

---

[20] NK 6/2, 170; cf. TI Expeditions §30 and EH Wise §8.

4
Nietzsche on Christianity and the Mysteries

In section 34 of *The Anti-Christ* Nietzsche presents Christ as an essentially symbolic figure, but he does not refer to him as Christ or as Jesus, but instead uses the biblical expression 'Son of Man' (or, in German, *des Menschen Sohn*). In the New Testament the phrase 'Son of Man' occurs only in the Gospels – with the exception of one occasion in the Acts of the Apostles (Acts 7:56) and two occasions in the Book of Revelation (Rev. 1:13; 14:14). The expression is, in the words of the commentary in the NJB, the 'favourite self-designation' of Jesus, used (for example) in one of his most famous sayings, 'The foxes have holes, and the birds of the air nests: but the son of man hath not where to lay his head' (Matt. 8:20).

In the Gospel of Mark, the expression is frequently used, as in 'the Son of man hath power on earth to forgive sins' (Mark 2:10), 'the Son of man is Lord also of the Sabbath' (Mark 2:28), 'the Son of man must suffer many things' (Mark 8:31), and 'you shall see the Son of man siting on the right hand of the power of God, and coming with the clouds of heaven' (Mark 14:62). Nietzsche's understanding of this and related expressions needs to be understood against the background of the biblical context in which it is presented. In order to appreciate the significance of Nietzsche's argument, we need to remind ourselves of what he would have taken for granted that we as his readers would know, though nowadays this is not necessarily the case.

Son of Man (AC §34)

In the Gospel of John, Christ applies the expression 'Son of Man' to himself at the conclusion of his conversation with Nathanael which leads to the latter's conversion (John 1:51); and in the course of his conversation with Nicodemus, Christ declares: 'And no man hath ascended into heaven, but he that hath descended from heaven, the Son of man, who is in heaven. And as Moses lifted up the serpent in the desert, so must the Son of man be lifted up: That whosoever believeth in him, may not perish, but may have life everlasting' (John 3:13–15). (This passage is, of course, dense with allusions to the Hebrew Bible.)[1] The phrase 'Son of Man' also features in the discourse at the synagogue at Capernaum, where Christ describes himself as 'the bread of life' (John 6:35), and upsets his listeners when he tells them: 'Amen, amen, I say to you: Unless you eat the flesh of the Son of man, and drink his blood, you shall not have life in you' (John 6:54).

After he has entered Jerusalem as the Messiah (John 12:12–19) and foretold his death and subsequent glorification (John 12:20–36), the crowd question him about what this expression means: 'We have heard of the law, that Christ abideth for ever: and how sayest thou, The Son of man must be lifted up? Who is this Son of man?' (John 12:34). The answer given is an indirect one (John 12:35–6), but the expression is used on one further occasion in this Gospel at the outset of the extensive farewell discourses that follow the washing of the apostles' feet and the foretelling of Judas's treachery. After Judas has taken the morsel of bread dipped in sauce, he leaves, and Christ announces, 'Now is the Son of man glorified: and God is glorified in him' (John 13:31).

As a New Testament expression, 'Son of Man' clearly refers back to the prophetic books of the Hebrew Bible, where the origin of this phrase can be found. In the Book of Ezekiel, for instance, the expression is used by Yahweh when he addresses the prophet directly before revealing the vision of the scroll:

---

[1] Specifically, to the bronze serpent fashioned by Moses in the desert of Num. 21:409; cf. Wis. 16:5–14.

'This was a vision of the likeness of the glory of the Lord. And I saw, and I fell upon my face, and I heard the voice of one that spoke. And he said to me: Son of man, stand upon thy feet, and I will speak to thee' (Ezek. 2:1–2). This designation by God of his prophet as 'Son of Man' is a major characteristic of the Book of Ezekiel (cf. NJB, OT, 1409, note b). Then again, in the Book of Daniel the prophet has a remarkable dream – the vision of the four beasts, of the One most venerable, and of the Son of Man: 'I beheld, therefore, in the vision of the night, and lo, one like the Son of man came with the clouds of heaven, and he came even to the ancient of days: and they presented him before him' (Dan. 7:13). The Hebrew expression *ben 'adam* appears frequently in the Hebrew Bible, primarily meaning – as the Aramaic *bar nasha'* does here – simply 'man', as it does in Psalm 8, 'What is man, that thou art mindful of him? or the son of man, that thou visiteth him?' (Ps. 8:5). In the Book of Daniel, however, the expression 'allusively signifies something further', as the commentary in the NJB puts it – namely, it indicates an individual.

For it is in this sense that one finds the phrase being used in such early Jewish apocryphal writings as the Book of Enoch and the Second Book of Esdras. In the Book of Enoch, for instance, Enoch sees 'another, whose face had the appearance of a man, and his face was full of grace, like one of the holy angels', a figure identified by one of those angels as 'the Son of Man who has righteousness, and with whom righteousness dwells', who will 'reveal all the treasures of that which is secret' and 'rouse the kings and the powerful from their resting-places, and the strong from their thrones, and will loose the reins of the strong, and will break the teeth of the sinners' (En. 46:1–4, in Sparks [ed.] 1984: 227). In the Second Book of Esdras, also known as the Fourth Book of Ezra, the scribe has the following apocalyptic dream: 'And, lo, there arose a wind from the sea, that it moved all the waves thereof. And I beheld, and lo, that man waxed strong with the thousands of heaven; and when he turned his countenance to look, all the things trembled that were seen under him' (2 Esdr. 13:2–4).

Not surprisingly, then, the figure of the Son of Man also emerges in Christian apocalyptic literature in the Book of Revelation, where John the Apostle, in exile on the Greek island of

Patmos, falls into an ecstatic state and, hearing behind him 'a great voice, as of a trumpet', turns round and sees 'seven golden candlesticks, And in the midst of the seven golden candlesticks, one like to the Son of man, clothed with a long garment, and girded about the paps with a golden girdle' (Rev. 1:12–14). In its presentation of the Messiah as judge, this text draws on earlier biblical texts: his long robe symbolises his priesthood (Exod. 28:4; 29:5; Zech. 3:4) and the golden cord around his waist signifies royalty (1 Macc. 10:89), while other elements – his white hair as a symbol of eternity, the feet of burnished bronze, the brighness of his legs and face, his eyes 'like a burning flame' – draw on details from Daniel (7:9; 10:5–6) as well as one of the Psalms most frequently used in the liturgy, Psalm 149, *Cantate domino*: 'The saints shall rejoice in their glory: they shall be joyful in their beds. The high praises of God shall be in their mouth: a two-edged swords in their hands: To execute vengeance upon the nations, chastisements among the people' (Ps. 149:5–7).

The expression 'Son of Man' returns towards the end of the Book of Revelation, when angels announce the Day of Judgement, prior to the hymn of Moses and the Lamb, the vision of the seven bowls of plagues, the punishment of Babylon, the destruction of the unbelievers, and the vision of the heavenly Jerusalem of the future. 'And I saw, and behold a white cloud: and upon the cloud one sitting like to the Son of man, having on his head a golden crown, and in his hand a sharp sickle', John records (Rev. 14:14). Again, echoes of the Book of Daniel (Dan. 7:13) inform the presentation of this figure, explicitly associated here with the harvest and vintage of the gentiles (i.e., the non-Jewish peoples).

In other words, the figure of the Son of Man is clearly one that undergoes a process of evolution, shifting from its origins in the Jewish apocalyptic tradition to become a significant self-designation used by Christ himself. To an extent, the figure of the Son of Man is a *textual* one, emerging from a dense network of intertextual references across documents over a couple of centuries. It is this aspect of the figure that Nietzsche seems to have understood when, in *The Anti-Christ*, he writes that 'the concept of "the Son of Man" does not connote a concrete person in history, an isolated and definite individual, but an "eternal" fact, a psychological symbol set free from the concept of time' (AC §34). As we shall see, this symbolic aspect is also central to Nietzsche's understanding of two other New Testament concepts, the 'kingdom of God' and the 'son of God'.

Kingdom of God (AC §34)

One of the most famous passages in the New Testament can be found in the Gospel of Luke, where an account is given of a conversation between Christ and the Pharisees about the coming of the kingdom of God. 'And being asked by the Pharisees, when the kingdom of God should come? he, answering them, said: The kingdom of God cometh not with observation. Neither shall they say: Behold here, or behold there: for, lo, the kingdom of God is within you' (Luke 17:20–1). The function of this text is to stage a confrontation between differing conceptions of the Messiah: on the one hand, the Messiah as a political or military figure, a conqueror or a monarch, a revenger of the wrongs done to Israel; and, on the other, as a spiritual figure in the sense that Christianity understood the Messiah. Yet how should the preposition 'within' be understood in the context of this remark about the kingdom of God being 'within you'?

It is easy to interpret this text as a negation of the political in favour of the spiritual or religious, yet the scholarly consensus among biblical scholars suggests that this would be to miss the point. While older translations render the phrase as meaning that the kingdom of God is 'within you' (KJV, DRV), other versions translate it as 'among you' (JB, NJB) or as 'in your midst' (New International Version, New American Standard Bible). For the point of the passage is that the Messiah has *already* come, or in other words that he is *with* you. In the Gospel of John, John the Baptist declares that 'there hath stood one in the midst of you, whom you know not' (John 1:26), and the emphasis is on the actual presence of the Messiah. Hence the NJB commentary glosses the kingdom of God being 'among you' as meaning that it is something 'already present and active', noting that the translation 'within your grasp' is an attractive one, while describing the conventional translation, 'within you', as inadequate as it does not provide an answer to the Pharisees' question as to *when* the kingdom of heaven would come (NJB, NT, 1719).

This biblical crux caught the attention of C. G. Jung, who was fascinated in *Aion: Researches into the Phenomenology of the Self* (1951) by the different descriptions applied to the kingdom of heaven – 'the pearl of great price, the treasure buried in the field, the grain of mustard which will become a great tree, and the heavenly city' – as well as by it being 'in' us as Christ 'is in us' and indeed as 'we in him' (§69, in Jung 1968: 36). Jung notes that, according to one of the papyrus fragments from Oxyrhynchus, this text reads, 'The kingdom of heaven is within you, and whosoever knoweth himself shall find it. Know yourselves' (§69, n. 4, in Jung 1968: 37).[2] In his paper 'The Visions of Zosimos' (1938; 1954), Jung quotes extensively from a medieval alchemical tract, the *Waterstone of the Wise* (*Das Wasserstein der Weysen*) by Johann Ambrosius Siebmacher (1561–1611), in which one reads: 'For as Christ says [. . .] Behold, the kingdom of God is within you – from which it is clearly seen that knowledge of the light in man must emerge in the first place from within and cannot be placed there from without' (§141, in Jung 1983: 106; trans. R. T. Llewellyn). And in a letter to Eugene M. E. Rolfe of 3 March 1949, Jung cited another version of this passage from Oxyrhynchus Papyrus 654, 'Strive therefore to know yourselves [. . .] and ye shall know that ye are in the city of God and ye are the city' (Jung 1973: 524).[3]

One does not have to be a Jungian to see that Jung has put his finger on something immensely important and suggestive about this biblical expression. Similarly, in *The Anti-Christ* Nietzsche argues that 'nothing could be more un-Christian than the *crude ecclesiastical* notions [. . .] of a "kingdom of God" that is to come, of a "kingdom of heaven" beyond [. . .]', since 'the "kingdom of heaven" is a state of the heart – not something to come "beyond

---

[2] James (ed.) 1924: 26: 'the kingdom (of heaven) is within you: (and whosoever) knoweth (. . .) shall find it (. . .) know yourselves'.

[3] James (ed.) 1924: 28: 'the kingdom (of heaven) is within you (and whosoever) knoweth (God) shall find it: (for if ye know him) ye shall know yourselves (and shall know that) ye are (sons) of the Father that is (perfect: and likewise) ye shall know yourselves (to be citizens in heaven). And ye are the city (of God)'.

the world" or "after death"' (AC §34). In short, he concludes, 'the "kingdom of God" is not something that men wait for; it had no yesterday and no day after tomorrow, it is not going to come at a "millennium" – it is an experience of the heart, it is everywhere and it is nowhere' (AC §34). This reading is really quite close to the psychological or existential one proposed by Jung, when he interprets it as meaning that 'if you are a really integrated personality [. . .] then you have a hope to be the truth, namely truly yourself' (Jung 1973: 524).

So it is not surprising to learn that this biblical passage also provided Leo Tolstoy (1828–1910) with the title of a philosophical work that was completed in 1893 and published in Germany in 1894, translated into English as *The Kingdom of God Is Within You*. In this text, Tolstoy proposed a gospel of pacifism, non-violence and Christian anarchism, set out as the basis for a new kind of society. Nietzsche would probably have been appalled.

Son of God (AC §34 and §37)

Just as he rejects what he terms such '*crude ecclesiastical* notions' as 'God as a *person*', a '"kingdom of God" that is to come' and 'a '"kingdom of heaven" beyond', so Nietzsche rejects the concept of a 'son of God' as 'the *second person* of the Trinity' (AC §34). The doctrine of the Trinity is notorious for its complexity; St Augustine is said to have told the story of how he was walking along the seashore while contemplating the doctrine of the Trinity when he saw a small boy trying to fill a hole in the sand with water using a seashell. When Augustine asked what he was doing, the boy answered that he was trying to pour the ocean into the hole. To Augustine's response that this was an impossible task, the boy replied that it was no more impossible than trying to understand the mystery of the Trinity. This episode is the subject of numerous depictions, including works by Guercino in the Prado and by Fra Filippo Lippi in the Hermitage.[4]

---

[4] On the Trinity, see Augustine 2002; Ayres 2011.

Nietzsche would have none of this. Nor would he have any truck with more subtle interpretations of the notion of filiation such as those proposed by Bertrand Vergely, who argues that 'Christianity has so often spoken about the Son that we sometimes forget what it means' (Vergely 2004: 132). On Vergely's account, the Son is not an 'exterior son', i.e., a son 'born of a father situated in time, in space, with a certain nationality, a certain culture, a certain identity', nor is he a 'passive son', i.e., 'an heir who receives name, property, a memory' (or in other words an inheritance), but 'the interior Son, someone whom the Father, the source of life, has begotten, and above all someone who has allowed himself to be begotten by the Father, the source of life' (2004: 132). Vergely contrasts the traditional notion of filiation, i.e., a lineage founded on natural continuity by blood, and the modern notion of filiation, i.e., a lineage founded on recognition by an act of will, to the idea of 'divine filiation', i.e., the proclamation by Christ that he is the son of God (2004: 136–7).

Instead, Nietzsche suggests that 'the word "Son" expresses *entrance* into the feeling that there is a general transformation of all things (beatitude), and "Father" expresses that *feeling itself – the* sensation of eternity and of perfection' (AC §34). True, this sounds almost Gnostic in its formulation, but Nietzsche would insist that it is *symbolic*. In section 37, he returns again to the symbolic dimension of Christianity, a dimension which he regards as more significant than – and, in fact, temporally prior to – its historical dimension. Instead of the conventional view (as represented more recently by G. A. Wells) that 'the *crude fable of the wonder-worker and Saviour* constituted the beginnings of Christianity' and that 'everything spiritual and symbolical in it only came later', Nietzsche inverts this account and argues that precisely the reverse is true: 'The whole history of Christianity – from the death on the cross onward – is the history of a progressively clumsier misunderstanding of an *original* symbolism [*ursprünglichen Symbolismus*]' (AC §37).

As a result of this misunderstanding and of the suppression of the symbolic, a markedly different kind of symbolism takes the place of this 'original symbolism' – the kind of symbolism developed in his theological writings by St Paul, one of Nietzsche's major targets (and arguably the chief target) in *The Anti-Christ*. In sections 42 and 44, the notion of symbol is used in the context of Paul in an entirely negative sense (see Chapter 6 below). Allegedly falsifying the history of Christian beginnings (by shifting the centre of gravity from the figure, teaching and way of life of the Saviour to 'a place *behind* this existence – in the *lie* of the "risen" Jesus') and falsifying the history of Israel (and thereby laying the foundation for the Church's falsification of the history of humankind), Paul wanted 'power', and had use only for 'such concepts, teachings and symbols as served the purpose of tyrannizing over the masses and organizing mobs' (AC §42). Extending this analysis from Paul to Christianity as a whole, Nietzsche declares that 'the underlying will to make use only of such concepts, symbols and attitudes as fit into priestly practice' is 'not only tradition, it is *inheritance*', and this will instinctively repudiates 'every *other* mode of thought, and every other method of estimating values and utilities' (AC §44).

These statements build on earlier reflections by Nietzsche about the symbolic. For instance, in an aphorism entitled 'Christianity as Antiquity' in *Human, All Too Human*, Nietzsche lamented that the figure of the Cross was 'a symbol in an age that no longer knows the purpose and ignominy of the Cross' (HAH I §113), and ten years later in *The Anti-Christ* Nietzsche was asking in section 51 with even more urgency of 'God on the Cross', 'is man always to miss the frightful inner significance of this symbol?' (AC §51). And in section 58, Nietzsche saw in 'the symbol of "God on the Cross"' the means by which St Paul had kindled 'a world conflagration', amalgamating all the secret seditions and anarchist intrigues in the Roman Empire into one immense power (AC §58). Suggesting that Christianity had become Paul's formula for 'exceeding *and* summing up' all the subterranean cults of the Roman Empire – for instance, the cults of Osiris, of the Great Mother and of Mithras – Nietzsche hints at the significant relation between Christianity and the ancient Mystery religions. In order to understand what is at stake in this argument, we need to remind ourselves what the ancient Mysteries were (or might have been).

Nietzsche, Christianity and the Mysteries (AC §37)

It is curious that some figures make it into the (academic) pantheon, whereas others do not. In his lifetime, Nietzsche was – at least, as a philosopher – almost entirely ignored, and it was only after his death that his reputation grew. (This reception confirms his observation in the preface to *The Anti-Christ* that 'some people are born posthumously'.) Today the body of commentary on Nietzsche's thought is immense, covering thousands of pages of books and journal articles. That Nietzsche's reputation as a philosopher not only grew but, over time, acquired a particular ideological coloration is due to his sister, Elisabeth Förster-Nietzsche. Thanks to her, Nietzsche's posthumous fame acquired a thoroughly meteoric character; thanks to her also, alas, he acquired a reputation as an anti-Semite and a right-wing thinker, a reputation which has, despite the best efforts of Walter Kaufmann in the 1960s, never entirely disappeared.

It is one of the curiosities of the history of ideas that Nietzsche's reception is intertwined with the intellectual development of another figure who has never been and probably never will be accepted as canonical: Rudolf Steiner (1861–1925).[5] Yet before Steiner discovered Madame Blavatsky, became a theosophist, and then split from her to form his own school of anthroposophy, he was involved with the early years of the Nietzsche Archive established in Weimar by Elisabeth Förster-Nietzsche and with the editing of Nietzsche's *Nachlass*. Hence he is a significant figure in the history of Nietzsche reception, and can help us grasp some of the ways in which Nietzsche was understood in the years immediately following the composition of *The Anti-Christ*; Steiner is, if you like, a kind of intellectual seismograph.[6] After

---

[5] For an account of Steiner that highlights his pivot towards Nietzsche in 1895 and subsequent shift away, see Leijenhorst 2006.

[6] Thomas Mann talked about the function of the writer or the philosopher as 'a reporting instrument. Seimograph, medium of sensitivity' (Mann 1961: 43). Mann adds that such an individual 'lack[s] clear knowledge of his organic function and therefore [is] quite capable of wrong judgments also'. The same image was used by Nicolaus Harnoncourt when, at the opening of the Salzburg Festival in 1995, he declared that 'the artist has always been a kind of seismograph of the intellectual situation of his time' (*Der Künstler ist seit jeher eine Art Seismograph der geistigen Situation seiner Zeit*) (Harnoncourt 2020: 166).

all, Steiner's short study, *Friedrich Nietzsche, Fighter for Freedom* (1895), was, along with the study *Nietzsche in his Works* by Lou von Salomé (1861–1937), one of the earliest critical assessments of Nietzsche's thought and intellectual achievement (Steiner 1960; 1963; Andreas-Salomé 1983; 2001).

For the same reason it is useful to consult a work written by Steiner just over a decade after Nietzsche had written *The Anti-Christ*, a study entitled *Christianity as Mystical Fact* (1902; 2nd edn, 1910). This study should be seen in the context of a series of other – and, at the time, far more respectable – academic works by leading anthropologists of the time, such as James George Frazer (1854–1941). Born in Glasgow, Frazer became a Fellow in Classics at Trinity College, Cambridge, and was knighted in 1914. One of the founding fathers of the modern discipline of anthropology, Frazer published his most famous study, *The Golden Bough*, in 1890, just two years after Nietzsche had composed *The Anti-Christ* (in 1888) and five years before its first publication (in 1895). First published in two volumes as *The Golden Bough: A Study in Comparative Religion* and in a second edition (in three volumes) as *The Golden Bough: A Study in Magic Religion* (1900), its third edition was published in 12 volumes (1906–15). An abridged edition was published in one volume in 1922; tellingly, this edition excised Frazer's references to Christianity. For at the core of Frazer's book lay a controversial argument about the origins of Christianity.

Frazer's work takes its title from book 6 of Virgil's *Aeneid*, which gives an account of Aeneas's descent to the underworld. Deiphobe, the Sibyl of Cumae, agrees to accompany him on his visit to the shade of his dead father. But before he can begin his descent, Aeneas must obtain the golden bough and present it to Proserpina, the queen of Pluto, the king of the underworld. When, aided by two doves sent by Venus, his mother, Aeneas finds the bough and pulls it from the tree, another golden bough immediately springs up to replace it. Nietzsche knew this story, or at least its Homeric model, as his aphorism 'The Journey to Hades' in *Human, All Too Human*, where he identifies with Odysseus, makes clear (HAH II AOM §408).

Frazer's central thesis was that pagan religions had derived from fertility cults, rituals that re-enact the worship and sacrifice of a sacred king. Within this schema, Frazer found place to discuss numerous ancient ritual phenomena, including human sacrifice, the scapegoat and the dying-and-rising god. This god was incarnated as the king, who then underwent the same pattern of death and resurrection. Frazer identified the god as a solar deity, wedded to the goddess Earth, who died at harvest time and was resurrected in the spring. What began as an investigation into what Frazer later described as 'a single rule of an ancient Italian priesthood', i.e., the pre-Roman priest-king at the temple of Nemi, turned into an all-encompassing, indeed universal, archetypal interpretation – and one which, controversially, could be applied to Christianity too. On this account, the Passion, Crucifixion and Resurrection of Christ are structurally identical to the pagan vegetation rites Frazer described elsewhere.

Frazer's thesis proved to be remarkably influential, providing a source of ideas for, among others, T. S. Eliot in his poem *The Waste Land* (1922); H. P. Lovecraft in his short story 'The Call of Cthulhu' (1928); Naomi Mitchison in her novel *The Corn King and the Spring Queen* (1931); Robert Graves in his study of the Muse-Goddess, *The White Goddess* (1948); and Camille Paglia in her study of 'art and decadence' from Nefertiti to Emily Dickinson, *Sexual Personae* (1990). In *From Ritual to Romance* (1920) by Jessie L. Weston (another major influence on Eliot's *Waste Land*), it was argued that Arthurian myths in general and the Grail legend in particular provided evidence of a connection between paganism and Christianity. In short, the question of the relation between Christianity and paganism was very much in the air at the time when Nietzsche was crafting his polemic against Christianity. More recently, the solar thesis has been taken up and restated, although without reference to Frazer, in various ways – from the popular conspiracy theory film *Zeitgeist: The Movie* (2007), to Michael Onfray who, noting the astrological and astronomical significance of much traditional Christian architecture, has in *Cosmos* (2015) described Christianity as a 'solar shamanism' (Onfray 2015: 349–67).

Frazer's and Steiner's work did not, however, spring into being from nothing. The nineteenth century saw an explosion of interest in the ancient world, reflected in the work of Friedrich Creuzer (1771–1858) and his *Symbolik und Mythologie der alten Völker, besonders der Griechen* (4 vols, 1810–12; 2nd edn, 1821–36); in the work of F. W. J. Schelling and his treatise *Über die Gottheiten von Samothrake* (1815); and in the work of Nietzsche's colleague at Basel, Jacob Burckhardt, whose first published work, *Die Zeit Constantins des Grossen* (1853), discussed the period of transition from paganism to antiquity that occurred during the reign of the Emperor Constantine. This interest carried through into the twentieth century in the work of the German classical philogist and comparative religionist Richard Reitzenstein (1861–1931), one of the leading figures in the history of religions school (or, in German, *religionsgeschichtliche Schule*) and the author of, among other books, *Die hellenistischen Mysterienreligionen: Ihre Grundgedanken und Wirkungen* (1910; 3rd edn, 1927) and *Das iranische Erlösungsmysterium: Religionsgeschichtliche Untersuchungen* (1921).[7]

In 1812 the Russian classical scholar Sergey Uvarov (1786–1855) published an influential study, *Essai sur les mystères d'Eleusis*, the second edition (1816) of which was translated and published as *Essay on the Mysteries of Eleusis* (1817).[8] In the preface to the first edition, Uvarov argued that 'the study of antiquities is not an isolated study; whenever it raises itself above the dead letter, this noble science becomes the history of the human mind' (Ouvaroff 1817: viii). In 1816 the English Neoplatonist Thomas Taylor (1758–1835) published a second and updated edition of his study on *The Eleusinian and Bacchic Mysteries*, first published in 1790. He claimed that the Lesser Mysteries had, in his view, been 'designed by the ancient theologists, their founders, to signify occultly the condition of the unpurified soul invested with an earthly body, and enveloped in a material and physical nature' (Taylor 2001: 60). As for the Greater Mysteries of Eleusis, their ceremonies are said by Taylor to have 'obscurely intimated, by mystic and splendid visions, the felicity of the soul both here and hereafter, when purified from the defilements of a material nature, and constantly elevated to the realities of intellectual [spiritual] vision' (Taylor

---

[7] According to Steiner's translator, Andrew Welburn, his emphasis on an Iranian-Zoroastrian thread in the Mysteries as in Christianity is 'more subtle and restrained' than Reitzenstein's; these are adjectives that are not usually applied to Steiner (Welburn, 'Introduction' in Steiner 1997: xvii).

[8] Ouvaroff 1816; for a survey of literature on the Eleusis cult, see Boyancé 1962.

2001: 77). For Steiner's translator, Andrew Welburn, the spirit of the Eleusinian Mysteries is 'brilliantly captured' by the French esoteric publicist Édouard Schuré (1841–1929) in his study *Sanctuaires d'Orient* (1898) (Steiner 1997: 221, n. 85).

In Germany there was intense interest in the ancient Mysteries towards the end of the nineteenth century. Here, the ancient Greek cults in general and the Mystery cult at Eleusis in particular were treated at length by such scholars as Otto Gruppe (1851–1921) in *Die griechischen Kulte und Mythen in ihren Beziehungen zu den orientalischen Religionen* (1887), Otto Rubensohn (1867–1964) in *Die Mysterienheiligtümer in Eleusis und Samothrake* (1892) and Gustav Anrich (1867–1930) in *Das antike Mysterienwesen in seinem Einfluss auf das Christentum* (1894); the first of these studies appeared at the time when Nietzsche was working on *Twilight of the Idols*, where he touched on the Mystery cults (TI Ancients §4), and on *The Anti-Christ*. Between 1864 and 1878 the art historian and archaeologist Karl Bötticher (1806–89), who worked extensively on classical architecture (see *Die Tektonik der Hellenen*, 2 vols, 1844–52), published a series of 11 articles under the title *Ergänzungen zu den letzten Untersuchungen auf der Akropolis in Athen* in the journal *Philologus: Zeitschrift für das klassische Alterthum*, including a detailed account of the layout of the sanctuaries at Eleusis.

What were the sanctuaries at Eleusis all about, and why would Nietzsche have bothered to mention them in *The Anti-Christ*? Without going into details, the scholarly consensus is that the cult of Demeter and Persephone at Eleusis was probably established in 1500 BCE, and it became one of the most influential and famous of the Mysteries in the ancient world.[9] During the Hellenic era it was a major festival, and its rites were even celebrated in Rome. Those rites involved the abduction of Persephone and her descent into the underworld, the search to retrieve her, and her subsequent ascent and reunion with her mother, Demeter. Yet the precise nature of these rites has always remained a mystery, because a strict vow of silence was enjoined on those who participated in them.

---

[9] For further discussion, see Meyer (ed.) 1987; Foley (ed.) 1994: 65–75; Bremmer 2014; Stein 2016.

Evidence suggests, however, that the Eleusinian Mysteries were divided into two kinds, the Lesser and the Greater. The Lesser Mysteries were celebrated during the month of Anthesteria, overseen by the *archon basileus* (or sovereign magistrate) of Athens. Participants sacrificed a piglet to Demeter and Persephone, and underwent ritual purification in the river Illisos. Upon successful completion of the Lesser Mysteries, these initiates were now admitted to the Greater ones. These were celebrated in Boedromion, the third month of the Attic calendar (around September or October), and lasted ten days. This time the rites involved a procession from Eleusis to the Eleusinion, a temple at the base of the Acropolis in Athens, ritual washing in the sea at Phaleron, and a festival for Asklepios, the god of healing at Epidauros. Participants then processed from the Athenian cemetery (or the Kerameikos) back to Eleusis along the 'Sacred Way', swinging branches and shouting obscenities, and eventually arriving at the great hall or Telesterion, containing the Anaktorin which only the hierophants could enter. Inside the Telesterion, at the culmination of the ceremonies, the *mystai* or initiates saw – what? We simply do not know, which has not prevented (and has even encouraged) speculation.

The Mysteries survived the sacking of the Temple of Demeter by the Sarmatians in 170 CE (it was rebuilt by Marcus Aurelius), and Julian, the last pagan emperor of Rome, tried to restore the popularity of the Mysteries amid the rise of Christianity, but the end was now in sight. In 392 CE, Theodosius ordered the closure of the sanctuaries, and what traces remained of the Mysteries were wiped out by the desecration of the sacred sites by Alaric, the Arian king of the Goths. In other words, the disappearance of the Mysteries marks a turning point in the history of the West, and correspondingly the Mysteries remained a source of fascination for scholars and historians, no more so than in the eighteenth and nineteenth centuries. Friedrich Schiller, for example, wrote a poem entitled 'The Festival of Eleusis' (1798), and penned a lament ostensibly ascribed to Ceres, the goddess of agriculture (the Roman counterpart to Demeter) (see 'Lament of Ceres' [1796]).

As well as serving as an intellectual seismograph of the age for which Nietzsche was writing, Rudolf Steiner can act as a kind of psychopomp or guide for the soul in the afterlife (a role for which he is perhaps better suited). After all, in his account of the ancient Mysteries in relation to Christianity, Steiner suggested that 'the spirit of mysteriosophy', i.e., the knowledge or wisdom relating to the ancient Mysteries, the core of all religions and spiritual heritages, both Eastern and Western, was 'all-pervasive' in the festivals celebrated at Eleusis (Steiner 1997: 82). Steiner was entirely unabashed by the Mysteries of Eleusis, describing the mythology of Demeter and Persephone as 'not hard to interpret' (1997: 84)! On his account, the figure of Demeter represents 'the essential source out of which human consciousness arises', while the myth of Persephone expresses the conviction of 'the immortality of the human soul' (1997: 84–5). Interestingly, Steiner notes that, at Eleusis, alongside Demeter and Persephone, the god Dionysos was also honoured – 'the divine presence in the world, which assumes an endless variety of forms', 'the god poured out into cosmic existence, torn apart in order to be reborn spiritually', and in this respect, a rather Nietzschean god (1997: 85).

In the early twentieth century, Steiner was not alone in his interest in the ancient Mystery cults, as is demonstrated by the work of K. H. E. de Jong (1872–1960) entitled *Das antike Mysterienwesen in religionsgeschichtlicher, ethnologischer und psychologischer Beleuchtung* (1909), or of Ferdinand Noack (1865–1931) in his *Eleusis: Die baugeschichtliche Entwicklung des Heiligtums* (2 vols, 1927). These studies, among others, prompted the vitalist philosopher Ludwig Klages (1872–1956) to discuss the ancient Mysteries at some length in his treatise *Of Cosmogonic Eros* (1922; 2nd edn, 1926). Klages was profoundly influenced by the thought of Nietzsche, to whom he dedicated a study in 1926 entitled *Die psychologischen Errungenschaften Nietzsches*.[10] (That said, Klages regarded himself as not simply building on Nietzsche, but transcending him, as this title suggests: Nietzsche's achievements are *psychological*, rather than *philosophical*, ones.) Klages is, in other words, another seismograph, revealing hidden contours of Nietzsche's impact on his contemporaries.

---

[10] See Klages 1926a; for further discussion, see Bishop 2002; 2002/2003; 2018: 20–8.

In the appendix discussing the sources for his book *Of Cosmogonic Eros*, Klages is characteristically dismissive of previous work in the field, claiming that none had brought about 'a decisive change in our understanding of the "primitive" state of consciousness' (Klages 1926b: 238). True, he described *Psyche: The Cult of Souls and the Belief in Immortality among the Greeks* (2 vols, 1890–94) – the famous work by Nietzsche's student friend Erwin Rohde in which the sixth chapter was devoted to 'The Eleusinian Mysteries' – as 'indispensable' for a deeper understanding of the beliefs of Greek antiquity, and he praised its 'magnificent, richly documented description of the Dionysian orgy' in its second volume, in which he detected the 'archaeological impact' of Nietzsche's *The Birth of Tragedy*. Yet Klages argues that Rohde failed to go beyond Nietzsche's insights, and he specifically criticises Rohde's discussion of Eleusis as 'sketchy' (1926b: 238).

In the sixth chapter discussing the cult of the ancestors in the ancient world, Klages argued that 'all burial customs, symbols, and myths of the soul' point to a phenomenon that was widespread in the pre-prehistoric (or, to use his terminology, the Pelasgian) world and later became restricted to the initiation rites – the 'ecstatic *epopteia*', the final initiation rite in the Eleusinian Mysteries. On this account,

> a drama that compelled its viewers to become involved (or more accurately forced them inwardly to participate) transposed the Eleusinian *mystai* temporarily into a state of non-bodily vision, and from this he emerged with the experience of the reality of the images [*Wirklichkeit der Bilder*] and the presence of the deceased [. . .] (1926b: 172–3)

As a result of this experience, Klages concluded, the initiand would have 'the unshakeable certainty of the ceaselessly renewing *soul* of life' (1926b: 173).

Later in this chapter, Klages introduces an important distinction. He points out that the purpose of the Eleusinian Mysteries was not to guarantee so-called 'eternal life' or immortality, but rather to guarantee a *blessed* life after death. Citing the Homeric hymn to Demeter (ll. 480–2) and an Eleusinian tomb inscription,

Klages argues that immortality was a presupposition in the cult, and he insists on the difference between a desire for immortality and the eternalisation of life (1926b: 188–9). In this respect, Klages is moving into highly Nietzschean territory: after all, in 'The Drunken Song' in *Thus Spoke Zarathustra*, the Higher Men all join in singing Zarathustra's roundelay, which concludes: 'But joys all want eternity, / Want deep, profound eternity!' (TSZ IV 19 §12), and Zarathustra himself is 'the teacher of the eternal return' (TSZ III 13 §2).

In the final chapter in *Of Cosmogonic Eros*, Klages links the Eleusinian Mysteries with the signature concept of his book when he writes that what was desired and intuited in the earliest days of the cult at Eleusis was 'cosmogonic Eros' (1926b: 200) – a concept and term derived from Hesiod's *Theogony* (ll. 116–22), found also in the Orphic tradition (cf. Orphic Hymn, no. 5), and understood in a metaphysical sense by Aristotle (*Metaphysics*, book 1, section 4, 984b–985a). The figure of Eros is central to Nietzsche's thinking as well (see below). In other words, the nexus of 'Mysteries' – 'Dionysos' – 'Eros' is more central to Nietzsche's critique of Christianity than might initially appear.

More recent studies of Eleusis include the work of the Hungarian philologist and mythologist Carl Kerényi (1897–1973), who explored in some detail the significance of the Mysteries on the basis of various ancient depictions in *Eleusis: Archetypal Image of Mother and Daughter* (1967); a study by Walter Burkert of *Ancient Mystery Cults* (1987); Hugh Bowden's work on *Mystery Cults of the Ancient World* (2010); and Jan N. Bremmer's *Initiation into the Mysteries of the Ancient World* (2014). This is not to mention those studies that propose entheogenic theories of the Eleusinian Mysteries, suggesting that the power of the *kykeon*, an ancient Greek drink consumed during the rituals, derived from psychedelic agents or psychoactive mushrooms used in its concoction; see, for example, R. Gordon Wasson, Albert Hofmann and Carl A. P. Ruck's *The Road to Eleusis: Unveiling the Secret of the Mysteries* (1978); Terence McKenna's *Food of the Gods: Search for the Original Tree of Knowledge* (1993); and Harold R. Willoughby's *Pagan Regeneration: A Study of Mystery Initiations in the Graeco-Roman World* (2003).

Of all these studies it is worth recalling the older ones, because they set the tone for the kind of approach to the Mysteries with which Nietzsche would, as a classical scholar, have been familiar. For his part, Nietzsche clearly knew of the Eleusinian Mysteries – indeed, as a classicist, how could he not have done? – for in his account of the Dionysian in *The Birth of Tragedy*, he wrote that the human being is no longer 'an artist' but becomes 'a work of art': 'The noblest clay, the most costly marble, the human being, is here kneaded and cut, and to the sound of the chisel-strokes of the Dionysian world-artist rings out the cry of the Eleusinian mysteries, "Do you prostrate yourselves, millions? Do you sense your Maker, world?"' (BT §1). (Here, the cry of the Eleusinian Mysteries is, in fact, a line from Schiller's famous ode, 'To Joy'.) In fact, Nietzsche uses the image of the primordial maternal in a more substantial way as part of his argument when, in section 16 of *The Birth of Tragedy*, he depicts the voice of nature crying out in Dionysian art and its tragic symbolism: '"Be as I am! Amid the ceaseless flux of phenomena I am the eternally creative primordial mother, eternally finding satisfaction in this change of phenomena!"' (BT §16).

For now, let us leave aside the significance attached by the anthroposophical movement to Steiner's work, and his own belief that, around the turn of the century, 'a conscious knowledge of real Christianity' had begun to dawn within him, enabling him to stand 'spiritually before the Mystery of Golgotha in a deep and solemn celebration of knowledge' (Steiner 2006: 188). For Steiner's account of the relation between the initiation of the ancient Mysteries and the Christian tradition provides a useful summary of the *Stand der Forschung* at the end of the nineteenth century and on the cusp of the twentieth. Reviewing this account can allow us better to appreciate the specificities of Nietzsche's own approach to the Mysteries, which was developed at roughly the same time as he was writing *The Anti-Christ* and is a product of a similar cultural background. The argument here is not that Nietzsche is wrong and Steiner is right, or vice versa, but rather to constellate both their approaches and so gain a deeper understanding of what is characteristic about Nietzsche's.

Steiner begins by noting how it is 'as though a veil of secrecy is drawn over the way in which, in the civilisations of the ancient world, those who sought a deeper religious life and knowledge than could be found in the popular religions were able to satisfy their spiritual needs' (Steiner 1997: 1). Such a veil only attracts Steiner's attention, of course, even if (or maybe precisely because) 'an inquiry into how those needs were met leads us immediately into the obscurity of those ancient cults' (1997: 1). In order to understand the Mysteries, Steiner introduces a distinction between two kinds of 'reality' – not unlike the kind of dual ontology associated with Plato about which, as we know, Nietzsche was so scathing.[11] This dualism is, however, rather more subtle than the crude version of Platonism rejected by Nietzsche: it distinguishes between 1) 'reality' in the sense of our 'immediate environment', whose 'processes' are 'registered by our senses of touch, hearing, and sight'; and 2) 'reality' in the sense of 'the images that surface from the spiritual life of the psyche', correspondingly reducing the degree of actuality ascribed to the sense-impressions (hearing, touching, seeing) (1997: 3–4).

The perception of these psychic images depends, Steiner continues, on the 'spiritual eye' – a suspicious phrase, perhaps, except that it is widely used by such eminently *non*-mystical thinkers as Johann Wolfgang Goethe and Ernst Cassirer.[12] Thus the entire issue of the Mysteries is transformed by Steiner into one of *perception*; or, as he puts it, 'how to realize and feel the truth of what is seen' (1997: 5). True, some people 'deny living response and feeling to everything except what the senses tell them', and such people dismiss the 'higher vision' as 'mere fantasy'. For those others, however, who have 'transformed [their] perceptions and attitudes toward reality', the 'solid structure' of sensory truth loses 'its unconditional and unquestioned character' and leaves room for 'something else' – for 'the world of the spirit', which begins to 'animate the space that is thus left open' (1997: 5–6).

---

[11] For a useful collection (in French) of Nietzsche's writings on Plato, see Nietzsche 2019.
[12] In *On Morphology* (1817–24), for example, Goethe writes that 'we learn to see with the eyes of the spirit' (*wir lernen mit Augen des Geistes sehen*) (Goethe, *Werke* [Weimare Ausgabe]: vol. II.8, 37). As Cassirer points out, when Goethe wrote this he was drawing attention to the role of the 'productive imagination' not just in scientifically determined or artistically formed intuition, but in simple empirical intuition as well (Cassirer 1957: 134–5). For further discussion, see Förster 2001.

On Steiner's account, this dimension is not just perceptual, but also experiential. If one reaches the point in understanding where 'the spirit reveals all of life to be death', then 'one has descended into Hades' (1997: 6). After death and the underworld can only come, on this account, birth or rebirth: about which Steiner recalls the remarks on the experience of the Mysteries attributed to Menippus (in Lucian of Samosata's satire *Menippus or The Descent into Hades*), those by Aristides (in his *Sacred Orations*) and by Plato (in the *Phaedo*, 69a); in a fragment ascribed to Sophocles; and by Plutarch in his treatise 'On the E at Delphi'. When Steiner recalls what happened to the *mystai*, we have to remember that the word means 'initiate', not 'mystic' (analogous to the distinction in German between *der Myste* and *der Mystiker*). The goal of the Mysteries was 'divinisation' (*Vergöttung*), a kind of *apotheosis* or *theothenai*, 'becoming god' (1997: 15; cf. xx), in the sense of creating 'something higher than the senses can grasp, something for which the personality is mere instrument of its creative power, something in humanity that is divine' (1997: 15).

This kind of language sounds distinctly un-Nietzschean, and in some senses it is. In fact, it sounds very much like St Gregory of Nazianzus, who writes in his *Orations* (14.23–5): 'Acknowledge that you have been made a son of God, a co-heir with Christ. Acknowledge [. . .] that you have been made divine' (Gregory of Nazianzus 2003: 55–6); or like St Athanasius of Alexandria, who writes in his treatise *On the Incarnation of the Word of Christ*: 'He, indeed, assumed humanity that we might become God. He manifested Himself by means of a body in order that we might perceive the Mind of the unseen Father. He endured shame from men that we might inherit immortality' (Athanasius 2009). Indeed, in the wake of Origen (*Contra Celsum*, book 3, §28),[13] there developed – particularly in the tradition of Eastern Christian theology – the notion of *theosis* or deification, to which St Gregory of Nyssa (in his *Catechetical*

---

[13] In his polemic against Celsus, the second-century Greek philosopher and early opponent of Christianity, Origen wrote that believers see that 'from [Jesus] there began the union of the divine with the human nature, in order that the human, by communion with the divine, might rise to be divine [. . .] [and] enter upon the life which Jesus taught, and which elevates to friendship with God' (Roberts, Donaldson and Coxe [eds] 1885: 475).

Oration, §25, and *On the Making of Man*, ch. 4, where he speaks of humankind partaking with the Godhead 'both in rank and name'), St Gregory Palamas (who maintained that humankind is, 'by virtue of the body created in the likeness of God [. . .] higher than the angels'), and St Macarius also contributed.[14]

At the same time, it is worth noting that these Christian writers have important pagan antecedents, such as Plato, whose Socrates urges Theodorus (= 'gift of the gods') in *Theaetetus* 176b: 'We should make all speed to take flight from this world to the other, and that means becoming like the divine so far as we can' (Plato 1989: 881); or Plotinus, who describes his concern as being 'not to be out of sin, but to be god' in *Enneads* I.2, §6;[15] or Iamblichus, who declares in his *Protrepticus* that '[k]nowledge of the Gods is Virtue and Wisdom and perfect Felicity, and makes us similar to the Gods' (Iamblichus 1988: 25).[16]

At the same time, this kind of language is *also* highly Nietzschean; after all, Nietzsche describes the composition of *Zarathustra* as nothing less than a *revelation*:

> The idea of revelation, in the sense that something which profoundly convulses and upsets one becomes suddenly visible and audible with indescribable certainty

---

[14] For further discussion, see Payne 1958: 306 (for Gregory Palamas), and 171, 174 and 306 (for Macarius); Inge 1918: 356–68 (Appendix C, 'The Doctrine of Deification'); and Lot-Borodine 1970, cited in Patrides (ed.) 1969: 19.

[15] 'If, then, there is still any element of involuntary impulse of this sort, a man in this state will be a god or spirit who is double, or rather who has with him someone else who possesses a different kind of virtue: if there is nothing, he will simply be god, and one of those gods who follows the First [i.e., Zeus, the leader of the procession of souls in the *Phaedrus*, 246e]' (Plotinus 1989: 143).

[16] For the Cambridge Platonists, of course, these two traditions – one pagan, one Christian – were to be regarded as entirely compatible. In one of his sermons, Benjamin Whichcote (1609–83) urged his listeners to look '*in our selves*; in our *Nativity from above*; in *Mental Transformation*, and DEIFICATION', referring to such texts as 2 Pet. 1:4, Eph. 4:24 and Heb. 1:6; while in his sermon preached before the House of Commons in 1647, Ralph Cudworth cited both 2 Pet. 1:4 and St Athanasius when speaking of God as 'descending into the World in *Our Form* [. . .] that he might allure, and draw us up to God, and make us partakers of his *Divine Form* [. . .] that is [. . .] make us *partakers of the Divine nature*' (cited in Patrides [ed.] 1969: 70, 101).

and accuracy – describes the simple fact. One hears – one does not seek; one takes – one does not ask who gives: a thought suddenly flashes up like lightning, it comes with necessity, without faltering – I have never had any choice in the matter. (EH Z §3)

In *Ecce Homo* Nietzsche emphasises that the experience of writing *Zarathustra* was a visible and auditory one: it involved him becoming 'the mere incarnation' – incarnation! – or the mere 'mouthpiece, or medium of an almighty power'. Paradoxically, as the highest experience of a feeling of freedom, it involves an overwhelming sense of necessity, and this sense of necessity is strongly present in the rest of Nietzsche's description of his experience, where he does not shy away from using precisely the terms 'ecstasy', 'absoluteness', and even 'divinity':

> There is an ecstasy so great that the immense strain of it is sometimes relaxed by a flood of tears, during which one's steps now involuntarily rush and anon involuntarily lag. There is the feeling that one is utterly out of hand, with the very distinct consciousness of an endless number of fine thrills and titillations descending to one's very toes; – there is a depth of happiness in which the most painful and gloomy parts do not act as antitheses to the rest, but are produced and required as necessary shades of colour in such an overflow of light. There is an instinct for rhythmic relations which embraces a whole world of forms [. . .] Everything happens quite involuntarily, as if in a tempestuous outburst of freedom, of absoluteness, of power and divinity. (EH Z §3)

What Nietzsche says in *Ecce Homo* is confirmed by other sources. According to his sister, Elisabeth Förster-Nietzsche, 'my brother had the figure of Zarathustra in his mind from his very earliest youth: he once told me that even as a child he had dreamt of him', and she relates these dream encounters to his decision to name this figure Zarathustra:

At different periods in his life, he would call this haunter of his dreams by different names; 'but in the end', he declares in a note on the subject, 'I had to do a *Persian* the honour of identifying him with this creature of my fancy. Persians were the first to take a broad and comprehensive view of history. Every series of evolutions, according to them, was presided over by a prophet; and every prophet had his Hazar, his dynasty of a thousand years.' (Förster-Nietzsche 1954: xix)

Förster-Nietzsche – possibly a better biographer of her brother than an interpreter of his works – records that he 'often used to speak of the ecstatic mood in which he wrote "Zarathustra"; how in his walks over hill and dale the ideas would crowd into his mind, and how he would note them down hastily in a note-book from which he would transcribe them on his return, sometimes working till midnight', adding that he told her in a letter: 'You can have no idea of the vehemence of such composition' (Förster-Nietzsche 1954: xxix; see Jung 1998: 10–11, 24).

In *Ecce Homo* Nietzsche talks about *Entzückung* (ecstasy) as a feeling of *Außer-sich-sein* (being-outside-of-oneself), and it is instructive to compare this passage from *Ecce Homo* with Plutarch's description of what the soul experiences at the moment of death in terms of what the initiate underwent in the Eleusinian Mysteries, based on the principle that 'the verbs *teleutân* (die) and *teleisthai* (be initiated), and the actions they denote, have a similarity':

> In the beginning there is straying and wandering, the weariness of running this way and that, and nervous journeys through darkness that reach no goal, and then immediately before the consummation every possible terror, shivering and trembling and sweating and amazement. But after this a marvellous light meets the wanderer, and open country and meadow lands welcome him; and in that place there are voices and dancing and the solemn majesty of sacred music and holy visions. And amidst these, he walks at large in new freedom, now perfect and fully initiated, celebrating the sacred rites, a garland upon his head, and converses

with pure and holy men [...] (Stobaeus, *Anthologium*, 4.52.49; in Plutarch 1969: 317–19, Fragment 178)[17]

In other words, the experiential dimension of initiation explored by Steiner is really not so far removed from the sphere of reference usually associated with Nietzsche.

In fact, Nietzsche can be read as a staunch defender of paganism (and perhaps this is one of the sources of the frequent misperception of him as a right-wing thinker). For in *The Anti-Christ* Nietzsche is nothing less than scathing about the assimilation of paganism by Christianity:

> With every extension of Christianity among larger and ruder masses, even less capable of grasping the principles that gave birth to it, the need arose to make it more and more *vulgar* and *barbarous* – it absorbed the teachings and rites of all the *subterranean cults* of the *imperium Romanum*, and the absurdities engendered by all sorts of sickly reasoning. (AC §37)

Indeed, in a fragment from the *Nachlass* for the period November 1887 to March 1888, Nietzsche suggested that 'Christian doctrine continually changes its *emphasis*', so that 'the "Christian" type step-by-step re-accepts everything which he originally negated' and 'the entire life of the Christian is finally precisely the life *from which Christ preached redemption*' (KSA 11[364], 160–1). And he reflected on the forces that had 'come to rule over Christianity': Judaism (in the form of Paul), Platonism (in the form of Augustine), the Mystery cults (in the form of the doctrine of redemption and the emblem of the 'Cross'), and aceticism (in the form of an hostility towards 'nature', 'reason', 'senses' – in short, 'the Orient') (KSA 11[364], 160–1).[18]

---

[17] For further discussion, see Foley (ed.) 1994: 70–5.
[18] For further discussion of Nietzsche's view of the persistence of paganism in Christianity, see Biebuyck, Praet and Vanden Poel 2004; Rempel 2010.

Yet in his work from around the same time, *Twilight of the Idols*, Nietzsche spends a significant amount of time discussing the concept of the Dionysian and the figure of Dionysos, the god in whose name one set of ancient Mysteries was celebrated.[19]

Nothing to do with Dionysos?

This interest in Dionysos goes back, of course, to Nietzsche's earliest published work on the origin of Greek tragic drama, *The Birth of Tragedy* (1872). In this work Nietzsche emphasised the role of the ancient Dionysian Mysteries (as well as, in turn, the more fundamental role of music in those Mysteries themselves). In his unpublished notes (or *Nachlass*) from the time he was working on *The Birth of Tragedy*, Nietzsche observes that 'the Mysteries' involved a 'new mechanism' – new, that is, in relation to Pythagorean philosophy or the cult of Apollo. 'Here the sense of atonishment about existence was not weakened, it was deeply lamented as the tearing-apart of the god', he wrote, adding: 'A strong metaphysics finally brought joy to the face again' (KSA 7, 7[62], 152).

In this context, Nietzsche foregrounded the role of individuation in relation to art: 'Individuation – then the hope of rebirth of the one Dionysos. Everything will become Dionysos. Individuation is the *martyrdom* of the god – no initiate mourns more. Empirical existence is something which should not be. Joy is possible in hope of this restitution', he writes, adding: 'Art is just such a beautiful hope' (KSA 7, 7[61], 152). At this point, Nietzsche makes the following somewhat gnomic remark, based on the following equation: '*Dionysos omistis* and *agronios* = *Zagreus*. It is to him that Themistocles offers three youths as a sacrifice before the Battle of Salamis' (KSA 7, 7[61], 152).

In so writing, Nietzsche was developing a line of thought that he had begun to elaborate during the period of winter 1869–70 and spring 1870 (cf. KSA 7, 3[82], 82) when – on the basis of the work of the classical philologist and linguist Georg Curtius (1820–85), *Grundzüge der griechischen Etymologie* (3rd edn, 1869) – he considered the etymology of the names 'Zeus' (the ancient Greek god of

---

[19] See Hatab 2019: 13–16; and for background, see Henrichs 1984.

the sky and thunder, the king of the gods on Mount Olympus) and 'Zagreus' (a god worshipped by the followers of Orpheus as the son of Zeus and Persephone who is torn apart by the Titans and reborn – and is later merged with the figure of Dionysos himself). (The episode involving Themistocles to which Nietzsche here alludes is recounted by Plutarch in the chapter of his biographical *Parallel Lives* devoted to the famous Athenian politician and general [§13].)

In these notes we find the core idea of how something Dionysian emerged from the Apollonian, although Nietzsche presents this idea in a way that might surprise us: 'The Hellenic world of Apollo is gradually subjugated by the Dionysian forces from within. Christianity *was* already present' (KSA 7, 7[3], 137; see Nietzsche 2009: 33). Or in other words, the early Nietzsche construed Christianity as something 'Dionysian' in nature, an idea he also presents in this form: 'The *Gospel according to St John* born out of Greek atmosphere, out of the soil of the Dionysian: its influence on Christianity in contrast to Judaism' (KSA, 7[13], 139; see Nietzsche 2009: 33).

In another *Nachlass* fragment, Nietzsche considers the meaning of the Temple of Apollo at Delphi, the home to the Pythia or high priestess who acted as the oracle based at this famous site (KSA 7, 7[122], 174–5). In this case Apollo manifested himself, not (yet) as an 'artistic deity' (*Kunstgott*), but as a 'healing, reconciling, warning god-of-the-state [*Staatengott*]' (KSA 7, 7[122], 175), as well as in the form of an individual (*Einzelner*), and even in the form of Homer (who presents Apollo as a terrible god or δεινὸς θεός, and as a god who brings healing), of Lycurgus (the law-giver of Sparta who reformed the city state in accordance with the advice of the Apollonian Oracle at Delphi), and of Pythagoras (said to have been the son of Apollo and born to Parthenis, a virgin) (KSA 7, 7[122], 175). Yet out of this Apollonian world, the forces of Dionysos are said to have emerged:

> All these Apollonian apparatuses have something of the character of the Mysteries about them [. . .] Yet whilst the Apollonian individual is protected from the terrifying knowledge that this confusion of suffering beings that are tearing themselves apart has its goal and its purpose in him,

the *Dionysian* will uses precisely this knowledge to bring its individuals to an even higher level and to be glorified in them. Thus next to the completely veiled Apollonian order of Mysteries runs a Dionysian one alongside, the symbol of a world that can be revealed to only a few individuals, a world that could only be spoken about to the Many in a language of images. (KSA 7, 7[122], 175–6)

At this point in his argument, Nietzsche turns away from his reflections on Apollo and presents his thesis that 'this rapturous ecstasy of the Dionysian orgies spun itself as it were into the Mysteries':

That 'noble simplicity and quiet grandeur' which made Winckelmann enthusiastic remains something inexplicable if one disregards the essence of the metaphysical Mysteries, continuing to work in the depths. Here the Greek had an unshakeable, credible certainty, while he could deal with his Olympian gods more freely, sometimes playful, sometimes doubtful. For this reason he considered the profanation of the Mysteries as the one and only cardinal crime, which seemed to him to be more dreadful than the break-up of the city-state. (KSA 7, 7[122], 176)

In the spring–summer of 1875, Nietzsche noted a detail from the lectures on Greek culture given by Jacob Burckhardt and published as *Vorlesungen über griechische Kulturgeschichte* (a transcript of the course given in Basel which he read in its entirety): 'The first grain at Eleusis, the first vine shoot at Thebes, the first olive tree, fig tree' (KSA 8, 5[67], 59; see Burckhardt 1910: 20). Burckhardt was still very much on Nietzsche's mind when, over a decade later in 1888, he returned to the question of the Dionysian in *Twilight of the Idols*, where he claimed that he had been 'the first for the purpose of understanding the older, still copious, and even overflowing Hellenic instinct, to take seriously that wonderful phenomenon which bears the name of Dionysos' – namely, as explicable only as 'a surplus of energy' (TI Ancients §4). For in contrast to the approach to the Mysteries taken by the German classical scholar Christian August Lobeck (1781–1860) in his *Aglaophamus* (1829), which in turn argued, against the view of Creuzer in his *Symbolik*, that the religion of the Greek mysteries was national and non-esoteric, Nietzsche aligned himself with the approach taken by Burckhardt in his *Culture of the Greeks*, by which he presumably means the lecture course on *Griechische Kulturgeschichte* (translated as *The Greeks and Greek Civilization*) (Burckhardt 1998). Although Burckhardt did not dedicate a specific chapter to Dionysos, nevertheless certain aspects of Nietzsche's account of the Dionysian as found in *The Birth of Tragedy* informed Burckhardt's thinking.[20] As Nietzsche understands this view of the Dionysian, at its centre lies an experience that is essentially orgiastic: 'That element out of which Dionysian art evolved' is, he asserts, 'the orgy' (TI Ancients §4).[21]

Leaving aside at this point Nietzsche's polemics against the kind of classicising approach to the Dionysian that – rightly or wrongly – he associates with Johann Joachim Winckelmann (1717–68) and Goethe, what does Nietzsche understand here by the orgy? He goes on to explain:

> For only in Dionysian mysteries, in the psychology of the Dionysian condition, does the *fundamental fact* of Hellenic instinct – its 'will to life' – express itself. *What* did the Hellene pledge himself for with these mysteries? *Eternal* life, eternal recurrence of life; the future promised and consecrated in the past; the triumphing affirmation of life beyond death and change; true life, as the universal continuation of life by generation, by the mysteries of sexuality. (TI Ancients §4)

In line with this view – and as a riposte to Schopenhauer, who had argued in *The World as Will and Representation* (vol. 1, §60) that 'the

---

[20] See Felix Stähelin's remarks in his introduction to Burckhardt 1930–31 (cited in NK 6/1, 575).

[21] Compare with the importance attached to the orgy in the second volume of Erwin Rohde's *Psyche*, over and beyond which Rohde argued that primitive immortality cults had developed from the sense of mystical or primordial unity experienced during their rituals.

genitals are the real *focus* of the will' and 'the life-preserving principle assuring to time endless life [. . .] worshipped by the Greeks in the *phallus*, and by the Hindus in the *lingam*' (Schopenhauer 1966: vol. 1, 33) – Nietzsche foregrounds the phallus as the major symbol of importance to the ancient Greeks:

> On that account, the sexual symbol was to the Greeks the symbol venerable in itself, the intrinsic profundity within all ancient piety. Every detail in the act of generation, in pregnancy, and in birth, awakened the most exalted and solemn sentiments. In the doctrine of mysteries pain is pronounced holy: the 'pains of travail' sanctify pain in general, all becoming and growing, all pledging for the future, involves suffering . . . In order that the eternal delight of creating may exist, that the will to life may assert itself eternally, there must also exist eternally the 'pains of travail'. (TI Ancients §4)

Even here, in the midst of his most intensive engagement with Greek antiquity, Nietzsche's cultural grounding in German classicism is unmistakable. For the phrase 'pains of travail' (*Wehen der Gebärerin*) derives directly from Schiller's work as a translator of Euripides' play *The Phoenician Women* (NK 6/1, 578).

Yet this is no casual intertextual reference, and the image resounds across Nietzsche's work. For instance, in 'On the Blissful Islands', Zarathustra declares: 'For the creator himself to be the new-born child, he must also be willing to be the child-bearer, and endure the pangs of the child-bearer. / Verily, through a hundred souls went I my way, and through a hundred cradles and birth-throes' (TSZ II 2). And in his later seminars (of 1937 and 1944) on Nietzsche, Martin Heidegger picked up on this relation between the 'pains of travail' and 'joy in creating' (*Lust des Schaffens*) (Heidegger 2004: 208). Consequently, Nietzsche concludes:

> All this is implied by the word Dionysos: I know of no higher symbolism than this *Greek* symbolism of *Dionysia*. In them the deepest instinct of life, the instinct for the future of life, for the eternity of life, is felt religiously – the way

itself to life, procreation, is recognised as *the sacred* way . . . (TI Ancients §4)

As Nietzsche goes on to explain in section 5, the psychology of the orgy as 'an exuberant feeling of life and energy, in which pain even operates as a stimulus, gave me the key to the concept of *tragic* feeling'; and he insists: 'The affirmation of life, even in its most unfamiliar and most severe problems, the will to live, enjoying its own inexhaustibility in the *sacrifice* of its highest types, – *that* is what I called Dionysian, *that* is what I divined as the bridge to a psychology of the *tragic* poet' (TI Ancients §5).

The goal of the tragic poet – and, by extension, the goal of Nietzsche himself – was thus, 'beyond terror and pity, *to realise in fact* the eternal delight of becoming, – that delight which even involves in itself the *joy of annihilating*' (TI Ancients §5). For this reason Nietzsche, as the author of *The Birth of Tragedy*, reaffirms his identity as 'the last disciple of Dionysos the philosopher' and as 'the teacher of eternal recurrence' (TI Ancients §5). Precisely this Dionysian outlook is the one that Nietzsche opposes to the Christian outlook when, at the end of *Ecce Homo*, he asks: 'Have you understood me? – *Dionysos versus the Crucified*' (EH Destiny §9).

Nietzsche's embrace of a Dionysian outlook is accompanied in *Twilight of the Idols* by a savage critique of Christianity, thoroughly in line with his rhetoric in *The Anti-Christ*: 'It is only Christianity, with its *resentment against* life in its foundations, which has caused sexuality to be regarded as something impure: it cast *dirt* on the commencement, on the prerequisite of our life' (TI Ancients §4). This line of critique rings throughout the entirety of Nietzsche's writings in his middle and late periods. In section 76 of *Daybreak*, Nietzsche laments the way in which Christianity 'has succeeded in transforming Eros and Aphrodite – sublime powers, capable of idealization – into hellish genii and phantom goblins, by means of the pangs which every sexual impulse was made to raise in the conscience of the believers', and he asked: 'And must we call Eros an enemy?' (D §76):

The sexual feelings, like the feelings of pity and adoration, possess the particular characteristic that, in their case, one being gratifies another by the pleasure he enjoys – it is but rarely that we meet with such a benevolent arrangement in nature. And yet we calumniate and corrupt it all by our bad conscience! We connect the procreation of man with a bad conscience! (D §76)

In *Beyond Good and Evil*, Nietzsche reprised this analysis in the following trenchant aphorism: 'Christianity gave Eros poison to drink. He did not die of it but degenerated – into a vice' (BGE §168).

Nietzsche's chief accusation against Christianity is that it is, in his view, against *life*; and hence it is opposed to *eros*, to pleasure and to joy. For his part, Nietzsche's objective was always the opposite, or as he put it in *The Gay Science*: while science might be known for depriving humankind of its joys, it has the capacity to become 'the great *pain bringer*', thereby uncovering as its counterpart 'its immense capacity for making new galaxies of enjoyment beam forth!' (GS §12). In an aphorism written in Genoa, Nietzsche says that 'living in the midst of this confusion of streets, of necessities, of voices' gave him 'a melancholy happiness': 'It makes me happy to see that men do not want to think at all of the idea of death! I would fain do something to make make the idea of life even a hundred times *more worthy of their attention*' (GS §278). As will be discussed in more detail in the next chapter, this critique of Christianity informs Nietzsche's view of the fall of the Roman Empire as it is presented in section 58 of *The Anti-Christ*. Here Christianity is presented as 'the vampire of the *imperium Romanum*', and as an essentially destructive force that undermined the achievements of ancient pagan culture. If Chateaubriand talked about 'the genius of Christianity', then for Nietzsche it was an evil genius, or something truly diabolical. Hence Nietzsche's praise for Epicurus as someone who waged war against Christianity *and* its ideological precursors, that is, against the religion of revenge *and* the subterranean cults: 'He combated the *subterranean* cults, the whole of latent Christianity – to deny immortality was already a form of genuine *salvation*. – Epicurus had triumphed, and every respectable intellect in Rome was Epicurean – *when Paul appeared . . .*' (AC §58).²²

While there is a tension between this praise for Epicurus and Nietzsche's earlier critique of Epicureanism as 'the theory of salvation of paganism' and as a kind of pain-fearing *décadence* that could only give rise to 'a *religion* of love' (AC §30), this points to a tension within Epicurus' thought between hedonism and asceticism. Yet Nietzsche is unwavering in his critique of Paul, which ties into his critique of Christianity as

> the formula for exceeding *and* summing up the subterranean cults of all varieties, that of Osiris, that of the Great Mother, that of Mithras, for instance: in his discernment of this fact the genius of St Paul showed itself [. . .] he *made* out of [the 'Saviour'] something that even a priest of Mithras could understand. (AC §58; see Chapter 5 below)²³

In his famous seminar on Nietzsche's *Zarathustra* given between 1934 and 1939, Jung argued that an experiential dimension underpinned the composition of *Zarathustra*, describing the work as 'the Dionysian experience *par excellence*' and adding that 'in the latter part, that Dionysian *ekstasis* comes in' (Jung 1998: 10). It seems that Jung meant this in a very literal sense, and believed that *Zarathustra* had 'really led [Nietzsche] up to a full realization of the mysteries of the cult of Dionysos': 'He had already ideas about it' – from his

---

²² For an earlier engagement with Epicurus, see the section entitled 'The "Life After Death"' in *Daybreak*: 'Christianity found the idea of punishment in hell in the entire Roman Empire: for the numerous mystic cults have hatched this idea with particular satisfaction as being the most fecund egg of their power. Epicurus thought he could do nothing better for his followers than to tear this belief up by the roots: his triumph found its finest echo in the mouth of one of his disciples, the Roman Lucretius, a poet of a gloomy, though afterwards enlightened, temperament' (D §72). For an analysis of this entire section, see Rempel 2012.

²³ In April 1877, Nietzsche made a trip to Capri, with its Mithraic grotto. His imagination seems to have been caught by the Grotto Azzurra and the cult of Mithras: in the 'madness of Mithraism' (*Mithraswahn*) he saw an appealing idea, 'life as a *festival*' (KSA 8, 28[22] and 28[34], 507–8). For further discussion, see Köhler 2002: 103–9.

time as a philologist – 'but *Zarathustra* was the experience *which made the whole thing real*' (1998: 10; my emphasis).

Indeed, in his paper on the archetype of rebirth (first given as an Eranos lecture in 1939), Jung related the chapter entitled 'At Noontide' – which, occupying a central position in part 4, relates how Zarathustra fell asleep beneath an old tree embraced by a grape-vine and had a dream, or a vision, or an ecstatic experience of some sort, described as a 'strange drunkenness' – to the Eleusinian Mysteries; he cites, for instance, the Homeric Hymn to Demeter, 'Blessed is the mortal on earth who has seen these rites, / but the uninitiate who has no share in them never / has the same lot once dead in the dreary darkness' (Foley [ed.] 1994: 26), and he refers to a text that he identifies as one of the Eleusinian epitaphs: 'Truly the blessed gods have proclaimed a most beautiful secret: / Death comes not as a curse, but as a blessing to men' (§205, n. 2, in Jung 1969: 115). For Jung, the midday vision experienced by Zarathustra in 'At Noontide' falls into the category of archetypal experiences of rebirth that involve the transcendence of life, and constitutes a classic example of the spontaneous, ecstatic or visionary experience.

'Nietzsche, as we know', Jung argues, 'substitutes for the Christian mystery the myth of Dionysus-Zagreus, who was dismembered and came to life again. His experience has the character of a Dionysian nature myth: the Deity appears in the garb of Nature, as classical antiquity saw it' – Jung refers to the passage about 'an old, bent and gnarled tree, hung with grapes' – 'and the moment of eternity is the noonday, sacred to Pan' (§210, Jung 1969: 118): 'Hath time flown away? Do I not fall? Have I not fallen – hark! – into the well of eternity?' In the image of the 'golden ring', the 'ring of return', Jung believes (and here he draws on the interpretation of Ernst Horneffer (1871–1954) for support [see Horneffer 1900]) that Nietzsche saw 'a promise of resurrection and life' (§211, Jung 1969: 118). According to Jung, this kind of 'spontaneous, ecstatic, or visionary experience' can offer 'all that the mystery drama represents and brings about in the spectator'; and, on the basis of this reading of 'At Noontide', Jung confidently concludes that 'it is just as if Nietzsche had been at a performance of the mysteries' (§210, Jung 1969: 118).

In Chapter 6, we shall turn to Nietzsche's critique of St Paul but, before doing so, in the next chapter we shall consider the controversial case of the Lawbook of Manu, an ancient legal text about which Nietzsche is enormously enthusiastic, yet which he only knew through a corrupt French translation; we will examine his account of the demise of the Roman Empire (according to the American science fiction novelist Philip K. Dick, 'the Empire never ended',[24] but Nietzsche would have emphatically disagreed); and we conclude by discussing the significance for Nietzsche of the much-misunderstood concept of nobility in *The Anti-Christ*, the resurgence of which is a goal of (or even something actually achieved by) this text.

---

[24] This single line is repeated like a refrain in Dick's novel *Valis* (1981). In his *Exegesis* (posthumously published in 2011), Dick explored the hypothesis that history had stopped in the first century CE, that we are living in a continuation of the Empire that he called the 'black iron prison', and that US President Richard Nixon was the Emperor of Rome incarnate.

5
Nietzsche on Hinduism, the Roman Empire and Nobility

The Manusmṛiti (as it is known in Sanskrit), also called the Mānava-Dharmaśāstra or Laws of Manu, is an ancient legal text that belongs to the genre of Hindu treatises called Dharmaśāstras (see Olivelle 2005: 18–19, 41). Although it is a religious text, it is also a political one, as it was used as the basis for Hindu law by the British colonial government in India. In 1876, the French barrister and colonial judge Louis Jacolliot (1837–90) made a translation of the work, including it in a work entitled *Les Législateurs religieux: Manou, Moïse, Mahomet* (1876).[1] In 1888, Nietzsche came across Jacolliot's translation and he quickly became enthusiastic about it, telling his correspondent Heinrich Köselitz that 'everything else we possess in the nature of great moral codes is simply an imitation or even a caricature of this work':

> This absolutely *Aryan* product, a sacerdotal code of morality built upon the foundations of the Vedas, the idea of castes, and almost prehistoric in its antiquity and not at all pessimistic although very sacerdotal completes my ideas about religion in the most remarkable manner [...] Even Plato strikes me as being, in all important points, merely the well-schooled *chela* of a Brahmana. (Nietzsche 1921: 228–9)

---

[1] For Nietzsche's reception of this work, see NK 6/1, 365–71; NK 6/2, 265–79; and Liebscher 2012.

In relation to the Laws of Manu, Nietzsche added, 'everything else we possess in the nature of great moral codes is simply an imitation or even a caricature of this work: above all Egypticism',[2] and 'the Jews seem to be a Chandala race, that has learned from its masters, the principles according to which a priesthood can prevail and organize a people' (Nietzsche 1921: 229).

Nietzsche on the Lawbook of Manu (AC §§56–7)

Some terms in this letter require explanation. To begin with, the Aryans (or the 'nobles') was a term used by Indo-Iranian peoples in India in the Vedic period, c. 1500–c. 500 BCE, to refer to themselves. In the nineteenth century, when Nietzsche was writing, the term was used to refer to Proto-Indo-Europeans, thought to have been the prehistoric people of Europe and Asia; this predates the racial-ideological sense in which the word was used by Arthur de Gobineau (1816–82), Houston Stewart Chamberlain (1855–1927) and the Nazis. A *chela* is a disciple or pupil in Hinduism (although this term was introduced by the translator, Oscar Levy; in the original German, Nietzsche wrote that Plato had been 'well educated' by a Brahmin, i.e., a priest or teacher of sacred doctrine, and a member of the highest caste in Hinduism). A *chandala* is the Sanskrit word for someone who is 'untouchable', the lowest of the positions in the ancient Indian caste system known as Varna, based on the Vedas.

However, there is a problem. Jacolliot's work is now regarded as being such a poor translation that it is no exaggeration to describe it as a falsification (see Etter 1987). And it has also been argued that Jacolliot – who had only spent three years in India – was simply not knowledgeable enough about Sanskrit and Tamil, let alone Indian culture and mythology, to have produced an adequate translation (see Vinson 1888). Jacolliot was not a neutral scholar; in fact, Andreas Urs Sommer describes his translation of

---

[2] By 'Egypticism', Nietzsche means a predilection for 'concept mummies', i.e., seeing the world as something static and unchanging (TI 'Reason' §1; cf. D §72; and TI Ancients §2). For further discussion, see NK 6/1, 287–8; and Huddleston 2018.

the Manusmṛiti as 'a dubious, shoddy product of enthusiasm for a fantasy version of India, which in its extensive notes propagates extremely strange theories of history which even a non-expert reader should have been immediately able to expose' (NK 6/1, 366). Bad enough, except that Nietzsche appears to have taken this work at face value, citing passages from it in *Twilight of the Idols* and *The Anti-Christ* that appear only in Jacolliot's translation – not in the original.

In *Twilight of the Idols*, Nietzsche praises the Manu lawbook for its proposed task of 'breeding no fewer than four races simultaneously' (TI 'Improvers' §3), i.e., the Brahmins (priests, scholars and teachers), the Kshatriyas (rulers and warriors), the Vaishyas (merchants) and the Shudras (workers and labourers). Nietzsche is boundless in his admiration: 'One draws a breath of relief when coming out of the Christian sick-house and dungeon atmosphere into this healthier, higher, *wider* world', he writes, adding: 'How paltry the "New Testament" is compared with Manu, how ill it smells!' (TI 'Improvers' §3). Here we find Nietzsche deploying the olfactory metaphor he enjoys using elsewhere; in, for instance, *On the Genealogy of Morals*: 'At this point I cannot suppress a sigh and a last hope. What is it that I especially find unendurable? That I cannot cope with, that makes me choke and faint? Bad air! Bad air! The approach of some ill-constituted thing: that I have to smell the entrails of some ill-constituted soul!' (GM I §12); and not least in *The Anti-Christ*: 'One would as little choose "early Christians" for companions as Polish Jews: not that one need seek out an objection to them . . . Neither has a pleasant smell' (AC §46).[3]

This admittedly problematic metaphor has to be understood in relation to its positive counterpart, found in *Ecce Homo*, where

---

[3] On the motif of bad smells in the repertoire of Nietzsche's metaphors, see NK 6/2, 215–16, where Andreas Urs Sommer comments on how these lines 'seek to transfer negative affects from a primary object (the Jews) into a secondary one (the Christians), while without exonerating the primary object [. . .] What is paradoxical about the comparison of Polish Jews and the first Christians is that it does not establish a relation between something unknown and something which really is known, since most readers will, like Nietzsche, have never smelled "early Christians" nor "Polish Jews" (in fact, the only "Polish Jew" whom Nietzsche knew was Siegfried Lipiner)' (NK 6/2, 216).

Nietzsche exlaims: 'And in what does one really recognize that someone has *turned out well!* In that a human being who has turned out well does our senses good: that he is carved out of wood at once hard, delicate and sweet-smelling' (EH Wise §2). Elsewhere in *Ecce Homo*, Nietzsche makes a virtue out of his 'perfectly uncanny sensitivity of the instinct for cleanliness, so that I perceive physiologically – *smell* – the proximity or – what am I saying? – the innermost parts, the "entrails", of every soul' (EH Wise §8); or as he memorably expressed it, 'my genius is in my nostrils' (EH Destiny §1). And as part of his polemic against his usual metaphysical and religious targets, Nietzsche declares: 'He who not only understands the word "Dionysian," but understands *himself* in that term, does not require any refutation of Plato, or of Christianity, or of Schopenhauer – for his nose *scents decomposition*' (EH BT §2).

The cause for Nietzsche's admiration is the struggle undertaken by this law code, not with the 'beast' (*Bestie*) – i.e., the 'blond beast', to use the term introduced by Nietzsche in *On the Genealogy of Morals* (GM I §11),[4] and used again in *Twilight of the Idols* (TI 'Improvers' §2) – but its *antithesis*, i.e., 'the non-bred human being, the hotchpotch human being [*dem Mischmasch-Menschen*], the Chandala' (TI 'Improvers' §3). At this point, Nietzsche cites – with evident approval – a series of edicts from the *Avadana-Shastra*, advocating a whole series of measures to be taken in relation to this caste, including dietary restrictions, limited access to water, denying them assistance in childbirth, and even advocating (along with male circumcision) female genital mutilation, and prescribing rules for how they are to write by hand. (The fact that some of these edicts derive not from the original Dharmaśāstra, but from Jacolliot, is irrelevant to the question, how seriously is Nietzsche to be taken? Some of these recommendations would be enough to have Nietzsche added to a human rights watch-list . . .)

---

[4] As Hollingdale notes, the term 'blond beast' means 'man considered as an animal', exemplified by the Roman, Arab, Teutonic and Japanese nobility, the Homeric heroes, the Scandinavian Vikings and the Athenians of the age of Pericles, and it is not fully intelligible with reference to Nietzsche's psychology of the will-to-power and his concept of sublimation (see Hollingdale, footnote in Nietzsche 1968b: 56).

Nietzsche hails these recommendations as an expression 'for once' of '*Aryan* humanity, quite pure, quite primordial' (TI 'Improvers' §4), and in so doing he adopts for his own use the notion of Aryanism found in nineteenth-century scholarship in general and Jacolliot in particular. As problematic as this term sounds to our ears today, it is anachronistic to hear in it an affirmation of white supremacy; rather, it is similar to the notion of the Celts, another nineteenth-century Romantic invention, albeit one whose associations and connotations are more benign.[5] Indeed, in *On the Genealogy of Morals*, Nietzsche affirms that the Celts were 'definitely a blond race' (GM I §5). Nevertheless, it remains problematic that, in so writing about the Aryans, Nietzsche employs a biologistic concept of race, and one that was, even then, contaminated with anti-Semitism (NK 6/2, 369); even though he made it clear in his letter of 29 March 1887 to Theodor Fritsch (1852–1933), an avowedly anti-Semitic writer and the editor of the journal *Antisemitische Correspondenz*, that he in no way shared his political programme:

> This disgraceful chiming-in of *noioso* dilettantes about the *value* of human beings and races, this submission to 'authorities' which are rejected by every more prudent mind with cold contempt (e.g., E. Dühring, R. Wagner, Ebrard, Wahrmund, P. de Lagarde – who of these is the most unreliable, the most unjust in questions of morality and history?), these constant, absurd falsifications and adjustments of such vague concepts as 'Germanic', 'Semitic', 'Aryan', 'Christian', 'German' – all this could in the long run really infuriate me and bring me out of the ironic indulgence with which I have hitherto viewed the virtuous velleities and Phariseeisms of the current Germans. And finally, how do you think I feel when anti-Semites use the name *Zarathustra*? (KSB 8, 51)

By contrast, Nietzsche believes that 'the hatred, the Chandala hatred for this "humanity" has been immortalized' and 'become

---

[5] For further discussion, see Chapman 1992; Collis 2003.

religion' and 'become genius' in another people (TI 'Improvers' §4). Nietzsche does not name them, but they can only be, as they are in Jacolliot, the Jews. Even if not intended to be anti-Semitic, Nietzsche's interweaving of a biologistic discourse of race and a cultural or ideological discourse of hierarchy is, seen from the perspective of the twenty-first century, a fatal error (even or especially if it is one whose consequences he could never have foreseen). As evidence for this judgement about the Jews, Nietzsche points to the Gospels, as well as – perhaps less predictably – the apocryphal Book of Enoch (TI 'Improvers' §4).

This work is ascribed by tradition to a biblical figure from the antediluvian period (i.e., the time before Noah's flood), identified as the son of Jared, the father of Methuselah, and the great-grandfather of Noah, called Enoch. Of him it is said in the Book of Genesis that he lived to be 365 years old – 'he walked with God, and was seen more: because God took him' (Gen. 5:21–4) – but the Book of Enoch named after him is not part of the biblical canon, neither for Jews nor Christians. Consisting of five sections (known as the Book of Watchers, the Book of Parables, the Astronomical Book, the Book of Dreams and the Epistle of Enoch), it contains – and perhaps this is the reason for Nietzsche's choice of this work – such imprecatory passages as the following: 'And behold! He comes with ten thousand holy ones to execute judgement upon them, and to destroy the impious, and to contend with all flesh concerning everything which the sinners and the impious have done and wrought against him' (En. 1:9, in Sparks [ed.] 1984: 185; cf. Jude 1:14–15). Another reason might have been that, in 1886–87, that is, shortly before the composition of *The Anti-Christ*, two extensive manuscripts of Enoch in Greek were discovered in a monk's tomb in Akhmim in Egypt; in other words, there may have been scholarly or philological motivations.[6]

---

[6] Until the discovery of the Ahkmim fragments, the main editions of the Book of Enoch were those of August Dillmann (1823–94) (Dillmann 1851; 1853); the Akhmim fragments were published by Urbain Bouriant (1849–1903) and Adolphe Lods (1867–1948) (Bouriant 1892; Lods 1892). Further fragments of Enoch in Aramaic were found at Qumran in 1952.

In the following passage from *Twilight of the Idols*, which clearly anticipates the argumentational thrust of *The Anti-Christ*, Nietzsche summarises his views about 'the Chandala hatred' in the Gospels and in the Book of Enoch in a way that interweaves a biologistic and a cultural discourse, and yet is not dependent on this conjunction:[7]

> Christianity springing out of a Jewish root, and only comprehensible as a growth of this soil, represents the movement counter to every morality of breeding, of race, and of privilege: it is the *anti-Aryan* religion *par excellence*: Christianity, the transvaluation of all Aryan values, the triumph of Chandala values, the gospel preached to the poor and lowly, the collective insurrection against the 'race' of all the down-trodden, the wretched, the ill-constituted, the misfortunate, undying Chandala revenge as the *religion of love* . . . (TI 'Improvers' §4)

These arguments or assertions are taken up and developed in *The Anti-Christ*, written immediately after *Twilight of the Idols*. In fact, Nietzsche's discussion begins with a notion that links directly into section 5 of 'The "Improvers" of Mankind', the notion of the 'pious fraud' (see Chapter 3 above), 'the great, the *uncanny* problem' of 'the psychology of the "improvers" of mankind' (TI 'Improvers' §5). In sum, Nietzsche believes that '*all* the measures hitherto used for the *purpose* of moralizing humankind, have been fundamentally *immoral*' (TI 'Improvers' §5).

At the end of section 55 of *The Anti-Christ*, Nietzsche picks up on precisely this point: 'The "holy lie" – common alike to Confucius, to the Code of Manu, to Mohammed and to the Christian Church – is not even wanting in Plato. "Truth is here": this means, no matter and where it is heard, the *priest lies*' (AC §55). As Nietzsche dramatically puts it in *Ecce Homo*, attributing this insight to Zarathustra: '*good men never tell the truth. The good taught you to follow false shores and false securities: you were born and kept in the lies of the good. Everything has been distorted and twisted down to its very bottom through the good*' (EH Destiny §4).

---

[7] For further discussion, see Moore 2002.

As becomes clear in section 56, what Nietzsche objects to is not the lie *per se* as much as the reason for which the lie is uttered: 'In the last analysis it comes to this: what is the *end* of lying? The fact that, in Christianity, "holy" ends are not visible is *my* objection to the means it employs' (AC §56). Nietzsche's objection is that the ends or purposes of Christianity are bad ones – 'the poisoning, the calumniation, the denial of life, the despising of the body, the degradation and self-contamination of the human being by the concept of sin' – and *therefore* its means are also bad (AC §56). And it is at this point that he returns to his encomium of the Lawbook of Manu. As in *Twilight of the Idols*, the excellence of the Manusmṛiti serves an explicit function: to illustrate the *lack* of excellence, as Nietzsche sees it, of the Bible: 'I have a contrary feeling when I read the Code of Manu, an incomparably more intellectual and superior work, which it would be a sin against the spirit to so much as *name* in the same breath with the Bible' (AC §56).

Nietzsche underscores his evaluation with a biblical allusion to those passages in the New Testament which talk about the sin against the Holy Spirit (see Matt. 12:30–2; Mark 3:28–30; Luke 12:8–10).[8] And he follows it up with another uncomfortably expressed contrast between the 'genuine philosophy' of the Manusmṛiti and 'the foul-smelling *Judain* of rabbinism and superstition', echoing a term used by the German orientalist Paul de Lagarde (1827–91) (see Lagarde 1887: 272; 1878–81: vol. 1, 31). (*Judain* also echoes one of Nietzsche's own neologisms, *Moralin* and *moralinfrei*.) Nietzsche goes on to define 'the central point, the fundamental difference between it and every type of Bible' as being that 'by means of it the *nobles*, the philosophers and the warriors, keep the whip-hand over the majority; it is full of noble valuations, it shows a feeling of perfection, an acceptance of life, and triumphant feeling toward self and life – the *sun* shines upon the whole book' (AC §56). The sun is emphatically *not* the Platonic sun, a metaphor for the Good;

---

[8] According to the *Catechism of the Catholic Church*, §1864, 'anyone who deliberately refuses to accept [God's] mercy by repenting, rejects the forgiveness of his sins and the salvation offered by the Holy Spirit', and 'such hardness of heart can lead to final impenitence and eternal loss' (1997: 509).

rather it is a Camusian sun, the sun of Tipasa as described in the first of the four essays by Albert Camus (1913–60) published as *Noces* (*Nuptials*) (1938).[9]

What the Manusmṛiti casts particular light upon is – perhaps not surprisingly, given Nietzsche's focus in *Twilight of the Idols* on 'the orgy' as 'the element' out of which 'Dionysian art' evolved, on 'the mysteries of sexuality', and on 'the *sexual* symbol' as 'the symbol venerable as such' – precisely the field of sexual desire. Nietzsche takes exception to Paul's advice in his First Letter to the Corinthians that 'because of fornication let every man have his own wife, and let every woman have her own husband [. . .] for it is better to marry than to burn' (1 Cor. 7:2, 9). The precise context of these remarks is likely to have been – as St Jerome (*Against Jovinianus*, book 1, §7 and §9) and St John Chrysostom (*Homilies on the First Epistle of St Paul to the Corinthians*, no. 19) suggested – whether or not Christians were, after conversion, bound to abstain from their infidel wives, rather than the more general question of whether or not it is expedient to marry (a question which, as Haydock notes, 'the sages of antiquity had frequently taken into consideration'; Haydock 2006: 1507). Indeed, Andreas Urs Sommer has defended this Pauline passage, seeing in it 'neither dark renunciation nor a demonization of the sexual'; no link is established here, he suggests, between the Fall of Man and sexuality (NK 6/2, 268).

Yet Nietzsche is surely right to suggest that this passage is not exactly a celebration of sexuality, and it is not difficult to see it as emblematic of what Michel Onfray has described as Paul's 'misogynist, phallocratic, sexist, and homophobic' attitude towards Christianity (Onfray 2017: 99). That attitude, found in the early Christian enthusiasm for virginity for example,[10] finds a

---

[9] Compare with the following juxtaposition of the sun in Camus with the sun in Paul Valéry (1871–1945), a Platonically inspired writer: 'Camus's sun, unlike Valéry's, is not the manifestation of a spherical form of being, closed in on itself . . . It is always the sun shining on the ruins of Tipasa, the sand beach of *The Stranger*, or the sea. It is light felt not as a distant purity, but as a fecundating bath. It is the unifying force of the cosmos' (Doubrovsky 2003: 98).

[10] See St Jerome's comments on marriage and virginity in Letter 22 to Eustochium, Letter 130 to Demetrias and his treatise *Against Jovinian*; and St Augustine's treatise, *On Virginity* (*De virginitate*).

fitting symbol in the gesture made by Origen in Alexandria in 215 CE when he castrated himself (Onfray 2017: 99–114); or in the doctrine, to which Nietzsche himself makes explicit reference, of the *Immaculata Conceptio*, that is, the doctrine that the Virgin Mary was conceived in the usual biological way in the womb of her mother, St Anne, but preserved free from original sin ('by reason of the merits of her son').[11] By contrast, Nietzsche finds in the Manusmṛiti – or rather in Jacolliot's 1876 translation – passages that say 'many delicate and kindly things about women', illustrating 'a way of being gallant to women that it would be impossible, perhaps, to surpass' (AC §56). And it is true that there is a certain wistful charm about these passages, even if they have been invented by Jacolliot:

> 'The mouth of a woman [. . .] the breasts of a maiden, the prayer of a child and the smoke of sacrifice are always pure.' [. . .] 'There is nothing purer than the light of the sun, the shadow cast by a cow, air, water, fire, and the breath of a maiden.' [. . .] 'All the orifices of the body above the navel are pure, and all below are impure. Only in the maiden is the whole body pure.' (AC §56)

Or is that final quotation, Nietzsche wonders, just another 'holy lie'?

In section 57, Nietzsche continues (and concludes) his comparison of the ethics of Christianity and the Manusmṛiti, seeking to demonstrate the 'unholiness' of the former and the holiness of the latter; holiness residing here in conformity to a 'natural order' (*Natur-Ordnung*) explored later in this section (see NK 6/2, 269). He begins by explaining that the superiority of the Manusmṛiti lies in its origins – in the way it 'epitomizes the experience, the sagacity and the ethical experimentation of long centuries', the prerequisite for which is 'recognition of the fact that the means which establish the authority of a slowly and painfully attained *truth* are fundamentally different from those which one would make use of

---

[11] See the *Catechism of the Catholic Church*, §492, referring to the encyclical *Lumen gentium*, §53 and §56 (1997: 138).

to prove it' (AC §57). In short, Nietzsche is following the principle of genealogy as he had set it out in *On the Genealogy of Morals*, that is, 'A law-book never recites the utility, the grounds, the casuistical antecedents of law' (AC §57; see NK 6/2, 269).

According to Nietzsche, at a certain point in the development of any people, the class with the greatest insight declares the experiences according to which all shall live to be concluded, and that the goal is now to prevent any further experimentation. In order to do this, this class sets up a 'double wall', consisting of *revelation* and *tradition*. On his account, the claim made by *revelation* is that the reasoning behind the law is 'of divine ancestry' and 'came into being complete, perfect, without a history, as a free gift, a miracle' (AC §57). And the claim made by *tradition* is that 'the law has stood unchanged from time immemorial' and its authority is thus grounded on the following thesis – 'God gave it, and the fathers *lived* it' (AC §57).

Behind revelation and tradition lies, Nietzsche says, a 'higher reason' (*höhere Vernunft*) that seeks to achieve, as he puts it, 'a perfect automatism of the instinct' (or, in Sommer's words, 'human actions should become automatised through a process of habituation' [NK 6/2, 271]). In other words, the point of religion is to accustom people to such a degree that they do not realise that this has happened, and this instinctual automatisation is 'the precondition for every kind of mastery, for every kind of perfection in the art of life' – the notion of a *Kunst des Lebens* being associated by Nietzsche in particular with Epicurus.[12] For Nietzsche, the superiority of the Manusmṛiti lies in the fact it is, in his eyes, precisely an exercise in this *Kunst des Lebens*:

> To draw up such a law-book as Manu's means to lay before a people the possibility of future mastery, of attainable perfection – it permits them to aspire to the highest reaches of the art of life [*die höchste Kunst des Lebens zu ambitioniren*]. *To that end it must be made unconscious:* that is the aim of every holy lie. (AC §57)

---

[12] See KSA 13, 12[1], 197: 'Philosophy [as] art of life, *not* art of discovering the truth'; cf. NK 6/2, 271.

So does this mean that the 'holy lie' is not quite the problem that Nietzsche had thought it was? Is the 'holy lie' justified if it is maintained to permit aspiration to the highest art of life? Indeed, might Socrates have been right after all when he said in *The Republic* that the noble lie was 'a contrivance for one of those falsehoods that come into being in case of need, of which we were just now talking, some noble one' (414b–c)?

It is fascinating to compare with Plato's *Republic* what Nietzsche (in the rest of this section) says about hierarchy, despite his critique of Plato in his earlier writings. And on this point concerning hierarchy, so difficult for our ears to hear today, Nietzsche could not be clearer: '*The order of castes*, the highest, the dominating law, is merely the sanction of an *order of nature*, of a natural law of the first rank, over which no arbitrary caprice, no "modern idea", can exert any influence' (AC §57). As Sommer points out, Nietzsche could have been confirmed in his thoughts in this respect by his reading of *Gedanken über Goethe* (1888; repub. 1921) by the German-Baltic cultural historian Victor Hehn (1813–90). In a chapter entitled 'Natural Forms of Human Life', Hehn reminds his readers that Aristotle considered slaves to be an essential component of human society and necessary to the household in the process of growth of social life.[13] For Hehn, 'the difference between the races' is simply part of the 'order of nature', and this 'natural order' forms the basis of Aristotle's political thought. Hehn may be right to trace this kind of thinking back to Aristotle; of course, this does not mean that Aristotle was right. Be that as it may, what this 'natural law of the first rank' means in practice is now explained by Nietzsche at some length.

Every healthy society, he says, can be divided into three 'physiological types', and he insists that this division arises, not from Manu, but from nature itself. These types are first, those who are chiefly intellectual; second, those are chiefly characterised by muscular strength and temperament; and third, those who chiefly have no distinctions, i.e., the mediocre. Further on, Nietzsche insists that this division is essential, not just for life, but for the development of higher forms of life: 'The order of castes,

---

[13] See Hehn 1921: 278; cf. Aristotle, *Politics*, 1252a15–1252b9, in Barker (ed.) 1952: 3–4.

the order of rank, simply formulates the supreme law of life itself; the separation of the three types is necessary to the maintenance of society, and to the evolution of higher types, and the highest types — the *inequality* of rights is essential to the existence of any rights at all' (AC §57).

It is hard not to hear in this threefold division an echo of Plato's *Republic* and its tripartite division of society (into producers, guardians and philosopher-kings) (cf. *Republic*, 435b), to which there corresponds a tripartite division of the soul (into the appetitive part, the spirited part and the rational part). And Nietzsche's detailed description of each of these three types makes these echoes all the more audible. These echoes may appear, at first sight, surprising, given Nietzsche's reputation for having an anti-Platonic stance. Yet on 22 October 1883, just five years before he was working on *The Anti-Christ*, Nietzsche remarked to Franz Overbeck in relation to his reading of the German philosopher Gustav Teichmüller: 'I am increasingly struck rigid with astonishment about how *little* Plato I know and how much Zarathustra πλατονίζει [i.e., platonises]' (KSB 6, 449; cf. NK 6/2, 275; Foley 2015).

The first group, or the highest caste, is described by Nietzsche as '*the fewest*' and, as such, as enjoying 'the privileges of the few' – i.e., happiness, beauty, goodness on earth. Indeed, their privileges can be summed up as Nietzsche does in a quotation from Horace's *Satires*: 'few men are noble = beauty is for the few' (*pulchrum est paucorum hominum*) (book 1, §9, l. 44.)[14] This intellectual, spiritual, *geistig* instinct only knows affirmation; its outlook is summed up in the phrase, 'the world is perfect', an allusion, perhaps, to the chapter entitled 'At Midday' in part 4 of *Thus Spoke Zarathustra* (TSZ IV 10).[15] This outlook is so affirming that it can even affirm what is beneath or below it; in other words, it expresses the *amor fati* of which Nietzsches writes elsewhere: 'I want more and more to perceive the necessary characters in things as the beautiful: – I shall thus be one of those who beautify things. *Amor fati*: let that

---

[14] See Horace 1942: 109. Cf. TI What the Germans Lack §5; HAH II AOM §118; CW §6. For further discussion, see NK 6/1, 387; Sommer 2000: 575–6.
[15] For further discussion, see Bishop 2017.

henceforth be my love ! [. . .] Some day I wish to be only a yes-sayer' (GS §276). Compare this with his cry in *Ecce Homo*:

> My formula for greatness in a human being is *amor fati*: the fact that one wishes nothing to be different, either forwards or backwards, or for all eternity. Not only must the necessary be borne, and on no account concealed, – all idealism is falsehood in the face of necessity, – but it must also be loved . . . (EH Clever §10)

And in *Twilight of the Idols*, Nietzsche answers his questions, 'What alone can our teaching be?', as follows:

> We are necessary, we are part of destiny, we belong to the whole, we exist in the whole, there is nothing which could judge, measure, compare, or condemn our being, for that would be to judge, measure, compare, and condemn the whole . . . *But there is nothing outside of the whole!* (TI Errors §8)

The consequence of this teaching, i.e., 'that no one be made responsible any longer, that the mode of being be not traced back to a *causa prima*, that the world be not regarded as a unity, either as sensorium or as "spirit"', leads to '*the great liberation*' and to the restoration of 'the *innocence* of becoming' (TI Errors §8).

In *The Anti-Christ* Nietzsche summarises the strengths and ascetic qualities of these Horatian 'happy few' in the following terms:

> The most intellectual people, as they are the *strongest*, find their happiness where other people would find their downfall: in a labyrinth, in being hard towards themselves and towards others, in effort; their enjoyment is in self-constraint; in them asceticism is their nature, a necessity, an instinct. The difficult task is for them a privilege, and to play with burdens that would crush others is a *recreation* . . . Knowledge – a form of asceticism. (AC §57)

What gives this class of human beings the right to rule? As the 'most venerable' type of people and at the same time the 'most cheerful' and the 'most amiable', they rule, not 'because they want to, but because they *are*' (AC §57). They are born leaders, so to speak; and, as such, they 'are not at liberty to be second' (AC §57). Or as Socrates puts it in *The Republic*:

> Neither city nor regime will ever become perfect, nor yet will a man become perfect in the same way either, before some necessity chances to constrain those few philosophers who aren't vicious, those now called useless, to take charge of a city, whether they want to or not, and the city to obey. (499b; Bloom 1968: 178–9)

For all the potential (and real) political problems that might arise in a society by having such 'natural-born' leaders, one can also see the continuing influence of this idea in contemporary management theory . . .

The second group or type of human beings considered by Nietzsche are called the custodians of the law or the guardians; they are 'the keepers of order and of security, the more noble warriors', and hence above all *the king* – 'as the highest form of warrior, judge, and preserver of the law' (AC §57). (One can tell that *The Anti-Christ* was written by a former German academic: in his order of ranking, the intellectual is higher than even the king . . .) While adopting the categorisation of *The Republic* that assigns the guardians to the second class and the philosopher-king to the first, Nietzsche tweaks this distinction, and preserves the first class very much for intellectuals; the king (of all), in relation to whom and on whose account 'everything exists', a fact that is 'the cause of all that is beautiful' (as Plato puts it in his Second Letter, 312e; Plato 1989: 1566), is here placed firmly in the second category. Of this second class Nietzsche has the following to say: 'They are the executive arm of the intellectuals, the next to them in rank, taking from them all that is *rough* in the business of ruling – they are their attendants, their right hand, their best pupils' (AC §57).

Last and (by their nature) very much least is the third group of human beings. Nietzsche envisages an essentially pyramidal structure of society. In an early lecture (with an implicitly political theme) entitled 'The Greek State' (1871/1872), Nietzsche had argued that '*slavery belongs to the essence of a culture*', since 'in order for there to be a broad, deep, fertile soil for the development of art, the overwhelming majority has to be slavishly subjected to life's necessity in the service of the minority, *beyond* the measure that is necessary for the individual' (Nietzsche 2007: 166). In 'The Greek State' he had asserted that 'through war, and in the military profession, we are presented with a type, even perhaps with the *archetype of the state*', and he went on to argue: 'Here we see, as the most general effect of the war tendency, the immediate separation and division of the chaotic masses into *military castes*, from which there arises the construction of a "war-like society" in the shape of a pyramid on the broadest possible base: a slave-like bottom stratum' (Nietzsche 2007: 172).

In *The Anti-Christ*, Nietzsche reaffirms this hierarchical view: 'A high culture is a pyramid: it can only stand on a broad base, its primary prerequisite is a strong and soundly consolidated mediocrity' (AC §57). While apparently keeping a straight face, Nietzsche informs us that the mediocre enjoy privileges too, inasmuch as 'life becomes increasingly harder the *higher* up you go, – it gets colder, there are more responsibilities' (AC §57). Yet how does Nietzsche understand mediocrity? The third caste of the mediocre is defined as follows:

> The handicrafts, commerce, agriculture, *science*, the greater part of art, in brief, the whole range of *occupational* activities, are compatible only with mediocre ability and aspiration; such callings would be out of place for exceptional people; the instincts which belong to them stand as much opposed to aristocracy as to anarchism. To be publicly useful, to be a wheel, a function, is evidence of a natural predisposition; it is *not* society, but the only sort of happiness that the majority are capable of, that makes them intelligent machines. (AC §57)

In other words, the description that Nietzsche gives of the mediocre means that nearly all of this book's readers will fall into this category! And, to be honest, from the point of view that Nietzsche appears to be advocating, most of us *are* slaves, in the terms in which Nietzsche defines slavery. In *Human, All Too Human* Nietzsche remarks: 'As at all times, so now too, men are divided into the slaves and the free; for he who does not have two-thirds of his day to himself is a slave, let him be what he may otherwise: statesman, businessman, official, scholar' (HAH I §283).

These reflections from Nietzsche's transitional period belong to a significant, if often unnoticed, thematic thread in his writings on the problem of work or labour. In an unpublished note from 1869–70, Nietzsche identified modernity with barbarism, noting that 'the division of labour is the principle of barbarism' (KSA 7, 3[44], 73). In his *Untimely Meditation* on the German liberal Protestant theologian David Friedrich Strauss (1808–74), Nietzsche ponders the choice in *The Old Faith and the New* (1872) of an industrial metaphor to describe how 'soothing oil' offers consolation to the worker in the grip of the merciless cogs of the universal machine (UM I §6).[16] And in his second *Untimely Meditation* entitled 'On the Uses and Disadvantages of History for Life', Nietzsche laments how 'the jargon of the slave-owner and employer of labour' has come to be used to describe 'things which in themselves ought to be thought of as free of utility and raised above the necessities of life', so that the words '"factory", "labour market", "supply", "making profitable" [. . .] come unbidden to the lips when one wishes to describe the most recent generation of men of learning' (UM II §7).

In the second volume of *Human, All Too Human*, Nietzsche asks whether property can be squared with justice, proposing that 'we should keep open all the paths of work for small fortunes, but should prevent the effortless and sudden acquisition of wealth', that 'we should take all the branches of transport and trade which favour the accumulation of large fortunes – especially, therefore, the money market – out of the hands of private persons or private

---

[16] In his excerpts from Strauss's *The Old Faith and the New*, Nietzsche noted 'lubricating oil' (*Schmieröl*) (NK 1/2, 141).

companies', and that we should 'look upon those who own too much, just as upon those who own nothing, as types fraught with danger to the community' (HAH II WS §285). And in *Daybreak*, he utters nothing less than a revolutionary call to the working class, calling upon the workers of Europe to 'make it clear that their position as a class has become a human impossibility, and not merely, as they at present maintain, the result of some hard and aimless arrangement of society', and to 'bring about an age of great swarming-forth from the European beehive such as has never yet been seen, protesting by this voluntary and huge migration against machines and capital and the alternatives that now threaten them either of becoming slaves of the State or slaves of some revolutionary party' (D §206).

At the same time we should see Nietzsche's statements, despite or because of their provocative discourse, in terms of a tradition of German *Kulturkritik* to which, for instance, Friedrich Schiller (1759–1805) belongs. In the six of his letters *On the Aesthetic Education of Humankind* (1795), Schiller addressed directly the problem of the division of labour, writing that

> once the increase of empirical knowledge, and more exact modes of thought, made sharper divisions between the sciences inevitable, and once the increasingly complex machinery of state necessitated a more rigorous separation of ranks and occupations, then the inner unity of human nature was severed, and a disastrous conflict set its harmonious powers at variance. (Schiller 1982: 33)

In fact, Schiller uses exactly the same imagery as Nietzsche does in *The Anti-Christ* of being a part of a clockwork or a 'cog in a wheel', when in this letter he continues:

> That polypoid character of the Greek states, in which every individual enjoyed an independent existence but could, when need arose, grow into the whole organism, now made way for an ingenious clock-work, in which, out of the piecing together of innumerable but lifeless parts, a mechanical kind of collective life ensued. (Schiller 1982: 35)

Ironically, it is from this same tradition that Karl Marx (1818–83), usually seen as Nietzsche's political antipode, derived his vision of the alienation brought about by bourgeois capitalist society, to which he famously opposed a contrasting picture of human activities that constitutes a communist idyll: no longer forced, under the division of labour, to decide whether he or she is a hunter, a fisherman, a herdsman or a cultural critic, the human being can choose to go hunting in the morning, to go fishing in the afternoon, to rear cattle in the evening, and – after dinner, of course – to be a critic.[17]

Despite – or *precisely* because of – his elitist discourse, Nietzsche can easily be aligned with the school of critical theory that arose out of Marxist thought. In *Dialectic of Enlightenment* (1944; 1947), Theodor W. Adorno (1903–69) and Max Horkheimer (1895–1973) explained how the culture industry and mass entertainment taught the workers to *enjoy* their oppression.[18] This point was taken up and pushed to its extreme by the postmodernist thinker Jean-François Lyotard (1924–98), in his *Libidinal Economy* (1974):

> [T]he English unemployed did not become workers to survive, they [. . .] *enjoyed* the hysterical, masochistic, whatever exhaustion it was of *hanging on* in the mines, in the foundries, in the factories, in hell, they enjoyed it, enjoyed the mad destruction of their organic body which was indeed imposed on them, they enjoyed the decomposition of their personal identity, the identity that the peasant tradition had constructed for them, enjoyed the dissolution of their families and villages, and enjoyed the new monstrous *anonymity* of the suburbs and the pubs in the morning and evening. (Lyotard 2004: 109–10)

---

[17] See *The German Ideology*, in Marx 1983: 177. For further discussion, see Rippere 1981; Jaeggi 2014.
[18] See 'The Culture Industry: Enlightenment as Mass Deception', in Adorno and Horkheimer 2002: 94–135.

As usual, however, such later thinkers are articulating an insight that we first find in Nietzsche:

> To the mediocre, mediocrity is a form of happiness; they have a natural instinct for mastering one thing, for specialization. It would be altogether unworthy of a profound intellect to see anything objectionable in mediocrity itself. It is, in fact, the *first* prequisite to the appearance of the exceptional: it is a necessary condition to a high degree of civilization. When an exceptional person treats a mediocre one more delicately than he treats himself or his equals, this is not just courtesy of the heart, – it is simply his *duty* . . . (AC §57)

This phrase 'courtesy of the heart' (*Höflichkeit des Herzens*) is one of Nietzsche's favourites.[19] Its source is Goethe's novel *Elective Affinities* (*Die Wahlverwandtschaften*, 1809), where Ottilie writes in her notebook: 'There is a politeness of the heart, akin to love. From it derives the easiest politeness of outward behaviour' (Goethe 1994: 151). What Nietzsche (and Goethe) here call 'politeness of the heart' in the attitude of the 'superior' to the 'inferior' is something one might today call *condescension*; although the etymology of this word (as recorded in the OED) might give us pause for thought, implying as it does that one person 'accedes' to, 'agrees' to, or (literally) *stoops* to another person.

Here, then, lies the source of Nietzsche's quarrel with the political Left. Some thinkers have proposed a libertarian reading of Nietzsche in a sense of a *nietzschéisme de gauche*, though not without being contested for doing so.[20] And one critic has ingeniously argued that Nietzsche, as an essentially right-wing thinker, was nevertheless aiming to infiltrate and thereby undermine the Left (see Waite 1996). Nevertheless, Nietzsche is perfectly open about his political sentiments when, at the end of this section, he writes:

---

[19] See HAH I §49; BGE §122 and §245; EH Wise §5.
[20] For a left-wing/libertarian reading of Nietzsche, see Onfray 2006a; 2011: 175–338. And for the case against, see Monville 2007.

Whom do I hate the most among the rabble of today? The Socialist-rabble, the Chandala-apostles, who undermine the workers' instincts and pleasures, their feelings of contentment with their petty existence, – who make them envious and teach them revenge . . . Injustice never lies in unequal rights, it lies in the claim to '*equal*' rights . . . What is *bad*? But I have already said: all that proceeds from weakness, from envy, from revenge . . . The anarchist and the Christian are descended from the same lineage . . . (AC §57)

And here lies the intersection in Nietzsche's thinking – in both senses of the word, a critical one – between religion and politics.

It turns out that, in fact, Nietzsche has no problem with the noble or the holy lie, depending, that is, on the cause that this lie is supporting. Or, as he puts it at the beginning of section 58, which opens up the wider political and cultural dimension of the triumph of Christianity over paganism: 'In point of fact, the end for which one lies makes a great difference: whether one thereby sustains or *destroys*. *Christians* and *anarchists* are perfectly identical: their goal, their instinct is only to destroy' (AC §58). This contention forms the basis of two comparisons: first, as we have already seen, between Christianity and the Manusmṛiti; second, as we shall now see, between Christianity and the Roman Empire.

Nietzsche on the Roman Empire (AC §58)

From its beginnings, the Roman Empire has been an object of admiration for many – and Nietzsche is no exception. Although the founding of Rome is associated with the earliest days of civilisation, reflected in the myth that the city was established in 753 BCE by Romulus and Remus, the half-divine twins of Mars (the Roman god of war) who had been raised by a she-wolf, historians today place its founding in 624 BCE. Its history is usually divided into three periods: first, the period of kings (625–510 BCE); second, Republican Rome (510–31 BCE); and third, Imperial Rome (31 BCE –476 CE).

In response to an Etruscan invasion, villagers in an area of ancient Italy known as Latium joined with settlers from the surrounding hills. In its first period, the settlement so founded, Rome, was governed by kings, but such historians as Livy and others record that, after the last of its seven kings, Tarquin the Proud, was deposed by Lucius Junius Brutus, a system of elected magistrates and representative assemblies was established known as the Republic. Over the period of the Republic, Rome expanded its political control over the entire Italian peninsula, and during the Punic Wars (264–146 BCE) it gained control of Carthage and Corinth, establishing itself as the supreme maritime power in the Mediterranean. Roman society was divided into four classes: the nobles of Rome, or the 'patricians', in political control; the 'equestrians' (i.e., riders), wealthy individuals who defended Rome on horseback; 'plebeians', the majority of individuals who were free but had no power; and slaves, the class of individuals lacking any kind of rights at all. While the Roman Republic was successful, and lasted nearly five hundred years, political unrest initiated a shift towards imperialism, and in 60 BCE, the last of the dictators of the Republic and the first of the Roman emperors, Julius Caesar, came to power.

Under Julius Caesar, the Romans conquered Celtic Gaul and the Empire's borders now spread beyond the Mediterranean. Following his assassination in 44 BCE, Julius Caesar was replaced by Octavian who, taking over control of Egypt from Mark Antony in 31 BCE, assumed the title of Augustus, inaugurating the age of Imperial Rome. During the age of Imperial Rome, from its inception in 31 BCE until the fall of Rome in 476 CE, the Empire's borders expanded to include Asia Minor, northern Africa and most of Europe. The Romans faced down the challenge of the Carthaginians, a powerful force in northern Africa, despite the march of the Carthaginian general Hannibal across the Alps in order to invade Italy. As it expanded, the Roman Empire integrated the many cultures it conquered, in particular adopting and adapting Greek culture in terms of literature, architecture and religion. The Roman pantheon of the gods was largely based on the Greek; Mystery religions, such as Mithraism, expanded into new territories as the Empire grew.

In 286 CE, the Empire was split into Eastern and Western empires, each with its own emperor. In the west, the empire fell prey to several Gothic invasions; in 452, Attila and his Huns invaded Italy, and in 455 the Vandals sacked Rome. The great migrations of people across its territories proved too great for the Romans to control, and in 476 Rome itself was conquered by Odoacer, a Visigoth mercenary in the service of Roma, the leader of the Germanic soldiers in the Roman army, and the western Roman emperor, Romulus Augustus, was deposed; the western empire was over. In the east, the Roman Empire, which became known as the Byzantine Empire, survived for many more centuries; its capital, Constantinople (modern-day Istanbul), was eventually conquered by the Turks under Mehmed II in 1453.

Nietzsche was more interested in the Roman Empire than in the Roman Republic;[21] part of the reason for his admiration was the absence of democracy in the Empire. In *Human, All Too Human*, vol. 1, Nietzsche had written, in an important aphorism entitled 'Religion and government':

> The belief in a divine order in the realm of politics, in a sacred mystery in the existence of the state, is of religious origin: if religion disappears the state will unavoidably lose its ancient Isis veil and cease to excite reverence. Viewed from close to, the sovereignty of the people serves then to banish the last remnant of magic and superstition from this realm of feeling; modern democracy is the historical form of the *decay of the state*. (HAH I §472)

Indeed, in *Twilight of the Idols* it becomes clear that Nietzsche wants to use Imperial Rome as a foil to modernity in general and to modern democracy in particular:

> In order that there may be institutions, there must be a species of will, instinct, or imperative, anti-liberal even to malignity: a will for tradition, for authority, for responsibility throughout centuries, a will for the *solidarity* of chains

---

[21] For a recent reappraisal and appreciation of various aspects of Roman life and thought, see Onfray 2019.

of generations forward and backward *in infinitum*. When this will exists, something establishes itself like the *Imperium Romanum* [. . .] (TI Expeditions §39)

Nietzsche's emphasis here on *tradition* and *authority* stands in a tension with the religious abuse (as he sees it) of 'revelation' and 'tradition' in *The Anti-Christ*; it is a good example of the tension between different propositions of which Karl Jaspers (1883–1969) famously spoke, when he said that '*self-contradiction* is the fundamental ingredient in Nietzsche's thought': 'For nearly every single one of Nietzsche's judgments, one can also find an opposite. He gives the impression of having two opinions about everything. Consequently it is possible to quote Nietzsche at will in support of anything one happens to have in mind' (Jaspers 1977: 10).[22] (In terms of the political situation of his day, Nietzsche pointed to Imperial Russia as a counter-example to 'that pitiable European petty-state politics and nervousness' out of which, he argued, the German *Reich* had emerged.) As usual, however, Nietzsche is more concerned with the broader picture:

> The entire Western world no longer possesses those instincts out of which institutions grow, out of which the *future* grows; perhaps nothing is so much against the grain of its 'modern spirit'. We live for the present, we live very fast, we live very irresponsibly: this is precisely what we call 'freedom'. That which *makes* institutions in reality is despised, hated, and repudiated: wherever the word 'authority' even becomes audible, people believe themselves in danger of a new slavery. *Décadence* goes so far in the appreciative instinct of our politicians and political

---

[22] This statement has been used to justify approaching Nietzsche as essentially a stylist, not a philosopher (and certainly not someone to take seriously), as well as the postmodernist, anything goes reading of Nietzsche. Yet Jaspers's point was that one should read Nietzsche carefully: 'It is the task of the interpreter to be forever dissatisfied until he has *also* found the contradiction, to search out contradictions in all their forms, and then, if possible, to gain direct experience of their necessity. Instead of being occasionally provoked by contradiction, one should pursue contradictoriness to its source' (Jaspers 1977: 10).

parties, that *they prefer instinctively* what disintegrates, what hastens the end . . . (TI Expeditions §39)

Although written in 1888, much of Nietzsche's political and cultural critique could equally apply today, and alarmingly so; and in *The Anti-Christ* Nietzsche returns to this critique made in *Twilight of the Idols* and develops it. His core thesis involves the identification of a common motive or instinct in religion and politics, i.e., in Christianity and in anarchism, and in his view this instinct is one to destroy:

> Christianity found its mission in putting an end to such an organization [the Roman Empire], *because life flourished under it*. There the benefits that reason had produced during long ages of experiment and insecurity were applied to the most remote uses, and an effort was made to bring in a harvest that should be as large, as rich and as complete as possible; here, on the contrary, the harvest is *blighted* overnight . . . (AC §58)

Nietzsche's encomium of Imperial Rome begins with a quotation from one of the representative writers of the age of Augustus, the Roman lyric poet called Quintus Horatius Flaccus (65–27 BCE), known as Horace. One of his *Odes* (book 3, §30) opens with these lines about the monument that he as a poet has left:

> *Exegi monumentum aere perennius*
> *Regalique situ pyramidum altius,*
> *Quod non imber edax, non Aquilo impotens*
> *Possit diruere aut innumerabilis*
> *Annorum series et fuga temporum.*

> I have finished a monument more lasting than bronze,
> more lofty than the regal structure of the pyramids,
> one which neither corroding rain nor the ungovernable North Wind
> can ever destroy, nor the countless
> series of the years, nor the flight of time. (Horace 2004: 216–17)

Thus Horace concluded the first three books of his *Carmina* with the hope that he had secured immortal renown as the man who had spun the 'Aeolian song' of Sappho and Alcaeus into Latin poetry. Nietzsche liked this phrase, *aere perennius*, more lasting than bronze or brass,[23] so much that, in the chapter of *Twilight of the Idols* entitled 'What I Owe to the Ancients', he borrowed it and applied it to himself: 'In my writings, up to my Zarathustra, a very strenuous ambition to attain the *Roman* style, the *"aere perennius"* in style will be recognised' (TI §1). Nietzsche's admiration for Horace knows no bounds, as he declares that, 'up to the present, I have not received from any poet the same artistic rapture as was given to me from the first by an Horatian ode'; in fact, Horace serves Nietzsche as an emblem for 'Roman style' in general:

> That lingual mosaic[24] where every word, as sound, as position, and as notion, diffuses its force right, left, and over the whole, that *minimum* in the compass and number of signs, that *maximum* thus realized in their energy, – all that is Roman, and, if you will believe me, it is *noble par excellence*. All other poetry becomes somewhat too popular in comparison with it, mere sentimental loquacity. I am not at all under obligation to the Greeks for any similarly strong impressions, and, to speak out candidly, they *cannot* be to us what the Romans are. We do not *learn* from the Greeks: their mode is too foreign, it is also too unstable to operate imperatively or 'classically'. Who would ever have learned to write from a Greek! Who would ever have learned it *without* the Romans! (TI Ancients §§1–2)[25]

Instead of the conventional nineteenth-century German historiographical view of the inevitable decline of paganism and its

---

[23] Cf. *Daybreak* §71, entitled 'The Christian revenge on Rome'.
[24] The metaphor of the mosaic that Nietzsche uses here – as he does elsewhere as part of his critique of the decadent style (TI Expeditions §7; NK 6/1, 563, drawing on Bourget 1883: 23–32) – itself derives from Horace, *Satires*, book 2, §4, in Christoph Martin Wieland's translation (NK, 6/1, 563; cf. Horace 1786, vol. 2: 145–6).
[25] For Nietzsche's reception of Horace, see NK 6/1, 561–3.

replacement with a Christian-Germanic worldview, Nietzsche's view of the fate of Roman Empire is closer to Edward Gibbon's account of its 'rise and fall' (see NK 6/2, 280):

> That which stood there as *aere perennius*, the *imperium Romanum*, the most magnificent form of organization under difficult conditions that has ever been achieved, and compared to which everything before it and after it appears as patchwork, bungling, *dilettantism* – those holy anarchists made it a matter of 'piety' to destroy 'the world', *which is to say*, the *imperium Romanum*, so that in the end not a stone stood upon another – and even Germans and such other louts were able to become its masters . . . (AC §58)

On the basis of this historical analysis, Nietzsche reaffirms his equation of Christianity and anarchism, a term which he typically does not define more closely. In intellectual-historical terms, anarchism is associated with the thought of William Godwin (1756–1836), the author of *Political Justice* (1793), and the French thinker Pierre-Joseph Proudhon (1809–65), the author of *What is Property?* (1840); it is a complex tradition, and in some respects, by its very nature, hard to define (see Onfray 2011b). Nietzsche constellates both Christianity and anarchism around one of his major concepts, *décadence*:[26]

> The Christian and the anarchist: both are *decadents*; both are incapable of any act that is not disintegrating, poisonous, degenerating, *blood-sucking*; both have an instinct of *mortal hatred* of everything that stands up, and is great, and has durability, and promises life a future . . . (AC §58)

At this point Nietzsche returns to the image used earlier of Christianity as a form of vampirism; there he had protested against 'a vampirism of pale, subterranean leeches' (AC §49); here he exclaims, 'Christianity was the vampire of the *imperium Romanum*, – overnight it destroyed

---

[26] For further discussion, see Kuhn 2000: 213–15.

the vast achievement of the Romans of laying the ground for a great culture *that had time*' (AC §58).

The image of vampirism is not an attractive one, but it is one of Nietzsche's favourites. In an aphorism entitled 'Saviour and Physician' in 'The Wanderer and his Shadow' in *Human, All Too Human*, vol. 2, Nietzsche observes that traditional Christian advice to repress one's sensuality cannot succeed, and that the sensuality one has sought to repress 'still lives in an uncanny, vampire form, and torments [the Christian] in hideous disguises' (HAH II WS §83). In *The Gay Science*, Nietzsche is contemptuous about what he calls the 'philosophizing vampirism' he associates with Spinoza, which reduces the concept of God to 'nothing but bones and their rattling [. . .] categories, formulae, *words*': 'what is *amor*, what is *deus*, when they have lost every drop of blood?', he asks (GS §372). And in *Ecce Homo* Nietzsche insisted:

> Everything which until then was called truth, has been revealed as the most detrimental, most spiteful, and most subterranean form of life; the holy pretext, which was the 'improvement' of humankind, has been recognized as a ruse for *draining* life of its energy and of its blood. Morality conceived as *vampirism* . . . (EH Destiny §8; cf. NK 6/2, 232)

Its sources may be traced back to Julian the Apostate's *Against the Galileans* and to Renan's *Marc-Aurèle et la fin du monde antique* (1882) (see Julian 1923; Renan 1904, cited in NK 6/2, 232). It forms part of a network of imagery that runs throughout *The Anti-Christ*, linking vampirism with such associated images as darkness and the subterranean.

As the section unfolds, so Nietzsche develops his fundamental antithesis of, on the one hand, Imperial Rome and a flourishing of life, and, on the other, Christianity and its cult of death. Nietzsche's praise of Imperial Rome knows no bounds:

> The *imperium Romanum* that we know, and that the history of the Roman provinces teaches us to know better and better, – this most admirable of all works of art in the grand manner was merely the beginning, and the structure

to follow was not to *prove* its worth for thousands of years. To this day, nothing on a like scale *sub specie aeterni* has been brought into being, or even dreamed of! – This organization was strong enough to withstand bad emperors: the accident of personality has nothing to do with such things – the *first* principle of all genuinely great architecture. But it was not strong enough to stand up against the *corruptest* of all forms of corruption – against Christians . . . (AC §58)

In this section of *The Anti-Christ*, the Horatian epithet of *aere perennius* is removed from its aesthetic context and inserted into a political-metaphysical, or more precisely a political-theological, one (NK 6/2, 282). Sommer compares the approach to the Roman Empire taken by Nietzsche in *The Anti-Christ* with that of Jacob Burckhardt in *The Age of Constantine the Great* (1853; rev. 1880). As Nietzsche does in section 58 of *The Anti-Christ*, Burckhardt suggests that 'the great masses were attracted by the emphasis on the forgiveness of sins, through the promise of a blissful immortality, through the mystery which surrounded the sacraments and for some was certainly only a parallel to the pagan mysteries' (Burckhardt 1880: 138; cf. NK 6/2, 282). And as Nietzsche also does in section 58 of *The Anti-Christ*, Burckhardt argues that the belief in personal immortality was a crucial element in Christianity's appeal to the mentality of late antiquity (1880: 140; cf. NK 6/2, 282).

Unlike Nietzsche in *The Anti-Christ*, however, Burckhardt argues that 'theocrasia', i.e., the mixing of the attributes of several deities and their fusion into one single deity, a phenomenon which occurred as non-Greek and non-Roman cults grew in popularity, took place independently of St Paul and demonstrates the ease with which Christianity could adapt various elements (1880: 151; cf. NK 6/2, 282–3). Burckhardt, who devoted a large section of his book to the belief in immortality and to the Mysteries (see Chapter 4 above), went so far as to say that, in late antiquity, everyone was concerned with eternal bliss, whether or not he or she was Christian; on this account, the success of Christianity was due to the simplicity of its conception and offer of salvation (1880: 183–245, esp. 186–7; cf. NK 6/2, 283). And unlike Nietzsche in section 58 of *The Anti-Christ*, Burckhardt disputed that Christianity was responsible for the decline of Rome (1880: 250; cf. NK 6/2, 283).

In fact, Burckhardt notes that there were many indications of the age and depravity of Rome, not just the remark of Arnobius of Sicca (died c. 330 CE) in his *Adversus gentes* (*Against the Pagans*) (book 7) when asked whether anyone could believe in the gods of a city who, 'that one state might be pre-eminent, having been born to be the bane of the human race, subjugated the guiltless world?' (Arnobius 1871: 364; cf. NK 6/2, 283). Sommer puts forward the suggestion that Arnobius, an early Christian apologist during the reign of Diocletian whom Nietzsche had read in German translation in 1887–88, might have been a source of this unbridgeable opposition between Rome and Christianity (NK 6/2, 283–4).

By speaking about the Roman Empire as a work of art (*Kunstwerk*) Nietzsche is more obviously making an allusion to Burckhardt's *The Culture of the Renaissance in Italy* and to its first section, 'The State as Work of Art'. As Sommer has noted, in his late writings an noticeable shift in Nietzsche's thinking takes place – away from his earlier interest in the archaic qualities of Homer, the Presocratics and tragedy, and towards ancient Rome as the source of his enthusiasm for antiquity (NK 6/2, 284). Yet whereas in the section of *Twilight of the Idols* entitled 'What I Owe to the Ancients', he sets up the Romans as an example of stylistic excellence (§1), only to recur to tragedy and to the Dionysian in terms of the actual relevance of antiquity for the present day (§§4–5), in *The Anti-Christ* Nietzsche has, apart from a few significant hints at the end of section 58, relatively little to say about the Dionysian. This absence of the Dionysian in *The Anti-Christ* prompts Sommer to wonder: Why does Nietzsche *not* attack Christianity for its rejection of the Dionysian and its embrace of the Apollonian? Does this suggest that Nietzsche constructs his model of antiquity simply in accordance with the needs of his argumentation (NK 6/2, 284)?

By the same token, Nietzsche's characterisation of Christianity in section 58 astonishes by its devastating inventiveness and its unrelenting negativity:

These stealthy worms, which under the cover of night, mist and duplicity, crept upon every individual, sucking him dry of all earnest interest in real things, of all instinct for reality – this cowardly, effeminate and sugar-coated gang gradually alienated all 'souls', step by step, from that colossal edifice, turning against it all the meritorious, manly and noble natures that had found in the cause of Rome their own cause, their own serious purpose, their own *pride*. The sneakishness of hypocrisy, the secrecy of the conventicle, concepts as black as hell, such as the sacrifice of the innocent, the *unio mystica* in the drinking of blood, above all, the slowly rekindled fire of revenge, of Chandala revenge – all that sort of thing became master of Rome [. . .] (AC §58)

This characterisation or caricature (depending on one's point of view) of Christianity draws in part on *Histoire des origines du christianisme*, where Renan drew attention to the parallels between, on the one hand, the cult of Mithras and other Mystery cults and, on the other, aspects of Pauline Christianity. The *unio mystica* to which Nietzsche refers is the experience of union with God or the Absolute, although this is not a notion in any way exclusive to Christianity (Neoplatonism, for instance, envisages a experience of union or oneness which it calls *henosis*).[27] In 1887, Nietzsche told his friend, the theologian Franz Overbeck, how he had been reading the commentary on the *Enchiridion* of Epictetus by Simplicius of Cilicia,[28] and how he found in it the entire philosophical schematic on which Christianity had based itself. He wrote, 'the *falsification* through morality of everything factual stands there in its full glory': its psychology was miserable, the philosopher was

---

[27] For further discussion, see McGinn 2005.
[28] Simplicius was a sixth-century Neoplatonist who wrote several commentaries on Aristotle and a commentary on the *Manual* by Epictetus, the great Stoic philosopher of the mid-first to second century. His commentaries adopt an anti-Christian stance, particularly towards the Christian Neoplatonist John Philoponus (see NK 6/2, 285).

reduced to a country parson – 'And all of it is *Plato's* fault! – he *is still* Europe's greatest misfortune!'[29]

At this point in section 58, Nietzsche moves a new figure to the front of his argumentation – the ancient Greek philosopher Epicurus (341–270 BCE) (see Chapter 6 below). Earlier in section 30 Nietzsche had been negative in his attitude towards Epicurus, describing him as 'a typical *décadent*' and Epicureanism as 'the theory of salvation of paganism' (AC §30). Here, however, Epicurus is presented as a combatant of Christianity in its pre-existent form (AC §58):

> One has but to read Lucretius to know *what* Epicurus made war upon – *not* paganism, but 'Christianity', which is to say, the corruption of souls by means of the concepts of guilt, punishment and immortality. – He combatted the *subterranean* cults, the whole of latent Christianity – to deny immortality was already a form of genuine *salvation*. (AC §58)

The text by Lucretius (c. 99–c. 55 BCE) to which Nietzsche refers is, of course, his *De rerum natura* (*On the Nature of Things*), and Nietzsche's argument as a whole here recapitulates his earlier understanding of the intellectual-historical role of Epicurus in a section of *Daybreak* entitled 'The "after death"' (D §72). Here we find an early statement of the opposition between the Epicurean and the Christian as it later recurs in *The Anti-Christ*:

> Christianity found the idea of punishment in hell in the entire Roman Empire: for the numerous mystic cults have hatched this idea with particular satisfaction as being the most fecund egg of their power. Epicurus thought he could do nothing better for his followers than to tear this belief up by the roots: his triumph found its finest echo in the mouth of one of his disciples, the Roman Lucretius, a poet of a gloomy, though afterwards enlightened, temperament.

---

[29] See Nietzsche's letter to Franz Overbeck of 8 January 1887; KSB 8, 9; cf. KSA 12, 10[150], 539. For further information about the relationship between Nietzsche and Overbeck, see Meyer and von Reibnitz (eds) 1999; Overbeck 2012.

Alas! his triumph had come too soon: Christianity took under its special protection this belief in subterranean horrors, which was already beginning to die away in the minds of men; and that was clever of it. For, without this audacious leap into the most complete paganism, how could it have proved itself victorious over the popularity of Mithras and Isis? In this way it managed to bring timorous folk over to its side – the most enthusiastic adherents of a new faith! (D §72)

Whether Epicurus wanted to free his followers from the fear of punishment in the afterlife or from an incorrect assessment of the intention of the gods is open to question: was Epicurus ever *really* an opponent of the cults of Mithras or of Isis?

While correctly noting the pagan (and, in this sense, un-Jewish)[30] nature of the idea of hell, Nietzsche primarily rejects it as un-Epicurean:

In other places, where the impulse towards life was not so strong as among the Jews and the Christian Jews, and where the prospect of immortality did not appear to be more valuable than the prospect of a final death, that pagan, yet not altogether un-Jewish addition of Hell became a very useful tool in the hands of the missionaries: then arose the new doctrine that even the sinners and the unsaved are immortal, the doctrine of eternal damnation, which was more powerful than the idea of a *final death*,

---

[30] In earlier Jewish culture, the dead descended to She'ol, a place of shadowy darkness; but, by the time of the Second Temple period (c. 500 BCE –70 CE), the notion of a place of punishment in the afterlife arose, reflected in the account of the seven martyrs whom Antiochus IV Epiphanes tried to force to eat pork (2 Macc. 7). Similarly, the account of how Judas Maccabaeus organised a sacrifice for the fallen (2 Macc. 12:38–45) – and the reflection that 'it is therefore a holy and wholesome thought to pray for the dead, that they may be loosed from sins' (2 Macc. 12:46) – both marked a new stage in Jewish theology (NJB, OT, 741, note j) by implying a belief in the resurrection of the dead, and was later used as 'proof' for the possibility afforded to the souls of those who die in the state of grace to make expiation for unforgiven venial sins, or for the temporal punishment due to venial and mortal sins that have already been forgiven.

which thereafter began to fade away. It was science alone which could overcome this idea, at the same time brushing aside all other ideas about death and an after-life. We are poorer in one particular: the 'life after death' has no further interest for us! an indescribable blessing, which is as yet too recent to be considered as such throughout the world. And Epicurus is once more triumphant! (D §72)

In between the victory of Epicurus over pagan notions of a life after death and his renewed victory in the form of modern science, a less happy episode (as far as Nietzsche is concerned) takes place. 'Epicurus had triumphed, and every respectable intellect in Rome was Epicurean', he writes in *The Anti-Christ*, '*when Paul appeared*' (AC §58).

In *Daybreak*, Nietzsche presents the Pauline doctrine of (selective) immortality from the perspective of what this would have meant in an early Christian context:

Thoughts of eternal damnation were far from the minds of the early Christians: they thought they were delivered from death, and awaited a transformation from day to day, but not death. (What a curious effect the first death must have produced on these expectant people! How many different feelings must have been mingled together astonishment, exultation, doubt, shame, and passion! Verily, a subject worthy of a great artist!) St. Paul could say nothing better in praise of his Saviour than that he had opened the gates of immortality to everybody – he did not believe in the resurrection of those who had not been saved: more than this, by reason of his doctrine of the impossibility of carrying out the Law, and of death considered as a consequence of sin, he even suspected that, up to that time, no one had become immortal (or at all events only a very few, solely owing to special grace and not to any merits of their own): it was only in his time that immortality had begun to open its gates and only a few of the elect would finally gain admittance, as the pride of the elect cannot help saying. (D §72)

In *The Anti-Christ*, however, Nietzsche is even less compromising in his criticism of Paul. Repeating a phrase from the Gospel of John, 'salvation is of the Jews' (John 4:22), spoken by Christ in his conversation with the Samaritan woman at the well, and echoed by Paul in his emphasis in his Letter to the Romans on the privileges of Israel (Rom. 9:1–5), Nietzsche presents Paul as nothing less than the antipode of Epicurus:

> Paul, the Chandala hatred of Rome, of 'the world', in the flesh and inspired by genius – the Jew, the *eternal* Jew *par excellence* . . . What he saw was how, with the aid of the small sectarian Christian movement that stood apart from Judaism, a 'world conflagration' might be kindled; how, with the symbol of 'God on the cross', all secret seditions, all the fruits of anarchistic intrigues in the empire, might be amalgamated into one immense power. 'Salvation is of the Jews.' (AC §58)

Unlike in *Daybreak*, Nietzsche presents the Pauline doctrine of the salvific significance of the Crucifixion as a reaction and a response to the pagan cults of the Mysteries: Christianity is, he says, 'the formula for exceeding *and* summing up the subterranean cults of all varieties, that of Osiris, that of the Great Mother, that of Mithras, for instance: in his discernment of this fact the genius of St Paul showed itself [. . .] he *made* out of [the 'Saviour'] something that even a priest of Mithras could understand' (AC §58) (see Chapter 4 above). Osiris, whose corpse is cut by his brother Set into sixteen pieces and restored to life by Isis; Cybele, an Anatolian mother goddess, who was worshipped in Phrygia, and known in Rome as Magna Mater ('Great Mother'); and Mithras, who kills the bull (the scene of the 'tauroctony' commemorated in all Mithraic temples) and thereby saves the world – thanks to Paul, Christianity absorbs key ideas from these Mystery cults and, in so doing, replaces them with its own (in Nietzsche's view, anti-vitalist) doctrine of salvation:

> His instinct was here so sure that, with reckless violence to the truth, he put the ideas which lent fascination to every

sort of Chandala religion into the mouth of the 'Saviour' as his own inventions, and not only into the mouth – he made out of him something that even a priest of Mithras could understand . . . This was his revelation at Damascus: he grasped the fact that he needed the belief in immortality in order to rob 'the world' of its value, that the concept of 'hell' would master Rome – that the notion of a 'beyond' is the death of life . . . (AC §58)

Rome, as a political enterprise; paganism, as a religious enterprise: both meet their downfall at the hands of Christianity, a downfall which, in the sphere of politics and in the sphere of religious belief alike, Nietzsche can only lament – and describe as 'nihilist', i.e., having no values. 'Nihilist and Christian: they rhyme, and they do more than rhyme' (AC §58), and the rhyming of the words *Christ* and *nihilist* in German serves as a linguistic confirmation of his argument in these two complex sections, 57 and 58, and in *The Anti-Christ* as a whole. And for Nietzsche, no figure in the Christian tradition was more nihilistic than St Paul.

Theme of nobility (AC §24, §37, §45 and §§60–2)

In section 24 of *The Anti-Christ* Nietzsche begins his account of the origin of Christianity, but he breaks off in the third paragraph of this section to introduce a complementary topic – the origin of morality, or as he had called it in his work of 1887, *On the Genealogy of Morals*. In this work, Nietzsche returned to and developed a theme that had concerned him in *Human, All Too Human* (cf. GM Preface §2) and in *Beyond Good and Evil*, that is, 'the *origin* of our moral prejudices' (GM Preface §3). For the reader of *The Anti-Christ* Nietzsche summarises the conclusions as he had reached them in the *Genealogy*:

> In my *Genealogy of Morals* I give the first psychological explanation of the concepts underlying those two antithetical things, a *noble* morality and a *ressentiment* morality, the second of which is a mere product of the denial of the former. The Judaeo-Christian moral system belongs to the

second division, and in every detail. In order to be able to say Nay to everything representing an *ascending* evolution of life – that is, to well-being, to power, to beauty, to self-approval – the instincts of *ressentiment*, here become downright genius, had to invent an *other* world in which the *acceptance of life* appeared as the most evil and abominable thing imaginable. Psychologically, the Jews are a people gifted with the very strongest vitality, so much so that when they found themselves facing impossible conditions of life they chose voluntarily, and with a profound talent for self-preservation, the side of all those instincts which make for *décadence* – *not* as if mastered by them, but as if detecting in them a power by which 'the world' could be *defied*. (AC §24)

In fact, the notion of *nobility* is central to Nietzsche's critique of Christianity in its institutionalised form, and so we should consider in more detail how these passages envisage (in Dan Conway's words) a resurgence of nobility.[31]

Nietzsche's distinction between 'master morality' and 'slave morality' is bound up with his distinction between two sets of opposites: on the one hand, good versus bad, and, on the other, good versus evil.[32] In *Human, All Too Human*, Nietzsche introduces this distinction, identifying the opposition 'good versus bad' with 'the soul of the ruling tribes and castes', and mapping 'good versus bad' on to the opposites of noble and low, or master and slave. (Consequently, in Homer, the Greeks and the Trojans are, while enemies, both good.) By contrast, the opposition 'good versus evil' is associated with 'the soul of the oppressed, the powerless', which regards everything (or everyone) *other* as evil, an outlook which leads to 'the ruination of individuals, their tribes and races' (HAH I §45). On this occasion, Nietzsche argues that contemporary morality has 'grown on the soil of the *ruling* tribes and castes' (HAH I §45).

---

[31] For further discussion, see 'Resurgent Nobility and the Problem of False Consciousness', in Conway (ed.) 2019: 181–204.
[32] For further discussion, see Ottmann (ed.) 2000: 253–5.

In *Beyond Good and Evil*, Nietzsche returns to this distinction in section 260, suggesting that modern morality is a mixture of 'master morality' and 'slave morality': 'In all the higher and more mixed cultures', he writes, 'there also appear attempts at mediation between these two moralities', and 'at times they occur directly alongside each other – even in the same human being, within a *single* soul' (BGE §260). And in his treatise *On the Genealogy of Morals*, Nietzsche dedicates the first essay to this distinction between 'good and evil' and 'good and bad'. By this stage, however, Nietzsche has reversed his earlier position in *Human, All Too Human* and regards contemporary morality as the triumph of 'slave morality', using the notion of 'the slave revolt in morality' – the moment 'when *ressentiment* itself becomes creative and gives birth to values' – to explain the ascendancy of slave morality (GM I §10).

In the third essay of the *Genealogy* on the meaning of 'ascetic ideals', Nietzsche links the way in which 'the ascetic ideal springs from the protective instinct of a degenerating life' to two symptoms of the sickness he diagnoses in contemporary human beings – nausea and pity. These interrelated symptoms occur in *Thus Spoke Zarathustra*, a work that stands in a close relationship to *Beyond Good and Evil* and *On the Genealogy of Morals*. For Nietzsche once wrote that *Beyond Good and Evil* had said 'the same things' as *Zarathustra* but very differently (KGB 7, 254), and intended the *Genealogy* as a 'supplement and clarification' of *Beyond Good and Evil* (KSA 14, 377), while its third essay was conceived as a 'commentary' (of sorts) on an aphorism from a passage in *Zarathustra* (GM Preface §8; cf. TSZ I 217).[33] In 'Of the Rabble', Zarathustra reintroduces the theme of nausea, which subsequently recurs in later chapters (TSZ I 6), while another chapter is entitled 'Of the Pitying' (TSZ I 3). In part 4, after he has overcome his nausea for humankind, Zarathustra faces his ultimate temptation – *pity*.

Much earlier in *The Anti-Christ*, in section 7, Nietzsche had advanced his critique of pity in relation to Christianity by describing it as 'the religion of *pity*' (AC §7). In so doing, Nietzsche is reprising a phrase and a critique that can be found earlier in

---

[33] For further discussion, see Janaway 2007: 165–85.

The Gay Science.³⁴ Section 338 of *The Gay Science* summarises Nietzsche's view in a positive way, as a wish to make his friends 'more courageous, more enduring, more simple, more joyful', and to do so by 'teach[ing] them that which at present so few understand, and the preachers of fellowship in sorrow least of all: – *fellowship in joy*!' (GS §338). By contrast, in *The Anti-Christ* Nietzsche highlights its negative aspect: 'Pity stands in opposition to all the tonic passions that augment the energy of the feeling of aliveness: it is a depressant' (AC §7). Pity, in other words, is *anti-vitalist*.

'People have dared to call pity a virtue', Nietzsche writes, whereas 'in every *noble* morality it is considered a weakness' (AC §7). In support of his interpretation, Nietzsche draws on two other thinkers. First, he draws on Aristotle, who argues in his *Poetics* that the 'pity and fear' aroused in dramatic form allow tragedy to accomplish 'its catharsis of such emotions' (1449b 27–30), adding that while 'the tragic fear and pity may be aroused by the spectacle', they may also be aroused by 'the very structure and incidents of the play – which is the better way and shows the better poet' (1453b 1–3; see NK 6/2, 59). However, Nietzsche misrepresents Aristotle as insisting that pity is something *purely* negative, from which release (or purgation) must be found (see Schiaparelli and Crivelli 2012: 622–4).

Second, Nietzsche instrumentalises Schopenhauer for his own argumentational purposes. In section 20 of his treatise *On the Basis of Morals* (1840), Schopenhauer recognised just three fundamental drives of human action: namely, willing one's own well-being (i.e., egoism), willing someone else's woe (i.e., malice) and willing someone else's well-being (i.e., compassion or pity), arguing that these 'three ethical fundamental incentives [. . .] are present in everyone in various and incredibly different proportions' (Schopenhauer 2010: 253). And in *The World as Will and Representation* (vol. 2, ch. 49), Schopenhauer did not shrink from the conclusion that 'suffering expresses itself clearly enough to the whole of human existence as its true destiny', so that 'the more one suffers,

---

³⁴ See GS §338 and §377; BGE §202 and §206; and GM III §25.

the sooner is the true end of life attained' (Schopenhauer 1966: vol. 2, 635). While Nietzsche correctly rehearses Schopenhauer's position, however, he fundamentally disagrees with it (see NK 6/2, 57). For pity can only appear as a virtue to Schopenhauer because he was 'hostile to life' (AC §7).

Perhaps prompted by Aristotle's analysis (as Nietzsche sees it) of pity as 'a sickly and dangerous state of mind, the remedy for which was an occasional purgative' (in the form of tragic drama), Nietzsche relates his critique of Christianity to the medical discourse he employs throughout *The Anti-Christ*, writing: 'To be doctors *here*, to be unmerciful *here*, to wield the knife *here* – all this is *our* business, all this is *our* sort of humanity, by this sign we are philosophers, we Hyperboreans!' (AC §7); that is, by the sign of the rejection of pity, *not* by the sign of the Cross, as the Emperor Constantine saw in the sky before the Battle of the Milvian Bridge.³⁵

In section 37, Nietzsche challenges head-on the conventional view, found in nineteenth-century historians such as Renan in his *Vie de Jésus* (and restated by such later critics as G. A. Wells), that 'the *crude fable of the wonder-worker and Saviour* constituted the beginnings of Christianity – and that everything spiritual and symbolical in it only came later' (AC §37). In fact, precisely the reverse is true, he asserts, arguing that 'the whole history of Christianity – from the death on the Cross onward – is the history of a progressively clumsier misunderstanding of an *original* symbolism' (AC §37). As we have seen (in Chapter 3 above), this analysis in *The Anti-Christ* is underpinned by Nietzsche's insistence on the importance of the *symbolic* dimension of Christianity, a dimension he even seems prepared to defend. Yet this 'original symbolism' is gradually effaced as it was found necessary to '*vulgarize Christianity and make it barbaric*', using a strategy of 'soak[ing] up doctrines and rites from all the *subterranean* cults of the *imperium Romanum* and its nonsense from all kinds of sick reason' (AC §37). Nietzsche thus sets up an opposition between '*Christian* values',

---

³⁵ In his *Life of Constantine*, Eusebius gives an account of how Constantine was marching with his army when he looked up to the sun and saw a cross of light above it, and a Greek phrase usually translated into Latin as *in hoc signo vinces*, 'in this sign [you shall] conquer'.

identified with a '*sickly barbarism*' that is embodied in the Church as an embodiment of 'deadly hostility to all honesty, to all loftiness of soul, to all discipline of the spirit, to all spontaneous and kindly humanity', and '*noble* values' – Nietzsche calls this 'the greatest of all antitheses in value', which only he, and the other 'free spirits', have re-established (AC §37).

In section 45, Nietzsche parodies a number of New Testament passages, beginning with the Gospels (Mark, Matthew and Luke), before turning to the epistles of Paul (and, in particular, to the First Letter to the Corinthians). Nietzsche takes particular exception to a passage where Paul asks:

> Hath not God made foolish the wisdom of this world? For seeing that in the wisdom of God the world, by wisdom, knew not God, it pleased God, by the foolishness of our preaching, to save them that believe [. . .] For see your vocation, brethren, that there are not many wise according to the flesh, not many mighty, not many noble: But the foolish things of the world hath God chosen, that he may confound the wise; and the weak things of the world hath God chosen, that he may confound the strong. And the base things of the world, and the things that are contemptible, hath God chosen, and things that are not, that he might bring to nought things that are: That no flesh should glory in his sight. (1 Cor. 1:20–1, 26–9)

At this point Nietzsche refers the reader to the first essay of his *Genealogy*, '"Good and Evil", "Good and Bad"', in order to understand how Paul's letter constitutes 'a first rate example of the psychology underlying every Chandala-morality', since in this earlier work Nietzsche had expounded 'the antagonism between a *noble* morality and a morality born of *ressentiment*' (AC §45).

In the midst of his discussion of Islam, Nietzsche turns to a critique of the German aristocracy. The immediate context of these remarks is the Crusades, which Nietzsche describes as 'a higher form of piracy, nothing else!' (AC §60). For Nietzsche, the German nobility, which is 'fundamentally a Viking nobility', was 'in its element'; except that it was working, not in its own interests, but in those of the Church: 'The Church knew only too well how the German nobility was to be *won* . . . The German noble, always the "Swiss guard" of the Church, always in the service of every bad instinct of the Church – *but well paid*' (AC §60). Swiss mercenaries played an important role as regular troops in various armies, especially those of France and Spain, particularly during the Renaissance. Established in 1506, the Pontifical Swiss Guard is still in service today as the *de facto* military force of the Holy See, responsible for protecting the pope and Vatican City, even if only in a ceremonial way.

For Nietzsche, the role of the German aristocracy in the Crusades is but one example of its wider responsibility for the damage wrought (through its anti-nobility stance) by the Church: 'Consider the fact that it is precisely the aid of German swords and German blood and valour that has enabled the Church to carry through its war to the death upon everything noble on earth! The German nobility stands *outside* the history of higher culture' (AC §60). Nietzsche's explanation for this fact is, one might say, whimsical at best: 'The reason is obvious . . . Christianity, alcohol – the two *great* means of corruption' (AC §60).[36] But there is a more serious objection to Nietzsche's argument at this point (one which is made by Andreas Urs Sommer): why would one expect the 'German nobility' or 'German aristocracy' to have anything to do with 'the history of higher culture' in the first place, given that, in section 57, Nietzsche has argued (citing as his authority the Lawbook of Manu) that it is 'the few', i.e., the philosopher-priests, who are responsible for the creation of culture, whereas it is the second class, i.e., the guardians, who are 'the noble warriors' (AC §57)? As Sommer points out, 'no nobility in the world that has to concern itself with questions of power is primarily concerned with being culturally creative [*kulturschöpferisch*]', and this was just as much the case in the Middle Ages as at other times (NK 6/2, 297). (Of course, Nietzsche would point to Frederick II as an exception to this rule . . .)

---

[36] See Nietzsche's remarks on Germans and alcohol in *Ecce Homo* (EH Clever §1; EH HAH §2).

Sommer raises the question of whether the concept of culture as it is employed here by Nietzsche is claiming not just normativity, but objectivity too. After all, Nietzsche tends to talk about culture as if it were something scientifically determinable, and amenable to division into its 'higher' and 'lower' varieties (which is exactly what he does in section 5 of volume 1 of *Human, All Too Human*). Although Nietzsche never actually defines 'culture' in *The Anti-Christ*, it plays a decisive role in his evaluation of the Islamic Orient and the Christian West. In this section, Moorish Spain – like, elsewhere, the Roman Empire – is associated with culture.

In the case of the Roman Empire, scholarship and the state (*Staatswesen*) are mentioned by Nietzsche as expressions of 'higher culture'; in the case of Moorish culture, however, he only mentions 'rare and refined luxuriousness' (AC §60) – no mention is made of such achievements of al-Andalus as its advances in culture and science in general and its contributions to astronomy, pharmacology, surgery and trigonometry in particular. Viewed thus, Nietzsche's argument is essentially binary: Christianity is the inverse of culture, so everything else *is* culture. No account is taken of the specificities of, say, Islamic or Arabic culture (and no distinction is made between geographical and religio-cultural categories).

Thus in Sommer's eyes, Nietzsche's argument operates with a simple (and simplistic) dualism: Christianity is the absence of culture or *Unkultur*, so therefore everything that isn't Christian *must* be culture. This circular argumentation doesn't generate any useful definition of culture itself, however; a problem, as Sommer sees it, in Nietzsche's work as a whole. Even in such early works as *The Birth of Tragedy*, Nietzsche uses the concept of culture in an 'inflationary' way, and in his subsequent writings – including, by implication, *The Anti-Christ* – he neglects to give this concept any concrete meaning (NK 6/2, 297). From such a profound expert on Nietzsche's work as Andreas Urs Sommer, this is a devastating criticism. That said, one might note how, in *The Birth of Tragedy*, Nietzsche defined culture in close relation to myth: 'But without myth every culture loses the healthy natural power of its creativity: only a horizon defined by myths completes and unifies a whole cultural movement' (BT §23). Precisely what worried or even outraged Nietzsche about David Friedrich Strauss was his *insouciance* in the face of the collapse of the Christian myth; a collapse to which he, Strauss, contributed even further with his demythologised version of Christianity, which Nietzsche so greatly disliked.

In section 61, Nietzsche casts the net of his criticism of the Germans even wider, arguing that 'the Germans have destroyed for Europe the last great harvest of culture that Europe was ever to reap – the *Renaissance*' (AC §61). Nietzsche understands the Renaissance as an attempt to reactivate those noble values which elsewhere in *The Anti-Christ* he has been seeking to promote, and as a consequence he is full of praise for it as '*the transvaluation of Christian values*', that is, 'an attempt with all available means, all instincts and all the resources of genius to bring about a triumph of the *opposite* values, the more *noble* values' (AC §61).[37]

As the period in European history bridging the gap between the Middle Ages and the modern period (i.e., bridging the fourteenth and seventeenth centuries), the Renaissance marked the rediscovery of classical Greek philosophy and the renewal of humanism, embracing an integrated vision of the individual represented by the so-called 'Renaissance man', for example Leonardo da Vinci (1452–1519) or Michelangelo (1475–1564). (Like Goethe, Leonardo and Michelangelo are prototypes of what Nietzsche calls the *Übermensch*.)[38] Nietzsche understands the Renaissance almost as a military exercise, as 'the one great war of the past' and as 'a form of *attack*'; and as a military exercise, the Renaissance aimed to attack 'at the critical place, at the very seat of Christianity, and there enthrone the more noble values' (AC §61). In order to encapsulate what is at stake in this project, Nietzsche invokes a striking vision, whose implications might not be immediately clear:

---

[37] For discussion of the relation between Renaissance *virtù* and Nietzsche's project of revaluation, see Owen 2019.
[38] See, for example, Nietzsche's remarks in WP §380 = KSA 12, 9[157], 428 and WP §1018 = KSA 12, 5[91], 223–4. For Nietzsche's encomium of Goethe, see TI Expeditions §49.

I see before me the *possibility* of a perfectly heavenly enchantment and spectacle: – it seems to me to scintillate with all the vibrations of a fine and delicate beauty, and within it there is an art so divine, so infernally divine, that one might search in vain for thousands of years for another such possibility; I see a spectacle so rich in significance and at the same time so wonderfully full of paradox that it should arouse all the gods on Olympus to immortal laughter – *Cesare Borgia as pope!* (AC §61)

'*Cesare Borgia* as pope – that would be the *meaning* of the Renaissance, its actual symbol', Nietzsche wrote to Georg Brandes (1842–1927) on 20 November 1888 (KSB 8, 482).[39] Why was Nietzsche so attached to this idea? Who was Cesare Borgia?

The Borgias were a family from Valencia in Spain, who rose to prominence in ecclesiastical and political affairs in the fifteenth and sixteenth centuries, despite their sulphurous reputation for such crimes as bribery, simony, adultery, incest and murder. Yet they were also major patrons of the arts, particularly in the case of Rodrigo Lanzol y de Borja (1431–1503), who was consecrated as pope in 1492, taking the name of Alexander VI. Cesare Borgia (1475–1507) was one of the several children Alexander VI fathered by his various mistresses, in this case Vanozza dei Cattanei. Cesare was appointed bishop of Pamplona at the age of 15 and archbishop of Valencia at the age of 17, being elevated to the position of cardinal at the age of 18. His struggle for power is said to have been an important inspiration for Niccolò Machiavelli (1469–1527) in his political tract written in 1513 and published in 1532, *The Prince* (*Il Principe*), with its paradigm of the princely warrior type (*condottiero*);[40] and in *Beyond Good and Evil* Nietzsche had offered Cesare Borgia as an example of 'the beast of prey and the man of prey' (BGE §197).

---

[39] For Jacob Burckhardt's *The Civilisation of the Renaissance in Italy* as a stimulus for Nietzsche's thought-experiment of Cesare Borgia as pope, see Owen 2019: 75–85.

[40] See Loeb 2019: 98; and for a discussion of the significance of the *condottiero* as an embodiment of *virtù*, see Onfray 1993: 23–63; Emden 2019: 169–70.

As such, Cesare embodies the value of health and strength espoused by Nietzsche in ways that can be profoundly disturbing for modern readers: in a way, he is an embodiment of 'the will to power', understood by Nietzsche to be a 'fact of nature' and, in this sense, *beyond good and evil.* 'We misunderstand "nature"', Nietzsche wrote, 'as long as we still look for something "pathological" at the bottom of these healthiest of all tropical monsters and growths, or even for some "hell" that is supposed to be innate in them' (BGE §197). Could it be, Nietzsche asked rhetorically, that 'moralists harbour a hatred of the primeval forest and the tropics?' (BGE §197). So Cesare Borgia represents, in human terms, what for Nietzsche, in plant terms, the *Sipo matador* represents.[41]

In part 9 of *Beyond Good and Evil*, entitled 'What is noble', Nietzsche insists on several things that sit uneasily with our current outlook on issues of equality. He talks about the '*pathos of distance*' (BGE §257), about 'an *instinct for rank* which, more than anything else, is a sign of *high* rank' (BGE §263); he talks about how '*the noble soul has reverence for itself*' (BGE §287) – the values Nietzsche espouses are unashamedly, unabashedly *aristocratic*. As an emblem of 'a good and healthy aristocracy', defined for Nietzsche in terms of a fundamental belief that 'society must *not* exist for society's sake but only as the foundation and scaffolding on which a choice type of being is able to raise itself to its higher task and to a higher state of *being*', Nietzsche chooses the *Sipo matador*, one of those 'sun-seeking vines of Java [. . .] that so long and so often enclasp an oak tree with their tendrils until eventually, high above it but supported by it, they can unfold their crowns in the open light and display their happiness' (BGE §258). Nietzsche returns to this image a few sections later when he points to the ancient Greek *polis* or Renaissance Venice as examples of an 'aristocratic commonwealth', at the centre of which lies a highly Nietzschean conception of the individual – the individual as someone who 'dares to be individual and different' (BGE §262):

---

[41] For discussion of the image of the *Sipo matador*, see NK 5/1, 738–42; Onfray 2011a: 273–5; 2015: 129–30, 139–58.

At these turning points of history we behold beside one another, and often mutually involved and entangled, a splendid, manifold, junglelike growth and upward striving, a kind of *tropical* tempo in the competition to grow, and a tremendous ruin and self-ruination, as the savage egoisms that have turned, almost exploded, against one another wrestle 'for sun and light' and can no longer derive any limit, restraint, or consideration from their previous morality [. . .] The dangerous and uncanny point has been reached where the greater, more manifold, more comprehensive life transcends and *lives beyond* the old morality [. . .] (BGE §262)[42]

This is why Nietzsche objects to the Christian doctrine of 'equality of souls before God' (AC §62). This phrase, 'equality of souls before God', is derived from a passage of *Les moines de l'occident* where Charles Forbes René de Montalembert (1810–70) is talking about St Isidore of Seville's *Rule for Monks* (Montalambert 1860: 212; cf. NK 6/2, 313), but it is a preoccupation of Nietzsche's in previous sections (see AC §43, §45, §57).

As we have seen above, in his early writings Nietzsche envisages the structure of society as essentially pyramidal, and this notion of culture as a pyramid re-emerges in section 57 of *The Anti-Christ* and its reaffirmation of the hierarchical view that 'a high culture is a pyramid: it can only stand on a broad base, its primary prerequisite is a strong and soundly consolidated mediocrity' (AC §57). For Nietzsche the ideology of equality constitutes the link he makes, here as elsewhere (AC §57 and §58), between Christianity and anarchism: 'The "equality of souls" before God – this fraud, this *pretext* for the *rancunes* of all the base-minded – this explosive concept, ending in revolution, the modern idea, and the notion of overthrowing the whole social order – this is *Christian* dynamite' (AC §62). Yet in this respect one might respond to Nietzsche by pointing out that in Christian thinking the idea

---

[42] The core argument in this passage about the developmental process of civilisation as the exchange of one form of morality for another is taken up and restated by Jung in, for example, *Transformations and Symbols of the Libido* (1911–12), revised as *Symbols and Symbols of Transformation* (1952).

of the 'equality of souls' is one side of a doctrinal coin, the other side of which is the notion of the human being as enjoying an aristocratic, indeed royal, lineage.

The source of this idea can be found in the First Letter of Peter, where the apostle writes, 'But you are a chosen generation, a kingly priesthood, a holy nation, a purchased people: that you may declare his virtues, who hath called you out of darkness into his marvellous light' (1 Pet. 2:9). In so writing, Peter is echoing the words of Yahweh to Moses in Exodus: 'If therefore you will hear my voice, and keep my covenant, you shall be my peculiar possession above all people [. . .] And you shall be to me a priestly kingdom, and a holy nation' (Exod. 19:5–6), an idea taken up by Second Isaiah in the promise of the miracles of a new Exodus: 'I have given waters in the wilderness: rivers in the desert, to give drink to my people, to my chosen. This people have I formed for myself' (Isa. 43:20–1).

The injunction in Peter's First Letter to remember humankind's royal descent is seen as being of profound moral significance by the philosopher and Orthodox theologian Bertrand Vergely, who declares that 'this royal dignity is what makes us human' (Vergely 2004: 46), and, perhaps surprisingly, argues that Nietzsche understood this. For by distinguishing in *The Birth of Tragedy* between two kinds of relation to existence, the Apollonian and the Dionysian, Nietzsche sought to separate 'what arises from representation from what does not' – and thus 'what makes existence human from what restores to existence its vivid strangeness' (Vergely 2004: 47). Of course, Nietzsche was not a believer (to put it mildly!), but, as someone who meditated for a long time on the death of God, he concluded that 'making God human' had been the cause of that death and that 'what was human about God in the Western world [had] extinguished what was divine about God' – just as 'what is human has killed what was royal about humankind' (Vergely 2004: 47).

The idea of humanity's royal lineage is developed in the *Spiritual Homilies* of the Egyptian Christian hermit and monk Macarius of Egypt, also known as Macarius the Elder, Macarius the Great and the Lamp of the Desert. Born in Upper Egypt in around 300 CE, Macarius sought refuge from the world in the Nitrian Desert, where he visited St Anthony the Great, known as the Father of all

Monks. Returning to the Scetic Desert at the age of forty or so, he presided over its monastic community until his death in 391; his relics are in the Monastery of St Macarius the Great in Scetes in Egypt. The twenty-seventh of his *Homilies* begins, 'Know, O man, thy nobility and thy dignity, how honourable thou art, the brother of Christ, the friend of the King, the bride of the heavenly Bridegroom' (27, §1), and the core of the homily resides in the proclamation, 'Recognise therefore thy nobility, that thou art called to kingly dignity, a chosen generation, a royal priesthood, and a holy nation' (27, §4; see Macarius 1921: 200, 202).

In this injunction, Bertrand Vergely sees a response to the 'terrible statement' made by Nietzsche that 'slaves rule the world', and 'it is the logic of victimhood that is in power' (Vergely 2010: 119) – a statement that is indeed terrible if Nietzsche is right. In this formula of humanity's royal lineage as found in the homilies of St Macarius (as well as in St Gregory of Nyssa),[43] Vergely finds a way out of this logic of victimhood, the rule of slavery and the tyranny of suffering. In the injunction to recall our royal lineage Vergely sees an articulation of a fundamental moral law, one with which Nietzsche himself would most likely be in agreement: that 'to be a human being is something so precious that to be oneself is not simply a right, it is a duty' (2010: 120). And Vergely goes on to derive from this insight the following – in its own way, vitalist – conclusion:

> To lose one's dignity is not a right, otherwise slavery becomes a right and inhumanity has won [. . .] One delivers the world

---

[43] In his treatise *On the Making of Man*, Gregory of Nyssa declares: 'The best Artificer made our nature as it were a formation fit for the exercise of royalty, preparing it at once by superior advantages of soul, and by the very form of the body, to be such as to be adapted for royalty [. . .] So the human nature also, as it was made to rule the rest, was, by its likeness to the King of all, made as it were a living image, partaking with the archetype both in rank and in name, not vested in purple, nor giving indication of its rank by sceptre and diadem [. . .] but instead of the purple robe, clothed in virtue, which is in truth the most royal of all raiment, and in place of the sceptre, leaning on the bliss of immortality, and instead of the royal diadem, decked with the crown of righteousness; so that it is shown to be perfectly like to the beauty of its archetype in all that belongs to the dignity of royalty' (Schaff and Wace [eds] 1893: 389–90).

from tyranny and slavery by turning back into life. Here it is a question of the most generous act there can be. Anyone who goes back into life renounces making others suffer by preferring to live. He renounces above all the status of being a victim, since such a status permits one to seek vengeance. This is a supreme act of generosity. It can be so tempting to do things wrong in order to preserve the possibility of seeking revenge! (2010: 121)

The rejection of revenge pivots on the status of humankind, and forms a significant point of intersection with the cry to reject revenge as found in Nietzsche's writings and as passionately declaimed by Zarathustra. For one of the chapters in *Thus Spoke Zarathustra* is entitled 'Of the Tarantulas' – an idea echoed in *The Anti-Christ*'s reference to God 'as spider' (AC §18).[44] Here Zarathustra describes the 'preachers of *equality*' as 'tarantulas [. . .] and secretly revengeful ones' (TSZ II 7). But Zarathustra does not just harangue the tarantulas, whose black colour clearly recalls clerical garb, but he also bursts out with a passionate cry: 'Because, for man to be redeemed from revenge – that is for me the bridge to the highest hope, and a rainbow after long storms' (TSZ II 7).

These lines caught the attention of Martin Heidegger, in an essay entitled 'Who is Nietzsche's Zarathustra?' (first published in 1954). As Heidegger observes, these words must seem 'strange and puzzling' to 'the prevailing view of Nietzsche's philosophy that has been fabricated', a view structured around Nietzsche as the promoter of the will-to-power, of power politics and war, and of the frenzy of the 'blond beast' (Heidegger 1985: 69).

---

[44] 'In the Indian *Oupnakhat*, III.67.IV.80, God as a spider spins everything out of himself' (Menzel 1870: vol. 1, 142; cited in NK 6/2, 107). Cf. GM III §9: 'Our attitude toward God as some alleged spider of purpose and morality behind the great captious web of causality, is *hubris* – we might say, with Charles the Bold when he opposed Louis XI, "*je combats l'universelle araignée*", our attitude toward *ourselves* is *hubris*, for we experiment with ourselves in a way we would never permit ourselves to experiment with animals and, carried away with ourselves, we cheerfully vivisect our souls' (GM III §9). A possible word-play on Spinoza/*Spinne* has been suggested by Sommer (NK 6/2, 106), who also detects echoes of Lichtenberg and Heinrich Heine (NK 6/2, 107).

While Heidegger's reading of Nietzsche's text is characteristically idiosyncratic, two points he makes are relevant for our discussion here.

First, the question posed by the title of Heidegger's essay is answered in the chapter entitled 'The Convalescent', where Zarathustra's animals acclaim him as *'the teacher of the eternal recurrence'* (TSZ III 13 §2), thus confirming what Zarathustra himself had declared from the outset when he announced to the people in the market-place, *'I teach you the superman'* (TSZ Prologue §3). As Heidegger notes, it is 'in the peculiar structure' of *Thus Spoke Zarathustra* that the answer to the subsequent question, 'What bridge allows him to cross over to the Superman, and in that crossing allows him to take leave of man as he is until now, so that he frees himself from him?' (Heidegger 1985: 69), finds its answer in a chapter that precedes the animals' acclamation of Zarathustra as the teacher of eternal recurrence, i.e., 'Of the Tarantulas' and the passage quoted above. In other words, just as *Thus Spoke Zarathustra* must be read as a totality *and* in relation to Nietzsche's writing as a whole (including – and, one senses, for Heidegger, especially – the *Nachlass*), so we must read *The Anti-Christ* as a totality and in relation to Nietzsche's entire philosophy.

Second, in answering the two further questions, 'What does Nietzsche mean here by revenge?' and 'What does deliverance from revenge consist of?', Heidegger draws our attention to the chapter entitled 'Of Redemption', where Zarathustra declares:

> This, yea, this alone is *revenge* itself: the Will's antipathy to time, and its 'It was.'
>
> Verily, a great folly dwelleth in our Will; and it became a curse unto all humanity, that this folly acquired spirit!
>
> The spirit of revenge: my friends, that hath hitherto been man's best contemplation; and where there was suffering, it was claimed there was always penalty. (TSZ II 20)

In other words, without the doctrine of eternal recurrence, our relationship to time, and our inability to will backwards, suffuses our existence with the spirit of revenge: 'Thus did the Will, the emancipator, become a torturer; and on all that is capable of suffering it taketh revenge, because it cannot go backward' (TSZ II 20).

For reasons of space we cannot go here into Heidegger's attempt in his essay to examine Nietzsche's thought in terms of the Western metaphysical tradition, from Plato's understanding of thought (in *Theaetetus*, 189e, and *Sophist*, 263e) to F. W. J. Schelling's definition of the essential character of Being as willing (in his *Philosophical Investigations into the Essence of Human Freedom* of 1809). But the emphasis Heidegger places in the later part of his essay on the significance of love in Nietzsche's thought highlights the remarkable parallels between Nietzsche's philosophy and Christianity, which might explain the curious tension in *The Anti-Christ* between Nietzsche's outright rejection of St Paul (and of all ecclesiastical structures) and his positive conception of the figure of Christ himself.

On the one hand, in 'Of the Tarantulas' and in *The Anti-Christ* Nietzsche identifies Christianity with 'the spirit of revenge', and he analyses Judeo-Christian morality as 'slave morality' and as an ethical code that has arisen from 'the slave revolt in morality'. In his 'Attempt at a Self-Criticism' added to *The Birth of Tragedy* in 1886, two years before *The Anti-Christ*, Nietzsche described Christianity as 'the most prodigal elaboration of the moral theme to which humanity has ever been subjected' (BT Attempt §5). Behind Christianity's hostility towards art – shared, one might add, by Platonism – lies, Nietzsche senses, 'a *hostility to life* – a furious, vengeful antipathy to life itself', for 'all of life is based on semblance, art, deception, points of view, and the necessity of perspectives and error' (BT Attempt §5). Hence Christianity was 'from the beginning, essentially and fundamentally, life's nausea and disgust with life, merely concealed behind, masked by, dressed up as, faith in "another" or "better" life' (BT Attempt §5). Behind the 'Sabbath of Sabbaths' or Yom Kippur, the Day of Atonement, Nietzsche detects 'a sign of abysmal sickness, weariness, discouragement, exhaustion, and the impoverishment of life' (BT Attempt §5). 'Long ago', Nietzsche writes, his instinct had turned *against* morality, aligned itself *with* life, and discovered 'a fundamentally opposite doctrine and valuation of life' – one he defines as 'purely artistic' and '*anti-Christian*', thus anticipating the title of his later work.

On the other hand, Christianity presents itself as a departure from an ethic based on obligation and revenge to an ethic founded on love. Time and again, Christ emphasises that love is the real basis of the Law, and in his Epistles Paul distinguishes between the Law and the new ethic of love – as does, in his Epistles, St John. (Precisely this emphasis on love aroused the suspicions of such later critics of religion as Jung, who wrote extensively about this problem in his *Answer to Job* [1952].) True, the linear conception of time found in Judeo-Christianity is at odds with the pagan circularity embraced by Nietzsche's conception of eternal recurrence, but even more fundamental to both is their common insistence on an ethic of love. Heidegger cites a note from Nietzsche's *Nachlass* of spring 1844 which expresses his doctrine of eternal recurrence as a refrain, '*Love alone shall have jurisdiction*' (*nur die Liebe soll richten*), and describes this love as 'creative love which *forgets* itself in its works' (*die schaffende Liebe, die sich selber über ihren Werken vergißt*) (Heidegger 1985: 74; see KSA 11, 25[493], 143).

The unexpected subterranean affinities between Christian doctrine and Nietzschean philosophy help explain the fascination of this apparently hard-core materialist, unabashedly atheist thinker for theologians in the twentieth century.[45] In a sense, Nietzsche is obliged to affirm the way in which the Roman Empire is hijacked by Christianity since, in order to do so, he has to illuminate (and thereby activate) an unintended boon to the future nobility, those whom he associates with the way that he (and, by the same token, 'we') can emerge as 'Hyperboreans' and as 'good Europeans'. Has the 'harvest' – a term rich in biblical echoes – that has been denied to European modernity not been permanently cancelled, but merely delayed? After all, if we – as late moderns, as Hyperboreans – have not inherited the pagan, Epicurean-infused empire to which we are entitled, nevertheless we have received the gifts of *The Anti-Christ*. Are we sufficiently outraged at the historical crime that has been

---

[45] For discussion of 'certain ambiguities in Nietzsche's approach to divinity' in *The Anti-Christ*, arguing that 'within his persistent vilification of Christianity lies a gesture toward alternative conceptions of deification that are more consistent with natural existence', see Hatab 2019.

done to us to take it upon ourselves to install the post-Christian, pan-European empire that *The Anti-Christ* promises to inaugurate?

In the next chapter we turn to Nietzsche's great enemy in *The Anti-Christ*: not Jesus, but Paul of Tarsus (or *Saint* Paul, to those who venerate him). In 2008–09, Josef Ratzinger, Pope Benedict XVI, alluded to 'a true and proper denigration of Saint Paul' that emerged in the twentieth century; thinking, of course, primarily of Nietzsche, whom he describes as having 'derided the theology of Saint Paul's humility, opposing it with his theology of the strong and powerful man' (Benedict 2009: 130). Not surprisingly, Benedict immediately moved to 'set this aside', yet one of Nietzsche's key claims about Paul in *The Anti-Christ* is recapitulated by Benedict and attributed to historical-critical science when he argues that the importance placed on the concept of freedom in Pauline thought led to an emphasis on a differentiation between the proclamation of Jesus and that of Paul: 'And Saint Paul appears almost as a new founder of Christianity' (Benedict 2009: 130). We shall approach Paul through the logic of sacrifice that is discernible in his writings; through Nietzsche's remarks about Paul in his earlier work, *Daybreak*; and through the role that the figure of Paul plays in the argument of *The Anti-Christ*.

6
Nietzsche and St Paul

Separated as its origins are from us by nearly two millennia, and linguistically (and hence conceptually) obscured by the sociocultural changes that have taken place in the meantime, can we ever know the *truth* about Christianity? Can we ever know what its *real* history is? How far are the origins of Christianity accessible to us through such disciplines as archaeology and linguistics (i.e., philology)? In short, is it possible to carry out a *genealogy* (in Nietzschean terms) of Christianity?

In section 39 of *The Anti-Christ*, Nietzsche pauses a moment to resume the thread of his argument and undertakes to give what he calls 'the *authentic* history of Christianity' (AC §39). This historical account begins with a very simple proposition – 'there was really only one Christian, and he died on the Cross' (AC §39). With the death of Jesus, the argument goes, so the *evangelion* (or in Greek εὐαγγέλιον) – the 'gospel' or the good news – died as well. What has taken its place is, according to Nietzsche, a *dysevangelion* – i.e., *bad* tidings, the opposite of a gospel – which is the opposite of what Jesus, as Nietzsche conceives him, had represented.

Following the Crucifixion and the death on the Cross, the 'good news' which Jesus had brought, at least as that is imagined by Nietzsche, is faced with the almost impossible task of having to explain 'this unexpected and shameful death' (AC §40). '*Who was that? What was that?*' – these were the questions with which his disciples were faced (AC §40). As Nietzsche conceives of the gospel – as not about believing but doing, as '*not* faith but acts; above all, as an *avoidance* of acts, a different *state of being*' (AC §39) – it was not designed to cope with such an explanatory task. No wonder Nietzsche describes the reactions of the disciplines as a feeling of 'dismay, of profound affront and injury' (AC §40).

Then the questions asked suddenly changed. Not '*Who was that? What was that?*', but rather '*Who* put him to death? *Who* was his natural enemy?', and with those questions, 'cracks began to appear' (AC §40). Just as these questions 'jumped out like a bolt of lightning', so the answer resounds back like a roll of thunder. The answer to the questions, '*Who* put him to death? *Who* was his natural enemy?', turns out to be – 'the *Jewish* rulers, the upper class' (AC §40). This development is, in Nietzsche's eyes, a complete reversal of what Jesus' project had been about:

> All that Jesus could hope to accomplish by his death, in itself, was to offer the strongest possible proof, or *example*, of his teachings in the most public manner. But his disciples were very far from *forgiving* his death [. . .] On the contrary, it was precisely the most unevangelical of feelings, *revenge*, that now possessed them. (AC §40)

Revenge and *ressentiment* are, of course, two of Nietzsche's big themes. Their complement is guilt, so that we might say that Nietzsche objects to two chief characteristic human strategies: of saying 'You're wrong', i.e., *ressentiment*, and of saying 'I'm wrong', i.e., guilt.

The logic of revenge and *ressentiment* brings about the inversion of what Jesus' project had been about. So whereas the gospel had been about the 'kingdom of God' as something that enacted 'the existence, the fulfilment, the *actuality* of this kingdom', instead the 'kingdom of God' becomes caught up with notions of 'retaliation', 'judgement' and 'punishment', and turned into 'a historical moment', one associated with 'the popular expectation of a messiah'; from something alive and actual, it becomes 'a closing ceremony, a promise' (AC §40).

On this account, there is a concomitant shift in the way that Jesus is seen by his disciples and the Jewish people. The 'contempt and bitterness' in which they held the Pharisees and theologians was now redirected to create the figure of a master, who himself came to be made into a Pharisee and a theologian. At the same time, however, they take revenge on this master figure by distorting his teaching of equality and *elevating* Jesus 'in an extravagant manner', thereby distancing him from themselves. In the past, so Nietzsche argues, the Jews had 'taken revenge' on their enemies by 'separating off their God and raising him up into the heights' (AC §40). And so the same now happens with Jesus, who is transformed into being the son of God. In this way, Nietzsche concludes, 'the one God and the only Son of God' are 'both products of *ressentiment*' (AC §40). Tracing the logic (if that is the right word) of *ressentiment* leads Nietzsche into considering the logic of *sacrifice*.

The logic of sacrifice (AC §§39–40)

These days we tend to use the expression 'sacrifice' in a purely metaphorical sense, as when politicians congratulated citizens for having 'made sacrifices' during the coronavirus pandemic of 2020; or in a less figurative sense, as when thinking of hospital staff or workers who died while caring for those who had contracted the virus. But we tend not to use it in the sense of an act of slaughtering an animal or a person, or surrendering a possession, as an offering to a deity; and we very rarely use it in the sense of Christ's offering of himself in the Crucifixion. And yet the notion of sacrifice was fundamental for numerous human cultures and civilisations.[1]

The question of how such a thing as sacrifice became possible is one that was not just important for Nietzsche (above all in *On the Genealogy of Morals*), but that has occupied many contemporary thinkers too, including such twentieth-century thinkers as Georges Bataille (1897–1962), Jacques Derrida (1930–2004), Jean-Luc Nancy (b. 1940), René Girard (1923–2015) and Slavoj Žižek (b. 1949).[2] Seen thus in its historico-cultural as well as intellectual-historical context, Nietzsche's critique in *The Anti-Christ* (and elsewhere) of the Christian doctrine of sacrifice seems less obsessive than it might otherwise appear.

---

[1] See Burkert 1983; Girard 2005; Carter (ed.) 2003; Hamerton-Kelly (ed.) 1987.
[2] For further discussion, see Keenan 2005; Bubbio 2014.

After all, the notion of 'sacrifice' leads to the heart of religion in general and Judeo-Christianity in particular; the term *sacrificium* deriving from the concepts of *sacra* (or 'sacred things') and *facere* ('to do', 'to perform') – to sacrifice is, literally, to 'make holy'. In the nineteenth century, numerous thinkers tried to untangle the thinking bound up in the idea of sacrifice.[3] In England, for instance, the anthropologist Edward Burnett Tylor (1832–1917), the founder of cultural or social anthropology, proposed a theory based on the idea of cultural evolutionism, i.e., the view of culture, not as static, but as developing. Tylor envisaged a threefold pattern of development, from 1) savagery via 2) barbarism to 3) civilisation, suggesting in *Primitive Culture* (1871) that sacrifice had begun as a gift offered to the gods to secure their favour or placate their anger, then became a form of homage, and finally was understood as an act of renunciation. On Tylor's account, sacrifice was seen as something essentially transactional that later acquired a moral dimension.

In his *Prolegomena to the History of Israel* (1882; first published in 1878 as the *History of Israel*), the German biblical scholar and orientalist Julius Wellhausen suggested that sacrifice is a feeling that is at once universal and spontaneous. He argued that, among 'primitive' peoples, it was considered entirely natural to think of giving gifts to the gods or even of sharing a meal with them. This essentially idyllic conception became disrupted, he argued, when the *oral* cultural background to primitive sacrificial praxis became distorted by *written* sacrificial laws, reflected in the Bible by the organisation of sacrificial practices in the Book of Deuteronomy, with its focus on centralising cultic sacrifice around the temple in Jerusalem. Wellhausen concluded that the development of a priestly caste, first in Judaism, then in the form of the Church, had created a distorted form of the (divinely ordained) political state.[4]

In his *Lectures on the Religion of the Semites* (1889; 2nd edn, 1894), the Scottish orientalist and biblical scholar William

---

[3] See 'A Genealogy of Theories of Sacrifice', in Keenan 2005: 10–32.

[4] In turn, Wellhausen's critique reveals his own (liberal, Lutheran) political assumptions, as John Milbank has argued (1995: 20).

Robertson Smith (1846–94) proposed that the original function of sacrifice was to establish a sense of communion between the members of a group and, in turn, between the group and its god. Whereas Wellhausen had argued that sacrifice had originally been an individual or private gift with the aspect of communal sharing as only a secondary aspect, Robertson Smith emphasised the social, communal aspect of sacrifice. For evidence of his interpretation, Robertson Smith relied heavily on an account by St Nilus the Elder of Sinai, a fourth-century defender of St John Chrysostom. The story narrated by Nilus about how Bedouin Arab tribes made a sacrifice of a living camel attracted the interest of many commentators and scholars, including Sigmund Freud, who in 1913 in *Totem and Taboo* related the account as given by Robertson Smith (Freud 1990: 199–200; Eliade 1976: 6).

Perhaps the best-known theory of sacrifice can be found in *The Golden Bough: A Study in Magic and Religion* (1890) by the Scottish social anthropologist James George Frazer. In this work Frazer elaborated his theory – which later exercised a huge influence on Modernist thinkers and writers, notably T. S. Eliot – that the origin of sacrifice lay in magical practices involving the ritual slaying of a god in order to bring about the god's rejuvenation – reflected in the cry, 'the king is dead, long live the king!' Just as Robertson Smith explored the function of the totem (an animal or plant that served as an emblem of a family, clan or tribe) in his account of sacrifice, whereby the sacrifice allows the group to enter into communion with the totem and hence with the divinity of the tribe, so Frazer argued that the totem became a repository for the life force of the god-king. In defence of this position, he cited the episode of the 'golden bough' narrated by Virgil in book 5 of *The Aeneid*: Aeneas must take the golden bough as a gift to Proserpina to gain entrance to the underworld. After removing the bough, a second one springs up to replace it – the entire nexus of death and renewal is, for Frazer, symbolised in this iconic episode.

In 1899 – the same year as Nietzsche was working on *The Anti-Christ* – the French comparative sociologists Henri Hubert (1872–1927) and Marcel Mauss (1872–1950) published their study entitled *Sacrifice: Its Nature and Function*. Rather than focusing on the presumed function of the sacrifice in relation to the putative recipient, the god (that is, obtaining favour, as Tylor argued; or as a gift, as Wellhausen proposed; or as a means of establishing communion, as Robertson Smith believed), Hubert and Mauss considered the sacrifice in terms of its effect on the person(s) offering it. Sacrifice is, as they defined it, 'a religious act which, through the consecration of a victim, modifies the condition of the moral person who accomplishes it or that of certain objects with which he is concerned' (Hubert and Mauss 1964: 13). The consecration of the victim is achieved through its destruction, and the communion thereby achieved with the sacred world is celebrated in the form of a sacred meal or feast.

As they develop it, Hubert and Mauss's theory of sacrifice becomes quite complicated (or sophisticated, depending on one's point of view). On their account, the victim plays a mediating role between those who offer the sacrifice and the divinity to whom the sacrifice is offered, operating a 'single mechanism' that simultaneously sacralises the profane and desacralises the sacred. There is a complex relation between the sacrifice *of* the god and the sacrifice *for* the god; taking issue with the totemic hypothesis that sacrifice primarily involves sacrifice *to* the god, Hubert and Mauss identify the sacrifice *of* the god with the ideal of renunciation that forms the operative principle of the social system. The complexity inherent in their argument comes to the fore in Freud's *Totem and Taboo*, where Freud relates the sacrifical doctrines of Christianity to his principle of 'ambivalence', which he described as an 'inexorable psychological law' (Freud 1990: 216–17). In response to Hubert and Mauss's claim that 'the Christian imagination has built according to ancient blueprints' (cited in Keenan 2005: 18), the Belgian historian Marcel Detienne (1935–2019) has replied that while this may be true, 'it is no less true that the imagination of the sociologists, and others, has built according to Christian blueprints' (Detienne 1989: 223, n. 53). This rejoinder might also be thought applicable to Nietzsche, who concludes his *Ecce Homo* with the iconic opposition of Dionysos and the Crucified (EH Destiny §9).

In the years following Nietzsche's death and in the first few decades of the twentieth century, the theme of sacrifice continued to attract the attention of sociologists, anthropologists, historians, philosophers and psychoanalysts: from Émile Durkheim's *The Elementary Forms of Religious Life* (1912) via the 12-volume study *Der Ursprung der Gottesidee* (*The Origin of the Idea of God*) (1912–55) by the Austrian linguist (and Roman Catholic priest) Wilhelm Schmidt (1868–1954), which proposed a theory of primitive monotheism, according to which primitive religion was not polytheistic, but monotheistic, centring on the cult of a sky god, to Freud's *Totem and Taboo*, which includes a reprise of the work of Robertson Smith. Freud's thesis, which drew on Charles Darwin's hypothesis of the primal horde, was that sacrifice expressed a psychological ambivalence – simultaneously an aggressive desire to kill the father and a search for reconciliation with the father through the substitution of a victim (Freud 1990: 212).

In the second volume of his *Philosophy of Symbolic Forms* (1923–29), devoted to the topic of *Mythical Thought* (1925), the philosopher Ernst Cassirer drew on his neo-Kantian reading of G. W. F. Hegel to argue that the act of sacrifice constitutes a central point around which the practice of worship in particular and indeed intellectual activity in general could be constellated (Cassirer 1955: 219–31). In their *Dialectic of Enlightenment* (1944), Max Horkheimer and Theodor W. Adorno argued, from the fact of the ritual of sacrifice, that myth was, in fact, already Enlightenment (2002: 50). (In this respect they were, as Rolf Wiggershaus has suggested, following up an interpretative line previously opened up by Karl Kerényi and C. G. Jung [Wiggershaus 1994: 230].) Their reading of myth in general and sacrifice in particular comes across, inspired as it is by their fusion of Nietzsche and Marx, as curiously de-transcendentalised, abstract, lacking in blood and guts; it is in entirely in tune with their reading of modernity as an embodiment of the 'totally administered society'.

By contrast, the account of sacrifice developed by the German ethnologist Adolf Ellegard Jensen (1899–1965) in *Myth and Cult among Primitive Peoples* (1951) reactivated the theory that had originated at the turn of the century with the German ethnologist Leo Frobenius (1873–1938). In contrast to the notion that 'indigenous peoples' (*Naturvölker*) were the remnant of a primordial era – one thinks, for example, of the Pelasgians in whom the likes of Johann Jakob Bachofen (1815–87) and Ludwig Klages (1872–1956) were interested – the scholars associated with the *Kulturkreislehre*, sometimes referred to as 'cultural morphologists', sought to reintroduce history into the study of the timeless or the archaic, arguing that the similarities that existed among different cultures arose not because there had been a prehistoric, primordial humanity, but rather because of cultural diffusion or influence between different cultural areas or fields. Behind the cultic re-enactment involved in blood sacrifice, Jensen argued, lay an actual killing that took place in archaic cultures, associated with the myth of the slaying of what Jensen calls a 'Dema deity', a mythological figure identified as having been responsible for passing knowledge about crop cultivation, animal husbandry, craftsmanship or ritual worship to a people or community.[5] On this account, blood sacrifices are 'meaningless survivals' of earlier 'rituals of killing' that were, however, intensely 'meaningful'.

So Nietzsche's interest in sacrifice is part and parcel of a wider interest in this phenomenon at the time when he was writing, and in the immediate and not-so-immediate aftermath. (In fact, the question of sacrifice is one has continued to preoccupy postmodern thinkers, as the work of Luce Irigaray (b. 1930), Lacan, Žižek, Derrida and others bears out.) In *Beyond Good and Evil* and *On the Genealogy of Morals* Nietzsche develops nothing less than an entire theory of sacrifice,[6] but here – for reasons of space – we must concentrate on his argument as presented in *The Anti-Christ*.[7]

In *The Anti-Christ* Nietzsche claims that 'a nation that still believes in itself holds fast to its own god. In him it does honour to the conditions which enable it to survive, to its virtues' – as

---

[5] See the extract from *Myth and Cult Among Primitive Peoples* in Carter (ed.) 2003: 175–88.
[6] See 'Nietzsche: The Eternal Return of Sacrifice', in Keenan 2005: 59–73; and Bishop 2020.
[7] For instance, Zarathustra declares, 'I love those who do not first seek a reason beyond the stars for going down and being sacrifices, but sacrifice themselves to the earth, that the earth of the Superman may hereafter arrive'; 'Thus to die is best; the next best, however, is to die in battle, and sacrifice a great soul'; and: 'It is your thirst to become sacrifices and gifts yourselves: and therefore have ye the thirst to accumulate all riches in your soul' (TSZ Prologue §4; TSZ I 21; TSZ I 22), to mention but a few references.

Zarathustra had declared in 'Of the Thousand and One Goals' (TSZ I 15):

> it projects its joy in itself, its feeling of power, into a being to whom one may offer thanks. He who is rich will give of his riches; a proud people need a god to whom they can make *sacrifices* . . . Religion, within these limits, is a form of gratitude. One is grateful for one's own existence: to that end one needs a god. – Such a god must be able to work both benefits and injuries; he must be able to play either friend or foe [. . .] (AC §16)

However, there is an important difference between sacrifice in the context of 'noble' religion (GM II 19; cf. Young 2006: 177) and sacrifice in the context of (Pauline) Christianity, as becomes clear in the course of Nietzsche's critique of St Paul.

Paul in *Daybreak* (D §68)

Nietzsche's remark that 'there was really only one Christian, and he died on the Cross' (AC §39) reminds us of his earlier engagement in 1881 with the figure of Paul in a section of *Daybreak* entitled 'the first Christian' (D §68). Here Nietzsche contends that the Bible contains 'the history of one of the most ambitious and importunate souls, of a mind as superstitious as it was cunning', that is, 'the history of the apostle Paul' (D §68). In the rest of this lengthy aphorism, Nietzsche presents this history as the history of 'the *first* Christian, the inventor of Christianness [*Christlichkeit*]', before whom there had only been 'a few Jewish sectarians' (D §68). Because everything that Nietzsche says about Paul in *The Anti-Christ* presupposes familiarity with this analysis in *Daybreak*, we must spend some time examining his argument about Paul in this work.[8]

---

[8] For further discussion of Nietzsche's reception of Paul, see Salaquarda 1974; and for his reception of contemporary interpretations of Paul by such theologians as David Friedrich Strauss (1808–74), Karl Holsten (1825–97), Hermann Lüdemann (1842–1933), Willibald Beyschlag (1823–1900), Ernest Renan (1823–92) and Franz Overbeck (1837–1905), see Havemann 2001; 2002.

As the commentary by Jochen Schmidt in the *Nietzsche-Kommentar* suggests, Nietzsche's discussion of Paul draws on various non-biblical sources (NK 3/1, 151–6). In a letter to Franz Overbeck of 22 June 1880, Nietzsche asked to borrow from him two historical theological works, *Das Christenthum Justins des Märtyrers* (1878) by Moritz von Engelhardt (1828–81) and *Die Anthropologie des Apostels Paulus und ihre Stellung innerhalb seiner Heilslehre* (1872) by Hermann Lüdemann (1842–1933).[9] In his interpretation of Paul as an epileptic, Nietzsche drew on a work by the English psychiatrist Henry Maudsley (1835–1918), *Responsibility in Mental Disease* (1874), translated into German as *Die Zurechnungsfähigkeit der Geisteskranken* (1875). And he draws on volume 2, chapter 48, of Schopenhauer's *The World as Will and Representation*, entitled 'On the Doctrine of the Denial of the Will-to-Live', in which Schopenhauer emphasises – an emphasis later taken up and developed by Lüdemann – that Paul came to see the Jewish Law as beyond fulfilment (Schopenhauer 1966: vol. 2, 603–5). The context here is Schopenhauer's argument that 'the ancients, particularly the Stoics and also the Peripatetics and Academics, laboured in vain to prove that virtue is enough to make life happy', whereas 'experience loudly cried out against this' (1966: vol. 2, 603). What was really 'at the root of the attempt' of those philosophers, even though (so Schopenhauer argued) they were unaware of it, was 'the assumed *justice* of the case', i.e., that 'he who was *without guilt* ought to be free from suffering, and hence happy' (1966: vol. 2, 603).

Yet, according to Schopenhauer, 'the serious and profound solution of the problem is to be found in the Christian doctrine that works do not justify', a doctrine found in the writings of Paul (see Rom. 3:21–31), St Augustine and Martin Luther. These theologians all teach that 'works cannot justify, since we all are and remain essentially sinners' (Schopenhauer 1966: vol. 2, 603). In its embrace of the doctrine of original sin, Schopenhauer argues, 'the innermost kernel and spirit of Christianity is identical with that of Brahmanism and Buddhism', inasmuch as they

---

[9] KSB 6, 23; cf. letter to Overbeck of 19 July 1880 (KSB 6, 30–1).

'all teach a heavy guilt of the human race through its existence itself, only Christianity does not proceed in this respect directly and openly, like those more ancient religions' (1966: vol. 2, 604). After briefly considering Augustine's treatise *De libero arbitrio* (*On Free Choice of the Will*), Schopenhauer turns back to Paul: 'Paul says that no one is justified before the law; we can be transferred from the state of sinfulness into that of freedom and salvation only by the new birth or regeneration in Jesus Christ, in consequence of the effect of grace, by virtue of which a new man arises and the old man is abolished' (1966: vol. 2, 604–5). Yet Nietzsche's portrait goes considerably beyond these sources in the characteristically polemical verve and energy it displays.

In *Daybreak*, Nietzsche presents Paul as someone without whose 'singular history, without the tribulations and passions of such a mind, and of such a soul, there would have been no Christian kingdom', and 'we should have scarcely have even heard of a little Jewish sect, the founder of which died on the Cross' (D §68). At the same time, while the existence of Paul's writings are the precondition for the growth of Christianity, to understand them correctly would bring about the demise of Christianity:

> It is true that, if this history had been understood in time, if we had read, really read, the writings of St. Paul, not as the revelations of the 'Holy Ghost', but with honest and independent minds, oblivious of all our personal troubles – there were no such readers for fifteen centuries – it would have been all up with Christianity long ago. (D §68)

This reflection prompts Nietzsche to draw a comparison between Paul and Pascal: 'so searchingly do these writings of the Jewish Pascal lay bare the origins of Christianity, just as the French Pascal let us see its destiny and how it will ultimately perish' (D §68).

Nietzsche's reception of Blaise Pascal (1623–62) deserves a chapter in its own right, given the complex fascination exercised on him by this French mathematician and philosopher, and the insights it offers into his view of Christianity. In the 'descent into Hades' undertaken by Nietzsche, like Odysseus (*Odyssey*, book 11), in the second volume of *Human, All Too Human*, Pascal belongs – along with Epicurus and Montaigne, Goethe and Spinoza, Plato and Rousseau, and Schopenhauer – to those four pairs on whom Nietzsche fixes his eyes and whose eyes he sees 'fixed on me' (HAH AOM §408). In *Beyond Good and Evil*, Pascal serves Nietzsche as the great example of Christian spirituality in the form of its supreme sacrifice of the mind (*sacrifizio dell'intelletto*) for reasons of the heart (BGE §229; cf. Lampert 2001: 103). And in *Ecce Homo* Nietzsche describes Pascal as someone whom he *loves* and as 'the most instinctive sacrifice to Christianity, killing himself inch by inch, first bodily, then spiritually, according to the terrible consistency of this most appalling form of inhuman cruelty' (EH Clever §3).[10] In short, Pascal serves Nietzsche as an 'admirable *logician*' of Christianity, even if Pascal's relationship with his sister revealed the terrible consequences of that logic.[11]

But how, in Nietzsche's eyes, did Paul rescue or indeed create Christianity? The amswer is that he did so by removing it from its Jewish context or, as Nietzsche puts it: 'that the ship of Christianity threw over-board no inconsiderable part of its Jewish ballast, that it was able to sail into the waters of the heathen and actually did do so', is all thanks to 'the history of one single man, this apostle who was so greatly troubled in mind and so worthy of pity, but who was also very disagreeable to himself and to others' (D §68).

The starting point for understanding Paul is, in Nietzsche's eyes, two questions: first, 'What is the Jewish *law* really concerned with?'; and second, 'What is the *fulfilment of this law?*' (D §68). The 'law' in question is, of course, the Torah – the five books of the Pentateuch and the rabbinic commentaries on them. The Torah is the central reference point of Judaism, having been given, so it is asserted, by God directly to the Jews; so by questioning the law, Paul is questioning the essence of Judaism. At the outset, however, Paul's position is eminently orthodox:

---

[10] For further discussion, see Williams 1952; Donnellan 1979a; 1979b; Natoli 1985; Voegelin 1996; Boyd 2011; Lebreton 2017.

[11] See WP §388 = KSA 12, 10[128], 531, citing *La Vie de Monsieur Pascal, écrite par Madame Périer*, where Pascal criticises himself for being too lovable (Pascal 1963: 29; cf. Guyau 1887: 162–3).

> In his youth he had done his best to satisfy [the Law], thirsting as he did for that highest distinction which the Jews could imagine – this people, which raised the imagination of moral loftiness to a greater elevation than any other people, and which alone succeeded in uniting the conception of a holy God with the idea of sin considered as an offence against this holiness. (D §68)

And then, on Nietzsche's account, Paul suddenly hits upon a problem – he discovers that he is in fact unable to fulfil this law:

> Now, however, he was aware in his own person of the fact that such a man as himself—violent, sensual, melancholy, and malicious in his hatred—*could* not fulfil the Law; and furthermore, what seemed strangest of all to him, he saw that his boundless craving for power was continually provoked to break it, and that he could not help yielding to this impulse. (D §68)

Nietzsche suggests that Paul might have been a highly problematic individual, although he presents no evidence for this, and Paul's thinking now begins to move in the direction that his inability to fulfil the Law may not have so much to do with him as with the Law itself:

> As he suggests here and there, he had many things on his conscience – hatred, murder, sorcery, idolatry, debauchery, drunkenness, and orgiastic revelry, – and to however great an extent he tried to soothe his conscience, and, even more, his desire for power, by the extreme fanaticism of his worship for and defence of the Law, there were times when the thought struck him: 'It is all in vain! The anguish of the unfulfilled Law cannot be overcome.' (D §68)

At this point Nietzsche draws a parallel between Paul and another key figure in the history of Christianity – the German Protestant reformer Martin Luther (1483–1546):

Luther must have experienced similar feelings, when, in his cloister, he endeavoured to become the ideal man of his imagination; and, as Luther one day began to hate the ecclesiastical ideal, and the Pope, and the saints, and the whole clergy, with a hatred which was all the more deadly as he could not avow it even to himself, an analogous feeling took possession of St. Paul. (D §68)

Paul comes to the conclusion that the problem lies with the Law itself, and he turns his mind to how to destroy it. At the intersection between ideological frustration, spiritual despair and physiological sickness (in the form of an epileptic attack), he experiences a vision:

And at last a liberating thought, together with a vision – which was only to be expected in the case of an epileptic like himself – flashed into his mind: to him, the stern upholder of the Law – who, in his innermost heart, was tired to death of it – there appeared on the lonely path that Christ, with the divine effulgence on His countenance, and Paul heard the words: 'Why persecutest thou Me?' (D §68)

Here Nietzsche is drawing on the account of Paul's conversion found in the Acts of the Apostles, where a light from heaven shines around him, he falls to the ground, and he hears a voice saying, 'Saul, Saul, why dost thou persecute me?' (Acts 9:4; cf. 22:9–12).

This experience, identified by Nietzsche as an epileptic attack, proves a pivotal moment for Paul: 'The sufferer from anguished pride felt himself restored to health all at once, his moral despair disappeared in the air; for morality itself was blown away, annihilated – that is to say, *fulfilled*, there on the Cross!' (D §68). The breakthrough comes for Paul (on Nietzsche's account) in the need now to destroy the Law:

The enormous consequences of this thought, of this solution of the enigma, danced before his eyes, and he at once became the happiest of men. The destiny of the Jews, yea, of all mankind, seemed to him to be intertwined with this instantaneous flash of enlightenment: he held the thought of thoughts, the key of keys, the light of lights; history would henceforth revolve round him! For from that time forward he would be the apostle of the *annihilation of the Law*! (D §68)

Nietzsche does not provide a detailed reading of the Pauline epistles from this interpretative perspective, but he does allude to a couple of passages in support of his reading. The first is an allusion to the First Letter to the Corinthians:

To be dead to sin – that meant to be dead to the Law also; to be in the flesh – that meant to be under the Law! To be one with Christ – that meant to have become, like Him, the destroyer of the Law; to be dead with Him – that meant likewise to be dead to the Law. Even if it were still possible to sin, it would not at any rate be possible to sin against the Law: 'I am above the Law', thinks Paul [. . .] (D §68)

The context of this allusion is Paul's argument in his letter where he invokes his own example as an apostle (1 Cor. 9:19–21). The argumentational logic in this passage is quite complicated, but it operates with a distinction between the Jewish Law, whose ceremonies Paul practised after *his* conversion in order not to hinder *their* conversion, but which is a law he now regards as no longer obligatory, and the new law of Christ, set up in parallel to his behaviour with those who are 'without the law', i.e., the gentiles, who had never been under the Law of Moses (Haydock 2006: 1510).

The second passage cited by Nietzsche comes from the Letter to the Galatians, where Paul is discussing the gospel he has been preaching. The logic of Paul's argument is again complex (and the passage cited by Nietzsche becomes easier to understand when placed in its argumentational context):

But knowing that man is not justified by the works of the law, but by the faith of Jesus Christ; we also believe in

> Christ Jesus, that we may be justified by the faith of Christ, and not by the works of the law: because by the works of the law no flesh shall be justified. But if while we seek to be justified in Christ, we ourselves also are found sinners; is Christ then the minister of sin? God forbid. For if I build up again the things which I have destroyed, I make myself a transgressor. For I, through the law, am dead to the law, that I may live to God: with Christ I am nailed to the cross. And I live, now not I; but Christ liveth in me. And that I live now in the flesh: I live in the faith of the Son of God, who loved me, and delivered himself for me. I cast not away the grace of God. For if justice be by the law, then Christ died in vain. (Gal. 2:16–21, DRV)

Paul's argument here is described by the commentary in the NJB as being 'so laconic as to be obscure', and two possible ways are suggested of understanding it: first, in the sense that Christians, crucified with Christ, are dead with Christ and therefore, like Christ, dead to the Mosaic Law – indeed, they are dead in virtue of that Law. For this reason, Christians may already be said to share the life of the risen Christ (NJB, NT, 1927). And second, in the sense that Christians are dead to the Mosaic Law inasmuch as they exhibit obedience to a higher law, the law of faith and of the Spirit (NJB, NT, 1927). So how does Nietzsche understand this passage?

> 'I am above the Law', thinks Paul; adding, 'If I were now to acknowledge the Law again and to submit to it, I should make Christ an accomplice in the sin'; for the Law was there for the purpose of producing sin and setting it in the foreground, as an emetic produces sickness. God could not have decided upon the death of Christ had it been possible to fulfil the Law without it; henceforth, not only are all sins expiated, but sin itself is abolished; henceforth the Law is dead; henceforth 'the flesh' in which it dwelt is dead – or at all events dying, gradually wasting away. To live for a short time longer amid this decay! this is the Christian's fate, until the time when, having become one with Christ,

he arises with Him, sharing with Christ the divine glory, and becoming, like Christ, a 'Son of God'. (D §68)

Here Nietzsche's reading is remarkably close to those proposed by the commentators of the NJB; in fact, it is almost a synthesis of the two readings offered in the NJB commentary. Yet the conclusion Nietzsche draws from this interpretation is obviously one that is radically opposed to the one implicit in the NJB commentary: 'Then Paul's exaltation was at its height, and with it the importunity of his soul – the thought of union with Christ made him lose all shame, all submission, all constraint, and his ungovernable ambition was shown to be revelling in the expectation of divine glories' (D §68).

So Nietzsche rejects the Pauline ambition to live one's life as if crucified with Christ, so that Christ lives in the believer who becomes, like Christ, a 'son of God'. Thus Nietzsche would also reject the injunction found in one of the *Orations* of St Gregory of Nazianzus, 'Acknowledge that you have been made a son of God, a co-heir with Christ. Acknowledge [. . .] that you have been made divine' (Gregory of Nazianzus 2003: 55–6); and he would equally reject the proposition made by St Basil the Great in his treatise *On the Holy Spirit* that the action of the Spirit endows the souls it illumines with 'foreknowledge of things future, understanding of mysteries, apprehension of things hidden, distribution of spiritual gifts, citizenship in heaven, the dance with the angels, unending joy, divine largesse, likeness to God' – and even 'the desire of all desires, to become god' (Palmer, Sherrard and Ware [eds] 2010: 572).

The role of Paul of Tarsus (AC §§41–3)

Recall that the argumentational context established in section 40 of *The Anti-Christ* had been the shift in the wake of the Crucifixion from such questions as 'Who was that? What was that?' to such questions as 'Why this, of all things' and then 'Who put him to death? Who was his natural enemy?' (AC §40). Now the focus of these questions shifts yet again – this time to 'How *could* God have allowed that?' (AC §41). And at this point the answer is introduced, 'God gave his son as a *sacrifice* for the forgiveness of sins', an answer that Nietzsche describes as 'terrifying in its absurdity' (AC §41). With this doctrine, Nietzsche asserts, the good tidings or the gospel came once and for all to an end – and was replaced by 'the *guilt sacrifice*, and in fact in its most revolting, barbaric form, the sacrifice of the *innocent* for the sins of the *guilty*!' (AC §41). Nietzsche dismisses this doctrine as 'appalling paganism', since on his account Christ had done away precisely with the concept of 'guilt', denying that there was 'a gulf' fixed between humankind and God; indeed, the entire life of Jesus had been an expression of 'this unity between God and human beings', and therein lay the essence of his 'glad tidings' (AC §41).

With the introduction of the doctrine of sacrifice, Nietzsche contends, a whole slew of other doctrines followed, distorting and corrupting Christ's status as a redeemer or saviour: the doctrine of the Second Coming and the Last Judgement, the doctrine of death as a sacrifice, and the doctrine of the Resurrection. All these doctrines project the notion of 'blessedness' away from the present moment and into the future, into a putative state *after* death. And this doctrinal shift is associated for Nietzsche with one figure in particular – St Paul. In his First Letter to the Corinthians, in a long discourse discussing the resurrection of the dead, Paul summarises his stance with arresting succinctness: 'And if Christ be not risen again, your faith is vain' (1 Cor. 15:17). Nietzsche cites this passage, but he omits to quote the remainder of the sentence: 'your faith is in vain, for you are yet in your sins'. This phrase is glossed by the NJB commentary in relation to the argument made by Paul in his letters to the Romans (Rom. 5:12) and to the Philippians (Phil. 2:6) to the effect that 'what makes sin disappear is the new life, particularly in the life of the risen Christ' (NJB, NT, 1909) – a view that is surely not so far removed from Nietzsche's insistence on 'blessedness' as 'the whole and only reality of the gospels' (AC §41). Yet for Nietzsche this moment marks the beginning of one of the most problematic aspects of Christianity as he sees it, 'the *shameless* doctrine of personal immortality', taught by Paul as a 'reward' (AC §41).

This also marks the 'fundamental difference', as Nietzsche sees it, between, on the one hand, Buddhism and, on the other,

Christianity: both are, in his view, 'religions of decadence', but whereas Buddhism 'promises nothing, yet actually fulfils', Christianity 'promises everything, yet *fulfils nothing*' (AC §42). And against this backdrop Nietzsche commences his portrait in *The Anti-Christ* of the figure who is in some ways presented quite literally as an *anti*-Christ, Paul of Tarsus – the embodiment or incarnation of 'the antithesis of the "bringer of glad tidings", the genius in hatred, in the vision of hatred, in the merciless logic of hatred' (AC §42). Nietzsche's invective is so ferocious that it is memorable; when in 1983 Karen Armstrong presented her landmark TV series on Paul on Britain's Channel 4, it was Nietzsche's words that she used at the outset to summarise her misgivings about him:

> *What*, indeed, has this dysangelist sacrificed to hatred! Above all, the Saviour: he nailed him to *his own* cross. The life, the example, the teaching, the death of Christ, the meaning and the law of the whole gospels – nothing was left of all this after that counterfeiter in hatred had reduced it to his uses. (AC §42; cf. Armstrong 1983: 15)

Such a view of Paul is, of course, in the starkest possible contrast to the respect in which he is held in Christian doctrine, arguably across all denominations. Paul's pre-eminence in Roman Catholicism is reflected in the fact that he is remembered on two feast days, the Feast of the Conversion of St Paul (25 January) and the shared Feast of Saints Peter and Paul (29 June) (with, in the former liturgical calendar, a extra commemoration of Paul the Apostle on 30 June), while for good measure a separate feast commemorates the dedication of the basilicas of Saints Peter and Paul (18 November).[12] On Malta, a special holiday observed on 10 February commemorates the Feast of St Paul's shipwreck, as described in Acts 28. In the Orthodox tradition, Paul is celebrated as (together with Peter) one of the two holy, glorious

---

[12] On the liturgical significance of the Feast of Saints Peter and Paul, see Guéranger 2000b: 311.

and all-praised leaders of the apostles, and the fast of these two saints is one of the four seasonal fasts, that is, the summer fast that commences nine days after Pentecost and continues until their joint feast day on 29 June. And throughout the history of theology Paul has served as the inspiration for numerous thinkers and movements, including Augustine, Luther, John Calvin (1509–64), Karl Barth (1886–1968) and the Second Vatican Council (1962–65).

As is his wont, Nietzsche tells us very little about St Paul, relying on the fact that the reader will know all about him – which today may very well *not* be the case. Paul was born in Tarsus in Cilicia, today part of Turkey; in Paul's time, however, it was one of the largest trading centres on the coast of the Mediterranean, and home to a renowned university, an important centre of Stoic philosophy. (The fusion of the Greek concept of *logos* with the figure of Christ was a crucial step in the development of Christian theology, as Pope Benedict XVI reminded an audience in 2007.)[13] Yet Paul originally identified himself as a Jew, writing in his Letter to the Philippians: 'Being circumcised the eighth day, of the stock of Israel, of the tribe of Benjamin, a Hebrew of the Hebrews, as to the law a Pharisee, as to zeal, persecuting the church of God, as to the justice that is in the law, conversing without blame' (Phil. 3:5–6). To the extent that he regarded himself as a Jew, Paul had much in common with Jesus, who, however, spent all his life in the Holy Land. In the case of Paul, however, there were important Greco-Roman aspects to his life and thought (and appreciating these is crucial for understanding both his theology and Nietzsche's objections to it).

First, as a son of an economically thriving and intellectually sophisticated Greek city, Paul spoke – and wrote – in Greek. As such, he would have known the scriptures not in Hebrew, but in their Greek translation, the Septuagint, so named after the seventy (or 72) Jewish scholars who translated the Torah into Greek at the instigation of Ptolemy II Philadelphus. This is an important

---

[13] See the General Audience given on 21 March 2007, focusing on the figure of Justin Martyr (c. 100–165) (Benedict 2008: 20–1).

philological point: in effect, Paul's knowledge of Jewish scripture (written in Hebrew) would have been through the linguistic prism of Greek. Yet curiously, Paul seems to have had no interest in the Greek philosophical tradition; the attribution to him of a correspondence with Seneca, a leading Stoic philosopher, is spurious (Grant 1915). Indeed, in some of his remarks Paul apparently shows himself to be positively anti-intellectual. In the first chapter of his First Letter to the Corinthians, Paul equates human wisdom with folly, writing (in words that echo the prophet Isaiah):

> For the word of the cross, to them indeed that perish, is foolishness; but to them who are saved, that is, to us, it is the power of God. For it is written: I will destroy the wisdom of the wise: and the prudence of the prudent I will reject. Where is the wise? Where is the scribe? Where is the disputer of this world? Hath not God made foolish the wisdom of this world? (1 Cor. 1:18–90; cf. Isa. 29:14; 32:18)

And in the third chapter of this letter Paul returns to this theme, warning: 'Let no man deceive himself: if any man among you seem to be wise in this world, let him become a fool that he may be wise. For the wisdom of this world is foolishness with God. For it is written: I will catch the wise in their own craftiness' (1 Cor. 3:18–19; cf. Job 5:18).

Second, Paul was a Roman citizen. At the time, the Romans were the occupying force in the Holy Land, a usurpation of the territory of the 'chosen race' that had both religious and political implications. The Roman occupation is in the background to the New Testament narrative – Herod the Great (born c. 74 BCE, ruled 37–4 BCE), a vassal king of Judea, had rebuilt the Temple in Jerusalem, and features in the New Testament as the king who is involved in the visit of the Magi, the flight into Egypt and the massacre of the Innocents (Matt. 2:1–18). One of his sons, Herod Antipas (born 21 BCE, ruled 4 BCE –39 CE), the tetrarch of Galilee and Peraea (the figure known in the New Testament outside the infancy narrative as King Herod), appears in the New Testament in relation to the beheading of John the Baptist (Matt. 14:1–12; Mark 6:14–29; Luke 3:1–20) and the mocking of Christ before his crucifixion (Luke 23:8–12). It is Herod the tetrarch whom Christ describes as a wily 'fox' (Luke 13:31–3), in one of those passages where Christ himself uses strong invective.

Being a Roman citizen gave Paul important privileges: when he was arrested in Jerusalem, for instance, it enabled him to demand to be tried by a Roman court, and it is after he was sent under escort by Festus the procurator to Rome where he lived for two years that our knowledge of his life based on biblical sources ends. The fact that the Romans had constructed an empire with trading routes connecting its different parts allowed Paul to travel – and to spread the word, so to speak, of the gospel. In this respect, Paul is known as the 'apostle to the gentiles', whereas Peter and many of the other apostles preached largely to fellow Jews.

Paul's preaching began after his famous conversion, before which he had built a reputation for himself as one of the fiercest persecutors of the early Christians. Paul was involved, for instance, in the martyrdom of Stephen (Acts 7:58; 22:20). Yet when he was on the road to Damascus, circa 34 CE, he underwent a miraculous conversion, described by Luke in the Acts of the Apostles (Acts 9:3–16) and alluded to by Paul himself in his Letter to the Galatians (Gal. 1:12, 15–16) and possibly in his Second Letter to the Corinthians (2 Cor. 12:1–6). Thereafter Paul dedicated himself to serving Christ as one of his followers, writing in his Letter to the Philippians:

> Not as though I had already attained, or were already perfect: but I follow after, if I may by any means apprehend that in which I am also apprehended by Christ Jesus. Brethren, I do not count myself to have apprehended. But one thing *I do*: forgetting the things that are behind, and stretching forth myself to those that are before, I pursue towards the mark, for the prize of the supernal vocation, of God in Christ Jesus. (Phil. 3:12–14)

After spending some time in Arabia (Armstrong 1983: 56–7), Paul returned to Damascus where he began preaching. After a short visit to Jerusalem, Paul set off for Syria and Cilicia, until he was brought back to Antioch by another apostle, Barnabas, from where they set sail on Paul's first missionary journey. It was on this journey that Paul started using his Greek name, Paul, rather than Saul, and in 49 CE he went to Jerusalem with Barnabas as deputies from Antioch, a meeting that cemented the strategy whereby Paul and Barnabas would serve as the apostles to the gentiles, while the leaders of the church in Jerusalem would act as 'the apostles to the circumcised' (Gal. 2:90). Subsequently Paul set out on two further missionary journeys, in 50–52 CE from Syria to Macedonia and Greece and in 53–58 CE from Syria to Galatia, Macedonia, Greece, Ephesus and Jerusalem, respectively. In 58 CE, Paul was arrested in Jerusalem and imprisoned at Caesarea Palestinae; sent to Rome where he stayed for two years, tradition has it that his case was dismissed for lack of evidence and he travelled again in the East, and possibly to Spain. According to tradition, he was imprisoned a second time in Rome and ended his life as a martyr in 67 CE.

None of this detail is mentioned by Nietzsche, who presumably took it for granted that it would be familiar to his readers; and indeed, we need to know it in order to understand the case that he builds against Paul. In part, that critique is all the more remarkable for what it does *not* say about Paul, so let us consider first why Nietzsche rejects Paul of Tarsus as a 'dysangelist' and as a 'genius in hatred' (AC §42). The chief objection made by Nietzsche is that Paul was responsible for the falsification of history, or in his words: 'Once more the priestly instinct of the Jew perpetrated the same old master crime against history – he simply struck out the yesterday and the day before yesterday of Christianity, and *invented his own history of Christian beginnings*' (AC §42). Not only did Paul invent for himself a history of the first Christianity, he went further and 'treated the history of Israel to another falsification, so that it became a mere prologue to *his* achievement: all the prophets, it now appeared, had referred to *his* "Saviour"' (AC §42). In effect, Nietzsche is restating his objection to Christianity on *philological grounds*, and the manoeuvre that Nietzsche associates with Paul was to become a blueprint for the later argumentation of the Church Fathers: 'Later on the Church even falsified the history of man in order to make it a prologue to Christianity' (AC §42). The operational shift effected by Paul was, in Nietzsche's view, a massive one – from the entire life of Christ as it had been lived and experienced to a single, unique focus on his death:

> The figure of the Saviour, his teaching, his way of life, his death, the meaning of his death, even the consequences of his death – nothing remained untouched, nothing remained in even remote contact with reality. Paul simply shifted the centre of gravity of that whole life to a place *behind* this existence – in the *lie* of the 'risen' Jesus. At bottom, he had no use for the life of the Saviour – what he needed was the death on the Cross, *and* something more. (AC §42)

Nietzsche notes that Paul's home town had been Tarsus, 'at the centre of the Stoical enlightenment' (AC §42), but he regards Paul's thinking as influenced not so much by Stoic philosophy as by his own personal psychology: as someone who had 'convert[ed] an hallucination into *proof* of the resurrection of the Saviour' – or had even gone so far as make up '[t]his tale that he suffered from this hallucination' (AC §42). On Nietzsche's account, Paul was someone who 'willed the end'; and '*therefore* he also willed the means' (AC §42). Thus for Nietzsche, Paul was someone who was fundamentally dishonest, and prepared to deceive as many people as possible in order to gain one thing – power:

> What *he* wanted was power; in Paul the priest once more reached out for power – had use only for such concepts, teachings, and symbols as served the purpose of tyrannizing over the masses and organizing mobs [. . .] Paul's invention, his device for establishing priestly tyranny and organizing the mob: the belief in the immortality of the soul – that is to say, the *doctrine of 'judgment'*. (AC §42)

For Nietzsche, these two doctrines, the immortality of the soul and the doctrine of judgement, are two sides of the same erroneous coin – a coin which elsewhere he identifies as one of the four great errors and defines as 'the error of free will' (TI Errors §7).

The consequence of this error, so he goes on to argue in section 43 of *The Anti-Christ*, is nihilism.

Nihilism, for Nietzsche, arises 'when the centre of gravity of life is placed, *not* in life itself, but in "the beyond" – in *nothingness* – then one has taken away its centre of gravity altogether' (AC §43).[14] As opposed to the Goethean vitalism espoused by Nietzsche which says that 'the point of life is life',[15] the Christian doctrine developed by Paul, i.e., personal immortality, evacuates all meaning from life in general and our instinctual life in particular:

> The vast lie of personal immortality destroys all reason, all natural instinct – henceforth, everything in the instincts that is beneficial, that fosters life and that safeguards the future is a cause of suspicion. So to live that life no longer has any meaning. *This* is now the 'meaning' of life . . . (AC §43)

In other words, Nietzsche's argument is that belief operates a reorientation of one's existential priorities in a way that is profoundly detrimental to one's well-being, individual and collective.

To explain what he means, Nietzsche refers back to an episode found in the Gospel of Luke, the famous story of Martha and Mary. In this episode (which attracted the attention of, for instance, Meister Eckhart in at least two of his sermons),[16] Jesus comes to a village and is welcomed into her house by a woman called Martha. Martha has a sister, Mary, who sits down at Jesus' feet and listens to him as he speaks. (The fact that these two sisters also appear in the story of the raising of Lazarus, found in John 11:1–44, suggests that we are dealing with two separate narrative traditions which have somehow become interlinked.) Martha is

---

[14] For further discussion of the concept of nihilism in *The Anti-Christ*, see Young 2007; Brock 2015; van Tongeren 2018; Emden 2019.

[15] See Goethe's letter to Johann Heinrich Meyer of 8 February 1796 (in *Briefe* [Hamburger Ausgabe], vol. 2, 215).

[16] See, in the sermons as translated by Walshe, sermon 8 (= Pfeiffer 8; Quint, *Deutsche Werke*, 2) and sermon 9 (= Pfeiffer 9; Quint, *Deutsche Werke*, 86; Evans, II.2). See Meister Eckhart 1987: 71–8 and 79–90. For further discussion of Nietzsche and Meister Eckhart, see Schoeller-Reisch 1998.

distracted by all the serving, and she complains that her sister is not helping her. Far from acknowledging the justice of her complaint, Jesus gently chides her: 'Martha, Martha, thou art careful, and art troubled about many things. But one thing is necessary. Mary hath chosen the best part, which shall not be taken away from her' (Luke 10:41–2).

This phrase, 'one thing is needful', was picked up by Nietzsche earlier in *The Anti-Christ* in the context of his discussion of Buddhism in section 20 (see Chapter 3 above). There, Nietzsche had related the phrase to the way in which Buddhism, in his view, relates everything back to the person, making a duty of egoism. Here, Nietzsche uses the phrase to capture an attitude that is inimical to everything he considers to be beneficial: 'Why be public-spirited? Why take any pride in descent and forefathers? Why labour together, trust one another, or concern one's self about the common welfare, and try to serve it? . . . Merely so many "temptations", so many strayings from the "straight path" –' (AC §43).

As becomes clear, Nietzsche objects to the doctrine of personal immortality, not simply because it is (in his view) not true, but because of what he regards as its *political* implications – the doctrine of '*equal* rights for everyone' (AC §43). Nietzsche's argument here is that the doctrine of personal immortality translates into the political doctrine of equality, conferring on *everyone*, irrespective of rank or worth, an equal claim to the possibility of eternal 'salvation' – so that 'insignificant bigots and the three-fourths insane may assume that the laws of nature are constantly *suspended* on their behalf' (AC §43). This is the error that Nietzsche had identified in *Twilight of the Idols* as 'the error of imaginary causes', a concept under which 'the entire realm of morality and religion falls' (TI Errors §6). And so Nietzsche returns to some of his favourite themes: the triumph of *ressentiment*, the erosion of the *pathos of distance* and the abolition of *noble* values:

> The poisonous doctrine, '*equal* rights for all', has been propagated as a Christian principle: out of the secret nooks and crannies of bad instinct Christianity has waged a deadly war upon all feelings of reverence and distance between man and man, which is to say, upon the first *prerequisite* to every

step upward, to every development of civilization – out of the *ressentiment* of the masses it has forged its chief weapons against *us*, against everything noble, joyous and high spirited on earth, against our happiness on earth . . . To allow 'immortality' to every Peter and Paul was the greatest, the most vicious outrage upon *noble* humanity ever perpetrated. (AC §43)

Thus Nietzsche's critique of Paul turns out to be a special instance of his more general critique of Judeo-Christianity, a critique that regards Christianity as 'a revolt of all creatures that creep on the ground against everything that is lofty: the gospel of the "lowly" lowers' (AC §43).

In section 45, Nietzsche reveals his talent for humour (albeit humour of a dark and rather twisted kind) by selecting various passages from the New Testament and offering an ironic commentary on them. After a sequence of passages from the Gospels, Nietzsche turns to the letters of Paul. The First Letter to the Corinthians provides him with several occasions for barbed remarks (see 1 Cor. 3:16 and 1 Cor. 6:2), culminating in a lengthy quotation from the end of this letter's first chapter (1 Cor. 1:20–1, 26–9). At this point, Nietzsche advises the reader to consult the first essay in *On the Genealogy of Morals*, which advances the distinction between 'good and evil' and 'good and bad', in order that the reader may '*understand* this passage' as 'a first rate example of the psychology underlying every Chandala-morality' (AC §45) – the morality, that is, of those who deal with the disposal of corpses and are thus, within the Hindu caste system, the lowest caste, considered to be untouchable. For in the *Genealogy*, Nietzsche claims, he had exposed for the first time 'the antagonism between a *noble* morality and a morality born of *ressentiment* and impotent vengefulness' (AC §45). As such, Nietzsche regards Paul as 'the greatest of all apostles of revenge' (AC §45).

From this perspective, Nietzsche argues that 'one had better put on gloves before reading the New Testament' (AC §46), and one recalls that, in *On the Genealogy of Morals*, Nietzsche had contrasted the 'Old Testament' (and its 'great human beings, a heroic landscape, and [. . .] the incomparable naïveté of the *strong heart*' and 'a people') with the New (and its 'petty sectarianism, mere rococo of the soul, mere involutions, nooks, queer things, the air of the conventicle, not to forget an occasional whiff of bucolic mawkishness that belongs to the epoch (*and* to the Roman province) and is not so much Jewish as Hellenistic') (GM III §22). In particular, he had made a jibe at St Peter: 'An "immortal" Peter: who could stand him?' (GM III §22). Here Nietzsche sets up an opposition between Paul and Petronius, the Roman satirist who wrote a celebrated novel during the reign of Nero, the *Satyricon*. Nietzsche applies to Petronius the words attributed to Domenico (= Giovanni) Boccaccio in conversation with the Duke of Parma about Cesare Borgia, '*è tutto festo*', i.e., 'all is festive' (AC §46).[17] 'Immortally healthy, immortally cheerful and sound' – whatever one makes of the writings of Paul, 'festiveness' is not really one of their striking qualities.

Hence Nietzsche's disdain for Paul's attacks on the 'wisdom of this world ' (1 Cor. 1:20), for his desire to be 'chosen by God' (1 Cor. 1:27), to be a 'temple of God' (1 Cor. 3:16), or to be a 'judge of angels' (1 Cor. 6:2), all of which Nietzsche regards as being in opposition to 'every *other* criterion, whether based upon honesty, upon intellect, upon manliness and pride, or upon beauty and freedom of the heart', all of which are rejected by Paul and his followers as 'worldly', indeed as '*evil in itself*' (AC §46). Against the figure of Paul, Nietzsche sets up the Roman governor, Pontius Pilate, as the '*one* figure worthy of honour' in the New Testament, since 'to regard a Jewish imbroglio *seriously* – that was quite beyond him' (AC §46).

Aside from this provocative act of comparison, Nietzsche recurs to his argument that Paul's attack on the 'wisdom of this world' is, in fact, an attack on *science* – or scholarship. 'A religion such as Christianity, which does not touch reality at a single point and which goes to pieces the moment reality asserts its rights at any point' can only be opposed to *Wissenschaft*, but Nietzsche has a particular 'science' in mind – philology. Paul's enemies, Nietzsche claims, are 'the *good* philologians and physicians of the

---

[17] On the confusion of names, see NK 6/2, 216–17.

Alexandrian School – on them he makes his war' (AC §47).[18] Herein lies the essence of Nietzsche's argument and the thinking behind the title of his book: 'As a matter of fact no man can be a *philologian* or a physician without being also *Antichrist* [*anti-Christian*]' (AC §47). And this is because 'as a philologian one looks *behind* the holy books, and as a physician one looks *behind* the physiological degeneration of the typical Christian' – where the physician sees something that is 'incurable', the philologist sees something that is in many ways for Nietzsche much worse – 'fraud' (AC §47).

In opposition to Paul, Nietzsche later sets up the figure of the ancient Greek philosopher Epicurus (341–270 BCE), the founder of the school of Epicureanism. In section 58, Epicurus is presented as combating '*not* paganism, but "Christianity", which is to say, the corruption of souls by means of the concepts of guilt, punishment and immortality' (AC §58). On Nietzsche's account, 'Epicurus had triumphed, and every respectable intellect in Rome was Epicurean – *when Paul appeared* . . .' (AC §58); and, with the appearance of Paul, everything is said to go into reverse:

> Paul, the Chandala hatred of Rome, of 'the world', in the flesh and inspired by genius [*der Fleisch-, der Genie-gewordne Tchandala-Hass gegen Rom, gegen die „Welt"*] – the Jew, the *eternal* Jew *par excellence* . . . What he saw was how, with the aid of the small sectarian Christian movement that stood apart from Judaism, a 'world conflagration' might be kindled; how, with the symbol of 'God on the cross', all secret seditions, all the fruits of anarchistic intrigues in the empire, might be amalgamated into one immense power. 'Salvation is of the Jews.' (AC §58)

---

[18] By the Alexandrian School, Nietzsche is not thinking so much of the syncretic mix of Jewish theology and Greek Neoplatonic philosophy found in the writings of Clement of Alexandria and Origen, as of the flowering of literature, philosophy, medicine and sciences in Alexandria during the Hellenistic and Roman periods, reflected in the remarkable collection built up in the great Library of Alexandria. See NK 6/2, 223–4.

By giving substance – for example, in Romans 9:4–5 – to the words recorded in the Gospel of John as having been spoken by Christ in his conversation with the Samaritan woman (John 4:22), Paul substitutes in Nietzsche's eyes the *ressentiment*-laden theology of Judaism for the nobility of Epicurean hedonism. This substitution is carried out through Paul's rereading and reinterpretation of Hebrew scripture.[19]

Thus Nietzsche's charge against Paul is *philological* – and it is significant that there are other possible charges against him that Nietzsche chooses *not* to make. After all, there is plenty of material in the life and thought of Paul that would make him a fit subject for the kind of critique that Nietzsche endorses, i.e., a psychological one (cf. AC §42). Michel Onfray has, for example, contrasted the radically anti-hedonist stance found in the writings of Paul – a hatred of the body, of life, of women and of sexuality – with the surprising absence of such an anti-hedonist stance in the sayings of Jesus, who does not express opposition to marriage, does not embrace the ascetic ideal, does not offer prescriptions about sexuality or food, and in fact sings the praises of being meek, mild and gentle (Onfray 2006b: 11–45; 2007a: 131–9; 2017: 65–82).

Indeed, Onfray describes Paul as certifiably hysterical, someone who persecutes the Church to the extent of being involved with the stoning of Stephen, and whose conversion on the road to Damascus hints at significant hysterical traits or disorders. First, he demonstrates a histrionic personality disorder (he falls down in public); second, he suffers a temporary amaurosis fugax (blinded by a light, he loses his sight for three days); third, he suffers from sensory hallucinations coupled with a tendency to mythomaniac or pathological lying (he claims to have heard the voice of Jesus, speaking to him); fourth, he suffers from ageusia and anosmia, the loss of taste and the loss of sense of smell (he goes for three

---

[19] It is surely no coincidence that Nietzsche adverts to this language again in *Ecce Homo* when he uses this phrase to describe his own revaluation of all values, his name for his project to undo (or creatively exploit) the damage done by Pauline Christianity; or, as Nietzsche puts it, '*the transvaluation of all values*, this is my formula for humankind's greatest step towards coming to its senses – a step which in me became flesh and genius [*der in mir Fleisch und Genie geworden ist*]' (EH Why I am a Destiny §1).

days without eating or drinking anything); his mythomania, *pseudologia fantastica* or pathological lying is demonstrated once again when he recovers his sight after the imposition of hands in the house of Judas by Ananias, a Christian believer whom God has sent; and finally, he evinces moral exhibitionism when he subsequently recovers, sits down to eat, regains his strength and sets off to preach the gospel across the Roman world.

In terms of his physical appearance, Paul is said to have been small, bald, thin, bearded,[20] and tormented by a mysterious affliction that he describes in the Second Letter to the Corinthians: 'There was given me a string of my flesh, an angel of Satan, to buffet me' (2 Cor. 12:7). Various interpretations of this 'thorn in the flesh' have been suggested, from the resistance of Paul's Jewish brothers to the Christian faith to some kind of a disease that led to severe, unforeseeable attacks (NJB, NT, 1923). Haydock suggests a whole variety of interpretations: a violent headache or pain, or some kind of distemper of the body, as St Augustine suggests in his commentaries on Psalm 98[99] and on Psalm 130[131]; the opposition Paul met from his enemies and the enemies of the gospel, as St John Chrysostom believes; or 'troublesome temptations of the flesh, immodest thoughts, and representations suggested by the devil, and permitted by Almighty God for [Paul's] greater good' (Haydock 2006: 1533). To the extent that there was a sexual dimension to this 'thorn in the flesh', then it would be consistent with the diagnosis of Paul as an hysteric to conclude that he suffered from a weak or absent libido; or from excessive libido, leading him to see sexual matters everywhere. In fact, hysteria is said to result from a struggle with repressed anxieties arising from one's sexuality, and it might involve a partial realisation of these anxieties under the narrative of the conversion experience.

Onfray suggests that the psychology behind Paul's thinking was very simple, in that Paul solved the problem of how to live with a neurosis by turning the whole world into a neurosis. Because Paul was born with a body he detested – in his

---

[20] While the NT offers no information about Paul's physical appearance, several descriptions can be found in apocryphal texts.

first Letter to the Corinthians, he famously describes himself as 'one born out of due time' or an abortion (1 Cor. 15:8) – he sought to rid himself of this self-hatred or self-loathing by anathematising everything to do with sexuality, both his own and everyone else's. So when Paul tells the Corinthians, 'But I chastise my body, and bring it into subjection' (1 Cor. 9:27), this self-mortification and self-denial are offered as a model for others to follow.

Onfray sees a connection between the portrait of Paul as he finds it in the New Testament – as someone who is a fanatic, as someone who is sick, misogynist and masochistic, someone dominated by the death drive – and the kind of world to which this belief-system has given rise: its ideological brutality, its intellectual intolerance, its cult of ill-health, its hatred of the body and its ecstasies, its disdain for women, its pleasure in inflicting pain, and its devalorisation of this world in relation to the putative next. All these characteristics and qualities can be found in the celebrated passage in the Second Letter to the Corinthians where Paul declares, 'Therefore I take pleasure in my infirmities, in reproaches, in necessities, in persecutions, in distresses for Christ's sake. For when I am weak, then I am strong' (2 Cor. 12:10).

Although Haydock notes its proximity to a pagan outlook, as found in Seneca's *calamitas virtutis occasio est*, or Pliny's *Optimos nos esse, dum infirmi sumus*,[21] for Onfray, this is a quintessentially Christian, i.e., Pauline, sentiment – it is an expression of an essentially masochistic outlook. In this second Corinthian epistle, Paul lists the physical abuse he has suffered: flagellated five times (thirty-nine lashes on each occasion); beaten with sticks three times; even stoned on one occasion (in Lystra in Anatolia); shipwrecked three times, once spending an entire night and a day in the open sea; in addition to which, he spent two years in prison (2 Cor. 11:23–5). He vividly evokes the dangers of his travels: in danger from rivers, in danger from brigands, in danger from his fellow Jews and from

---

[21] 'Calamity is virtue's opportunity' (Seneca, *De providentia*, ch. 4, §6); and 'We are most virtuous when we are in bad health' (Pliny, *Epistles*, book 7, letter 26); see Haydock 2006: 1533.

the gentiles, in danger in the towns and in danger in the open country, in danger at sea and in danger from people pretending to help him. He tells of how he has worked with unsparing energy, often without sleep, without food or drink, without clothing – tired, cold, hungry and thirsty (2 Cor. 11:26–7). After all this, for Paul to be imprisoned, and finally decapitated, in Rome forms the culmination of a masochist's life.

Like Nietzsche, Onfray sees Paul's thought as a thought informed by hatred; a hatred of himself that becomes projected into three other areas – a hatred of women, a hatred of freedom and a hatred of intelligence. On this account, Pauline thought recycles the Jewish misogyny of the Hebrew scriptures, as reflected in the story of the Garden of Eden in which Eve is responsible for the original sin. The misogynistic view of women as being a weaker sex, representing a danger of temptation or seduction for men, is reflected in Paul's injunctions to women to obey men in silent submission, to fear their husbands, and not to teach or make laws. The route to salvation for women from this perspective lies solely in maternity.

A second worrying aspect of Pauline thought is its hatred of freedom. On this account, Paul is responsible for implicitly supporting the institution of slavery, through his celebration of cultivating a submissive and obedient attitude. More generally, Paul is responsible for valorising submission to those in political authority. On the basis that to disobey those in authority means to disobey God, divine approval is thus given to poverty, misery and unjust inequality. Paul seems to have gone out of his way to flatter the Romans, and to offer no resistance whatsoever to the imperial authorities. The passage on civil obedience in Paul's Letter to the Romans (Rom. 13:1–7) equates submission to civil authority with submission to God, and can be used as a justification for paying taxes to tax collectors, obeying the army and the police, and respecting, regardless of whether they deserve it or not, all magistrates, ministers and kings.

The third area where Paul expresses his hatred has to do with his hatred of intelligence. In part, this is part of his cultural inheritance from the Book of Genesis, with its opposition between the Tree of Life and the Tree of Knowledge (of Good and Evil). As a Jew, Paul would have known the Hebrew scriptures (albeit in their Greek form), but he would not have made an in-depth study of them. According to the Acts of the Apostles, Paul's professional occupation was as a tent-maker (Acts 18:1–3), and the literary style of his Greek is generally considered to be rough and comparatively unsophisticated; as the introduction to the writings of Paul in the NJB puts it, he 'never attempted Attic elegance' (NJB, NT, 1852). Sometimes his grammar is wrong and his sentences unfinished; sometimes his thought is too fast, too emotional; and often he did not write letters but (as was common practice at the time) dictated them.

While the commentary in the NJB sees in these stylistic infelicities a reflection of Paul's deliberate avoidance of rhetoric so as to convince his audience not by the *form* but by the *content* of his religious message (NJB, NT, 1852), Onfray sees them as evidence of Paul's lack of culture and learning. This very lack of education becomes, however, an integral part of his message: in his letters to the Corinthians and to Timothy, his readers are invited to reject philosophy outright. The members of his audience would have been equally uneducated, even illiterate: weavers, dyers, craft workers, carpenters. To these people Paul's message would have been: turn away from intelligence – turn away from yourselves, from the world, from women, from freedom, from education, from culture.

Although Onfray might share Nietzsche's rejection of Christianity, it is clear from this portrait that he paints of Paul that his critique of Pauline thought is far more wide-ranging than Nietzsche's. At the same time, consideration of his arguments exposes some of the possible flaws not just in his critique but in Nietzsche's as well. For Paul presents us with a paradox: while, on the one hand, a tradition of theological commentary has developed that doubts the authenticity of Paul's letters and indeed his very existence, on the other, the Pauline writings continue to offer a resource for philosophical and theological reflection.

From the time that Nietzsche was working on *The Anti-Christ* (1887–88), there are notes that were included in the selection of *Nachlass* material that came to be known as *The Will to Power*. In one of these sections, which in the estimation of Walter Kaufmann contains formulations that 'seem better than any of the parallel passages in Nietzsche's works' (Nietzsche 1968c: 103), Nietzsche offers 'a psychology of Paul', emphasising that his approach is an essentially *psychological* one (WP §171 = KSA 13, 14[57], 244–5). (This approach was later turned against Nietzsche himself by Ludwig Klages in his 1926 study of the 'psychological achievements' of Nietzsche [Klages 1926a].) This *psychological* approach is, however, just one side of the coin of Nietzsche's critique of Paul in particular and Christianity in general, the other of which is *philological*. So in the next and final chapter we must turn to the role played by philology in Nietzsche's approach to Christianity in general and in *The Anti-Christ* in particular, considering in turn his critique of philology and his own philological strategies.

7
Nietzsche on Philology

In section 52 of *The Anti-Christ*, Nietzsche turns to consider '*unfitness for philology*' as a chief characteristic of theologians, listed second only to their '*impulse to lie*' (AC §52). What does Nietzsche mean by philology? In this section, anticipating his later remarks in section 59, Nietzsche defines philology as 'the art of reading well, – to be able to read facts *without* falsifying them through interpretations, *without* letting the desire to understand make you lose caution, patience, subtlety' (AC §52). In fact, philology as a discipline had long been one of Nietzsche's greatest concerns.[1] In *Daybreak*, he mused, 'I have not been a philologist in vain, perhaps I am one yet' (*Man ist nicht umsonst Philologe gewesen, man ist es vielleicht noch*) (D Preface §5), and Nietzsche's philological training is evident in his philosophical instrumentarium of such concepts as 'text', 'genealogy', 'interpretation', 'perspectivism', and not least in his rejection of Christianity.

Nietzsche's critique of philology

As Christian Benne has argued, in *The Anti-Christ* Nietzsche stages a confrontation between the culture of Hellenistic scholarship in Alexandria and the Stoic-based approach of allegoresis (AC §47), proposing instead a 'sceptical science' – symbolised by the term

---

[1] For further discussion, see William Arrowsmith's introduction to 'We Classicists' (Nietzsche 1990: 307–20); Porter 2000; the linking passages in Bishop (ed.) 2012, as well as Benne 2005; and Balaudé and Wotling (eds) 2012.

ephexis or a 'suspension of judgement' – that derives from the Bonn School of historical-critical philology (AC §52; see Benne 2005). In *Ecce Homo*, Nietzsche expressed the hope that he would find 'a reader such as I deserve, and one who reads me just as the good old philologists used to read their Horace' (EH Books §5); elsewhere, he explains that such a reader would possess 'delicate fingers and eyes' (*mit den zarten Fingern und Augen*) and 'a refined and excellent tact and taste' (*der gute, der feine Takt*) (D Foreword §5; AC §59). As becomes clear from his letter to Paul Deussen of 4 April 1867, Nietzsche attached an almost ethical value to philology as a discipline— 'every great task [. . .] has an ethical influence', for 'the effort of concentrating material and shaping it harmonically is a stone falling into the life of our soul: from the narrow circle many other further ones emerge' (KSB 2, 206) – while in *Daybreak* Nietzsche hailed the 'passion for truth' (cf. KSA 9, 6[457], 6[459], 6[461], 316), describing it as 'one of our most recent virtues, not yet quite mature, frequently misconstrued and misunderstood' and as 'a virtue in process of becoming' (D §456; cf. Vivarelli 2007: 430).

In his lecture material from 1870–71, published as *Encyclopädie der klassischen Philologie*, Nietzsche urged his students that, 'because how something is handed down is usually the text itself, we have to learn to *read* again', and insisting: 'We have to learn to *read* again: something which, with the predominance of the printed word, we have forgotten how to do' (§8; KGW II.3, 373; cf. 404; cited in Benne 2005: 152). In the concluding section of his *Encyclopädie*, Nietzsche summarised the significance (in his eyes) of classical philology as follows:

> However dark the world might be: if one suddenly introduces into it a piece of Hellenic life, it immediately brightens up. They [the Greeks] transfigure the history of antiquity and are in fact a place of refuge for every serious human being. So I hope I have showed you the task of philology: as a means of transfiguring one's existence and that of the rising generation. (KGW II.3, 437; cited in Wilson 1996: 115)

In the second of his *Untimely Meditations*, 'On the Uses and Disadvantages of History for Life', Nietzsche praised the (antiquarian) historian for having 'an ability to feel his way back and sense how things were, to detect traces almost extinguished, to read the past quickly and correctly no matter how intricate its palimpsest may be – these are his talents and virtues' (UM 2 §3). He associates this with Goethe's admiration in his essay 'On German Architecture' (1773) for Erwin von Steinbach (c. 1244–1318), the main architect responsible for the construction of Strasbourg Cathedral; with Jacob Burckhardt's famous account, *The Civilization of the Renaissance in Italy*; and with Barthold Georg Niebuhr's history of ancient Rome (UM 2 §3). And in *Human, All Too Human*, Nietzsche defines 'the historic sense' as being 'that out of given instances we can quickly reconstruct such systems of thoughts and feelings, just as we can mentally reconstruct a temple out of a few pillars and remains of walls accidentally left standing' (HAH I §274). The historical approach undertaken by philology is later extended by Nietzsche into his preference for using *genealogy* to understand morality (Benne 2005); in short, it is no exaggeration to talk about the birth of Nietzschean philosophy from the spirit of philology (Sommer 2007: 400).

Indeed, Nietzsche's blend of philological and philosophical concepts is one of the reasons for his position in intellectual history as a key figure in the history of hermeneutics and deconstruction (Schrift 1990). In his *Nachlass* for the period November 1887 to March 1888, Nietzsche summarised the rejection (for philological reasons) of Christianity that underpinned his condemnation of it in such coruscating tones in *The Anti-Christ*:

> Here every word is a symbol [= *Symbol*]; basically there is no reality any more. There is an extreme danger of making a mistake about these symbols. Nearly all ecclesiastical concepts and evaluations lead one astray: one cannot misunderstand the New Testament more fundamentally than the Church has misunderstood it. It lacked all prerequisites for an understanding: the historian's neutrality which does not give a damn about whether 'the salvation of souls' depends on the word. (KSA 13, 11[302], 128)

And he went on to declare:

> The Church has never had the good will needed to understand the New Testament: it wanted to use it to prove itself. It searched and searches behind it for a theological system: it presupposes it, – it believes in the One Truth. Not until the nineteenth century – le siècle d'irrespect[2] – was it possible to regain some of the most provisional conditions to read the book as a book (and *not* as the truth), in order to recognize this story not as a 'sacred story', but as a devilish mix of fable, tidying up, forgery, palimpsest, confusion, in short as *reality* . . . (KSA 13, 11[302], 128)

Nor should this preoccupation with philology be a surprise. After all, Nietzsche's professional career had been precisely as a philologist or a classicist. After his school studies at Schulpforta, he had originally gone to university in Bonn to study theology. But his school-leaving dissertation on the sixth-century BCE Greek lyric poet Theognis of Megara, entitled 'Theognis as a Poet', served as a reminder of what was now his real passion: classical philology. Thus his subsequent change from theology to philology, undertaken in 1865, formalised in curricular terms a switch of focus that had already taken place. And when his favourite lecturer, the great classical scholar Friedrich Ritschl, moved from Bonn to Leipzig, Nietzsche decided to switch universities as well; Ritschl's exclamation on spotting his student among the audience at his inaugural lecture, entitled 'On the Value and Use of Philology' – 'Look! Nietzsche is here, too!' (*Ei da ist ja auch Herr Nietzsche!*) – expresses that sense of intellectual excitement in his and Nietzsche's shared endeavour, until the latter gradually began to question precisely the value and use of philology;[3] as Zarathustra would put it, 'One requiteth a teacher badly if one remain merely a pupil' (TSZ I 22 §3).

At Bonn, Nietzsche was able to witness the great *Philologenstreit*, sometimes even called *Philologenkrieg*, between Ritschl and his rival, Otto Jahn (1813–69), and Nietzsche's decision to follow

---

[2] See *Journal des Goncourt*, I, 63 (see KSA 14, 756).
[3] For further discussion of this period of Nietzsche's life, see Heise 2000.

Ritschl to Leipzig rather than remain in Bonn with Jahn reflects his investment in one side of this dispute about philology (Jensen 2014). Ritschl was the leading representative of the so-called *Bonner Schule* of philology, whose approach was characterised by 'the linking of textual criticism with the study of prosody, metre, epigraphy, and literary history' (Benne 2005: 59). Concretely this meant a focus on the study of historical sources (*Quellenforschung*), establishing texts and critically interpreting them in order to determine how they have been handed down (Benne 2005: 59). The Bonn School prided itself on the forensic discipline of its methodology, insisting not so much on its purely formal rigour as on the critical distance maintained towards its own scientific imagination (Benne 2005: 59). As a consequence, the outlook of the Bonn School was empirical, anti-metaphysical and anti-theological in temperament, and Christian Benne has listed its eight chief characteristics (2005: 59, 60–8).

First, philology was regarded as being rigorous in its method and its ethical outlook. In an anecdote related by Friedrich Paulsen (1846–1908), during a lecture on Homer Ritschl once suddenly paused, unsure about his own reading of a difficult passage. The following day he declared that he *had* been right after all, a conclusion reached after having spent the night reading Homer – *all* of Homer! Second, although philology aimed to gain a comprehensive knowledge of antiquity, its practical work was focused on individual aspects for examination in the most thorough way possible, despising what Ritschl is reported by Otto Ribbeck (1827–98) to have called 'that superficial, lazy universality that has no real home'. Third, in its treatment of these individual aspects, the Bonn School aimed at an almost artistic perfection in its academic presentation. In *Ecce Homo*, Nietzsche recalled: 'My old master Ritschl went so far as to declare that I planned even my philological treatises after the manner of a Parisian novelist – that I made them absurdly thrilling' (EH Books §2).

Fourth, philology as practised by the Bonn School was never purely formal, but demanded the use of intuition, intimate knowledge and far-reaching textual expertise. Or in Ribbeck's words, it demanded 'educated feeling, healthy commonsense, and a careful eye'. Fifth, philology was essentially textual criticism (*Textkritik*), partly because texts are the most important monuments by which antiquity is handed down to us; and partly because of philology's essentially pedagogical function, developing such key skills as critical consciousness and a critical imagination. Sixth, in methodological terms, philology *à la* Bonn meant a balance between criticism and hermeneutics. Seven, philology meant reading – slow reading, careful reading, the kind of reading that responded to the fifth of Ritschl's 'Ten Commandments of classical philologists', *thou shalt learn to read* . . . And eighth, this emphasis on wide reading combined with philosophical abstinence points to the final key element of Bonn School philology: a sound empirical underpinning. In one of his early lectures at Bonn, Ritschl lamented 'the mutual lack of respect that is expressed between representatives of natural sciences [*Naturwissenschaften*] and the so-called humanities [*Geistesiwissenschaften*]', and this embrace of empirical science (and its concomitant rejection of theology and metaphysics) was a position that Nietzsche himself made his own in *Human, All Too Human* (Benne 2005: 60–5).

Under Ritschl's supervision, Nietzsche undertook and published a number of projects: a long article (published in instalments in the *Rheinisches Museum für Philologie*) on the sources used by Diogenes Laertius, the author of the famous *Lives and Opinions of the Philosophers*; a paper on Simonides' *Danae* and a study of Theognis (again, published in the *Rheinisches Museum*); an analysis of the sources of Suidas; a draft of an essay on Democritean *spuria*; a paper on the satire of Varro and Menippus; and a comprehensive index of twenty-four years' editions of the *Rheinisches Museum*. During his two years in Leipzig, Nietzsche was entirely committed to the ideals of philology: together with fellow students Heinrich Wilhelm Wisser, Wilhelm Heinrich Roscher and Richard Arnold, he founded a philological society, the *Philologischer Verein*; and he met regularly with friends in Café Kintschy to discuss philology and philosophy. Through another philological society, the *Ritschlsche Sozietät*, Nietzsche met fellow-student Erwin Rohde, with whom a close friendship developed.

On the strength of the philological excellence of his publications in the *Rheinisches Museum*, Ritschl – one of the co-editors of that journal – urged his colleagues in Basel to appoint Nietzsche to their Chair for Greek language and literature. Ritschl wrote to his colleague, the Horace specialist Adolf Kießling (1837–93), in December 1868 that, of all the 'young talent' he had seen in the previous thirty-nine years, he had never come across someone who had been 'so mature, while so early and so young', as Nietzsche, and he hailed him as 'the idol and (without wishing to be) the leader of the world of young philologers here in Leipzig' (cited in Stroux 1925: 32). And so Nietzsche became a classics professor in Basel; to be precise, in April 1869 he was appointed Extraordinary Professor of Classical Philology at the University of Basel, at the age of 24.

Yet if, as we have seen, Nietzsche had had doubts about religion, he was now also beginning to have doubts about philology. Writing to Rohde on 3 or 4 May 1868, Nietzsche told his friend that

> we cannot live for ourselves [. . .] but for our part let us see to it that the young philologists conduct themselves with the necessary scepticism, free from pedantry and overvaluation of their discipline, as true promoters of humanistic studies. *Soyons de notre siècle* – a standpoint which no one forgets more easily than the classicist-to-be. (KSB 2, 307; cf. KSA 2, 329)

And in the months leading up to his appointment to Basel, he had in fact been developing a plan to abandon philology and study chemistry (see his letter to Rohde of 16 January 1869; KSB 2, 359–60).

Despite (or perhaps because of) all the help he had received from Ritschl in landing his job in Basel, Nietzsche's attitude towards his *Doktorvater* was ambivalent: Ritschl, so Nietzsche wrote to Rohde on 1–3 February 1868, was 'a pimp' (*ein Kuppler*) whose only desire was 'to hold us in the toils of Madame Philology', adding: 'I have a surprising desire in the essay I have just written *in honorem Ritscheli* to tell the philologists a number of bitter truths' (KSB 2, 248). To Deussen he wrote in October 1868: 'If I were to speak mythologically, I should view Philology as an abortion begotten on the Goddess Philosophy by an idiot or a cretin' (KSB 2, 329).

And on 20 November 1868, after his first meeting with Richard Wagner in the Brockmann household, Nietzsche wrote a letter to Rohde in which his dissatisfaction with scholars and with his academic colleagues was expressed with some force:

> Now that I see once more the swarming breed of philologists at close range – so that I must daily observe all the mole-like efforts, the full cheek-pouches and the blind eyes, the joy over the captured worm and the utter indifference to the true and highest problems of life – it seems even clearer to me that we two, if we remain uncompromisingly loyal to our genius, will not proceed along life's path without being struck by it and thwarted in many ways. (KSB 2, 344)

In some ways, Nietzsche's critique of philology anticipates his critique of religion in the *The Anti-Christ*: both Christianity and classicism are – albeit in different ways and to different degrees – deemed to be fundamentally anti-life in their outlook. In a letter to Carl von Gersdorff (1844–1904) of 11 April 1869, Nietzsche contrasts the kind of humanistic education he was now beginning to envisage – and the kind of vitalist outlook he was gradually beginning to espouse – with the professional occupation of philology:

> To be a philistine, ἄνθρωπος ἄμουσος [an illiterate or uncultured person], a man of the crowd – may Zeus and the Muses preserve me from that! [. . .] To infuse my discipline with fresh blood, to convey to my audience that Schopenhauer-like seriousness which is stamped on the brow of the high-minded man – this is my wish, my dearest hope. I want to be something more than a taskmaster to virtuous little philologists: the production of teachers of the present, the care for the growing brood that is coming, all this is before my mind. (KSB 2, 385–6)

In short, Nietzsche's intellectual trajectory shifts from the desire to produce better philologists to the desire to will the Superman; *Thus Spoke Zarathustra* stands at the end of this trajectory, and

The Anti-Christ reasserts that ideal while seeking to quarrel with and condemn its opponents.

The disquiet that Nietzsche was beginning to feel about philology had repercussions in his public discourse and published writings; gradually, and increasingly perceptibly. If his inaugural lecture at Basel of 1869, 'Homer and Classical Philology', took the form of a sceptical defence of philology, in a follow-up series of public lectures given in 1872 entitled *On the Future of Our Educational Institutions* he no longer pulled any punches (Nietzsche 2014). In its own way, *The Birth of Tragedy from the Spirit of Music* (1871) was the great act of leave-taking from the academic establishment and the world of classical philology; at any rate, its reception sealed Nietzsche's fate and effectively ended his career.[4]

The Birth of Tragedy – its birth, as the subtitle of the first edition of 1872 emphasised, 'out of the spirit of music' – was a complex, difficult, subtle work, whose central lines of strategic argument can be summarised as follows. From Johann Joachim Winckelmann, via Goethe (who, for instance, had told Eckermann to 'study Molière, study Shakespeare; but, above all things, the ancient Greeks, and always the Greeks'),[5] to Hegel, the culture of ancient Greece had fascinated German writers, thinkers and artists, classical and Romantic alike.[6] To his subject Nietzsche brought the opposition between the Dionysian and the Apollonian, an opposition from which, so he told Rohde on 4 August 1871, he believed he could derive much (KSB 3, 215). Prior to Nietzsche, other thinkers and scholars (including Friedrich Schlegel, Friedrich Creuzer and F. W. J. Schelling) had attached significance to the god Dionysos.[7] In the case of Nietzsche, however, Apollo and Dionysos are

---

[4] For the documents from the debate on *The Birth of Tragedy*, see Gründer (ed.) 1989; Musgrave Calder III 1983.

[5] See Goethe's conversation with Eckermann of 1 April 1827; Eckermann 1981: 572.

[6] For further discussion, see Butler 1935; Valdez 2014.

[7] See Baeumer 1976; Frank 1982: 73–106. As James Porter remarks, Nietzsche's 'uses of Dionysus' are both 'a product of the Dionysian tradition that runs from Herder to Friedrich Schlegel, Creuzer, Schelling, Heyne, Bachofen, and beyond' – 'a fact that his contemporaries could see in a way we no longer do' – and 'a polemical commentary on this tradition, which is to say on the German obsession with Germanic traits, in the guise of Hellenism and Dionysianism' (Porter 2000: 262–3).

referred to in *The Birth of Tragedy* as gods or 'art deities' (*Kunstgottheiten*), as creative human drives or *Triebe*, and as physiological states, namely *Traum* (dream) and *Rausch* (frenzy) (BT §1).

Yet the book's immediate reception showed no awareness of this subtlety and complexity. True, Wagner loved it – 'I have never read anything more beautiful than your book!', he enthused – and this delighted Nietzsche (KSB 3, 272–3). Indeed, according to his sister Elisabeth, the publication of *The Birth of Tragedy* made Nietzsche literally want to dance (Förster-Nietzsche 1915: 95). But the response of his professional colleagues was silence and then rejection. On 30 January 1872, Nietzsche wrote an indignant letter to his former mentor in Leipzig, expressing his surprise at Ritschl's lack of response (KSB 3, 281–2); for his part, Ritschl wrote to Wilhelm Vischer-Bilfinger (1808–74), the senior philologist in Basel, on 2 February 1872: 'But our Nietzsche! – this is a really sad story [. . .] he is too giddyingly high-flying for me'; what annoyed Ritschl most, however, was 'his impiety toward his own mother, who has suckled him at her breast: philology' (KGW II.7.1, 622). When the young Berlin philologist Ulrich von Wilamowitz-Moellendorff (1848–1931) published an attack on *The Birth of Tragedy* entitled *Zukunftsphilologie* or *The Philology of the Future* (Berlin, 1872), Nietzsche's friend, Erwin Rohde, who had already reviewed *The Birth of Tragedy* in glowing terms, responded on his behalf with a vigorous defence entitled *Afterphilologie* (Leipzig, 1872), perhaps best translated as *Philology of the Posterior*. But Nietzsche now found himself, in effect, deprived of 'both mission and profession' (Brown 1990: 238). Composed amid the conflict of the Franco-Prussian War (1870–71), *The Birth of Tragedy* launched an academic war of words, and arguably it marks the beginning of Nietzsche's strategic withdrawal from the sphere of philology.

Behind the scenes, Nietzsche's scepticism about philology as a professional occupation had been growing, but his feelings were not simply negative ones. At the end of January and the beginning of February 1870 he wrote to Rohde:

> My love for Greek antiquity keeps on growing; there is no better way of approaching it than that of tirelessly shaping one's own small person. The stage I have reached in the

most shameful confession of my ignorance. The philologist's existence in any critical task whatever, but a thousand miles away from the Greek experience, is becoming more and more impossible for me. I doubt I will ever be able to become a true philologist. The unfortunate thing is that I have no model and I run the risk of going mad at my own hands. (KSB 3, 94)

The kind of 'model' that Nietzsche had in mind becomes clearer in a subsequent letter to Rohde, dated 28 March 1870: 'I have the best hopes for my own philology, only I must allow myself several years' time. I am approaching a unified perception of Greek antiquity, step by step and with a timid amazement' (KSB 3, 112). And a month later on 30 April 1870 he wrote again to Rohde:

When I have finished several minor tasks (on old topics), I want to gather my strength for a book for which new ideas keep coming to me. I am afraid that it will not make a scholarly impression, but how can I oppose my own nature? The period of scandal is beginning for me, after a period in which I aroused a certain benevolence because I was wearing the old, familiar slippers. Theme and title of the future book: Socrates and instinct. (KSB 3, 120)

This projected title with its emphasis on Socrates and the instincts points to a continuity in Nietzsche's interests between the earlier and the later periods of his writing; hence, a continuity in evidence in *The Anti-Christ* too.

For many years later, in *Twilight of the Idols* and *The Anti-Christ*, we find Nietzsche still waging his war against Socrates. In *Twilight* Nietzsche sets up a contrast between the idealised figure of the Greek aristocrat and the figure of the decadent Socrates: 'The same kind of degeneration was everywhere silently preparing itself: the old Athens was coming to an end [. . .] Everywhere the instincts were in anarchy' (TI Socrates §9). Rather than the instincts being regulated by what Nietzsche in *Ecce Homo* calls 'the organising "idea"' (EH Clever §9), the Athenian soul was threatened by chaos; or as Nietzsche put it, the Athenians became 'full of weariness with life, full of opposition to life', and life became regarded as a sickness (TI Socrates §1). In this context, Socrates functions both as a symptom and as a response. When Zopyrus reveals to Socrates that he is 'a cave of every evil lust', Socrates responds with 'a phrase that provides the key to him' – '"That is true", he said, "but I have become master of them all"' (TI Socrates §9).[8] So while he was 'the extreme case, only the most obvious instance of what had at that time begin to be the universal exigency', he proposed that 'a *counter-tyrant*' should oppose the tyranny of the instincts (TI Socrates §9). This new tyrant was *reason* and it exercised its power through the dialectic:

> The moralism of the Greek philosophers from Plato downwards is pathologically conditioned: likewise their estimation of dialectics. Reason = virtue = happiness means merely: one must imitate Socrates and counter the dark desires by producing a permanent *daylight* – the daylight of reason. One most be prudent, clear, bright at any cost: every yielding to the instincts, to the unconscious, leads *downwards* . . . (TI Socrates §10)

Or to put it another way, as Aaron Ridley summarises Nietzsche's argument, Socrates becomes an *idealist*, inasmuch as 'he accorded absolute value to a hypertrophied version of one human capacity, rationality, invented a realm of the Forms that would answer to it, and then used it as a rod with which to beat and denigrate the rest of human nature and the world' (Ridley 2012: 234). To this extent, what Plato and subsequently all philosophers have selected 'as an expedient, as a deliverance, is itself only another expression of *décadence*' (TI Socrates §11). Although Socrates portrays himself as a 'physician' and, even more, as a 'saviour' – a *soter*, like Christ – he is, in Nietzsche's view, nothing of the kind. Likewise, this entire argument is presented in a compact form in *The Anti-Christ* when, in section 20, he writes: 'Perhaps one will here recall that Athenian

---

[8] For the context of Zopyrus's remark, see NK 6/1, 270 (cf. Cicero, *Tusculan Disputations*, book 4, §37).

who also declared war upon pure "scientificity", to wit, Socrates, who elevated personal egoism even in the realm of problems into a morality' (AC §20).

In *The Anti-Christ* as in *Daybreak*, Nietzsche turns philology against Christianity, much as he had earlier turned philology against itself and quit the academic field. And this goes to the heart of one of his objections, if not his *chief* objection, to Christianity: we simply cannot know what it means. In *Beyond Good and Evil*, Nietzsche praises 'the Jewish "Old Testament"' as 'the book of divine justice, there are human beings, things, and speeches in so grand a style that Greek and Indian literature have nothing to compare with it' (BGE §52). In stark contrast is the New Testament, and 'to have glued this New Testament, a kind of rococo of taste in every respect, to the Old Testament to make *one* book, as the "Bible", as "the book par excellence" – that is perhaps the greatest audacity and "sin against the spirit"[9] that literary Europe has on its conscience' (BGE §52). Nietzsche's stylistic objection to the New Testament is not a *merely stylistic* one, given the existential importance that he attaches to style; 'one thing is needful', echoing that biblical phrase also found in *The Anti-Christ*, is the title of an aphorism in *The Gay Science*, which begins: 'To "give style" to one's character – that is a grand and a rare art!':

---

[9] In the New Testament Gospels, Christ warns on several occasions about 'the sin against the Holy Spirit', see Matt. 12:30–2; Mark 3:28–30; Luke 12:8–10. In his *Summa Theologiae* (II/II, 14, II), Thomas Aquinas specifies the following six sins as those that sin against the Holy Spirit: despair, presumption, resistance to known truth, envy of someone's spiritual good, impenitence and obstinacy. In the *Catholic Encyclopedia* the sin against the Holy Spirit or 'the unforgivable sin' is defined as follows: to 'sin against the Holy Ghost is to confound Him with the spirit of evil, it is to deny, from pure malice, the Divine character of works manifestly Divine'; so while 'sins against the Father' are those resulting from 'frailty' and 'sins against the Son' are those springing from 'ignorance', sins against the Holy Ghost 'are those that are committed from downright malice, either by despising or rejecting the inspirations and impulses which, having been stirred in man's soul by the Holy Ghost, would turn him away or deliver him from evil' (Forget 1910: 414–15). And according to the revised *Catechism of the Catholic Church*, there are no limits to the mercy of God, but anyone who deliberately refuses to accept his mercy by repenting rejects the forgiveness of his sins and the salvation offered by the Holy Spirit, and such hardness of heart can lead to final impenitence and eternal loss (§1864; *Catechism* 1997: 509).

> For one thing is needful: namely, that man should attain to satisfaction with himself – be it but through this or that fable and artifice: it is only then that man's aspect is at all endurable! He who is dissatisfied with himself is ever ready to avenge himself on that account: we others will be his victims, if only in having always to endure his ugly aspect. For the aspect of the ugly makes one mean and sad. (GS §290)

Rather, Nietzsche's objection involves whether it is actually – conceptually or philologically – *possible* for us to understand the origins of Christianity, given our lack of access to the historical, cultural and intellectual world in which it developed.

On the other hand, Nietzsche's struggle with philology in the 1870s also led him to question whether it was any longer possible to understand the Greeks! In response to Wilamowitz's critique of *The Birth of Tragedy*, Nietzsche mused to Rohde in a letter of 16 July 1872:

> The soft thesis of the Homeric world as a youthful world has begun to irritate me. *In the sense* in which it is expounded, it is false. That an enormous struggle – savage, of gloomy roughness and cruelty – precedes it; that Homer is, as it were, a conqueror at the close of this long and desolate period – this is for me one of my firmest convictions. The Greeks are much more ancient that anyone thinks. One can talk about springtime, provided one puts the winter before the spring. But this world of purity and beauty certainly didn't fall from the skies. (KSB 4, 23)

While the remarkable speed and extent of Nietzsche's academic promotion should not be underestimated, nor should his eventual and scathing disillusionment with the profession in which he had been so swiftly advanced. This led him to write (in a letter of 6 January 1889, addressed to his former colleague, Jacob Burckhardt) the bitingly satirical sentence: 'In the end I would much rather have been a professor at Basel than God' (KSB 8, 577).

Nietzsche spent the first half of 1875 working on an essay intended for his series of *Untimely Meditations*, entitled 'We Philologists' (KSA 8, 11–127) and devoted to his own professional class, but in the end he left it incomplete.[10] (Was the subject simply too painful for him to confront in full?) In his notes for this essay, Nietzsche achieves his final reckoning with philology, as this remark demonstrates: 'Ninety-nine classicists out of a hundred *shouldn't be* in the profession' (Nietzsche 1990: 330–1). And in part 2 of *Thus Spoke Zarathustra*, in the discourse entitled 'Of the Scholars', Nietzsche reiterated this critique in the characteristically playful language of this work: 'When I lay asleep, then did a sheep eat at the ivy-wreath on my head, – it ate, and said thereby: "Zarathustra is no longer a scholar." [. . .] For this is the truth: I have departed from the house of the scholars, and the door have I also slammed behind me' (TSZ II 16).

In addition to the early philological writings of Nietzsche's student days, the more mature work of his professional years, between 1869 and 1879, constitutes a constant, continuous and ever deepening reflection on philology: his lectures on Greek drama and on other classical subjects; his sketch, 'Introduction to the Study of Classical Philology'; his inaugural lecture at Basel; 'Homer's Contest'; various sections of *On the Future of Our Educational Institutions*; his notes for an unfinished 'untimely meditation', to be entitled 'We Classicists'; the *Birth of Tragedy* (which provoked an attack by Wilamowitz on Nietzsche, and a counter-attack on Wilamowitz by Rohde); and *Philosophy in the Tragic Age of the Greeks*. And throughout his philosophical writings, in *Human, All Too Human, Daybreak, The Gay Science* and *Twilight of the Idols*, no less than in *The Anti-Christ* itself, Nietzsche repeatedly returns to philological concerns and themes.

Nietzsche's philological strategies

Nietzsche develops two main techniques for approaching classical texts – and subsequently (as demonstrated in *The Anti-Christ*) for approaching biblical ones, too. First, there is the principle enunciated in his letter of 16 September 1882 to Lou von Salomé:

---

[10] See 'We Classicists', in Nietzsche 1990: 321–87.

> Your idea of reducing philosophical systems to the personal deeds of their originators is truly an idea from a 'kindred mind': I myself in Basel related the history of ancient philosophy in *this* way and I used to like to tell my audience: 'This system is refuted and dead – but the *person* behind it is irrefutable, the person always remains immortal' – for instance, Plato. (KSB 6, 259)

Throughout his writings and across the field of philosophy as a whole was how far Nietzsche sought to extend this principle, as he suggested in *Beyond Good and Evil*: 'Gradually I have understood what every great philosophy until now has been: namely, the personal confession of its originator, and a kind of involuntary and unnoticed memoir; equally, that the moral (and immoral) intentions in every philosophy constitutes the real germ-seed from which the entire plant has sprung' (BGE §6). And as his preface to the second edition (1887) of *The Gay Science* makes clear, this 'germ-seed' of every philosophy is essentially physiological: 'I have often enough asked myself, whether on the whole philosophy hitherto has not generally been merely an interpretation of the body, and a misunderstanding of the body' (GS Preface §2).

Second, there is an approach to a text which Nietzsche described as 'retrospective' or 'backward inference' (*Rückschluss*), and which he claimed to have derived from his engagement with the Greek thought of Epicurus and Christianity alike, inasmuch as he 'gradually began to understand Epicurus, the opposite of a Dionysian pessimist; – in a similar manner also the "Christian", who in fact is only a type of Epicurean, and like him essentially a Romanticist' (GS §370). Accordingly, Nietzsche defined this technique of backward inference as follows:

> My vision has always become keener in tracing that most difficult and insidious of all forms of *retrospective inference*, in which most mistakes have been made – the inference from the work to its author, from the deed to its doer, from the ideal to him who *needs it*, from every mode of thinking and valuing to the imperative want behind it. (GS §370)

What this meant in practice is explained by Nietzsche in *The Gay Science* and clarified in *Nietzsche contra Wagner* (1888), in which he reprised this passage:

> In regard to all aesthetic values I now avail myself of this radical distinction: I ask in every single case, 'Has hunger or superfluity become creative here?' [. . .] The desire for destruction, change and becoming, may be the expression of overflowing power, pregnant with futurity (my terminus for this is, of course, the word 'Dionysian'; but it may also be the hatred of the ill-constituted, destitute and unfortunate, which destroys, and must destroy, because the enduring, indeed, all that endures, in fact all being, excites and provokes it. (GS §370)

In the case of Goethe, for instance, one finds superabundance that has become creative; in the case of Flaubert, by contrast, hatred (NCW We Antipodes). Precisely these two principles of technique – which one could uncharitably describe as an approach *ad hominem* and as a vitalist psychologising reductionism – inform and underpin Nietzsche's argument in *The Anti-Christ*.

In an aphorism in *Daybreak*, Nietzsche had already launched an excoriating attack on 'the philology of Christianity', which opens with an assertion and a series of questions:

> How little Christianity cultivates the sense of honesty can be inferred from the character of the writings of its learned men [. . .] Their continual cry is: 'I am right, for it is written' – and then follows an explanation so shameless and capricious that a philologist, when he hears it, must stand stock-still between anger and laughter, asking himself again and again: Is it possible? Is it honest? Is it even decent? (D §84)

In *Daybreak*, Nietzsche chooses to focus on the way in which this 'dishonesty' is practised in Protestant pulpits – 'in what a clumsy fashion the preacher takes advantage of his security from interruption; how the Bible is pinched and squeezed; and how the people are made acquainted with every form of the art of false reading' – but at the same time he highlights how this philological practice is inherent in Christianity from its earliest forms, or what Nietzsche describes as 'a religion which, during the centuries when it was being firmly established, enacted that huge philological farce concerning the Old Testament'; and he went on to elaborate this charge: 'However strongly Jewish savants protested, it was everywhere sedulously asserted that the Old Testament alluded everywhere to Christ, and nothing but Christ, more especially His Cross' (D §84). The kind of interpretation that Nietzsche has in mind here is the one in which 'wherever reference was made to wood, a rod, a ladder, a twig, a tree, a willow, or a staff, such a reference could not but be a prophecy relating to the wood of the Cross' (D §84), and he goes on to allude to a number of biblical episodes – 'even the setting-up of the Unicorn and the Brazen Serpent, even Moses stretching forth his hands in prayer, indeed the very spits on which the Easter lambs were roasted: all these were allusions to the Cross, and, as it were, preludes to it!' (D §84).[11]

The fundamental question that Nietzsche puts to his readers is this: 'Has anyone who asserted this ever *believed* it?' (D §84). As a final example, Nietzsche cites the case of a disputed, even controversial, verse from the Book of Psalms, Ps. 96[95]:10, translated (in the DRV) as 'Say ye among the Gentiles, the Lord hath reigned' (DRV); or (in the NJB) as 'Say among the nations, "Yahweh is king"' (NJB); or (in the Coverdale translation of the Psalms) as 'Tell it out among the heathen that the Lord is King'. In their commentary on the Psalms, the Anglican clergymen John Mason Neale (1818–66) and Richard Frederick Littledale (1833–90)

---

[11] For the image of the unicorn or one-horned beast, see Deut. 33:17, where Moses blesses the tribes and says of Joseph, 'His beauty as of the firstling of a bullock, his horns as the horns of a rhinoceros', read by such Church Fathers as Augustine as applying to Christ as the first-born of creation and lifting up the nations on his cross, as it were with horns (Haydock 2006: 257); for the brazen or bronze serpent, see Num. 21:4–9, read as a figure of the crucified Christ and of the efficacy of faith in him against the serpent from hell (Haydock 2006: 184); and for the instructions for the preparation of the paschal lamb, seen as a prefiguration of Christ as redeeming through his death, see Exod. 12:1–14. In yet another philological turn, Nietzsche derived these examples from Moritz von Engelhardt's *Das Christenthum Justins des Märtyrers* (1878) (see NK 3/1, 167–9).

offer the following remarks on this text: 'In the time of St Justin Martyr, and for a long time subsequently, the reading of the first member of this verse was, *The Lord hath reigned from the Wood*', and Justin Martyr 'explicitly charges the Jews with having quite recently cut out the latter words, as well as some expressions in Ezra and Jeremiah, as being too distinctly prophetic of Christ'.[12] In the hymn *Vexilla Regis* by Venantius Fortunatus, the idea is retained in the stanza which, translated (by J. M. Neale), runs: 'Fulfilled is all that David told / In true prophetic song of old; / Amid the nations God, saith he, / Hath reigned and triumphed from the Tree.'

Neale and Littledale note, however, that while Tertullian, St Cyprian and Lactantius, as well as St Augustine 'adopted' these words, they were not in the Hebrew manuscripts consulted by St Jerome, and Genebrardus 'inclines to the view that they were a paraphrase introduced by the Seventy' – i.e., the authors of the Septuagint – 'into the Greek text' (Neale and Littledale 1874: vol, 3, 235). In fact, Neale and Littledale suggest that the original reference, if it existed, was to the wood of the Ark of the Covenant, as the source of the power which overthrew Dagon, the idol of the Philistines, thus bringing about the return of the Ark itself to Israel. In an extensive footnote on this verse in Psalm 96[95], Haydock discusses the omission or alleged erasure of these words from the text, and concludes that

> whatever may be the decision on this important matter, it is certain that the reign of Christ was propagated *from the wood*, in a wonderful manner, as he there began to *draw all* to himself, and the prophet seems evidently to allude to the times when Christ proclaimed, *the kingdom of God is at hand*, and when the conversion of the Gentiles, and the institution of the blessed Eucharist, would fill all the world with rapture. (Haydock 2006: 764)

---

[12] Neale and Littledale 1874: vol. 3, 234. See Justin Martyr, *Dialogue with Trypho*, §73; cf. Pouderon, Salamito and Zarini (eds) 2016: 492, 1291.

Today in our postmodern (and post-Vatican II) world we might well be tempted to smile at these interpretations; yet in 1898 – only ten years after *The Anti-Christ* – it was possible for Joris-Karl Huysmans (1848–1907), the French novelist and art critic who converted to Catholicism and recorded his spiritual journey in a trilogy of novels (*Là-bas* [1891], *En route* [1895] and *La cathédrale* [1898]), to put the following words into the mouth of Durtal, his main autobiographical character:

> 'Argument is vain,' murmured Durtal, who was meditative. 'The Messianic prophecies are irresistible. All the logic of the Rabbins, the Protestants, the Freethinkers, all the ingenuity of the Germans, have failed to find a crack or to undermine the old rock of the Church.' (Huysmans 1997: 218)

– to which Durtal's interlocutor, Abbé Plomb, responds by confirming this view (1997: 218). Of course, the Germans, to whose 'ingenuity' Durtal alludes, are precisely those scholars whose (re)interpretation of scripture accompanied the 'search for the historical Jesus', part of the eighteenth- and nineteenth-century background to *The Anti-Christ*;[13] while the references to the Rabbins and the Protestants remind us of the anti-Semitic and sectarian aspects of Huysmans's discourse. In response to Durtal's question that, 'supposing the Gospels were to be annihilated, they could, I suppose, be restored, and a brief history written of the Saviour's life as they relate it merely by studying the Messianic announcements in the books of the Prophets?', Abbé Plomb again answers in the affirmative (1997: 219). In fact, Durtal's question and the answer it elicits from Abbé Plomb get close to how the New Testament may actually have come to be written.

As Michel Onfray has reminded us, the very names of biblical characters are replete with significance: the name Jesus means 'God saves, has saved, will save'; Bethlehem, the town where Jesus

---

[13] For discussion of Nietzsche's relation to the 'quest of the historical Jesus', as Albert Schweitzer (1875–1965) dubbed it (Schweitzer 1910), see Jensen 2019.

is said to have been born, means the 'house of bread'; while the name of Joseph of Arimathea, the man who according to all four Gospel sources took responsibility for the burial of Jesus after the Crucifixion, means 'Joseph, the one who buries' (Arimathea = 'after death') (Onfray 2017: 47, 59; 2007a: 128–9). This linguistic dimension is so dense that it defines the etymological origin of Christianity; it would be no exaggeration to describe it as a religion built out of texts. In *Daybreak* Nietzsche sees these philological interventions made by the Patristic writers in the interpretation of ancient Hebrew texts as something to be taken very seriously. With reference to the debate over the text of Psalm 96[95]:10, he remarks that 'the Church did not shrink from putting interpolations in the text of the Septuagint [. . .] in order that she might later on make use of these interpolated passages as Christian prophecies', for they were 'engaged in a struggle, and thought of their foes rather than of honesty' (D §84).

So when, in section 52 of *The Anti-Christ*, Nietzsche returns to this critique of the philology of Christianity, he does not need to give any specific examples, but can content himself with lamenting the way that philology is exercised as *'ephexis'* – i.e., suspension of judgement – 'in interpretation':

> The way in which a theologian, whether in Berlin or in Rome, is ready to explain, say, a 'passage of Scripture', or an experience, or a victory by the national army, by turning upon it the high illumination of the Psalms of David, is always so *daring* that it is enough to make a philologist run up a wall. (AC §52)

Here Nietzsche's objection is to the instrumentalisation of religion in general and biblical interpretation in particular for political purposes, in the way that, for example, the famous opening of Psalm 68[67], 'Let God arise, let his enemies be scattered', can be used in any given situation as an appeal for military intervention. At the same time, however, he objects to the way that religion is used – as it is, for instance, by some Evangelical Christians – to portray the world as somehow through prayer being at our beck and call, writing in *Daybreak*:

However small our piety, if we ever encountered a God who always cured us of a cold in the head at just the right time, or got us into our carriage at the very instant heavy rain began to fall, he would seem so absurd a God that he would have to be abolished, even if he existed. (D §52)

Today, we might call this conception 'the God of the parking space', a deity who intervenes miraculously to find someone a place to park their car, while curiously yet conspicuously failing to intervene in cases of famine, plague or war. In Nietzsche's terms, this is 'God as a domestic servant, as a letter carrier, as an almanac-maker – at bottom, he is a mere name for the stupidest sort of chance' (D §52). Given the importance that this etymological or philological dimension has for Nietzsche's critique of Christianity in *The Anti-Christ*, we must always remember the *textual* nature of Christianity, which substantiates Nietzsche's philological approach, and helps us understand why, given that philological approach, he came to the view that faith was no longer possible.

For the core of Nietzsche's quarrel with Christianity is this: having seen through the philological methods with which it supports its claims to truth, we *can* no longer believe in it. It is this loss of faith that is deleterious to life, and inclines us towards nihilism – arguably Nietzsche's real enemy in *The Anti-Christ*, inasmuch as he identifies Christianity with nihilism. Nevertheless, this has not prevented numerous Christian philosophers and theologians in the twentieth century – ranging from Paul Tillich (1886–1965) to Hans Küng (b. 1928), from Henri de Lubac (1896–1991) to Hans Urs von Balthasar (1905–88), via Max Scheler (1874–1928), Gabriel Marcel (1889–1973) and Emmanuel Mounier (1905–50), not to mention Romano Guardini (1885–1968), Erich Przywara (1889–1972), Cornelio Fabro (1911–95), Georges Morel (1920–89) and Paul Valadier (b. 1933) – from finding in Nietzsche a valuable source of precious theological insight (and, in some cases, even religious inspiration). Interestingly, but in line with the general fascination with Nietzsche in that country that continues to this day, a good number of these thinkers came from France.[14] And it is an intriguing paradox that it has been Christian writers and intellectuals who have most profoundly, extensively and fruitfully engaged with Nietzsche's anti-Christian arguments.

---

[14] For further discussion of the Catholic reception of Nietzsche in Germany, see Köster 1981/82; 1998; and for France (and elsewhere), see Ledure 1984.

Conclusion

As we saw in Chapter 7, the conclusion to which Nietzsche is nudging us, his readers, is not so much that we *should* no longer believe in Christianity as that we *can* no longer believe in it. Yet he is also aware that some of us (or, if not us, our neighbours, or friends, or relatives, or even work colleagues) still do believe; at least, some of them claim to, others think they do, and possibly some actually *do* believe in Christianity. For the most part, however, the problem seems to be that we, as late moderns in the history of Western civilisation, are still habituated to a set of beliefs to which we in practice no longer actually adhere. On Nietzsche's account, our practices and our beliefs are now fundamentally misaligned. After all, we are Hyperboreans (as he reminded us at the outset in AC §1).

In other words, Nietzsche is posing the problem of 'secularism' (and, by the same token, 'post-secularism'). This problem has been taken up by a number of thinkers, most notably Hans Blumenberg (1920–96) in such works as *Legitimacy of the Modern Age* (1966) and *The Genesis of the Copernican World* (1975). Against the fundamental view of secularisation – as proposed, for example, by Karl Löwith (1897–1973) – that the modern age stands in a relation of continuity to Antiquity, to the Middle Ages and to the early Renaissance, and that the notion of progress is simply a secularised version of Christian eschatology, Blumenberg argues that modernity represents a fundamental rupture with which we are still coming to terms. What characterises the modern age in Blumenberg's view is its rehabilitation, contrary to how it was considered during periods of theological absolutism in Antiquity and in the Middle Ages, of human curiosity, and the sense that history is legitimised by humankind's increasingly confident assertion of its sense of self-responsibility (Blumenberg 1983: 3–11).

The problem of legitimisation has been recognised by such other thinkers as the Austrian-born American sociologist and theologian Peter L. Berger (1929–2017) and the French sociologist Marcel Gauchet (b. 1946) (see Griffioen 2016). And it has also been explored by the German sociologist and philosopher Jürgen Habermas (b. 1929), a member of the third generation of the Frankfurt School, among whose early works one finds such titles as *Knowledge and Human Interests* (1968), *On the Logic of the Social Sciences* (1967) and *Legitimation Crisis in Late Capitalism* (1975). On 14 January 2004, the Catholic Academy of Bavaria in Munich invited Habermas and Cardinal Joseph Ratzinger (b. 1927) – at the time Prefect of the Congregation for the Doctrine of the Faith (an office previously known as the Inquisition), and subsequently elected Pope Benedict XVI – to a debate before a limited audience on the issue of secularisation. This discussion, subsequently published as *The Dialectics of Secularization*, showed not only how seriously the cardinal took philosophy, but how seriously the philosopher took religion (Habermas and Ratzinger 2006; 2005). At the heart of their discussion lies the status of reason, and what provides the ultimate grounding of reason. As Ratzinger argues, there is something circular about grounding reason on reason itself; already, he suggests, in submitting to reason, we are making an act of faith.

Significantly, Habermas conceded that Ratzinger had a point, and he has gone on to argue for a role for Judeo-Christian ethics in informing our society's culture, and to accept that the exclusion of religious voices from the public sphere is essentially 'illiberal'. Habermas points to a question often left undiscussed in academic circles: the question of the role that religion should play in the state. For as greatly as such New Atheists as Richard Dawkins and Christopher Hitchens might deplore it, a 'religious turn' is discernible in numerous contemporary thinkers, whether in Jacques Derrida and deconstruction (see Bradley 2006), in phenomenology, or in Habermas (see Habermas 2006; 2008). For Habermas, religious traditions have 'a special power to articulate moral intuitions, especially with regard to vulnerable forms of communal life' and, as a consequence, this potential 'makes religious speech a serious candidate for transporting possible truth contents, which can then be translated from the vocabulary of a particular religious community into generally accessible language'. Indeed, Habermas argues that 'the ostensibly critical overcoming of [. . .] a narrow secularist consciousness is itself an essentially contested issue – at least to the same extent as the demythologizing response to the cognitive challenges of Modernity' (Habermas 2006: 10, 16).

So where does this leave us with the problem as diagnosed by Nietzsche of the misalignment of our practices and beliefs? Or to put it another way, how do we achieve the desired realignment? Was *The Anti-Christ* intended to play a decisive, albeit unspecified, role in bringing about – or, indeed, even accelerating – the desired alignment, which would presumably result in the intellectual and affective upgrade to which Nietzsche aspired? Perhaps this is the task of a text that Nietzsche may (or may not) have intended to be included in *The Anti-Christ*, a text that would, if Nietzsche were teaching at a modern university, likely as not involve him in a brisk discussion with his HR managers before his dismissal. The text bears the title 'Law Against Christianity', and although the jury is out on whether it was supposed to be part of *The Anti-Christ*, it sets out, under the programmatic slogan 'War to the death against vice: the vice is Christianity', a road map for a post-Christian future in the form of seven propositions.[1] Here is a set of action points that very clearly map out what Nietzsche believed the initial steps should be as 'we' – that is, readers of Nietzsche – move forward from (and, above all, away from) Pauline Christianity.

The language of this 'Law' is bristling with hostility: its third proposition is that 'the execrable location where Christianity brooded over its basilisk eggs should be razed to the ground and, being the *depraved* spot on earth, it should be the horror of all posterity', while Nietzsche adds: 'Poisonous snakes should be bred on top of it.' And in its fifth proposition, Nietzsche writes, using the Sanskrit term for someone who is 'untouchable', the

---

[1] See NK 6/2, 315–20. The page with the text of the 'Law' seems to have been glued by Nietzsche to the final page of the manuscript of *The Anti-Christ*, but he may also have glued a blank sheet of paper over this one, covering it up.

lowest of the positions in the ancient Indian caste system: 'The priest is *our* Chandala, – he should be ostracized, starved, driven into every type of desert.' Yet despite this aggressive tone, even here we find a reprise of themes and ideas we have already encountered elsewhere in *The Anti-Christ*.

In his second proposition, Nietzsche urges that one should be 'harsher with Protestants than with Catholics, harsher with liberal Protestants than with orthodox ones', in line with his critique of liberal Protestantism as having downgraded Christianity into a symbolic faith and his protest at its transformation into a system of moral symbolism – a critique one also finds in the work of the French philosopher (and contemporary of Nietzsche), Jean-Marie Guyau.[2] And the image of basilisk eggs might be borrowed from the Book of Isaiah, where a penitential psalm in a part of the prophetic book once thought to have been written by a figure called Trito-Isaiah or Third Isaiah, but regarded today as a composite collection (see NJB, OT, 1170), includes the line, 'They have broken the eggs of asps, and have woven the webs of spiders: he that shall eat of their eggs, shall die: and that which is brought out, shall be hatched into a basilisk' (see NK 6/2, 321) (although a cognate image can be found in Pliny, who reports that the young of the viper 'burst through' its 'sides').[3]

A sketch of the 'Law' can be found in Nietzsche's *Nachlass* (KSA 13, 22[10], 588), and Éric Blondel (b. 1942) has argued that, behind the anti-clerical or anti-religious violence of the text that borders on delirium, its aim (especially in articles one, two, four and six) is, in fact, principally moral (Blondel 1994: 179). Taken together, however, the propositions of the 'Law Against Christianity' make it clear that the 'curse' on Christianity, pronounced by Nietzsche in the subtitle of *The Anti-Christ*, is but one ingredient in his larger, albeit ill-defined, political and geopolitical

---

[2] See NK 6/2, 320–1; cf. Guyau 1887: 133–6. For further discussion of Guyau, see Onfray 2011a: 49–174.

[3] Pliny, *Natural History*, book 10, §82; cf. Haydock 2006: 956. 'The viper is the only land animal that bears eggs inside it [. . .] After two days she hatches the young inside her uterus, and then bears them at the rate of about one a day, to the number of about twenty [. . .] the remaining ones get so tired of the delay that they burst open their mother's sides, so committing matricide' (Pliny 1967: 401).

designs in his final years. So should we sign up to this 'Law' and campaign for its immediate implementation?

Perhaps we should be careful what we wish for. However disruptive the coronavirus pandemic has been (and, at the time of writing, is continuing to be), other problems loom on our 'postmodern' (or, these days, 'post-postmodern') horizon. These include such issues as the consequences of climate change (Lea-Henry 2018), the promise (or threat) of AI (Bootle 2019), and the movement called transhumanism with its project to create an 'augmented humanity' in which the human will no longer be a natural individual but a mixture of nature and artificiality, thanks to the incorporation of new technologies.[4] In a series of books, including *The Age of Intelligent Machines* (1990), *The Age of Spiritual Machines* (1999) and *The Singularity Is Near* (2005), the Ametican inventor and futurist Ray Kurzweil (b. 1948), who is a director of engineering at Google, has predicted that, after the ages of polytheism and monotheism, a third religious age is beginning – what could be called the age of the Transcendent Human or the Man-God.[5]

From the transhumanist perspective, the 'death of God' acquires a new meaning. Now the answer to the question, 'Does God exist?', is: 'Not yet'. As the French philosopher and theologian Bertrand Vergely (b. 1953) has reminded us in a trilogy of essays entitled respectively *La Tentation de l'homme-Dieu* (2015), *Traité de résistance pour le monde qui vient* (2017) and *La Destruction du réel* (2018), the issues raised by transhumanism are profound. In this context Nietzsche's focus on the figure of the anti-Christ is revealed to have been even more prescient. For Vergely reminds us that such nineteenth-century Russian thinkers as Fyodor Dostoevsky (1821–81) reflected at considerable length on the figure of the anti-Christ, and their reflections were in turn taken up in the twentieth century by Vladimir Solovyov (1853–1900).[6]

---

[4] Although Nick Bostrom has downplayed the significance of Nietzsche as an ancestor of transhumanism (Bostrom 2005: 4), Stefan Lorenz Sorgner has detected several areas of conceptual affinities (Sorgner 2009).

[5] For further discussion, see Geraci 2008; later expanded in Geraci 2010.

[6] For further discussion of Dostoevsky and Solovyov, see the articles by George Pattison and Catherine Evtuhov respectively, in Emerson, Pattison and Poole (eds) 2020: 169–83, 205–18; and Grillaert 2008.

In recollections based on her notebook entries, the memoirist and translator Varvara V. Timofeyeva (1850–1931) recalls how Dostoevsky once lifted his head from the proofs of an article dealing with Prussia, Bismarck and the papacy, to declare of Timofeyeva's radical friends: 'They do not suspect that soon everything will come to an end – all their "progress" and chatter! They have no inkling that the Antichrist has been born . . . and is coming'. According to Timofeyeva, Dostoevsky spoke these words with an expression 'as if announcing [. . .] a terrible and grandiose secret', and when she expressed scepticism, he banged on the table with his fist and proclaimed 'like a mullah in his minaret': 'The Antichrist is coming! It is coming! And the end of the world is closer – closer than they think!' (Frank 2002: 48). As Dostoevsky's biographer, Joseph Frank, remarks, just how literally Dostoevsky believed in the anti-Christ can only remain 'a matter of speculation', but Timofeyeva was right to see that his greatest works had their origin in 'the eschatological imagination that could view the world in the looming shadow of such a possibility' (Frank 2002: 48).

In 'Tale of the Anti-Christ' (part of a work entitled *War, Progress, and the End of History: Three Conversations* [1900]), Solovyov – who, as a member of the Sophiological tradition to which Pavel Florensky (1882–1937) and Sergey Bulgakov (1871–1944) also belonged, concocted a syncretic philosophy that combined Hellenistic philosophy and Orthodox Christianity with Gnosticism, Kabbalah and Buddhism, focused on the figure of Sophia – imagined a futuristic scenario in which a Japanese empire has subsumed Asia and Europe. A charismatic leader appears who, following a nocturnal visit from a shadowy figure claiming to be his 'father', writes an all-encompassing treatise which, however, makes no mention of Christ. The objection of the Catholic, Orthodox and Protestant Churches to this omission sets the scene for their total destruction.

In his critique of the transhumanist movement, which seeks to enhance and transform the human condition by the use of technology, Bertrand Vergely suggests that Dostoevsky and Solovyov reflected on the figure of anti-Christ because they 'saw in the approaching revolutionary movement a will to save the world without God' (Vergely 2019: 38). This is a 'mad will', as the totalitarian systems of the twentieth century have shown, since 'the disasters it causes when it turns into something guiding the world' reveal the danger of presenting philosophy as 'a doctrine of salvation without God' (Vergely 2019: 38). In the case of Nietzsche, however, we find a reflection on the figure of anti-Christ, not to challenge it (as Dostoevsky and Solovyov did) but to champion it. Thus Nietzsche closes *The Anti-Christ* with the cry, 'War to the death against [. . .] Christianity'; just as, in *The Gay Science*, he announces 'the death of God' (GS §125); and in *On the Genealogy of Morals*, he extols the will-to-power as 'the essence of life' and 'the essential priority of the spontaneous, aggressive, expansive, form-giving forces that give new interpretations and directions' (GM II §12). God is dead, war on Christianity, the will-to-power: these are Nietzsche's slogans in the battle against nihilism.

In *Ecce Homo* Nietzsche presents himself as speaking on behalf of 'the party of life' (*die Partei des Lebens*) (EH BT §4), but for Nietzsche, life is a manifold, and to reduce it to a unity is to denaturalise it (Vergely 2019: 39). 'In the West, since Plato, God is the symbol of this de-naturalization', and 'behind the idea of God one can glimpse the project of an anxious will that desires to have "an order behind all that"' (Vergely 2019: 39). By the same token, life is not simply a manifold, it is a vital force, the affirmation of which involves a hardness that frightens us, and in order to protect ourselves against this we set up a morality of pity in the form of Christianity. Faced with the denaturalisation of life by God as well as by the Christian morality of pity, the only solution for Nietzsche is to 'return to the will-to-power, which is a will-to-life, open to the manifold and to the vital force, and extolling the latter' (Vergely 2019: 39). Astonishingly for a philosopher who is also an Orthodox theologian, Vergely agrees: he writes that Nietzsche's critique is fully justified, and that Christianity, originally 'a religion of life', has fallen into a state of 'decadence' and become 'a timid, conservative association, sprinkled with a bleak and bleating sentimentality' (2019: 39).

For Vergely, there is no doubt that we are in the age of the death of God, an age whose advent Nietzsche so ardently desired. Yet instead of an age which is more free, stronger, more powerful, our world in which God is dead is characterised by its emptiness.

When God exists, the world goes hand-in-hand with an invisible world, and life is not reduced to appearances – hence our efforts to transcend appearances so that life may be complete (Vergely 2019: 39–40). But when God no longer exists (because there is no 'other' world) and when everything is reduced to the body and to materiality, we fall into what the French philosopher and sociologist Gilles Lipovetsky (b. 1944) has called 'the era of the void, an era in which one no longer asks questions', and in which metaphysical questioning has disappeared (Lipovetsky 1983: 135).

An oft-quoted remark attributed to G. K. Chesterton (1874–1936) makes a similar point: 'When men stop believing in God they don't believe in nothing; they believe in anything.'[7] Although Vergely makes no reference to Jung, his analysis is confirmed by what the Swiss psychotherapist says in his seminar on *Zarathustra* (1934–39): 'So when Nietzsche declares that God is dead, instantly he begins to transform' (Jung 1998: 37). For Jung, however, this is an essentially *positive* transformation, for 'with that declaration he is no longer a Christian, he is an atheist or it doesn't matter what' and 'he immediately gets into the process of that archetype of rebirth', on the grounds that 'those vital powers in us which we call "God" are powers of self-renewal, powers of eternal change' (Jung 1998: 37). Yet Jung had not always been so positive: in 'The Psychology of the Unconscious' (1917; 3rd edn, 1926; 5th edn, 1943), he had argued that the case of Nietzsche 'shows, on the one hand, the consequences of neurotic one-sidedness, and, on the other hand, the dangers that lurk in this leap beyond Christianity' (§§40–1, in Jung 1953: 31–2). On this account, Nietzsche 'undoubtedly felt the Christian denial of animal nature very deeply indeed, and therefore he sought a higher human wholeness beyond good and evil', but whoever 'seriously criticizes the basic attitudes of Christianity also forfeits the protection which these bestow upon him' (§§40–1, in Jung 1953: 31–2).

---

[7] While widely attributed to Chesterton, this quotation can best be traced to the following remark: 'The first effect of not believing in God is to believe in anything' (Cammaerts 1937: 211).

So if we are living today in an epoch that is de-Christianising itself, does this mean we are more vital, stronger, more powerful? For his part, Vergely thinks this is not the case. And if we are living today in a world that extols the affirmation of the self as well as the will-to-power, does this mean we are more comfortable with ourselves? Once again, Vergely thinks not, and he argues that the affirmation of the *self* has turned into an affirmation of the *ego*, thanks to the development of a narcissistic hyper-individualism (Vergely 2019: 40). As the French psychoanalyst and priest Tony Anatrella (b. 1941) has pointed out, this hyper-individualism is extremely fragile (Anatrella 1983); and as Gilles Deleuze (1925–95) and Félix Guattari (1930–92) realised, behind the schizoid individual living in its ego by surfing on the wave of existence in a way that is rid of hang-ups and complexes, one finds an individual incapable of coping with lack and crumbling at the first sign of frustration (Deleuze and Guattari 1980).

On Vergely's account, precisely the values that Nietzsche defended – the death of God, the de-Christianisation of society, the affirmation of the self – have triumphed, inasmuch as they are in charge of today's world. Their triumph, however, has not brought success, inasmuch as the result has turned out not to be life, vitality and power, but emptiness, sadness and a febrile narcissism. How could this have happened? This failure derives, Vergely believes, from a crucial error that Nietzsche made and that we, for our part, are seemingly intent on reproducing. For when Nietzsche unleashed his philosophical project (and nowhere is this clearer than in *The Anti-Christ*), he demonised God and Christianity while idealising the will-to-power, but he did not see what *we* are in the process of discovering. Namely, that when God does not exist and when everything is possible, what arises is not greater freedom, but a new world-order – the world of the Man-God, not in the theological sense (of the God-Man or of the 'anointed one', i.e., the Christ) but in its transhumanist sense, all-powerful in its authority and in total control of existence.

Or as Vergely concludes, 'in this sense the anti-Christ wished for by Nietzsche is not the image of the liberator, but that of the oppressor', and Dostoevsky 'understood this' (Vergely 2019: 41). For when God exists and His place is taken, one cannot mistake oneself for Him; when He, however, no longer exists, His disappearance unleashes human pride – this is the message of the myth of the Grand Inquisitor in *The Brothers Karamazov* (1880). The reign of the limitless, of equality and of safety inaugurated by the Man–God illustrates this fact, yet while giving the impression of allowing humankind to become emancipated, in reality – by chaining us to ourselves – it prevents us from becoming precisely that.

Whether or not one agrees with Vergely's analysis of transhumanism; whether or not one agrees with René Girard (1923–2015) that 'the refusal of the real is the number one dogma of our time' (Girard 2001: 70); whether one is thrilled (or appalled) by the prospect mooted by the French essayist and entrepreneur Laurent Alexandre (b. 1960) that, 'with transhumanism, society will go from transgression to transgression to the very end of what technology will permit'; whether one is appalled (or thrilled) by the prospect that 'real life will soon no longer be one world among others [. . .] a reality no more nor less important than all the virtual universes in which we shall be immersed [. . .] these will be so realistic that there will be no difference between making love in real life and making love in a virtual way in an imaginary bed' (Alexandre 2015: 242, 98) – the issues, whether philological, theological or existential, raised by Nietzsche in *The Anti-Christ* could not be of more decisive relevance for our present age and for our future. Far from being 'untimely' (*unzeitgemäß*), Nietzsche – and *The Anti-Christ* – have never more been more timely than now.

Glossary of Key Terms

Anti-Christ [*der Antichrist*]: as the name suggests, this figure is the opposite of Christ, i.e., 'the anointed one', whose appearances will usher in the final days (see **eschatology**); in a wider sense, anyone who 'denieth the Father, and the Son' (1 John 2:22).

Atheism [*der Atheismus*]: deriving from the Greek *atheos* (ἄθεος), i.e. 'godless' or 'without gods', atheism originally meant a rejection of the gods (in the plural), but in the sixteenth century it acquired the meaning of rejecting belief in the monotheistic God of Judeo-Christianity or any kind of supreme being.

Bible [*die Bibel*]: derived from the Greek *tà biblía* (τὰ βιβλία). i.e., 'the books', the Bible is the core collection of texts in Judaism, comprising the Torah or Pentateuch (the 'five books' of Moses), the Prophets and the Writings (Psalms and Wisdom literature). In addition, Christianity recognises the New Testament, comprising the four Gospels, the Pauline and other letters (epistles) and the Book of Revelation, and reinterprets the Hebrew Bible in their light, describing them as the Old Testament.

Buddhism [*der Buddhismus*]: a term that embraces a variety and diversity of beliefs, originating in ancient India at some point between the sixth and fourth centuries BCE, which subsequently spread through large parts of Asia. While describing Buddhism and Christianity alike as 'nihilistic' and 'decadent' religions, Nietzsche seeks to show to the disadvantage of Christianity that these aspects are not inevitably ruinous.

Chandala [*Tschandala*]: a Sanskrit word for someone who is a member of the lowest of the Hindu castes; someone who disposes of corpses, and is thus 'untouchable'.

Christ [*Christus*]: the Greek equivalent, *Christos* or Χριστός, of the Hebrew term 'Messiah', meaning 'the anointed one'. According to the Christ myth theory (propounded by, among others, Bruno Bauer, Albert Kalthoff and Arthur Drews), Jesus of Nazareth never actually existed as an historical figure; or, if he did, he had nothing to do with the gospel accounts and the founding of Christianity. In *The Anti-Christ*, Nietzsche criticises Christianity and the Church, but makes great efforts not to criticise Christ himself, whose historical existence he seems not to question.

Death of God [*'Gott ist tot!'*]: in the parable of the madman in Nietzsche's *The Gay Science*, the madman declares: 'God is dead. God remains dead. And we have killed him' (GS §125). In *Thus Spoke Zarathustra*, this doctrine is simply taken for granted (see TSZ Prologue §2). So-called 'death of God theology' tries to think through the implications of this idea in relation to the challenges of secularism, the decline in traditional belief and the possibility of a revival of the sacred.

Dionysos [*Dionysos*]: the Greek god of fertility and ecstasy; contrasted by Nietzsche in *The Birth of Tragedy* to Apollo (BT §1), with whom he forms a 'fraternal union' (or *Bruderbund*) so that 'the highest goal of tragedy and of all art is attained' (BT §21); and opposed to the figure of the Crucified in the conclusion to *Ecce Homo* (EH Destiny §9).

Eschatology [*Eschatalogie*]: theological teaching about the final events of history, otherwise known as 'the end of the world'.

Gospel [*Evangelium*]: translated from the Greek *evangelion* (εὐαγγέλιον), meaning 'good news', the gospel consists in the news of the imminent arrival of the Kingdom of God; see Mark 1:14–15, 'Jesus came into Galilee, preaching the gospel of the kingdom of God; and saying, The time is accomplished, and the kingdom of God is at hand: repent, and believe the gospel.' According to Nietzsche, however, St Paul turns the *evangelion* into a *dysevangelion* – i.e., *bad* tidings, the opposite of a gospel.

Hyperboreans [*Hyperboreer*]: a mythical people, mentioned in Pindar's Tenth Pythian Ode and in book 4 of the *Histories* of Herodotus. Located beyond the Rhipean Mountains in the far north, they were said to inhabit a sunny, temperate climate, and to enjoy perpetual youth and unending happiness.

Israel [*Israel*]: a term used to refer to the tribes, kingdoms and dynasties formed by the ancient Jewish people in the Levant (an area equivalent today to Israel, Palestine, Lebanon, Jordan and Syria), and more specifically to two kingdoms – Israel (in the north) and Judah (in the south) – that constituted a united monarchy between 1047 BCE and 930 BCE and then split into two. *Shema Israel* (i.e., 'Hear, O Israel') is a Jewish prayer based on the words of the Torah (see Deut. 6:4), and expresses the monotheistic essence of Judaism. In section 25 of *The Anti-Christ* Nietzsche offers an outline of the history of Israel in terms of five stages of the 'denaturalisation' (*Entnatürlichung*) of 'natural values' or the values of nature (*Naturwerthe*).

Lawbook of Manu [*das Gesetzbuch des Manu*]: an ancient legal text known in Sanskrit as the Manusmṛiti (and also called the Mānava-Dharmaśāstra) that belongs to the genre of Hindu treatises called Dharmaśāstras; translated into French in 1876 by Louis Jacolliot and used by Nietzsche to establish a contrast with the Bible.

Messiah [*der Messias*]: a Hebrew term meaning 'the anointed one'; in Jewish theology, the Messiah is a future king of David's descent (i.e., descended from King David), who will be 'anointed' with holy oil, establish the kingdom of God and rule during the Messianic Age. In Christian theology, the Messiah is identified as (Jesus) Christ, as in the Petrine confession – Peter's cry in response to Jesus' question, 'Whom do you say that I am?': 'Thou art Christ, the Son of the living God' (Matt. 16:16)

Moraline-free [*moralinfrei*]: a neologism coined by Nietzsche to indicate an attitude 'free' of 'morality'.

Mystery religions [*der Mysterienkult*]: in the Greco-Roman world, Mystery religions were religious schools that reserved participation in their rites to initiates (*mystai*), reflecting the origin of the word in the Greek *mysterion* (μυστήριον), 'secret', probably derived from the Greek *myein* (μύειν), 'to close'. In the Christian tradition, the phrase 'mystery of faith' (or, in Latin, *mysterium fidei*) can be found in 1 Tim. 3:9 ('holding the mystery of faith in a pure conscience') as well as in the formula of consecration (or, these days, the memorial acclamation) in the Roman liturgy of the Mass.

Nobility [*die Vornehmheit*]: a topic that concerns Nietzsche in *Human, All Too Human* and in *Beyond Good and Evil*; in *The Anti-Christ* Nietzsche summarises his conclusions as he had reached them in the *Genealogy* as follows: 'In my *Genealogy of Morals* I give the first psychological explanation of the concepts underlying those two anithetical things, a *noble* morality and a *ressentiment* morality, the second of which is a mere product of the denial of the former. The Judaeo-Christian moral system belongs to the second division, and in every detail' (AC §24). The notion of *nobility* is central to Nietzsche's critique of Christianity in its institutionalised form, and it has been argued that in *The Anti-Christ* he proposes nothing less than a resurgence of nobility.

Philology [*Philologie*]: the study of oral and written historical sources, combining textual and literary criticism with history and linguistics. Nietzsche defines philology as 'the art of reading well, – to be able to read facts *without* falsifying them through interpretations, *without* letting the desire to understand make you lose caution, patience, subtlety' (AC §52). According to Nietzsche, however, a chief characteristic of theologians is their 'unfitness for philology' or, in other words, 'the impulse to lie' (AC §52).

Priest [*der Priester*]: the priesthood is an institution common to ancient Israel and the Church (especially the Catholic and Orthodox Churches) alike. Originally the priesthood was the class of male descendants from Aaron (the older brother of Moses), who offered sacrifice to Yahweh under the Law of Moses; but a separate line of priesthood runs from Melchizedek, the king of Salem, described as the priest of 'the most high God' (Gen. 14:18–20). In the Letter to the Hebrews attributed to Paul, Jesus Christ is identified as 'a priest forever, according to the order of Melchizedek' (Heb. 5:6; 6:20; cf. Ps. 109[110]:4). Nietzsche describes the priest as 'that *professional* denier, calumniator, and poisoner of life' (AC §8), but Zarathustra tells his disciples, 'Here are priests: but although they are mine enemies, pass them quietly and with sleeping swords!' (TSZ II §4).

Reformation [*die Reformation*]: the major movement associated with the figure of Martin Luther and his publication in 1517 of his *Ninety-five Theses* that challenged the Catholic Church and, in particular, the papacy on religious and political grounds in sixteenth-century Europe. Nietzsche attacked the Reformation as one among many examples of how the Germans created 'a futile substitute for something that once existed, for something *irrecoverable*' (AC §61).

Renaissance [*die Renaissance*]: the period in European history that marked the transition from the Middle Ages to the 'rebirth' of classical humanism in the fifteenth and sixteenth centuries. On Nietzsche's account, the Renaissance was '*the transvaluation of Christian values*, – an attempt with all available means, all instincts and all the resources of genius to bring about a triumph of the *opposite* values, the more *noble* values' (AC §61), but an attempt rendered null and void by the Reformation.

Roman Empire [*imperium Romanum*]: the ancient empire centred on the city of Rome; established in 31 BCE following the end of the Roman Republic, it lasted until the fifth century CE. Nietzsche presents the Roman Empire as a magnificent achievement, undermined from within by the growth of Christianity: 'Christianity was the vampire of the *imperium Romanum*, – overnight it destroyed the vast achievement of the Romans' (AC §58).

Semiotics [*Semiotik*]: literally, the study of signs, deriving from the Greek *sēmeiōtikos* (σημειωτικός), someone who is 'observant of signs' (cf. *sēmeion*, σημεῖον). Used more broadly by Nietzsche as cognate with 'sign language' [*eine Zeichenrede*] and speaking in 'parables' [*Gleichnissen*] (see AC §32).

Superman/Overman [*Übermensch*]: the future human being who will be the expression of non-metaphysical transcendence; in 'On the Blissful Islands', Zarathustra opposes the *Übermensch* to the monotheistic conception of God when he says, 'Once did people say God, when they looked out upon distant seas; now, however, have I taught you to say, Superman' (TSZ II 2).

Textual criticism [*die Textkritik*]: the scholarly study of the genesis of a text, especially through analysis of its textual variants, in order to reconstruct its original meaning(s). In the case of biblical criticism, the reconstruction of the original text is used to gain insight into the historical events they describe – or to reveal their non-historicity. In *Daybreak*, Nietzsche launches an excoriating attack on 'the philology of Christianity', in which he claims that 'how little Christianity cultivates the sense of honesty can be inferred from the character of the writings of its learned men'; focuses on the way in which this 'dishonesty' is practised in Protestant pulpits; and highlights how this philological practice is inherent in Christianity from its earliest forms, or what Nietzsche describes as 'a religion which, during the centuries when it was being firmly established, enacted that huge philological farce concerning the Old Testament' (D §84). The fundamental question that Nietzsche puts to his readers is this: 'Has anyone who asserted this ever *believed* it?' (D §84).

Theology [*die Theologie*]: deriving from the Greek *theologia* (θεολογία), composed of *theos* (Θεός, 'god') and *logia* (λογία, 'utterances, sayings'), this term literally means 'discourse about God'. Theology can (as, for example, in the case of Plato) be pagan, but in the Christian tradition it usually means thinking about Jesus Christ as God and the implications of the Incarnation and Resurrection.

Tübingen seminary [*Tübinger Stift*]: founded as Augustinian monastery in the Middle Ages, after the Reformation the Tübinger Stift was turned into a Protestant seminary to prepare pastors for clerical service in Württemberg. Among its famous alumni are several targets of Nietzsche's criticism, including G. W. F. Hegel and David Friedrich Strauss.

Guide to Further Reading on *The Anti-Christ*

Jessica N. Berry, 'Nietzsche's Attack on Belief: Doxastic Skepticism in *The Antichrist*': an essay on *The Anti-Christ* as an exercise in doxastic scepticism (i.e., scepticism as an attitude towards propositions of belief or disbelief).

Éric Blondel, 'Introduction' – 'Notes' – 'Bibliographie', in *L'Antéchrist*: for readers of French, a helpful introduction, explanatory notes and guide to further reading (in French), essential for anyone who wishes to take the 'French Nietzsche' seriously.

Daniel Conway (ed.), *Nietzsche and "The Antichrist": Religion, Politics and Culture in Late Modernity*: up-to-date series of essays representing a range of current approaches and historico-intellectual contexts to Nietzsche's work.

Giles Fraser, *Redeeming Nietzsche*: written from a religious perspective, suggests that Nietzsche was obsessed with the question of human salvation.

Dylan Jaggard, 'Nietzsche's *Antichrist*': examines *The Anti-Christ*, arguing for the importance of this work for understanding Nietzsche's critique of Christian moral values.

Paul Katsafanas, 'The Antichrist as a Guide to Nietzsche's Mature Ethical Theory': argues, contrary to the view of many commentators, that *The Anti-Christ* offers not just a critique of traditional morality but a substantive ethical theory that articulates positive ethical principles.

Dennis King Keenan, 'Nietzsche: The Eternal Return of Sacrifice', in *The Question of Sacrifice*: situates Nietzsche's thought in general and *The Anti-Christ* in particular in the context of a problematic concept, i.e., sacrifice.

Martin Liebscher, 'The Anti-Christ': offers a useful overview of some of the main themes and ideas of *The Anti-Christ* as part of a guide to Nietzsche's life and works.

Morgan H. Rempel, '*Daybreak* 68: Nietzsche's Psychohistory of the pre-Damascus Paul': discusses a text illuminating Nietzsche's later critique of Paul of Tarsus in *The Anti-Christ*.

Weaver Santaniello, 'Nietzsche's Hierarchy of Gods in the *Anti-Christ*': defends Nietzsche against the charge of anti-Semitism by arguing that his position aims to refute the fundamental position of anti-Semitic Christian theology.

Gary Shapiro, 'The Text as Graffito: Historical Semiotics (*The Antichrist*)': argues that Nietzsche anticipates Heidegger and Derrida by using the figure of *erasure* to designate his own relation to Christianity.

Andreas Urs Sommer, *Kommentar zu Nietzsches "Der Antichrist", "Ecce homo", "Dionysos-Dithyramben", "Nietzsche contra Wagner"* (NK 6/2): offers extensive commentary, contextualisation and analysis of all facets of Nietzsche's *The Anti-Christ* – albeit in German.

Andreas Urs Sommer, *Friedrich Nietzsches "Der Antichrist": Ein philosophisch-historischer Kommentar*: while a work in its own right, constitutes an earlier (and longer) version of Sommer's commentary as NK 6/2.

Julian Young, 'The Antichrist': part of a broader discussion of Nietzsche's philology of religion; ignores his vitriolic attacks on Christianity to examine his positive alternative – his view on the healthy society and the role of religion in it.

Bibliography

Adorno, Theodor W., and Max Horkheimer. 2002. *Dialectic of Enlightenment: Philosophical Fragments* [1944], ed. Gunzelin Schmid Noerr, trans. Edmund Jephcott. Stanford: Stanford University Press.
Alexandre, Laurent. 2015. *La Mort de la mort: Comment la techno-médicine va bouleverser l'humanité.* Paris: J. C. Lattès.
Anatrella, Tony. 1983. *Non à la société dépressive.* Paris: Flammarion.
Andreas-Salomé, Lou. 1983. *Nietzsche in seinen Werken* [1894], ed. Ernst Pfeiffer. Frankfurt am Main: Insel.
— 2001. *Nietzsche*, ed. and trans. Siegfried Mandel. Champaign: University of Illinois Press.
Armstrong, Karen. 1983. *The First Christian: St Paul's Impact on Christianity.* London: Pan.
Arnobius. 1871. *The Seven Books of Arnobius "Adverses Gentes"*, trans. Archibald Hamilton Bryce and Hugh Campbell. Edinburgh: Clark.
Ashworth, E. Jennifer. 2017. 'Medieval Theories of Analogy', in *The Stanford Encyclopedia of Philosophy* (fall 2017 edition), ed. Edward N. Zalta. <https://plato.stanford.edu/archives/fall2017/entries/analogy-medieval/>.
Athanasius. 2009. *On the Incarnation*, trans. Penelope Lawson. Grand Rapids: Christian Classics Ethereal Library.
Augustine. 2002. *The Trinity*, trans. Stephen MacKenna. Washington, DC: Catholic University of America Press.
Austin, J. L. 2013. 'Truth' [1950], *Proceedings of the Aristotelian Society*, virtual issue no. 1. <https://www.aristoteliansociety.org.uk/pdf/austin.pdf>.

Ayres, Lewis. 2011. 'Augustine on the Trinity', in *The Oxford Handbook of the Trinity*, ed. Gilles Emery and Matthew Levering. New York: Oxford University Press, 123–36.

Baeumer, Max. 1976. 'Nietzsche and the Tradition of the Dionysian', in *Studies in Nietzsche and the Classical Tradition*, ed. James C. O'Flaherty, Timothy F. Sellner and Robert M. Helm. Chapel Hill: University of North Carolina Press, 165–89.

Balaudé, Jean-François, and Patrick Wotling, eds. 2012. *«L'art de bien lire»: Nietzsche et la philologie*. Paris: Vrin.

Bamford, Rebecca (ed.). 2015. *Nietzsche's Free Spirit Philosophy*. New York: Rowman and Littlefield.

Barker, Ernest, ed. 1952. *The Politics of Aristotle*, trans. Ernest Barker. Oxford: Clarendon Press.

Barnes, Jonathan. 1987. *Early Greek Philosophy*. Harmondsworth: Penguin.

Bartha, Paul. 2016. 'Analogy and Analogical Reasoning', in *The Stanford Encyclopedia of Philosophy* (winter 2016 edition), ed. Edward N. Zalta. <https://plato.stanford.edu/archives/win2016/entries/reasoning-analogy/>.

Baur, F. C. 1876. *Paul the Apostle of Jesus Christ: His Life and Works, His Epistles and His Doctrine*, trans. Allan Menzies. 2 vols. London: Williams and Norgate.

Bazzano, Manu. 2006. *Buddha is Dead: Nietzsche and the Dawn of European Zen*. Eastbourne: Sussex Academic Press.

Benders, Raymond J., Stephan Oettermann et al. 2000. *Friedrich Nietzsche: Chronik in Bildern und Texten*. Munich: Hanser.

Benedict XVI [Josef Ratzinger]. 2008. *Die Kirchenväter – frühe Lehrer der Christenheit*. Regensburg: Pustet.

— 2009. *Saint Paul*. San Francisco: Ignatius Press.

Benne, Christian. 2005. *Nietzsche und die historisch-kritische Philologie*. Berlin: de Gruyter.

Bennett, Benjamin. 1979. 'Nietzsche's Idea of Myth: The Birth of Tragedy from the Spirit of Eighteenth-Century Aesthetics', *Publications of the Modern Languages Association of America*, 94.3: 420–33.

Berry, Jessica N. 2007. 'The Legacy of Hellenic Harmony', in *The Oxford Handbook of Continental Philosophy*, ed. Michael

Rosen and Brian Leiter. New York: Oxford University Press, 588–625.
— 2019. 'Nietzsche's Attack on Belief: Doxastic Skepticism in *The Antichrist*', *Journal of Nietzsche Studies*, 50.2: 187–209.
Bett, Richard. 2011. 'Nietzsche and the Romans', *Journal of Nietzsche Studies*, 42.1: 7–31.
Bianquis, G. 1929. *Nietzsche en France: L'influence de Nietzsche sur la pensée française*. Paris: Alcan.
Biebuyck, Benjamin, Danny Praet and Isabelle Vanden Poel. 2004. 'Cults and Migrations: Nietzsche's Meditations on Orphism, Pythagoreanism, and the Greek Mysteries', in *Nietzsche and Antiquity: His Reaction and Response to the Classical Tradition*, ed. Paul Bishop. Rochester, NY: Camden House, 151–69.
Bishop, Paul. 2002. 'Ludwig Klages's Early Reception of Friedrich Nietzsche', *Oxford German Studies*, 31: 129–60.
— 2002/2003. 'Ein Kind Zarathustras und eine nicht-metaphysische Auslegung der ewigen Wiederkehr', *Hestia: Jahrbuch der Klages-Gesellschaft*, 21: 15–37.
— 2009. 'Eudaimonism, Hedonism, and Feuerbach's Philosophy of the Future', *Intellectual History Review*, 19.1: 65–81.
— 2017. 'Just a Moment? Or, The Archaic as an Expression of the Eternal in Time', in *Time and the Psyche: Jungian Perspectives*, ed. Angeliki Yiassemides. London: Routledge, 87–105.
— 2018. *Ludwig Klages and the Philosophy of Life: A Vitalist Toolkit*. London: Routledge.
— 2020. 'Goethe, Nietzsche, Varoufakis: Why Did the Greeks Matter – and Still Do?', in *European/Supra-European: Cultural Encounters in Nietzsche's Philosophy*, ed. Marco Brusotti, Michael McNeal, Corinna Schibert and Herman Siemens. Berlin: de Gruyter, 19–48.
Bishop, Paul, ed. 2004. *Nietzsche and Antiquity: His Reaction and Response to the Classical Tradition*. Rochester, NY: Camden House.
— ed. 2012. *A Companion to Friedrich Nietzsche, Life and Works*. Rochester, NY: Camden House.
Blondel, Éric. 1994. 'Notes', in Friedrich Nietzsche, *L'Antéchrist*, ed. and trans. Éric Blondel. Paris: Flammarion, 135–80.

Bloom, Allan. 1968. *The Republic of Plato: Translated, with Notes, an Interpretive Essay, and a New Introduction*. 2nd edn. New York: Basic Books.

Blue, Daniel. 2016. *The Making of Friedrich Nietzsche: The Quest for Identity, 1844–1869*. Cambridge: Cambridge University Press.

Blumenberg, Hans. 1983. *The Legitimacy of the Modern Age* [1966], trans. Robert M. Wallace. Cambridge, MA: MIT Press.

Bonardel, Françoise. 2020. *Vacuités. Sortir du nihilisme grâce au bouddhisme?* Paris: Kimé.

Bootle, Roger. 2019. *The AI Economy: Work, Wealth and Welfare in the Robot Age*. London: John Murray.

Bostrom, Nick. 2005. 'A History of Transhumanist Thought', *Journal of Evolution and Technology*, 14.1: 1–25.

Bourget, Paul. 1883. *Essais de psychologie contemporaine*. Paris: Lemerre.

Bouriant, Urbain. 1892. *Fragments du texte grec du livre d'Énoch et de quelques écrits attribués à Saint Pierre*. Paris: Leroux.

Boyancé, Pierre. 1962. 'Sur les mystères d'Éleusis', *Revue des Études grecques*, 75.356–8: 460–82.

Boyd, Ryan. 2011. 'Pascal and Nietzsche', *Think*, 10.20: 59–70.

Bradley, Arthur. 2006. 'Derrida's God: A Genealogy of the Theological Turn', *Paragraph*, 29.3: 21–42.

Brandes, Wolfram, and Felicitas Schmieder (eds). 2010. *Antichrist: Konstruktionen von Feindbildern*. Berlin: Akademie Verlag.

Bremmer, Jan. N. 2014. *Initiation into the Mysteries of the Ancient World*. Berlin: de Gruyter.

Brock, Eike. 2015. *Nietzsche und der Nihilismus*. Monographien und Texte zur Nietzsche-Forschung, vol. 68. Berlin: de Gruyter.

Brown, Gary. 1990. 'Introduction' [to 'Richard Wagner in Bayreuth'], in Friedrich Nietzsche, *Unmodern Observations*, ed. William Arrowsmith. New Haven: Yale University Press, 227–52.

Bubbio, Paolo Diego. 2014. *Sacrifice in the Post-Kantian Tradition: Perspectivism, Intersubjectivity, and Recognition*. Albany: State University of New York Press.

Bultmann, Rudolf. 1971. *The Gospel of John: A Commentary*. Louisville, KY: Westminster John Knox Press.

Burckhardt, Jacob. 1880. *Die Zeit Constantin's des Grossen*. 2nd edn. Leipzig: E. A. Seemann.
— 1910. *Griechische Kulturgeschichte*, ed. Jakob Oeri. 5th edn, vol. 1. Berlin: Spemann.
— 1930–31. *Griechische Kulturgeschichte* [*Gesamtausgabe*, vols. 8–11], ed. Felix Stähelin and Samuel Merian. Berlin: Deutsche Verlagsanstalt.
— 1998. *The Greeks and Greek Civilization* [*Griechische Kulturgeschichte* 1898–1902], ed. Oswyn Murray, trans. Sheila Stern. New York: St Martin's Press.
Burkert, Walter. 1983. *Homo Necans: The Anthropology of Ancient Greek Sacrificial Ritual and Myth* [1972], trans. Peter Bing. Berkeley: University of California Press.
— 1985. *Greek Religion: Archaic and Classical* [1977], trans. John Ruffan. Oxford: Blackwell.
Burkitt, F. Crawford. 1915. 'Johannes Weiss: In Memoriam', *The Harvard Theological Review*, 8.3: 291–7.
Butler, E. M. 1935. *The Tyranny of Germany over Greece*. Cambridge: Cambridge University Press.
Cammaerts, Emile. 1937. *The Laughing Prophet: The Seven Virtues and G.K. Chesterton*. London: Methuen.
Carter, Jeffrey, ed. 2003. *Understanding Religious Sacrifice: A Reader*. London: Continuum.
Cassirer, Ernst. 1955. *The Philosophy of Symbolic Forms*, vol. 2: *Mythical Thought*, trans. Ralph Manheim. New Haven: Yale University Press.
— 1957. *The Philosophy of Symbolic Forms*, vol. 3: *The Phenomenology of Knowledge*, trans. Ralph Manheim. New Haven: Yale University Press.
Catechism of the Catholic Church, with modifications from the Editio typica. 1997. New York: Doubleday.
Chapman, Malcolm. 1992. *The Celts: The Construction of a Myth*. Basingstoke/New York: Macmillan/St Martin's Press.
Clement. 2003. *First Letter to the Corinthians*, in *The Apostolic Fathers*, vol. 1: *I Clement; II Clement; Ignatius; Polycarp; Didache*, trans. Bart D. Ehrman. Cambridge, MA: Harvard University Press, 34–151.
Collis, John. 2003. *The Celts: Origins, Myths and Invention*. Stroud: Tempus Publishing.

Conche, Marcel. 2007. *Nietzsche et le bouddhisme: édition augmentée.* Paris: encre marine.
Conway, Daniel, ed. 2019. *Nietzsche and "The Antichrist": Religion, Politics and Culture in Late Modernity.* London: Bloomsbury Academic.
Cupitt, Don. 1984. *The Sea of Faith: Christianity in Change.* London: BBC.
Currie, Robert. 1974. *Genius: An Ideology in Literature.* London: Chatto and Windus.
Deleuze, Gilles, and Félix Guattari. 1980. *Mille Plateaux.* Paris: Éditions de Minuit.
Detienne, Marcel. 1989. 'Culinary Practices and the Spirit of Sacrifice', in Marcel Detienne and Jean-Pierre Vernant, *The Cuisine of Sacrifice among the Greeks*, trans. Paula Wissing. Chicago: University of Chicago Press, 1–20.
Deussen, Paul. 1883. *Das System des Vedânta.* Leipzig: F. A. Brockhaus.
— 1887. *Die Sûtra's des Vedânta [. . .] aus dem Sanskrit übersetzt.* Leipzig: F. A. Brockhaus.
Dillmann, August. 1851. *Liber Henoch Aethiopice, ad quinque codicum fidem editus, cum variis lectionibus.* Leipzig: Vogel.
— 1853. *Das Buch Henoch übersetzt und erklärt.* Leipzig: Vogel.
Donnellan, Brendan. 1979a. 'Nietzsche and La Rochefoucauld', *The German Quarterly*, 52.3: 303–18.
— 1979b. 'Nietzsche and Pascal', *The Germanic Review*, 54.3: 89–97.
Doubrovsky, Serge. 2003. 'The Ethics of Albert Camus', in *Bloom's BioCritiques: Albert Camus*, ed. Harold Bloom. Philadelphia: Chelsea House, 95–111.
Eckermann, Johann. 1981. *Gespräche mit Goethe in den letzten Jahren seines Lebens*, ed. Fritz Bergemann. Frankfurt am Main: Insel.
Edward, Richard A. 1976. *A Theology of Q: Eschatology, Prophecy, and Wisdom.* Philadelphia: Fortress Press.
Eliade, Mircea. 1976. *Occultism, Witchcraft, and Cultural Fashions: Essays in Comparative Religion.* Chicago: University of Chicago Press.
Elman, Benjamin A. 1983. 'Nietzsche and Buddhism', *Journal of the History of Ideas*, 44.4: 671–86.
Emden, Christian J. 2019. 'Nihilism, Naturalism, and the Will to Power in Nietzsche's *The Antichrist*', in *Nietzsche and*

"The Antichrist", ed. Daniel Conway. London: Bloomsbury Academic, 159–80.

Emerson, Caryl, George Pattison and Randall A. Poole, eds. 2020. *The Oxford Handbook of Russian Religious Thought*. New York: Oxford University Press.

Etter, Annmarie. 1987. 'Nietzsche und das Gesetz-Buch des Manu', *Nietzsche-Studien*, 16: 340–52.

Foley, A. 2015. 'As Platonic as Zarathustra: Nietzsche and Gustav Teichmüller', *Archiv für Begriffsgeschichte*, 57: 217–23.

Förster, Eckart. 2001. 'Goethe and the "Auge des Geistes"', *Deutsche Vierteljahrsschrift für Literaturwissenschaft und Geistesgeschichte*, 75: 87–101.

Förster-Nietzsche, Elisabeth. 1915. *Wagner und Nietzsche zur Zeit ihrer Freundschaft*. Munich: Müller.

— 1954. 'Introduction [to *Thus Spake Zarathustra*]', in *The Philosophy of Nietzsche*, trans. Thomas Common. New York: Modern Library, xix–xxxii.

Foley, Helene P., ed. 1994. *The Homeric Hymn to Demeter: Translation, Commentary, and Interpretive Essays*. Princeton: Princeton University Press.

Forget, Jacques. 1910. 'Holy Ghost', in *Catholic Encyclopedia*, ed. Charles G. Herbermann et al. New York: Encyclopedia Press, vol. 7, 409–15.

Frank, Joseph. 2002. *Dostoevsky*, vol. 5: *The Mantle of the Prophet, 1871–1881*. Princeton: Princeton University Press.

Frank, Manfred. 1982. *Der kommende Gott: Vorlesungen über die Neue Mythologie*, vol. 1. Frankfurt am Main: Suhrkamp.

Fraser, Giles. 2002. *Redeeming Nietzsche: On the Piety of Unbelief*. London: Routledge.

Freud, Sigmund. 1990. *The Origins of Religion* [Penguin Freud Library, vol. 13], trans. James Strachey, ed. Albert Dickson. Harmondsworth: Penguin.

Fukuyama, Francis. 1992. *The End of History and the Last Man*. New York: Free Press.

— 1995. *Trust: Social Virtues and Creation of Prosperity*. New York: Free Press.

Geraci, Robert M. 2008. 'Apocalyptic AI: Religion and the Promise of Artificial Intelligence', *Journal of the American Academy of Religion*, 76.1: 138–66.

— 2010. *Apocalyptic AI: Visions of Heaven in Robotics, Artificial Intelligence, and Virtual Reality*. New York: Oxford University Press.

Gesthuisen, Johannes. 1985. *Das Nietzsche-Bild Hans Urs von Balthasars: Ein Zugang zur »Apokalypse der deutschen Seele«*. Rome: Gregorian Pontifical University.

Gibbon, Edward. 1840. *The History of the Decline and Fall of the Roman Empire*, ed. H. H. Milman, vol. 2. New York: Harper.

Giegerich, Wolfgang. 2004. 'The End of Meaning and the Birth of Man', *Journal of Jungian Theory and Practice*, 6.1: 1–66.

Girard, René. 2001. *I See Satan Fall Like Lightning* [1999], trans. James G. Williams. Maryknoll, NY: Orbis Books.

— 2005. *Violence and the Sacred* [1972], trans. Patrick Gregory. London: Continuum.

Goethe, Johann Wolfgang. 1994. *Elective Affinities*, trans. David Constantine. Oxford: Oxford University Press.

Grant, Frederick Clifton. 1915. 'St Paul and Stoicism', *The Biblical World*, 45.5: 268–81.

Gregory of Nazianzus. 2003. *Select Orations*, trans. Martha Pollard Vinson. Washington, DC: Catholic University of America Press.

Griffioen, Sjoerd. 2016. 'Modernity and the Problem of its Christian Past: The *Geistesgeschichten* of Blumenberg, Berger, and Gauchet', *History and Theory*, 55: 185–209.

Grillaert, Nel. 2008. *What the God-Seekers Found in Nietzsche: The Reception of Nietzsche's "Übermensch" by the Philosophers of the Russian Religious Renaissance*. Amsterdam: Rodopi.

Grimes, Pierre, and Regina L. Uliana. 1998. *Philosophical Midwifery: A New Paradigm for Understanding Human Problems with its Validation*. Costa Mesa, CA: Hyparxis Press.

Grottanelli, Cristiano. 1997. 'Nietzsche and Myth', *History of Religions*, 37.1: 3–20.

Gründer, Karlfried, ed. 1989. *Der Streit um Nietzsches "Geburt der Tragödie": Die Schriften von E. Rohde, R. Wagner, U. von Wilamowitz-Moellendorff*. Hildesheim: Olms.

Guéranger, Prosper. 2000a. *The Liturgical Year*, vol. 6: *Passiontide and Holy Week*, trans. Laurence Shepherd. Great Falls, MT: St. Bonaventura Publications.

— 2000b. *The Liturgical Year*, vol. 12: *Time After Pentecost: Book III*, trans. Laurence Shepherd. Great Falls, MT: St. Bonaventura Publications.
Guyau, Jean-Marie. 1887. *L'irréligion de l'avenir: Étude sociologique*. 2nd edn. Paris: Alcan.
— 1897. *The Non-Religion of the Future: A Sociological Study*. New York: Holt.
Habermas, Jürgen. 2006. 'Religion in the Public Sphere', *European Journal of Philosophy*, 14.1: 1–25.
— 2008. *Between Naturalism and Religion*, trans. C. Cronin. Cambridge: Polity.
Habermas, Jürgen, and Joseph Ratzinger. 2005. *Dialektik der Säkularisierung: Über Vernunft und Religion*. Freiburg im Breisgau: Herder.
— 2006. *The Dialectics of Secularization: On Reason and Religion* [2005], trans. Brian McNeil. San Francisco: Ignatius Press.
Hamerton-Kelly, Robert G., ed. 1987. *Violent Origins: Walter Burkert, René Girard & Jonathan Z. Smith on Ritual Killing and Cultural Formation*. Stanford: Stanford University Press.
Harnoncourt, Nikolaus. 2020. *Über Musik: Mozart und die Werkzeuge des Affen*. Salzburg: Residenz Verlag.
Harris, J. Rendel. 1925. 'Apollo at the Back of the North Wind', *Journal of Hellenic Studies*, 45.2: 229–42.
Hatab, Lawrence J. 2019. 'A Revived God in *The Antichrist*? Nietzsche and the Sacralization of Natural Life', in *Nietzsche and "The Antichrist"*, ed. Daniel Conway. London: Bloomsbury Academic, 7–20.
Havemann, Daniel. 2001. 'Evangelische Polemik: Nietzsches Paulusdeutung', *Nietzsche-Studien*, 30: 175–86.
— 2002. *Der "Apostel der Rache": Nietzsches Paulusdeutung*. Berlin: de Gruyter
Haydock, George Leo. 2006. *The Holy Catholic Bible with a Comprehensive Catholic Commentary*. Duarte, CA: Catholic Treasures.
Hayward, John, ed. 1964. *The Oxford Book of Nineteenth-Century Verse*. Oxford: Oxford University Press.
Heath, Peter. 1992. *Allegory and Philosophy in Avicenna (Ibn Sînâ)*. Philadelphia: University of Pennsylvania Press.

Hegel, G. W. F. 1956. *The Philosophy of History*, trans. John Sibree [1861, as *Lectures on the Philosophy of World History*]. Mineola, NY: Dover.
Hehn, Victor. 1921. *Gedanken über Goethe*. Darmstadt: Reichl.
Heidegger, Martin. 1985. 'Who is Nietzsche's Zarathustra?' [1964], in *The New Nietzsche: Contemporary Styles of Interpretation*, ed. David B. Allison. Cambridge, MA: MIT Press, 64–79.
— 1991a. *Nietzsche: Volume I: The Will to Power as Art. Volume II: The Eternal Recurrence of the Same*, trans. David Farrell Krell. San Francisco: HarperCollins.
— 1991b. *Nietzsche: Volume III: The Will to Power as Knowledge of Metaphysics. Volume IV: Nihilism*, trans. David Farrell Krell. San Francisco: HarperCollins.
— 2004. *Nietzsche: Seminare 1937 und 1944: Nietzsches metaphysische Grundstellung (Sein und Schein): 2. Skizzen zu Grundbegriffen des Denkens*, ed. Peter von Ruckteschell [*Gesamtausgabe*, Abt. 4, vol. 87]. Frankfurt am Main: Vittorio Klostermann.
Heise, Ulf. 2000. *»Ei da ist ja auch Herr Nietzsche«: Leipziger Werdejahre eines Philosophen*. Beucha: Sax-Verlag.
Hemming, Laurence Paul, Kostas Amiridis and Bogdan Costea, eds. 2011. *The Movement of Nihilism: Heidegger's Thinking After Nietzsche*. London: Continuum.
Henrichs, Albert. 1984. 'Loss of Self, Suffering, Violence: The Modern View of Dionysus from Nietzsche to Girard', *Harvard Studies in Classical Philology*, 88: 205–40.
Hesiod. 1982. *The Homeric Hymns and Homerica*, trans. Hugh G. Evelyn-White. Cambridge, MA/London: Harvard University Press/Heinemann.
Holland, John H., Keith J. Holyoak, Richard E. Nisbett and Paul E. Thagard. 1986. *Processes of Inference, Learning, and Discovery*. Cambridge, MA: MIT Press.
Hollingdale, R. J. 1969. 'Introduction', to Friedrich Nietzsche, *Thus Spoke Zarathustra*. Harmondsworth: Penguin, 11–35.
Horace. 1786. *Satyren*, trans. C. M. Wieland. 2 vols. Leipzig: Weidmanns Erben und Reich.
— 1942. *Satires; Epistles; and Ars Poetica*, trans. H. Rushton Fairclough. Cambridge, MA/London: Harvard University Press/Heinemann.

— 2004. *Odes and Epodes*, ed. and trans. Niall Rudd. Cambridge, MA: Harvard University Press.

Horneffer, Ernst. 1900. *Nietzsches Lehre von der ewigen Wiederkunft und deren bisherige Veröffentlichung*. Leipzig: Naumann.

— 1907. *Nietzsches letztes Schaffen*. Jena: Diederichs.

Hubert, Henri, and Marcel Mauss. 1964. *Sacrifice: Its Nature and Function*, trans. W. D. Halls. Chicago: University of Chicago Press.

Huddleston, Andrew. 2018. 'Against "Egypticism": Nietzsche on Understanding and "Defining" Concepts', in *The Nietzschean Mind*, ed. Paul Katsafanas. London: Routledge, 381–94.

Hultgren, Stephen. 2002. *Narrative Elements in the Double Tradition: A Study of Their Place within the Framework of the Gospel Narrative*. Berlin: de Gruyter.

Hume, David. 1975. *Enquiries Concerning Human Understanding and Concerning the Principles of Morals*, ed. L. A. Selby-Brigge. 3rd edn. Oxford: Clarendon Press.

Huskinson, Lucy. 2009. *The SPCK Introduction to Nietzsche: His Religious Thought*. London: SPCK.

Huysmans, J. K. 1997. *The Cathedral*, trans. Clara Bell [1898]. Sawtry: Dedalus.

Iamblichus. 1988. *The Exhortation to Philosophy: Including the Letters of Iamblichus and Proclus' Commentary on the Chaldean Oracles*, ed. Stephen Neuville [1907], trans. Thomas Moore Johnson. Grand Rapids: Phanes Press.

Inagaki, Hisao, trans. 2003. *The Three Pure Land Sutras*. Berkeley: Numata Center for Buddhist Translation and Research.

Inge, William Ralph. 1918. *Christian Mysticism: Considered in Eight Lectures* [1899]. 4th edn. London: Methuen.

Irenæus of Lyons. 2010. *Against Heresies: The Complete English Translation from the First Volume of "The Ante-Nicene Fathers"*. South Bend: Ex Fontibus.

Jaeggi, Rahel. 2014. *Alienation*, ed. Frederick Neuhouser, trans. Frederick Nouhouser and Alan E. Smith. New York: Columbia University Press.

Jaggard, Dylan. 2013. 'Nietzsche's *Antichrist*', in *The Oxford Handbook of Nietzsche*, ed. John Richardson and Ken Gemes. Oxford: Oxford University Press, 344–62.

James, M. R., ed. 1924. *The Apocryphal New Testament*. Oxford: Clarendon Press.

Janaway, Christopher. 2007. *Beyond Selflessness: Reading Nietzsche's "Genealogy"*. Oxford: Oxford University Press.

Jaspers, Karl. 1977. *Nietzsche: An Introduction to the Understanding of His Philosophical Activity* [1936], trans. Charles F. Wallraff and Frederick J. Schmitz. Baltimore: Johns Hopkins University Press.

Jensen, Anthony K. 2014. 'Friedrich Ritschl, Otto Jahn, Friedrich Nietzsche', *German Studies Review*, 37.3: 529–47.

— 2019. 'Nietzsche's Quest for the Historical Jesus', in *Nietzsche and "The Antichrist"*, ed. Daniel Conway. London: Bloomsbury Academic, 117–40.

Jensen, Anthony K., and Helmut Heit, eds. 2014. *Nietzsche as a Scholar of Antiquity*. Bloomsbury Studies in Philosophy. London: Bloomsbury Academic.

John Paul II. 2003. General Audience of Wednesday, 1 October 2003. <https://w2.vatican.va/content/john-paul-ii/en/audiences/2003/documents/hf_jp-ii_aud_20031001.html>. Accessed 18 May 2021.

Julian. 1923. 'Against the Galileans', in *Letters; Epigrams; Against the Galilaeans; Fragments* [*Works*, vol. 3], trans. William C. Wright. Cambridge, MA: Harvard University Press, 319–427.

Jung, C. G. 1953. *Two Essays on Analytical Psychology* [*Collected Works*, vol. 7], trans. R. F. C. Hull. London: Routledge and Kegan Paul.

— 1968. *Aion: Researches into the Phenomenology of the Self*. [*Collected Works*, vol. 9/ii], trans. R. F. C. Hull. Princeton: Princeton University Press.

— 1969. *The Archetypes and the Collective Unconscious* [*Collected Works*, vol. 9/i], trans. R. F. C. Hull. Princeton: Princeton University Press.

— 1971. *Psychological Reflections*, ed. Jolande Jacobi. London: Routledge and Kegan Paul.

— 1973. *Letters*, vol. 1, *1906–1950*, ed. Gerhard Adler and Aniela Jaffé, trans. R. F. C. Hull. Princeton: Princeton University Press.

— 1983. *Alchemical Studies*. [*Collected Works*, vol. 13], trans. R. F. C. Hull. Princeton: Princeton University Press.

— 1989. *Seminar on Nietzsche's "Zarathustra": Notes of the Seminar given in 1934–1939*, ed. James Jarrett. 2 vols. London: Routledge.
— 1998. *Seminar on Nietzsche's "Zarathustra": Abridged Edition*, ed. James L. Jarrett. Princeton: Princeton University Press.
— 2009. *The Red Book: Liber Novus*, ed. Sonu Shamdasani, trans. Mark Kyburz, John Peck and Sonu Shamdasani. New York: W. W. Norton.
— 2014. *The Symbolic Life: Miscellaneous Writings* [Collected Works, vol. 18], trans. R. F. C. Hull. New York: Routledge.
Katsafanas, Paul. 2018. '*The Antichrist* as a Guide to Nietzsche's Mature Ethical Theory', in *The Nietzschean Mind*, ed. Paul Katsafanas. London: Routledge, 83–101.
Kaufmann, Walter. 1950. *Nietzsche: Philosopher, Psychologist, Antichrist*. Princeton: Princeton University Press.
Keenan, Dennis King. 2005. *The Question of Sacrifice*. Bloomington: Indiana University Press.
Kelly, Henry Ansgar. 2006. *Satan: A Biography*. Cambridge: Cambridge University Press.
Klages, Ludwig. 1926a. *Die psychologischen Errungenschaften Nietzsches*. Leipzig: J. A. Barth.
— 1926b. *Vom kosmogonischen Eros*. 2nd extended edn. Jena: Diederichs.
Köhler, Joachim. 2002. *Zarathustra's Secret: The Interior Life of Friedrich Nietzsche* [1989], trans. Ronald Taylor. New Haven: Yale University Press.
Köster, Peter. 1981/1982. 'Nietzsche-Kritik und Nietzsche-Rezeption in der Theologie des 20. Jahrhunderts', *Nietzsche-Studien*, 10/11: 615–85.
— 1998. *Der verbotene Philosoph: Studien zu den Anfängen der katholischen Nietzsche-Rezeption in Deutschland (1890–1918)*. Berlin: de Gruyter.
— 2003. 'Letzte Haltungen? Hans Urs von Balthasars «Apokalypse der deutschen Seele»', in *Kontroversen um Nietzsche: Untersuchungen zur theologischen Rezeption*. Zurich: Theologischer Verlag, 365–78.
Kuhn, Elisabeth. 2000. 'Décadence', in *Nietzsche Handbuch: Leben – Werk – Wirkung*, ed. Henning Ottmann. Stuttgart and Weimar: Metzler, 215–17.

Lagarde, Paul de. 1878–81. 'Ueber das verhältnis des deutschen Staates zu Theologie, Kirche und Religion', in *Deutsche Schriften*. 2 vols. Göttingen: Dieterich, vol. 1, 5–54.

— 1887. *Mittheilungen*, vol. 2. Göttingen: Dieterich.

Lampert, Laurence. 1986. *Nietzsche's Teaching: An Interpretation of "Thus Spoke Zarathustra"*. New Haven: Yale University Press.

— 1993. *Nietzsche and Modern Times: A Study of Bacon, Descartes, and Nietzsche*. New Haven: Yale University Press.

— 2001. *Nietzsche's Task: An Interpretation of "Beyond Good and Evil"*. New Haven: Yale University Press.

Law, David R. 2012. *The Historical-Critical Method: A Guide for the Perplexed*. London: Continuum.

Layton, Bentley, ed. 1987. *The Gnostic Scriptures*. London: SCM Press.

— ed. 1989. *Nag Hammadi codex II,2– 7*, vol. 1: *Gospel according to Thomas, Gospel according to Philip, Hypostasis of the Archons, and Indexes*. Leiden: Brill.

Lea-Henry, Jed. 2018. 'Climate Change and the Joys of Punishment with David Deutsch and Friedrich Nietzsche', *Studia Philosophica Estonica*, 12: 99–114.

Lebreton, Lucie. 2017. 'Nietzsche, lecteur de Pascal: «le seul chrétien logique»', *Revue philosophique de la France et de l'étranger*, 142.2: 175–94.

Ledure, Yves. 1984. *Lectures «chrétiennes» de Nietzsche: Maurras, Papini, Scheler, de Lubac, Marcel, Mounier*. Paris: Le Cerf.

Leijenhorst, Cees. 2006. 'Rudolf Steiner', in *Dictionary of Gnosis & Western Esotericism*, ed. Wouter J. Hanegraaff et al. Leiden: Brill, 1084–91.

Leis, Mario. 2000. *Frauen um Nietzsche*. Reinbek bei Hamburg: Rowohlt.

Lessing, G. E. 1956. 'On the Proof of the Spirit and Power', in *Lessing's Theological Writings*, ed. Henry Chadwick. Stanford: Stanford University Press, 51–6.

Liebscher, Martin. 2012. 'The Anti-Christ', in *A Companion to Friedrich Nietzsche, Life and Works*, ed. Paul Bishop. Rochester, NY: Camden House, 339–60.

Lim, Timothy H., and John J. Collins, eds. 2010. *The Oxford Handbook of the Dead Sea Scrolls*. Oxford: Oxford University Press.

Lipovetsky, Gilles. 1983. *L'ère du vide: Essais sur l'individualisme contemporain*. Paris: Gallimard.

Lippert, Julius. 1881. *Die Religionen der europäischen Culturvölker, der Litauer, Slaven, Germanen, Griechen und Römer, in ihrem geschichtlichen Ursprunge*. Berlin: T. Hofmann.

Lods, Adolphe. 1892. *Le Livre d'Hénoch: Fragments grecs découverts à Akhmîm (Haute-Égypte), publiés avec les variantes du texte éthiopien*. Paris: Leroux.

Loeb, Paul S. 2019. 'Nietzsche's Critique of Kant's Priestly Philosophy', in *Nietzsche and "The Antichrist"*, ed. Daniel Conway. London: Bloomsbury Academic, 89–116.

Loman, A. D. 1887. 'Een Engelsche anonymus over den oorsprong des christendoms', *Theologisch Tijdschrift*, 21: 597–653.

Lot-Borodine, Myrrha. 1970. *La déification de l'homme selon la doctrine des pères grecs*. Paris: Le Cerf.

Lührmann, Dieter. 1969. *Die Redaktion der Logienquelle*. Neukirchen-Vluyn: Neukirchener Verlag.

Lyotard, Jean-François. 2004. *Libidinal Economy*, trans. Iain Hamilton Grant. London: Continuum.

Macarius of Egypt, St. 1921. *Fifty Spiritual Homilies of Saint Macarius the Egyptian*, trans. A. J. Mason. London: SPCK.

Maccoby, Hyam. 1991. *Paul and Hellenism*. Philadelphia: Trinity Press International.

Macdonald, Dennis R. 2000. *The Homeric Epics and the Gospel of Mark*. New Haven: Yale University Press.

Manktelow, K. I. 2009. *Reasoning and Thinking*. Hove: Psychology Press.

— 2012. *Thinking and Reasoning: An Introduction to the Psychology of Reason, Judgment and Decision Making*. London: Psychology Press.

Mann, Thomas. 1961. *The Story of a Novel: The Genesis of "Doctor Faustus"*, trans. Richard and Clara Winston. New York: Knopf.

Marx, Karl. 1983. *The Portable Marx*, ed. Eugene Kamenka. New York: Viking Penguin.

McGinn, Bernard. 2000. *Antichrist: Two Thousand Years of the Human Fascination with Evil*. 2nd edn. New York: Columbia University Press.

— 2005. 'Mystical Union in Judaism, Christianity, and Islam', in *Encyclopedia of Religion*. <https://www.encyclopedia.com/environment/encyclopedias-almanacs-transcripts-and-maps/mystical-union-judaism-christianity-and-islam>. Accessed 20 November 2018.

Meister Eckhart. 1987. *Sermons & Treatises*, vol. 1, ed. and trans. M. O'C. Walshe. Longmead: Element.

Menzel, Wolfgang. 1870. *Die vorchristliche Unsterblichkeitslehre*. 2 vols. Leipzig: Fues.

Meyer, Katrin, and Barbara von Reibnitz, eds. 1999. *Friedrich Nietzsche / Franz und Ida Overbeck: Briefwechsel*. Stuttgart: Metzler.

Meyer, Marvin W., ed. 1987. *The Ancient Mysteries: A Sourcebook of Sacred Texts*. Philadelphia: University of Pennsylvania Press.

Meyer, Matthew. 2019. *Nietzsche's Free Spirit Works: A Dialectical Reading*. Cambridge: Cambridge University Press.

Milbank, John. 1995. 'Stories of Sacrifice: From Wellhausen to Girard', *Theory, Culture & Society*, 12: 15–46.

Mistry, Freny. 1981. *Nietzsche and Buddhism: Prolegomenon to a Comparative Study*. Berlin: de Gruyter.

Montalembert, Charles Forbes de Tryon. 1860. *Die Mönche des Abendlandes vom h[eiligen] Benedikt zum h[eiligen] Bernhard*, trans. Karl Brandes, vol. 2. Regensburg: G. J. Manz.

Montinari, Mazzino. 1972. 'Ein neuer Abschnitt in Nietzsches "Ecce Homo"', *Nietzsche-Studien*, 1: 380–418.

— 1982. 'Nietzsches Nachlass von 1885 bis 1888 oder Textkritik und Wille zur Macht', in *Nietzsche lesen*. Berlin: de Gruyter, 92–119.

— 2003. 'A New Section in Nietzsche's Ecce Homo', and 'Nietzsche's Unpublished Writings from 1885 to 1888; or, Textual Criticism and the Will to Power', in *Reading Nietzsche*, trans. Greg Whitlock. Urbana: Illinois University Press, 2003, 103–40 and 80–102.

Monville, Aymeric. 2007. *Misère du «nietzschéisme de gauche»: De Georges Bataille à Michel Onfray*. Brussels: Aden.

Moore, Gregory. 2002. *Nietzsche, Biology and Metaphor*. Cambridge: Cambridge University Press.

Morrison, Robert G. 1999. *Nietzsche and Buddhism: A Study in Nihilism and Ironic Affinities*. New York: Oxford University Press.

Müller, August. 1885–87. *Der Islam im Morgen- und Abendland*. 2 vols. Berlin: Grote.

Müller, Max. 1881. 'Buddhism' [1862], in *Selected Essays on Language, Mythology and Religion*. London: Longmans, Green, vol. 2, 160–233.

— 1883. *India: What Can It Teach Us? A Course of Lectures Delivered Before the University of Cambridge*. London: Longmans, Green.

Murray, Gilbert. 2002. *The Five Stages of Greek Religion*. New York: Dover.

Murray, Peter, and Linda Murray. 2013. 'Preface', in *The Oxford Dictionary of Christian Art and Architecture*, ed. Peter Murray, Linda Murray and Tom Devonshire Jones. 2nd edn. Oxford: Oxford University Press, xviii–ix.

Musgrave Calder III, William. 1983. 'The Wilamowitz–Nietzsche Struggle: New Documents and a Reappraisal', *Nietzsche-Studien*, 12: 214–54.

Musurillo, Herbert, SJ. 1957. 'History and Symbol: A Study of Form in Early Christian Literature', *Theological Studies*, 18.3: 357–86.

Nagy, Gregory. 2013. *The Ancient Greek Hero in 24 Hours*. Cambridge, MA: Belknap Press of Harvard University Press.

Natoli, Charles M. 1985. *Nietzsche and Pascal on Christianity*. New York: Lang.

Neale, J. M., and R. F. Littledale. 1874. *A Commentary on the Psalms from Primitive and Mediæval Writers*. 4 vols. London: Masters.

Neymeyr, Barbara. 2020. *Kommentar zu Nietzsches "Unzeitgemässen Betrachtungen": I. David Strauss der Bekenner und der Schriftsteller; II. Vom Nutzen und Nachtheil der Historie für das Leben*. Historischer und kritischer Kommentar zu Friedrich Nietzsches Werken, vol. 1/2. Berlin: de Gruyter.

Nicholson, Ernest. 2002. *The Pentateuch in the Twentieth Century: The Legacy of Julius Wellhausen*. Oxford: Oxford University Press.

Nietzsche, Friedrich. 1899. *The Case of Wagner; Nietzsche Contra Wagner, The Twilight of the Idols; The Antichrist* [*Works*, vol. 3], trans. Thomas Common. London: T. Fischer Unwin.
— 1908. *Human, All Too Human*, trans. Alexander Harvey. Chicago: Kerr.
— 1911. *Ecce Homo (Nietzsche's Autobiography)*, trans. Anthony M. Ludovici. New York: Macmillan.
— 1920. *The Anti-Christ*, trans. H. L. Mencken. New York: A. A. Knopf.
— 1921. *Selected Letters*, ed. Oscar Levy. Garden City, NY: Doubleday, Page.
— 1924a. *The Dawn of Day*, trans. J. M. Kennedy. London: Allen and Unwin.
— 1924b. *The Joyful Wisdom*, trans. Thomas Common. New York: Macmillan.
— 1962. *Philosophy in the Tragic Age of the Greeks*, trans. Marianne Cowan. Washington, DC: Regnery.
— 1966. *Werke in drei Bänden*, ed. Karl Schlechta. 3 vols plus index. Munich: Hanser.
— 1967–. *Werke: Kritische Gesamtausgabe*, ed. Giorgio Colli and Mazzino Montinari, then Volker Gerhardt, Norbert Miller, Wolfgang Müller-Lauter, Karl Pestalozzi and the Berlin-Brandenburgische Akademie der Wissenschaften. 40 vols in 9 sections. Berlin: de Gruyter.
— 1967–77; 1988. *Sämtliche Werke: Kritische Studienausgabe*, ed. Giorgio Colli and Mazzino Montinari. 15 vols. Berlin/Munich: de Gruyter/Deutscher Taschenbuch Verlag.
— 1968a. *Basic Writings*, ed. and trans. Walter Kaufmann. New York: Modern Library.
— 1968b. *Twilight of the Idols/The Anti-Christ*, trans. R. J. Hollingdale. Harmondsworth: Penguin.
— 1968c. *The Will to Power*, ed. Walter Kaufmann, trans. Walter Kaufmann and R. J. Hollingdale. New York: Random House.
— 1969. *Thus Spoke Zarathustra*, trans. R. J. Hollingdale. Harmondsworth: Penguin.
— 1974. *The Gay Science*, ed. and trans. Walter Kaufmann. New York: Random House.

— 1975–. *Briefwechsel: Kritische Gesamtausgabe*, ed. Giorgio Colli and Mazzino Montinari. Berlin: de Gruyter.
— 1975–84. *Sämtliche Briefe: Kritische Studienausgabe*, ed. Giorgio Colli and Mazzino Montinari. 8 vols. Berlin/Munich: de Gruyter/Deutscher Taschenbuch Verlag.
— 1983. *Untimely Meditations*, trans. R. J. Hollingdale. Cambridge: Cambridge University Press.
— 1986. *Human, All Too Human*, trans. R. J. Hollingdale. Cambridge: Cambridge University Press.
— 1990. 'We Classicists', in *Unmodern Observations*, ed. William Arrowsmith. New Haven: Yale University Press, 321–87.
— 1992. *Ecce Homo*, trans. R. J. Hollingdale. Harmondsworth; Penguin.
— 1994 [1933–40]. *Frühe Schriften, 1854–1869*, ed Hans Joachim Mette, Karl Schlechta and Carl Koch. 5 vols. Munich: Beck.
— 1995. *Unpublished Writings from the Period of "Unfashionable Observations"*, trans. Richard T. Gray. Stanford: Stanford University Press.
— 2003. *Writings from the Late Notebooks*, ed. Rüdiger Bittner, trans. Kate Sturge. Cambridge: Cambridge University Press.
— 2007. 'The Greek State', in *On the Genealogy of Morality*, ed. Keith Ansell-Pearson, trans. Carol Diethe. Cambridge: Cambridge University Press, 164–73.
— 2009. *Writings from the Early Notebooks*, ed. Raymond Geuss and Alexander Nehamas, trans. Ladislaus Löb. Cambridge: Cambridge University Press.
— 2014. *On the Future of our Educational Institutions*, trans. J. M. Kennedy [1910]. Scotts Valley, CA: CreateSpace.
— 2019. *Platon* [*Ecrits philologiques*, vol. 8], trans. and ed. Anne Merker. Paris: Les Belles Lettres.
Novalis. 1978. *Das philosophisch-theoretische Werk* [*Werke, Tagebücher und Briefe*, vol. 1], ed. Hans-Joachim Mähl. Munich: Hanser.
Oldenberg, Hermann. 1881. *Buddha: Sein Leben, seine Lehre, seine Gemeinde*. Berlin: Hertz.
Olivelle, Patrick, ed. and trans. 2005. *Manu's Code of Law: A Critical Edition and Translation of the Mānava-Dharmásāstra*. New York: Oxford University Press.

Onfray, Michel. 1993. *La Sculpture de soi: La morale esthétique*. Paris: Grasset.
— 2006a. *La Sagesse tragique: Du bon usage de Nietzsche*. Paris: Le Livre de poche.
— 2006b. *Le christianisme hédoniste* [*Contre-histoire de la philosophie*, vol. 2]. Paris: Grasset.
— 2007a. *Atheist Manifesto: The Case Against Christianity, Judaism, and Islam*, trans. Jeremy Leggatt. New York: Arcade.
— 2007b. *Les Ultras des Lumières* [*Contre-histoire de la philosophie*, vol. 4]. Paris: Grasset.
— 2011a. *La Construction du surhomme* [*Contre-histoire de la philosophie*, vol. 7]. Paris: Grasset.
— 2011b. *Le Post-Anarchisme expliqué à ma Grand-mère*. 2 CDs. Vincennes: Frémeaux & Associés.
— 2015. *Cosmos: Une ontologie matérialiste* [*Brève encyclopédie du monde*, vol. 1]. Paris: Flammarion.
— 2017. *Décadence: Vie et mort du judéo-christianisme* [*Brève encyclopédie du monde*, vol. 2]. Paris: Flammarion.
— 2019. *Sagesse: Savoir vivre au pied d'un volcan* [*Brève encyclopédie du monde*, vol. 3]. Paris: Flammarion.
Orsucci, Andrea. 1996. *Orient – Okzident: Nietzsches Versuch einer Loslösung vom europäischen Weltbild*. Berlin: de Gruyter.
Osborn, Ronald E. 2017. *Humanism and the Death of God: Searching for the Good After Darwin, Marx, and Nietzsche*. Oxford: Oxford University Press.
Ottmann, Henning, ed. 2000. *Nietzsche Handbuch: Leben – Werk – Wirkung*. Stuttgart: Metzler.
Ouvaroff, M. 1816. *Essai sur les mystères d'Eleusis*. 3rd edn. Paris: Imprimerie Royale.
— 1817. *Essay on the Mysteries of Eleusis*, trans. J. D. Price. London: Rodwell and Martin.
Overbeck, Franz. 2012. *Erinnerungen an Friedrich Nietzsche: Mit Briefen an Heinrich Köselitz (Peter Gast)*. Berlin: Berenberg.
Owen, David. 2019. 'Nietzsche's Antichristian Ethics: Renaissance *Virtù* and the Project of Reevaluation', in *Nietzsche and "The Antichrist"*, ed. Daniel Conway. London: Bloomsbury Academic, 67–88.

Palmer, G. E. H., Philip Sherrard and Kallistos Ware, ed. and trans. 2010: *The Philokalia: The Complete Text*, vol. 4. London: Faber and Faber.

Panaïoti, Antoine. 2013. *Nietzsche and Buddhist Philosophy*. Cambridge: Cambridge University Press.

— 2019. 'Comparative Religion in *The Antichrist*: Pastiche, Subversion, Cultural Intervention', in *Nietzsche and "The Antichrist"*, ed. Daniel Conway. London: Bloomsbury Academic, 43–66.

Papias of Hierapolis. 1894. *The Oracles Ascribed to Matthew: A Contribution to the Criticism of the New Testament*. London: Longmans, Green.

Parkes, Graham, ed. 1991. *Nietzsche and Asian Thought*. Chicago: University of Chicago Press.

Pascal. 1963. *Œuvres complètes*, ed. Louis Lafuma. Paris: Seuil.

Patrides, C. A., ed. 1969. *The Cambridge Platonists*. London: Arnold.

Payne, Robert. 1958. *The Holy Fire: The Story of the Early Centuries of the Christian Church in the Near East*. Crestwood, NY: St Vladimir's Seminary Press.

Peerbolte, L. J. Lietaert. 1996. *The Antecedents of Antichrist: A Traditio-Historical Study of the Earliest Christian Views on Eschatalogical Opponents*. Leiden: Brill.

Pernet, Martin. 1995. 'Friedrich Nietzsche and Pietism', *German Life and Letters*, 48.4: 474–86.

Petrarca, Francesco. 2008. 'On His Own Ignorance and That of Many Others', in *Invectives*, trans. David Marsh. Cambridge, MA: Harvard University Press, 113–83.

Philo. 2000. *The Works of Philo*, trans. C. D. Yonge. Peabody, MA: Hendrickson.

Pindar. 1927. *The Odes of Pindar including the Principal Fragments*, trans. John Sandys. London/New York: Heinemann/Putnam.

Plato. 1989. *Collected Dialogues, including the Letters*, ed. Edith Hamilton and Huntington Cairns. Princeton: Princeton University Press.

Pliny. 1967. *Natural History*, vol. 3: *Books 8–11*, trans. H. Rackham. Cambridge, MA/London: Harvard University Press/Heinemann.

Plotinus. 1988. *Works VII: Enneads VI.6–9*, trans. A. H. Armstrong. Cambridge, MA/London: Harvard University Press/Heinemann.

— 1989. *Works I: Porphyry on Plotinus; Ennead I*, trans. A. H. Armstrong. Cambridge, MA/London: Harvard University Press/Heinemann.

Plutarch. 1969. *Moralia*, vol. 15: *Fragments from Other Named Works*, trans. F. H. Sandbach. Cambridge, MA: Harvard University Press.

Porter, James I. 2000. *Nietzsche and the Philology of the Future*. Stanford: Stanford University Press.

Pouderon, Bernard, Jean-Marie Salamito and Vincent Zarini (eds). 2016. *Premiers écrits chrétiens*. Paris: Gallimard.

Price, Robert M. 2016. *Blaming Jesus for Jehovah: Rethinking the Righteousness of Christianity*. Valley, WA: Tellectual Press.

Proclus. 1963. *The Elements of Theology: A Revised Text with Translation, Introduction and Commentary*, trans. E. R. Dodds. 2nd edn. Oxford: Clarendon Press.

Rempel, Morgan. 1998. 'Daybreak 68: Nietzsche's Psychohistory of the pre-Damascus Paul', *Journal of Nietzsche Studies*, 15: 50–8.

— 2010. 'Nietzsche, Mithras, and "Complete Heathendom"', *Comparative and Continental Philosophy*, 2.1: 27–43.

— 2012. 'Daybreak 72: Nietzsche, Epicurus, and the After Death', *Journal of Nietzsche Studies*, 43.2: 342–54.

Renan, Ernest. 1863. *Vie de Jésus*. Paris: Lévy.

— 1877. *Les Évangiles et la seconde génération chrétienne* [*Histoire des origines du Christianisme*, vol. 5]. Paris: Lévy.

— 1904. *Marcus Aurelius* [*Marc-Aurèle et la fin du monde antique*, 1882], trans. William G. Hutchison. London and Newcastle upon Tyne: Scott.

Richard of St Victor. 1979. *The Twelve Patriarchs; The Mystical Ark; Book Three of "The Trinity"*, ed. and trans. Grover A. Zinn. New York: Paulist Press.

Ridley, Aaron. 2012. 'Nietzsche: *The Anti-Christ, Ecce Homo, Twilight of the Idols*', in *Introductions to Nietzsche*, ed. Robert B. Pippin. Cambridge: Cambridge University Press, 215–39.

Rippere, Vickey. 1981. *Schiller and "Alienation"*. Berne: Lang.

Roberts, Alexander, James Donaldson and Arthur Cleveland Coxe, eds. 1885. *The Ante-Nicene Fathers*, vol. 4: *Fathers of the Third Century: Tertullian, Part Fourth; Minucius Felix; Commodian; Origen, Parts First and Second*. Grand Rapids: Eerdmans.

Robinson, James M. 1964. 'LOGOI SOPHON: Zur Gattung der Spruchquelle Q', in *Zeit und Geschichte: Dankesgabe an Rudolf Bultmann zum 80. Geburtstag*, ed. Erich Dinkler. Tübingen: Mohr, 77–96.

— 1971. '"Logoi Sophon": On the *Gattung* of Q', in *Trajectories through Early Christianity*, ed. James M. Robinson and Helmut Koester. Philadelphia: Fortress Press, 71–113.

Robinson, James M., ed. 1988. *The Naghammadi Library in English.* 3rd rev. edn. Leiden: Brill.

Salaquarda, Jörg. 1974. 'Dionysos gegen den Gekreuzigten: Nietzsches Verständnis des Apostels Paulus', *Zeitschrift für Religionsgeschichte*, 26: 97–124.

Salis-Marschlins, Meta von. 1897. *Philosoph und Edelmensch: Ein Beitrag zur Charakteristik Friedrich Nietzsches.* Leipzig: C. G. Naumann.

Santaniello, Weaver. 2000. 'Nietzsche's Hierarchy of Gods in the *Anti-Christ*', *Journal of Nietzsche Studies*, 19 [special issue: Nietzsche and Religion]: 89–102.

Sarrasin, Thilo. 2010. *Deutschland schafft sich ab: Wie wir unser Land auf Spiel setzen.* Munich: Deutsche Verlags-Anstalt.

— 2018. *Feindliche Übernahme: Wie der Islam den Fortschritt behindert und die Gesellschaft bedroht.* Munich: FinanzBuch Verlag.

Schaff, Philip, ed. 1888. *Nicene and Post-Nicene Fathers*, First Series, vol. 8. Buffalo: Christian Literature Publishing.

Schaff, Philip, and Henry Wace, eds. 1893. *Nicene and Post-Nicene Fathers*, Second Series, vol. 5: *Gregory of Nyssa: Dogmatic Treatises; Selected Writings and Letters.* Buffalo: Christian Literature Publishing.

Schelling, Friedrich Wilhelm Joseph. 1977. *Schelling's Treatise on "The Deities of Samothrace"*, trans. Robert F. Brown. Missoula, MT: Scholars Press.

Schenk, Wolfgang. 1981. *Synopse zur Redenquelle der Evangelien: Q – Synopse und Rekonstruktion in deutscher Übersetzung mit kurzen Erläuterungen.* Düsseldorf: Patmos.

Schiaparelli, Annamaria, and Paolo Crivelli. 2012. 'Aristotle on Poetry', in *The Oxford Handbook of Aristotle*, ed. Christopher Shields. New York: Oxford University Press, 612–26.

Schiller, Friedrich. 1844. 'The Gods of Greece' [1788], in *The Minor Poems of Schiller of the Second and Third Periods*, trans. John Herman Merivale. London: William Pickering, 16–21.

—— 1982. *On the Aesthetic Education of Man in a Series of Letters* [1794], ed. and trans. Elizabeth M. Wilkinson and L. A. Willoughby. Oxford: Clarendon Press.

Schlechta, Karl. 1966. 'Philologischer Nachbericht', in W 3, 1383–1432.

Schleiermacher, Friedrich. 1996. *Dialectic, or, The Art of Doing Philosophy: A Study Edition of the 1811 Notes*, ed. and trans. Terrence N. Tice. Atlanta: Scholars Press.

—— 2001. 'Über die Zeugnisse des Papias von unsern beiden ersten Evangelien' [1832], in *Kritische Gesamtausgabe*, ed. Hermann Patsch and Dirk Schmid, vol. 1.8: *Exegetische Schriften*. Berlin: de Gruyter, 227–54.

Schmidt, Jochen, and Sebastian Kaufmann. 2015. *Kommentar zu Nietzsches "Morgenröte"; Kommentar zu Nietzsches "Idyllen aus Messina"*. Historischer und kritischer Kommentar zu Friedrich Nietzsches Werken, vol. 3/1. Berlin: de Gruyter.

Schmithals, Walter. 1971. *Gnosticism in Corinth: An Investigation of the Letters to the Corinthians* [1956], trans John E. Steely. Nashville: Abingdon Press.

Schöll, Adolf. 1882. *Goethe im Hauptzüge seines Lebens und Wirkens: Gesammelte Abhandlungen*. Berlin: Hertz.

Schoeller-Reisch, Donata. 1998. 'Die Demut Zarathustras: Ein Versuch zu Nietzsche mit Meister Eckhart', *Nietzsche-Studien*, 27: 420–39.

Schömann, G. F. 1868. *Die Hesiodische Theogonie ausgelegt und beurtheilt*. Berlin: Weidmann.

Schopenhauer, Arthur. 1966. *The World as Will and Representation*, trans. E. F. J. Payne. 2 vols. New York: Dover.

—— 2010. *The Two Fundamental Problems of Ethics*, trans. David E. Cartwright and Edward E. Erdmann. Oxford: Oxford University Press.

Schrift, Alan D. 1990. *Nietzsche and the Question of Interpretation: Between Hermeneutics and Deconstruction*. London: Routledge.

Schulz, Siegfried. 1972. *Q: Die Spruchquelle der Evangelisten*. Zurich: Theologischer Verlag.

Schweitzer, Albert. 1910. *The Quest of the Historical Jesus: A Critical Study of its Progress from Reimarus to Wrede*, trans. W. Montgomery. London: Adam and Charles Black.

Scolari, Paolo. 2018. 'Gabriel Marcel and Nietzsche: Existence and Death of God', *Nietzsche-Studien*, 47: 398–409.
Seneca. 2009. *De Clementia*, ed. and trans. Susanna Braund. Oxford: Oxford University Press.
Seydel, Rudolf. 1882. *Das Evangelium von Jesu in seinen Verhältnissen zur Buddha-Sage und Buddha-Lehre*. Leipzig: Breitkopf und Härtel.
Shapiro, Gary. 1989. 'The Text as Graffito: Historical Semiotics (*The Antichrist*)', in *Nietzschean Narratives*. Bloomington: Indiana University Press, 124–41.
— 2016. *Nietzsche's Earth: Great Events, Great Politics*. Chicago: University of Chicago Press.
— 2019. 'Reading Dostoevsky in Turin: *The Antichrist*'s Accelerationism', in *Nietzsche and "The Antichrist"*, ed. Daniel Conway. London: Bloomsbury Academic, 229–52.
Skarsaune, Oskar. 1987. *The Proof from Prophecy: A Study in Justin Martyr's Proof-Text Tradition: Text-Type, Provenance, Theological Profile*. Leiden: Brill.
Soloviev, Vladimir. 1915. *War, Progress, and the End of History, Including a Short Story of the Anti-Christ: Three Discussions*, trans. Alexander Bakshy. London: University of London Press.
Sommer, Andreas Urs. 1998. 'Augustinus bei Franz Overbeck: Ein Rekonstruktionsversuch', *Theologische Zeitschrift*, 54: 125–50.
— 2000. *Friedrich Nietzsches "Der Antichrist": Ein philosophisch-historischer Kommentar*. Basel: Schwabe.
— 2007. '[Review of] Christian Benne, *Nietzsche und die historisch-kritische Philologie*', *Arbitrium: Zeitschrift für Rezensionen zur germanistischen Literaturwissenschaft*, 24.3: 399–401.
— 2012. *Kommentar zu Nietzsches "Der Fall Wagner"; "Götzen-Dämmerung"*. Historischer und kritischer Kommentar zu Friedrich Nietzsches Werken, vol. 6/1. Berlin: de Gruyter.
— 2013. *Kommentar zu Nietzsches "Der Antichrist"; "Ecce homo"; "Dionysos-Dithyramben"; "Nietzsche contra Wagner"*. Historischer und kritischer Kommentar zu Friedrich Nietzsches Werken, vol. 6/2. Berlin: de Gruyter.
— 2016. *Kommentar zu Nietzsches "Jenseits von Gut und Böse"*. Historischer und kritischer Kommentar zu Friedrich Nietzsches Werken, vol. 5/1. Berlin: de Gruyter.

Sorgner, Stefan Lorenz. 2009. 'Nietzsche, the Overhuman, and Transhumanism', *Journal of Evolution and Technology*, 20.1: 29–42.

Spariosu, Mihai I. 1989. *Dionysus Reborn: Play and the Aesthetic Dimension in Modern Philosophical and Scientific Discourse*. Ithaca: Cornell University Press.

Sparks, H. F. D., ed. 1984. *The Apocryphal Old Testament*. Oxford: Clarendon Press.

Spinoza, Benedict de. 1955. *On the Improvement of the Understanding; The Ethics; Correspondence*, trans. R. H. M. Elwes. New York: Dover.

Stack, George G. 1993. 'Nietzsche's Earliest Essays: Translation and Commentary on "Fate and History" and "Freedom of Will and Fate"', *Philosophy Today*, 37.2: 153–69.

Staniforth, Maxwell, trans. 1968. *Early Christian Writings*. Harmondsworth: Penguin.

Stein, Charles. 2016. 'Ancient Mysteries', in *The Cambridge Handbook of Western Mysticism and Esotericism*, ed. Glenn Alexander Magee. Cambridge: Cambridge University Press, 3–12.

Steiner, Rudolf. 1960. *Friedrich Nietzsche, Fighter for Freedom* [1895], trans. Margaret Ingram deRis. Englewood Cliffs, NJ: Rudolf Steiner Publications.

— 1963. *Friedrich Nietzsche, ein Kämpfer gegen seine Zeit* [1895]. Dornach: Rudolf Steiner Verlag.

— 1997. *Christianity as Mystical Fact* [1902], trans. Andrew Welburn. Hudson, NY: Anthroposophic Press.

— 2006. *Autobiography: Chapters in the Course of My Life 1861–1907*, trans. Rita Stebbing (revised). Great Barrington, MA: Steiner Books.

Stern, Tom. 2019. 'History, Nature, and the "Genetic Fallacy" in *The Anti-Christ*'s Revaluation of Values', in *Nietzsche and "The Antichrist"*, ed. Daniel Conway. London: Bloomsbury Academic, 21–42.

Stock, Brian. 1972. *Myth and Science in the Twelfth Century*. Princeton: Princeton University Press.

Straesser, Robert B., ed. 2008. *The Landmark Herodotus: The Histories*, trans. Andrea L. Purvis. London: Quercus.

Strong, Tracy. 2019. 'Nietzsche and the Critique of Religion', in *Nietzsche and "The Antichrist"*, ed. Daniel Conway. London: Bloomsbury Academic, 141–58.

— 2001. *Friedrich Nietzsche and the Politics of Transfiguration*. 3rd edn. Champaign: University of Illinois Press.

Stroux, Johannes. 1925. *Nietzsches Professur in Basel*. Jena: Frommann.

Suetonius. 1913–14. *The Lives of the Caesars*, vol. 1: *Julius. Augustus. Tiberius. Gaius. Caligula*, trans. J. C. Rolfe. Cambridge, MA: Harvard University Press.

Taylor, Thomas, trans. 1995. *Proclus: The Theology of Plato*. Thomas Taylor Series, vol. 8. Westbury: Prometheus Trust.

— trans. 1999. *Iamblichus: "On the Mysteries of the Egyptians, Chaldeans, and Assyrians" and "Life of Pythagoras"*. Thomas Taylor Series, vol. 17. Sturminster Newton: Prometheus Trust.

— trans. 2001. *Oracles and Mysteries*. Thomas Taylor Series, vol. 7. Frome: Prometheus Trust.

Teichmüller, Gustav. 1882. *Die wirkliche und die scheinbare Welt: Neue Grundlegung der Metaphysik*. Breslau: Koebner.

Tertullian/Minucius Felix. 1929. *Apology; De Spectaculis*, trans. R. R. Glover and Gerald H. Rendall. Cambridge, MA/London: Harvard University Press/Heinemann.

Theißen, Gerd. 1973. 'Wanderradikalismus: Literatursoziologische Aspekte der Überlieferung von Worten Jesu im Urchristentum', *Zeitschrift für Theologie und Kirche*, 70: 245–71.

— 1977. *Soziologie der Jesusbewegung: Ein Beitrag zur Entstehungsgeschichte des Urchristentums*. Munich: Kaiser.

Tolstoy, Leo. 1894. *The Kingdom of God Is Within You*, trans. Constance Garrett. New York: Cassell.

Tongeren, Paul van. 2018. *Friedrich Nietzsche and European Nihilism*. Cambridge: Cambridge Scholars Publishing.

Tylor, Edward Burnett. 1871. *Researches into the Development of Mythology, Philosophy, Religion, Art, and Custom*. 2 vols. London: John Murray.

Valdez, Damian. 2014. *German Philhellenism: The Pathos of the Historical Imagination from Winckelmann to Goethe*. New York: Palgrave Macmillan.

van der Braak, André. 2010. *Nietzsche and Zen*. Lanham, MD: Lexington Books.
— 2015. 'Zen and Zarathustra', *Journal of Nietzsche Studies*, 46.1: 2–11.
Vergely, Bertrand. 2004. *La Foi, ou la nostalgie de l'admirable* [2002]. Paris: Albin Michel.
— 2010. *Retour à l'émerveillement*. Paris: Albin Michel.
— 2019. *Transhumanisme: la grande illusion*. Paris: Le Passeur.
Vermes, Geza, ed. 1997. *The Complete Dead Sea Scrolls in English*. New York: Allen Lane/Penguin.
Vinson, Julien. 1888. 'Bibliographie' [review of Paul Gibier, *Le Spiritisme (Fakirisme occidental)*, 1887], *Revue de linguistique et de philologie comparée*, 21: 75–87.
Vivarelli, Vivetta. 2007. '[Review of] Christian Benne, *Nietzsche und die historisch-kritische Philologie*', *Orbis Litterarum*, 62.5: 430–3.
Voegelin, Eric. 1996. 'Nietzsche and Pascal', *Nietzsche-Studien*, 25.1: 128–71.
von Hellwald, Friedrich. 1877. *Culturgeschichte in ihrer natürlichen Entwicklung bis zur Gegenwart*, vol. 2. 2nd enlarged edn. Augsburg: Lampart.
Waite, Geoff. 1996. *Nietzsche's Corps/e: Aesthetics, Politics, Prophecy, or: The Spectacular Technoculture of Everyday Life*. Durham, NC: Duke University Press.
Wansbrough, Henry, ed. 1985. *The New Jerusalem Bible*. London: Darton, Longman and Todd.
Wellhausen, Julius. 1882. *Prolegomena zur Geschichte Israels* [3rd edn, 1886; Eng. trans., Edinburgh, 1883, 1891; 5th German edn, 1899; first published in 1878 as *Geschichte Israels*]. Berlin: G. Reimer.
Wells, G.A. 1971. *The Jesus of the Early Christians: A Study in Christian Origins*. London: Pemberton Books.
— 1975. *Who was Jesus?* London: Pemberton Books.
— 1988. *The Historical Evidence for Jesus*. Buffalo: Prometheus Books.
— 1989. *Who was Jesus? A Critique of the New Testament Record*. LaSalle, IL: Open Court.
Wiggershaus, Rolf. 1994. *The Frankfurt School: Its History, Theories, and Political Significance*, trans. Michael Robertson. Cambridge, MA: MIT Press.

Williams, W. D. 1952. *Nietzsche and the French: A Study of the Influence of Nietzsche's French Reading on his Thought and Writing*. Oxford: Blackwell.
Wilson, A. N. 1999. *God's Funeral*. London: Murray.
Wilson, John Elbert. 1996. *Schelling und Nietzsche: Zur Auslegung der frühen Werke Friedrich Nietzsches*. Berlin: de Gruyter.
Yarbrough, Robert W. 1983. 'The Date of Papias: A Reassessment', *Journal of the Evangelical Theological Society*, 26.2: 181–91.
Young, Julian. 2003. *The Death of God and the Meaning of Life*. London: Routledge.
— 2006. 'The Antichrist', in *Nietzsche's Philosophy of Religion*. Cambridge: Cambridge University Press, 177–89.
— 2007. 'Nihilism and the Meaning of Life', in *The Oxford Handbook of Continental Philosophy*, ed. Michael Rosen and Brian Leiter. New York: Oxford University Press. 463–93.
Zeller, Dieter. 1984. *Kommentar zur Logienquelle*. Stuttgart: Verlag Katholisches Bibelwerk.
Zeller, Edward. 1875. *The Contents and Origin of the Acts of the Apostles, Critically Investigated*, trans. Joseph Dare. London: Williams and Norgate.

Index

Abraham (Abram), 98–9
Acts of the Apostles, 112, 214, 222, 234
Adonis, 94–5
Adorno, T. W., 165, 207
aere perennius ('a monument more lasting than bronze'), 14, 34, 171–3, 175
al-Andalus, 86, 189
Al-Hakam II (Caliph), 86
Alaric, 126
Alexandre, L., 268
Alexandrian period, 54–5, 236
Alexandrian School, 229
allegoresis, 236
amor fati, 66, 159–60
Ananius of Damascus, 231
anarchism, 167, 175, 193
Anatrella, T., 267
Anrich, G., *Das antike Mysterienwesen in seinem Einluss auf das Christenthum*, 125
anti-Christ (theological concept), 40–7, 269
archons, 44–5
Aristides, *Sacred Orations*, 132
Aristotle, 54
   Metaphysics, 129
   Poetics, 185–6
   Politics, 158n,

Armstrong, K., 219
Aristeas (Greek poet), 47
Arnobius of Sicca, *Adversus gentes*, 176
Arnold, M., 1–2
Arnold, R., 20, 241
'art of life', 157
Aryans, 148, 151
Athanasius of Alexandra (Saint), 132, 133n
atheism, 63, 269
Attic period, 54
Augustine of Hippo (Saint), 42, 60–2, 136, 210–11, 220, 253n

Baal (deity), 100
Bachofen, J. J., 208
Bacon, F., *Essays, Civil and Moral*, 78
Balthasar, H. U. von, 257
Barnabas (Saint), 222–3
Barth, K., 220
Basil the Great (Saint), 217
Bataille, G., 203
Battle of the Milvian Bridge, 186
Benne, C., 236–7, 240
Berger, P. L., 260
Beyschlag, W., 209n
Blavatsky, Helena, 121
'blond beast', 150, 196

INDEX

Blondel, É., 262
Blue, D., 17–19
Blumenberg, H., 259–60
Bötticher, K., *Die Tektonik der Hellenen*, 125
Bonardel, F., 97
Bonn, 19–20, 239–40
Bonn School of philology, 240–1
Borgia, Cesare, 14, 191–2, 228
Bousset, W., 41
Bowden, H., 129
Bremmer, J. N., 129
Brockhaus, H., 20
'Buddha of Europe' (Nietzsche as), 81n
Buddhism, 10, 33, 76, 80–97, 218–19, 269
Bulgakov, S., 264
Bultmann, R., 73
Burckhardt, J., 21n, 249
　Die Zeit Constantins des Grossen, 124, 175–6
　The Culture of the Renaissance in Italy, 176, 238
　Vorlesungen über griechische Kulturgeschichte, 139–40
Burkert, W., 94–5, 129

Calvin, J., 220
Cambridge Platonism, 133n
Camus, A., 155n
Cassirer, E., 24–5, 131, 207
Catechism of the Catholic Church, 91n, 154n, 156n, 248n
catechisms, 51–2
Celsus, 31, 75, 132
Chamberlain, H. S., 148
chandala, 14, 148–53, 167, 177, 181, 269
Chateaubriand, F.-R. de, 143
Chesterton, G. K., 266
Christ (meaning of word), 7, 270

Christ (Nietzsche's portrait of), 63–74
classical education, 23, 28
Clement of Alexandria, 229n
Constantine (Emperor), 56, 124, 186
Conway, D., 4, 37, 49n, 183
Córdoba, 86
Corinthinans, First Letter to, 8, 72, 74, 155, 187, 215, 218, 221, 227, 232
Corinthians, Second Letter to, 74n, 110n, 222, 231, 232
'courtesy of the heart', 166
Creuzer, F., *Symbolik und Mythologie der alten Völker*, 123–4, 244
Cross, symbol of the, 20, 26–35, 119–20, 136, 181, 186, 253
Crusades, 187
Cupitt, D., 2
Cudworth, R., 133n
Curtius, G., *Grundzüge der griechischen Etymologie*, 137–8
Cyprian (Saint), 254
Cyril of Alexandria (Saint), 60
Cyril of Jerusalem (Saint), 42
Cyrus of Persia, 103

Daniel, Book of, 41–4, 113–15
Deleuze, G., 267
'death-drive' (thanatos), 107
'death of God', 63, 100, 194, 263–7, 270
'death of the symbol', 6
décadence, 170, 173, 183, 219, 247
'denaturalisation', 11, 97, 99, 101, 103, 107, 265
eternal recurrence (doctrine), 39, 140, 142, 197, 199
Dawkins, R., 260

Derrida, J., 203, 208
Detienne, M., 206
Deussen, P., 36, 39, 85, 96, 237, 242
Deuteronomic source, 98
Deuteronomy, Book of, 204
Diogenes Laertius, 241
Dick, P. K., 146
Dionysos, 137–45, 244–5, 270
'documentary hypothesis', 98
Dostoevsky, F., 263–4, 267–8
Durkheim, É., 207
doxastic scepticism, 275

Eckhart von Hochheim, 84, 225–6
Eckermann, J. P., 244
'Egypticism', 148
El (deity), 100
Eleusis, mysteries of (Greater and Lesser), 124–6, 128–9, 135, 139
Elijah, 100
Eliot, T. S., *The Waste Land*, 123, 205
Elohistic source, 98
Empedocles, 26
Engelhardt, M. von, 253n
Enoch, Book of, 114, 152–3
ephexis, 13, 237, 256
Epictetus, 31–2, 177
Epicurus, 12, 85, 157, 178–80, 212, 229–30, 251
'equal rights (for all)', 167, 226
'equality of souls before God', 193
Esdras, Second Book of, 114
Eusebius of Caesarea, 186n
Exodus, Book of, 8, 194
Ezekiel, 103
Ezekiel, Book of, 113–14
Ezra, 104, 114, 254
Ezra, Fourth Book of, *see* Esdras, Second Book of

Fabro, C., 257
Fichte, J. G., 10, 18
Flaubert, G., 252
Florensky, P., 264
Förster-Nietzsche, E., 19, 38, 69, 121, 134–5
Francis of Assisi (Saint), 65
Fraser, G., 34–5
Frazer, J. G., *The Golden Bough*, 122–3, 205
'free spirit', 12, 39, 50, 52, 74, 76–7, 110
Freud, S., *Totem and Taboo*, 107, 205, 206–7
Fritsch, T. (editor of *Antisemitische Correspondenz*), 151
Frobenius, L., 207
Fukuyama, F., 2

Galatians, Letter to, 215, 222
Galton, F., *Inquiries into Human Faculty and its Development*, 87
Gauchet, M., 260
Génébrard, G., 254
Genesis, Book of, 13, 152, 233
genius, Nietzsche's concept of, 67–8
Gersdorff, C. von, 243
Gibbon, E., *The Rise and Fall of the Roman Empire*, 58–9, 173
Gideon, 99
Girard, R., 203, 268
Gnosticism, 44, 119, 264
Gobineau, A. de, 146
Godwin, W., 173
Goethe, J.W., 34, 76, 84, 190, 212, 244, 252
  Elective Affinities, 166
  Faust, 5
  'On German Architecture', 238

INDEX

on 'spiritual eye', 131
on the Dionysian, 140
gospel (concept), 12, 32, 66–7, 72, 201–2, 218, 222, 227, 231, 270
Graf, K. H., 98
'grand style', 57
graves and resurrections, 37
Graves, R., 123
Great Mother, cult of, 120, 181
Gregory of Nazianzus (Saint), 132, 217
Gregory of Nyssa (Saint), 132–3, 195
Gregory Palamas (Saint), 133
Gruppe, O., 125, *Die griechischen Kulte und Mythen*, 125
Guardini, R., 257
Guattari, F., 267
Guyau, J.-M., 262
L'irréligion de l'avenir, 95, 212n

Habermas, J., 260–61
Harnoncourt, N., 121n
Hebrews, Letter to, 8, 72, 272
Hegel, G. W. F., 207, 244, 274
Hehn, V., 158
Heidegger, M., 29n, 38, 57–8, 97, 141, 196–7
hell, 12, 144, 177–9, 182; see also She'ol
'hellenic harmony', 45
Hellwald, F. von, 96
Heraclitus, 71
hero, 66–7
Herodotus, *Histories*, 47–8
Hesiod,
  Theogony, 93
  Works and Days, 93
'highest hope', 94
Hinduism, 73, 85, 147–67, 227

Hitchens, C., 260
Hobbes, T., 90
Hölderlin, F., 6
'holy lie', 153–4, 156–8, 167; see also 'noble lie'
Holsten, K., 209n
Homer, 48, 138, 176, 183, 240, 249
  Odyssey, 211
Horace, 33–4, 159, 171–2
Horkheimer, M., 165, 207
Horneffer, E., 145
Hubert, H., 205
Huysmans, J.-K., 255
Hyperboreans, 10, 15, 39, 47–51, 199, 259

Iamblichus of Apamea, 133, *On the Mysteries of the Egyptians, Chaldeans, and Assyrians*, 44–5
idiocy, Nietzsche on, 68–9
Irigaray, L., 208
Isaiah, 101–2, 104
Isaiah, Book of, 104, 194, 221, 262
Isis, cult of, 179
Islam, 3, 187
Isidore of Seville (Saint), 193
Israel, ancient, 97–108, 271

Jacolliot, L., *Les Législateurs religieux*, 147–9
Jahn, O., 239
Jaspers, K., 170
Jensen, A. E., *Myth and Cult Among Primitive Peoples*, 207
Jeremiah, 102
Jerome (Saint), 155
Job (biblical figure), 199
Job, Book of, 221,

John, Gospel according to, 33, 64, 69, 72, 113, 116, 138, 181, 230
John (the Apostle), 114, 199
John Chrysostom (Saint), 42, 70–1, 155, 205, 231
Jong, K. H. E. de, *Das antike Mysterienwesen*, 127
Joshua, 99
Josiah (King), 102
Judas Iscariot,
Judas (house-owner in Damascus), 231
Judas Isacariot, 113
Judas Maccabaeus, 179n
Julian (the Apostate), 60, 126, 174
Jung, C. G., 6, 30, 117–18, 207
  Aion, 117
  Answer to Job, 199
  'Concerning Rebirth', 145
  Seminar on Nietzsche's "Zarathustra", 17, 46–7, 81–2, 135, 144–5, 266
  'The Psychology of the Unconscious', 266
  The Red Book, 33n
  Transformations and Symbols of the Libido, 91, 193n
Jünger, E., 97
Justin Martyr (Saint), 29, 220n, 253n
  Dialogue with Trypho, 254

Kant, I., 10, 92n
Kaufmann, W., 121, 234–5
Kerényi, C., *Eleusis: Archetypal Image of Mother and Daughter*, 129, 207
Kießling, A., 242
'kingdom of God', 116–18, 202
'kingdom of heaven', 32, 70–1
Kings, First Book of, 100–1
Kings, Second Book of, 101
Klages, L., 208
  Die psychologischen Errungenschaften Nietzsches, 235
  Of Cosmogonic Eros, 127–9
Klopstock, F. G., 18
Koegel, F., 32, 40
Köselitz, H. (Peter Gast), 5, 40
Küng, H., 257
Kurzweil, R., 263

Lacan, J., 208
Lactantius, 254
Lagarde, P. de, 154
language, persistence of transcendence in, 30
Lampert, L., 49, 61
Lao-Tzu, 73
'Law Against Christianity' (Nietzsche), 14, 36, 40, 261–3
Lawbook of Manu, 13, 85, 147–67, 271
lectio divina, 9
Leipzig, 20, 239–42
Leonardo da Vinci, 6, 47, 190
Lessing, G. E., 75
Lipovetsky, G., 266
Lippert, J.,
  Christentum, Volksglaube und Volksbrauch, 89–90
  Die Religionen der europäischen Culturvölker, 90
Littledale, R. F., 253–4
liturgy, 8, 29, 115, 219
Livy, 168
Löwith, K.,
Lovecraft, H. P., 123
Lubac, H. de, 257
Lucian of Samosata, *Menippus*, 132
Lucretius, *De rerum natura*, 178

Lüdemann, H., 209n, 210
Luke, Gospel according to, 32, 68, 116, 187, 225
Luther, M., 13–14, 51, 75, 210, 213–14, 220, 273
Lyotard, J.-F., 165

Macarius of Corinth (Saint), 133
Macarius of Egypt (or the Elder) (Saint), 194–5
Maccabbees, Second Book of, 179n
Machiavelli, N., 191
Madame Blavatsky, *see* Blavatsky, Helena
magic, 25
Mähly, J., 21
Mann, T., 121n
Marcel, G., 257
Marcus Aurelius, 60, 126
Mark, Gospel according to, 72, 112, 187, 270
Marx, K., 165, 207
Martha and Mary, 84, 225–6
Matthew, Gospel according to, 30, 70–2, 187
Maudsley, H., 210
Mauss, M., 205
McKenna, T., 129
Meister Eckhart, *see* Eckhart von Hochheim
Merezhkovsky, D., 47
Messiah, 7, 29, 41–3, 110, 113, 115–16, 271
Meysenbug, M. von, 35, 40
methods, Nietzsche on, 52–63
Michelangelo, 190
Mitchison, N., 123
Mithras, cult of, 120, 144, 168, 177, 179, 181
modernity as barbarism, 2, 163
Molière, 244

Montaigne, M. de, 212
Montalambert, C. F. R., *Les moines de l'occident*, 193
Montaigne, M. de, 212
Montesquieu, 84
Morel, G., 257
mosaic metaphor, 172
Moses, 8–9, 64, 98–9, 113, 115, 194, 215, 253
Mounier, E., 257
Müller, M., 96
Murray, L. and P., 5–6
Mushacke, H., 20
mysteries, ancient (cults of), 121–37, 271
'mythical consciousness' (Cassirer), 24

Naumburg, 17–18
Nancy, J.-L., 203
Neale, J. M., 253–54
Nebuchadnezzar II, 103
Nehemiah, 64n, 104
Neoplatonism, 44, 177
Nero (Roman emperor), 27, 42, 44, 228
New Atheism, 260
Niebuhr, B. G., 238
Nietzsche, F.,
  LIFE:
  birth and baptism, 16–17
  early interest in philology and critique of Christianity, 23
  mental collapse, 40
  schooling, 17–19
  university education, 19–20
  IDEAS:
  eternal recurrence, 39, 140, 142, 197, 199
  on ancient Israel, 97–108
  on Buddhism, 82–97, 218–19
  on 'death of God', 63, 265

Nietzsche, F. (cont.)
  on 'genius', 67–8
  on 'idiocy', 68–9
  on loss of the symbolic
    dimension, 108–11
  on methods, 52–63
  on philology, 236–58
  on St Paul, 201–35
  on the Roman Empire, 167–82
  on theme of nobility, 182–200
  portrait of Christ, 63–74
  WORKS:
  Beyond Good and Evil, 28, 30,
    45, 89, 143, 182, 184, 192,
    248, 251
  Daybreak, 22, 28–9, 30, 91,
    107, 142–4, 180, 209–17,
    236–7, 248, 252–3, 256–7
  Der Gottesdienst der Griechen
    (lectures), 95
  Ecce Homo, 34, 62, 79, 83,
    133–5, 142, 149–50, 153,
    174, 206, 237, 240, 245, 265
  *Encyclopädie der klassischen
    Philologie*, 237
  'Fate and History', 18
  'Freedom of the Will and
    Fate', 18–19
  Human, All-Too-Human, 21–2,
    23–8, 55, 57, 75, 87, 91,
    108–11, 120, 163–4, 169,
    174, 182–3, 189, 211–2
  'Homer and Classical
    Philology', 21
  'Homer's Contest', 250
  'Introduction to the Study of
    Classical Philology', 250
  Nietzsche contra Wagner, 252
  'On the Future of Our
    Educational Institutions',
    244, 250
  On the Genealogy of Morals, 9,
    28, 30–1, 45, 85, 149–51,
    182, 184, 227–8, 265
  Revaluation of All Values
    (planned book), 35–6, 38–9
  'Sils Maria' (poem), 45
  'Socrates and Tragedy', 21
  The Anti-Christ,
    composition of, 39–40
    §13 and §59, 52–63
    §29 and §32, 63–74
    §20–§23, 82–97
    §24, §37, §45, §60–§62,
      182–200
    §25, 97–108
    §32 and §50, 74–9
    §34 and §37, 116–118,
      118–21, 121–7
    §39–§40, 203–09
    §41–§43, 217–35
    §56–§57, 148–67
    §58, 167–82
  The Birth of Tragedy, 54, 98,
    130, 198, 244–5, 249
  'The Dionysian World-View', 21
  The Gay Science, 55, 61, 63,
    75–6, 85, 100, 104, 143,
    174, 185, 248, 251–2, 265
  'The Greek Music Drama', 21
  'The Greek State', 162
  The Will to Power (Nachlass
    texts), 38–9, 57, 71, 234–5
  Thus Spoke Zarathustra, 17,
    35, 44, 61, 73, 81, 94, 129,
    133–4, 141, 159–60, 196,
    209, 243, 250
  Twilight of the Idols, 7, 29, 35,
    51n, 56, 67, 76–7, 78, 90,
    91–2, 105–6, 107, 108,
    125, 139–42, 149–54, 160,
    169–72, 176, 226, 246–7

Untimely Meditations, 2, 163, 237–8, 250
nietzschéisme de gauche, 166
nihilism, 82, 97, 182, 225, 257, 265
Nilus the Elder (Saint), 205
Noack, F., *Eleusis*, 127
nobility, theme of, 182–200, 272
'noble lie', 92, 158, 167; see also 'holy lie'
non-discursive faith, 74
Novalis, 87

Oldenberg, H., 81, 84
olfactory metaphor, 4, 62, 149–50
'one thing is needful', 84, 226, 249
Onfray, M., 67, 123, 155–6, 173, 230–4, 255
Origen, 31, 75, 88, 132n, 156, 229
Osiris, cult of, 120, 181
Otto, R., 104n
Overbeck, F., 4, 21, 40, 41, 53, 89–90, 159, 177
Ovid, *Metamorphoses*, 91
Oxyrhynchus fragments, 117

Paglia, C., 123
parables, 32, 73, 110–1, 273
'party of life' (*Partei des Lebens*), 265
Parzival/Parsifal, 111
Pascal, B., 61, 211–12
'pathos of distance', 192
Paul of Tarsus (Saint), 8, 30, 33–4, 42, 47, 72, 74, 120, 136, 144, 155, 180–2, 187, 199–200, 201–16, 217–35
Paulsen, F., 240
Peter, First Letter of, 194
Petrarch, F., *On His Own Ignorance and that of Many Others*, 69–70

Petronius, *Satyricon*, 228
Phidias, 54
Philippians, Letter to, 218, 220, 222
Philologenkrieg, see *Philologenstreit*
Philologenstreit, 239–40
philology, 7–9, 13, 15, 19–23, 28–9, 53–5, 79, 98, 102, 201, 223, 228–30, 235, 236–58, 272
Pindar, *Pythian Ode*, 10, 49
'pious fraud', 91, 153
Pirenne, H., 59
pity, 184–6
Plato, 54, 81n, 132–3, 153, 198, 212, 251
 Phaedrus, 133n
 The Republic, 13n, 92, 158–9, 161
 Second Letter, 161
 Sophist, 198
 Theaetetus, 133, 198
Platonism, 131, 136
Pliny, 232
 Epistles, 232n
 Natural History, 262
Plotinus, *Enneads*, 133
Plutarch, 135–6
 'On the E at Delphi', 132
Pontifical Swiss Guard, 188
Pontius Pilate, 13, 78–9
Praxiteles, 54
Priestly Code, 98
Proclus, *Theology of Plato*, 44
'proofs of strength', Pauline notion of, 74–9
Proudhon, P.-J., 173
Przywara, E., 257
Psalms, Book of, 29, 114–15, 231, 253–4, 256
pyramid metaphor, 162–3, 193

Ratzinger, J. (Benedict XVI), 200, 220, 260–1
Reitzenstein, R., *Die hellenistichen Mysterienreligionen*, 124
religionsgeschichtliche Schule, 41, 124
'Renaissance man', 190
Renan, E., 47, 60, 65–7, 70, 95, 174, 177, 186
ressentiment, 83, 182–84, 187, 202–3, 226–7, 230
Revelation, Book of, 43–4, 112, 114–15
Rheinisches Museum, 241
Ribbeck, O., 240
Ridley, A., 247
Ritschl, F., 20–1, 239–42, 245
Ritschle Sozietät, 241
Robertson Smith, W., 204–5, 207
Rohde, E., *Psyche*, 128, 241–2, 245–6, 249
Roman Empire, 14, 34, 42, 58–9, 88, 120, 167–82, 273
Romans, Letter to, 65, 181, 218, 233
Roscher, W. H., 20, 241
Rousseau, J.-J., 212
Rubensohn, O., *Die Mysterienheiligtümer in Eleusis and Samothrake*, 125

sacrifice, logic of, 203–9, 218
Salis-Marschlins, M. von, 70
Salomé, L. von, 250–1
Saoshyant, Nietzsche as, 46
Samson, 99
Samuel, 99
Sarrasin, T., 3
Saul (King), 99
Scheler, M., 257
Schelling, F. W. J., 244

Philosophical Investigations into the Essence of Human Freedom, 198
Über die Gottheiten der Samothrake, 124
Schiller, F., 141
On the Aesthetic Education of Humankind, 164
'The Gods of Greece', 2, 56, 58
'The Festival of Eleusis', 126
'Lament of Ceres', 126
'To Joy', 130
Schlegel, F., 244
Schleiermacher, F., 75
Schmidt, J., 210
Schmidt, W., 207
Schöll, A., 84
Schömann, G. F., 93
Schopenhauer, A., 20, 212
On the Basis of Morals, 185
The Two Fundamental Problems of Ethics, 55
The World as Will and Representation, 97, 185–6, 210
Schulpforta, 18–19
Schuré, É., *Sanctuaires d'Orient*, 125
secularism/secularisation, 259–60
Second Vatican Council, 220
seismograph, writer as, 121, 126–7
self vs ego, 267
semiotics, 73, 110
Seneca, 221, 232
She'ol, 179n; *see also* hell
Siebmacher, J. A., *The Waterstone of the Wise*, 117
Simonides, 241
Simplicius of Cilicia, 177
sin against the Holy Spirit, 154, 248
Sipo matador (plant), 192

Socrates, 54, 84, 92, 133, 158, 161, 246–8
Solovyov, V., 263–5
Sommer, H. U., 84, 87–8, 148–9, 155, 158, 175–6, 188–9
'son of God', 118–20, 217
'son of Man', 111, 113–16
Sophiological tradition, 264
spider, God as,
Spinoza, B., 10, 104, 174, 196, 212
Steiner, R., 121–7
   Christianity as Mystical Fact, 130–2
   Friedrich Nietzsche: Ein Kämpfer gegen seine Zeit, 122
Stobaeus (cited by Plutarch), 135–36
Stoicism, 31, 177, 210, 220–1, 224, 236
Strauss, D. F., 163, 190, 209n, 274
Strong, T., 55
symbolic dimension, loss of (Jung), 6
symbolic dimension, loss of (Nietzsche), 108–11
symbolism, 9, 19, 26, 31, 33, 120, 141, 155–6, 181, 186, 191, 229, 238

Taylor, T., *The Eleusinian and Bacchic Mysteries*, 124–5
Teichmüller, G., 96
Tertullian, 61, 254
textual criticism, 9, 240, 273
Theodoret of Cyrus, 42
Theodosius, 126
Theognis of Megara, 239
theosis (or deification), 132–3
Thessalonians, Second Letter to, 42

Thomas Aquinas (Saint), 61, 248n
Thucydides, 54, 55, 56
Tillich, P., 257
Timofeyeva, V.V., 264
Tolstoy, L., *The Kingdom of God is Within You*, 118
Torah, 212, 220, 269
'totally administered society' (Adorno), 207
transhumanism, 263–8
truth, 6, 12, 13, 19, 51, 57, 65, 74, 77–9, 93, 153, 157, 174, 237, 239, 257
Tübinger Stift, 10, 274
Tylor, E. B., 204

Usener, H., 21
Uvarov, S., *Essai sur les mystères d'Eleusis*, 124

Valadier, P., 257
Valéry, P., 155n
values (*Naturwerthe*), 97, 99, 103, 105
vampirism, 59–60, 104, 143, 173–4
Venantius Fortunatus, *Vexilla Regis*, 254
Vergely, B., 9, 30n, 119, 194–6, 263–8
Virgil, *Aeneid*, 122, 205
virtue (*virtù*), 52, 190n, 191n
virtues, theological, 11, 91–6
Vischer-Bilfinger, W., 245
vitalism, 195, 198, 225, 243, 252, 265
Voltaire, 81n

Wagner, R., 20, 111, 151, 243, 245
Wasson, R. G. et al., 129

Wellhausen, J., 97n
 Prolegomena to the History of Ancient Israel, 98, 204–5
 Skizzen und Vorarbeiten, 89, 98
Wells, G. A., 119, 186
Weston, J. L., 123
Whichcote, B., 133n
Wilamowitz-Moellendorff, U. von, 245, 249
Willoughby, H. R., 129
will-to-power, 150, 197, 265, 267
Winckelmann, J. J., 140, 244

Wisser, H. W., 20, 241
women, impact on Nietzsche's life, 17
work, 163–5

Yahweh (deity), 8n, 11, 98–104, 113, 194, 253
Yahwistic source, 98

Zarathustra, 45–6
Zeitgeist: The Movie, 123
Zerubbabel, 104
Žižek, S., 203, 208

EU representative:
Easy Access System Europe
Mustamäe tee 50, 10621 Tallinn, Estonia
Gpsr.requests@easproject.com

www.ingramcontent.com/pod-product-compliance
Lightning Source LLC
Chambersburg PA
CBHW050202240426
43671CB00013B/2220